ERIC B. HARE

SKYSCRAPERS

Daily Devotions for Juniors

365 Stories That Build You Up!

D1506803

IR

REVIEW AND HERALD® PUBLISHING ASSOCIATION

Since 1861 | www.reviewandherald.com

To order additional copies of *Skyscrapers,*
by Eric B. Hare, call 1-800-765-6955.

Visit us at www.reviewandherald.com
for information on other Review and Herald® products.

Copyright © 1964, 1986, 2009 by Review and Herald® Publishing Association

Published by Review and Herald® Publishing Association, Hagerstown, MD 21741-1119

Review and Herald® titles may be purchased in bulk for educational, business, fund-raising, or sales promotional use. For information, please e-mail SpecialMarkets@reviewandherald.com.

The Review and Herald® Publishing Association publishes biblically based materials for spiritual, physical, and mental growth and Christian discipleship.

The author assumes full responsibility for the accuracy of all facts and quotations as cited in this book.

Unless otherwise noted, all texts are from the New King James Version. Copyright © 1979, 1980, 1982 by Thomas Nelson, Inc. Used by permission. All rights reserved.

Texts credited to NIV are from the *Holy Bible, New International Version.* Copyright © 1973, 1978, 1984, International Bible Society. Used by permission of Zondervan Bible Publishers.

Bible texts credited to RSV are from the Revised Standard Version of the Bible, copyright © 1946, 1952, 1971, by the Division of Christian Education of the National Council of the Churches of Christ in the U.S.A. Used by permission.

This book was
Edited by Penny Estes Wheeler
Cover design by Ron J. Pride
Cover art by Thiago Lobo
Interior design by Heather Rogers
Typeset: Frutiger 9/12

PRINTED IN U.S.A.
13 12 11 10 09   5 4 3 2 1

Library of Congress Cataloging-in-Publication Data
Hare, Eric B.
  Skyscrapers : 365 stories that build you up : daily devotions for juniors / Eric B. Hare.
     p. cm.
  1. Teenagers—Prayers and devotions. 2. Devotional calendars—Seventh-day Adventists—Juvenile literature. I. Title.
  BV4850.H37 2009
  242'.63—dc22
                              2009012476

ISBN 978-0-8280-2466-2

Hi, Friends!

In the twentieth century one of the most beloved of Adventist storytellers was Eric B. Hare. Mention his name, and thousands of Adventists, young and old, instantly recall "Clever Queen," "The Haunted Pagoda," "Mee Mee," "Dr. Rabbit," "Silver and the Snake"—all stories from Hare's mission service in Burma (now Myanmar). He was a dramatic storyteller with a unique way of painlessly weaving a moral into each story.

Eric Hare was born in Australia in 1894. He and his wife, Agnes, spent some 20 years as missionaries in Burma. Following a few years of service in California, he was called to the Sabbath School Department of the General Conference. He retired officially from that post in 1962, but during a period of 14 years of "retirement," he met nearly 800 appointments! He passed to his rest in 1982.

With this daily devotional book, we suggest that each day you first read the entire Bible selection noted at the top left corner of that day's reading. This will give you the setting for the memory verse and the devotional thought.

In the beginning God created the heavens and the earth.
Genesis 1:1.

January 1

I'm so glad that the Bible begins with God. "In the beginning God . . . " We are at the beginning of a new year. Before us lies an unknown path. We want this to be the happiest year of our lives, and it can be if we will put God in "the beginning" of each day of the year. You'll find that people who make God first and last and best in their lives are the happiest people in the world.

You can make God first by picking up His precious Book and reading it each day.

There's a story in the *Review and Herald* of a lone traveler who was going along a foot trail over a hillside one stormy night. He carried a lantern in his hand to help him keep on the path, but it was so cold that at last he put the lantern under his heavy coat. This kept him warm, but in the darkness, without knowing it, he lost the way. Suddenly a gust of wind blew open his coat, and as the light shone out he was horrified to see that he was almost on the brink of a deep stone quarry. A few more steps without the light surely would have taken him to his death. He quickly found his way back to the trail, and you may be certain that he kept the light outside after that and followed it every step of the way.

Job made God first in his life, and God led him safely through sorrow, disaster, and sickness. Then He gave him "twice as much as he had before" (Job 42:10). Daniel made God first in his life, and God made him "ten times better" in wisdom than the other wise men, and He led him safely through temptation and the lions' den. You can easily believe that Daniel was one of the happiest people in all of Babylon. God wants to lead you this year and make you one of the happiest people in the world. Won't you make God first, the reading of His Word first, and prayer first, every day of this year?

"God's holy, educating Spirit is in His Word. A light, a new and precious light, shines forth from every page. Truth is there revealed, and words and sentences are made bright and appropriate for the occasion, as the voice of God speaking to the soul" (*Messages to Young People*, p. 246).

We need God in this new year. We need His light every step of the way.

GENESIS 3; 4

I will put enmity between you and the woman, and between your seed and her Seed; He shall bruise your head, and you shall bruise His heel. Genesis 3:15.

January 2

This is the first promise in the Bible. For 4,000 years it brought hope to the hearts of tired and discouraged men and women. Did you know that there are more than 3,000 promises in the Bible? Elder J. N. Loughborough, one of our Adventist pioneers, read the Old Testament through 69 times and the New Testament 71 times. His dear old Bible is kept at the General Conference. If ever you visit there, ask to see it. On one of the flyleaves you will see a list of the promises in the Bible. It is evidently his own counting, and it says:

Old Testament promises for the present, 2,253; for the future, 791.

Total Old Testament promises, 3,044.

New Testament promises for the present, 274; for the future, 253.

Total New Testament promises, 527.

Total promises in all the Bible, 3,571.

As I said above, today's text is the very first promise in the Bible. It gave hope to Adam and Eve in the hour of their great sorrow when they realized that their sin had brought death and a curse into the world. They memorized it and told it to their children and to their grandchildren. Then they, in turn, memorized it and told it to their children and grandchildren, and so on down to Moses. Moses wrote it down, and it became part of the Bible for everyone. It gave hope to all who heard it or read it, right on down to devout old Simeon, who took Baby Jesus in his arms and said, "My eyes have seen Your salvation" (Luke 2:30). But it does not end there. There is hope in that promise for you and for me, that through Christ we can overcome the devil and his temptations and bruise his head today and every day.

Solomon declared, "There has not failed one word of all His good promise, which He promised through His servant Moses" (1 Kings 8:56). And Peter says that these "exceedingly great and precious promises" "have been given to us" (2 Peter 1:4).

As you read through your Bible, keep your eyes open for the many precious promises. Underline them and treasure them. They were written for you.

Noah was a just man, perfect in his generations. Noah walked with God. Genesis 6:9.

January 3

What a wonderful feeling of security there is in walking with God! As Noah built the ark and preached for 120 years he kept his thoughts on God and talked to Him as a companion. That is the way Noah walked with God. Noah was mocked and he was abused, but God saved him and his family when millions of people who refused help were destroyed.

The three young Hebrew men walked with God in the same simple way—praying, reading the Scriptures, daily deciding to do nothing that God would not approve. The angry king threw them into the fire, but God joined them in the fire, and not a hair of their heads was even singed.

Have you heard of Desmond Doss? He was only a humble medic in World War II, but he too walked with God. He put God first every day of his life, by prayer and reading his Bible. At first the soldiers made fun of him and his Bible reading, and often called him a sissy and threw their boots at him. But when it came to danger, they soon changed their tune. There came the memorable battle of the precipice, when the United States armed forces were landing on Okinawa. There were 155 men who waited for Doss to say a prayer before they scaled the cliff on rope nets. After a few days only 55 came back down.

Doss was the last man. He dragged the wounded, man after man, to the cliff and lowered them down by a rope. "Come on down, Doss!" shouted the captain. "You'll only get yourself killed." But Doss replied, "Just give me a little more time. I can't leave these wounded men up here to die." And alone he lowered 75 men to safety. At last he himself was badly wounded, but he came home alive and was greatly honored. President Harry Truman personally presented to him the Congressional Medal of Honor—the highest award a grateful nation can bestow on a hero.

It pays to make God first. It pays to take God with you everywhere you go. It pays to keep away from places where God or the angels wouldn't go. Won't you decide to walk with God this year?

GENESIS 8; 9:1-17

I set My rainbow in the cloud, and it shall be for the sign of the covenant between Me and the earth. Genesis 9:13.

January 4

It was after the most awful storm and destruction that Noah and his family saw their first rainbow. What a comfort it must have been to them to know that the rainbow was the sign of God's promise that the waters should no more become a flood to destroy the entire earth. Only God could make a rainbow, and only God can comfort in a time of fear and sorrow.

Often we see a second rainbow just beneath the primary rainbow. But, strangely enough, though the red is on the outside of the arc of the primary rainbow, in the second rainbow the violet is on the outside of the arc. Only God would think of that. Bright moonlight can also form a rainbow. Have you ever seen a rainbow at night? I have.

It was years ago when our little school among the devil worshippers of Burma (now Myamnar) was struggling for existence. It seemed impossible for the gospel to break down the fear and the superstition of the jungle people. I had gone down the river to Moulmein for supplies. It had rained most of the day, but when the steamer reached the end of its journey that night a full moon was playing hide-and-seek with the clouds. I was standing on the deck with a government officer watching the logs and rubbish floating down the angry river when all of a sudden, there it was—a night rainbow! The officer beside me trembled. "It looks like a bad sign to me," he said. "I've never seen a rainbow at night before."

I replied, "It looks like a good sign to me. It reminds me of God's promises. I'm sure that in spite of floods, storms, fear, and superstitions all will be well someday." And sure enough, soon our mission work was well established.

Are there clouds of trouble or sorrow all around you today? Look for a rainbow and remember God's promises.

"Satan seeks to draw our minds away from the mighty Helper. . . . When Satan thrusts his threatenings upon you, turn from them, and comfort your soul with the promises of God. The cloud may be dark in itself, but when filled with the light of heaven, it turns to the brightness of gold; for the glory of God rests upon it" (*Messages to Young People*, pp. 109, 110).

There he built an altar to the Lord and called on the name of the Lord. Genesis 12:8.

January 5

It was Abraham's custom to call upon the name of the Lord wherever he was. We can rejoice to know that God hears our prayers wherever we are.

Elisha went into the house, shut the door, and prayed. Daniel opened the window and prayed. Peter went up to the housetop; Hannah went to the Temple; and Nehemiah breathed a quick prayer while he was before the king. Jonah prayed in the belly of a great fish, and Ba Twe prayed his first prayer at the top of a tall dead tree.

Ba Twe was a heathen boy who came to our mission school in Burma. During his first year he came to Sabbath school and to prayer meeting every week, but he would never take part. "Oh, no! I'm a heathen. God wouldn't listen to me," he said.

Then one day during the summer vacation, while minding his father's buffaloes, he lay down beside them as they rested in the shade and went to sleep. When he woke up, they were gone. "Oh, what will I do?" he said. "The buffaloes will wander into someone's garden and spoil it, and I'll get into plenty of trouble!" He ran down to the river and looked all around, but they were not there. He ran out to the rice fields, but they were not there. Just then he saw a tall dead tree. "I'll climb that tree and look all around," he said. From the top of the tree he saw other buffaloes with other boys driving them home, but his buffaloes were nowhere to be seen. "Oh, what will I do?" he cried.

And the little voice in his heart said, *Pray, pray, pray!*

"But God wouldn't listen to me," he argued. "I'm not a Christian."

But the little voice kept saying, *Pray, pray, pray!*

So he prayed, "O God, please, God, help me find my buffaloes." He was too frightened to say "for Jesus' sake. Amen." He almost expected God to strike him with thunder and lightning. He hurried down the tree as though to get away from God as quickly as possible. But as he jumped from the lowest limb, there were his buffaloes! "He heard me!" said Ba Twe in amazement. "Before I was a Christian, He heard me!" And right there, at that moment, Ba Twe gave his heart to Jesus.

Remember, wherever you are today, God is always near enough to hear your prayer.

GENESIS 13

Please let there be no strife between you and me . . .
for we are brethren. Genesis 13:8.

On this day, January 6, several large churches celebrate the visit of the Wise Men to Baby Jesus in Bethlehem. Of course, no one can be certain of the very day on which that visit occurred, but one thing is certain—Jesus came to bring peace to the world. Without Him there always will be strife and quarreling. It was the hope of the promised Savior that made Abraham so humble and kind that he let Lot choose land first, thus avoiding a quarrel.

The manager of the large plantation on which Elder Stahl had established the Metrano Mission became very angry and wrote a letter to General Cooper, the president of the corporation in Lima, Peru, demanding that the mission be closed. When Elder Stahl heard that General Cooper was coming to investigate, he rode down the trail to meet him. "I'm so glad I can have this opportunity of talking to you about the mission," said Brother Stahl.

"I don't want to talk to you," retorted the general.

Brother Stahl tried again. "The Indians used to be savages. Now they are leading new, clean lives."

"I told you I don't want to hear anything about the mission" was all he would say, so Elder Stahl bowed and went away. That night he was impressed to go over to the plantation headquarters. When he arrived, he found the general suffering from a head wound resulting from falling off his horse soon after he had refused to let Elder Stahl talk to him.

Elder Stahl treated the wound, and when the general was comfortable, he was glad to talk about the mission. Soon the hard feelings melted away, and the mission remained on the plantation. It was Jesus in Elder Stahl's heart that brought peace. "The warfare against self is the greatest battle that was ever fought," we read in *Steps to Christ*, page 43. When we humble ourselves and let Jesus come into our hearts, strife and quarreling vanish.

It takes two to make a quarrel. Our Burma Karens say, "You can't clap hands with one hand," and it's true. If you decide to be humble and kind, there will be no strife.

Won't you decide to follow this path to happiness and peace?

9

"And blessed be God Most High. . . . "
And he gave him a tithe of all. Genesis 14:20.

January 7

As we read this account it does not sound as if this was the first time Abram (Abraham) had returned tithe. Later, as we read of the tithing laws given to the children of Israel, the reformation in tithing at the time of Nehemiah, the blessings pronounced upon tithing by Malachi, and the affirmation given to it by Jesus, we can only conclude that this is one of God's paths to happiness that He has always planned for His children. And in every country of the world people are bearing witness to the happiness and blessings that come to the tithepayer.

Away across the sea in Barotseland (now a region in western Zambia) lived a dear old man named Shwebele. He and his kind old wife were the only Seventh-day Adventists in the village. One year at harvesttime they were both sick with malaria and unable to harvest their kaffir corn.

The village people were all busy harvesting their fields and beating dums and cans to keep the birds from devouring the grain. They dared not stop the noise from early morning to dark lest clouds of birds descend upon the fields and devour their grain.

Shwebele's friends wagged their heads and sadly said, "There is no hope for Shwebele's field. There is no one to reap and no one to beat the drum. The birds will eat up everything."

But Shwebele prayed, "O God, please take care of my fields. You promised to rebuke the devourer. I claim that promise, for I have paid a faithful tithe." And the birds did not settle in Shwebele's fields. The birds did not eat up his grain!

"He must have some magic medicine," said one.

"Yes, seven-day man's medicine from the mission," they agreed.

"Tell us," said the astonished village people, "what kind of medicine you used on your field that the birds dared not settle on your corn." Shwebele told them about his loving God and his angel watcher.

"Is that it!" they said. "We can't see the angel, but the birds can!" When the neighbors' harvesting was finished, they all kindly reaped Shwebele's field for him.

God wants you to follow this path to happiness. He wants you to prove Him so that He can pour out a blessing on you.

GENESIS 15

*And he believed in the Lord, and He accounted
it to him for righteousness. Genesis 15:6.*

January 8

This is the first time in the record of Abraham's experiences that we read the words "and he believed." God called him out of Ur, and he went forth. God called him into Canaan and promised to make him a great nation, and he departed. After Lot chose to live in the plain of Jordan, God renewed the promise to Abraham, and he came and dwelt in Hebron. After Abraham rescued Lot from his enemies, God renewed the promise again, and said that Abraham's children would number as many as the stars of heaven. Then we read that Abraham believed.

Is it hard for you to believe in God and have faith that He exists? Is it because you have never seen God? Most likely you never have seen the president of the United States or the queen of England—or the music star you especially like—yet you believe they are real people.

One evening a man went down into the basement of his house to get something. On his way back, at the foot of the stairs, he turned out the light. Just then he noticed his little 3-year-old daughter standing at the top of the stairs. The father, looking toward the lighted room, could see his little girl, but the little girl, looking down into the dark basement, couldn't see anything. "Daddy, where are you?" she asked.

"Down here, sweetheart," he replied. "Jump. I'll catch you."

"But I can't see you, Daddy," she said.

"But I can see you," said Daddy. "Come on and jump. I'll catch you." And she did jump—right into her own father's loving arms.

Why could the little girl believe and have faith that her daddy would catch her? She had learned to obey her daddy, and she loved him. That's the way it was with Abraham. He obeyed, and believing came easily. This is another pathway to happiness. Ellen White said it in these beautiful words: "All your happiness, peace, joy, and success in this life are dependent upon genuine, trusting faith in God. This faith will prompt true obedience to the commandments of God. Your knowledge and faith in God is the strongest restraint from every evil practice, and the motive to all good" (*Messages to Young People,* p. 410).

Won't you love, obey, and believe your heavenly Father today and every day?

Shall not the Judge of all the earth do right?
Genesis 18:25.

January **9**

In our Scripture texts today we have read of Abraham communing with God, the judge of all the earth, about saving the city of Sodom. "All the way up the steep road leading to eternal life are well-springs of joy to refresh the weary. Those who walk in wisdom's ways are, even in tribulation, exceeding joyful; for He whom their soul loveth walks, invsible, beside them" (*Messages to Young People,* p. 150).

In order for the children of God to be the happiest people in the world, God gave them the privilege of communing with Him along the way. As there can be no happy physical life if we don't keep breathing, so there can be no happy spiritual life without continual praying.

Abraham discovered this secret, and he *prayed* and *kept on* praying. The more he prayed, the bolder he became in prayer. You may be sure that Satan will try to stop you from praying. He may ridicule you, try to make you too busy, or discourage you by saying it's no use to pray.

That is when you need to pray more than ever. After writing, "Commit your way to the Lord," David continues, "Rest in the Lord, and wait patiently for Him" (Psalm 37:5, 7).

After attending a symphony concert in a large opera house, Mrs. Adams returned home to discover that she had lost an expensive diamond brooch. Frantically she telephoned the opera house and asked whether such a pin had been found. The manager asked her the number of her seat, then told her to hold the line while he went to look. He found the pin, but when he got back to the phone, Mrs. Adams had hung up. Perhaps she had gotten tired of waiting. Perhaps she had thought the manager wasn't coming back. Whatever the reason, he waited, hoping she would call again—but she didn't. He even advertised that he had found her treasure, but he never heard from her again. How happy she might have been if she had only held the line!

You will need God very much as you walk through this year. Determine that you will hold the line open between you and God every day.

GENESIS 19:1-28

*Get up, get out of this place; for the Lord will destroy this city!
Genesis 19:14.*

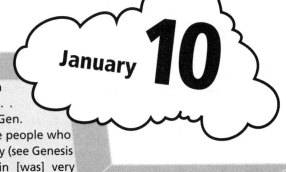

January 10

Sodom was a beautiful city in a plain that "was well watered . . . like the garden of the Lord" (Gen. 13:10). But it seems that most of the people who lived in Sodom were "evil continually (see Genesis 6:5)," for the Bible says their "sin [was] very grievous (Genesis 18:20, KJV)."

God never gives up on us unless there is no other choice, so we know that God had exhausted everything possible to save the people of Sodom. Even when He knew that He had to destroy the city, God told Abraham He would save the entire city if it had in it only 10 righteous people! How fortunate it was for Lot and his family that he heeded the message "Get up, get out of this place." How sad that his sons-in-law paid no heed to the warning message.

To us comes the same kind of message today. "Come out of her, my people" (Revelation 18:4). " 'Come out from among them and be separate,' says the Lord" (2 Corinthians 6:17). True Christians "will not desire to enter any place of amusement or engage in any diversion upon which [they] cannot ask the blessing of God. . . . No Christian would wish to meet death in such a place. No one would wish to be found there when Christ shall come" (*Messages to Young People*, p. 398).

It is good to keep in mind Paul's admonition that whatever is true, noble, right and pure—these are the things that should be in our minds (Philippians 4:8). It is not stretching Paul's advice to add that we should go only to places where we will experience what is true, noble, and pure. Yes, I know, that may mean you should drop some friends or, at the very least, be true to your own personal standards and ask that they don't swear around you or tell dirty jokes. And whatever is noble, right, and pure cuts out a lot of TV, song lyrics, and most movies shown in theaters or that come to you via DVD or on your computer.

If you are ever tempted to go to places where Christ and the angels do not go, stop and listen! You will hear the still small voice saying, "Get up, get out of this place." Make God first by keeping out of places of sinful pleasure, and you will be happy.

God has made me laugh.
Genesis 21:6.

January 11

Those whom God makes laugh are the happiest people in the world. We can't begin to imagine how happy Sarah was at this time. God had promised her and Abraham a son, but God had waited and waited, and Abraham and Sarah had grown older and older. Then when it looked humanly impossible, God fulfilled His promise—and Isaac was born. Do you know what the name Isaac means? It means "laughter"!

Let us always remember that with God nothing is impossible.

A young woman in the southern United States longed to go to school, but she had no money. She waited four years, but still there was no money. Then she walked 150 miles to one of our boarding schools, but the assistant principal said, "I'm sorry. All our student-aid fund is used up. I'm afraid you'll have to go home and try again next year."

But the young woman said, "I believe God wants me to be in school this year, for He opened the way for me to come even though I did have to walk."

"All right, then," the man said. "Go to the girls' dorm, find an empty room, and pray that some money will come in the next mail." Several hours went by. In the next mail delivery was a check to help support one more student. The assistant principal asked one of the teachers to go upstairs and find the girl and tell her the good news. The teacher went upstairs and found her—still on her knees, praying for God to send the money. It had seemed impossible—but there is nothing impossible with God.

"The power of God, combined with human effort, has wrought out a glorious victory for us. Shall we not appreciate this? All the riches of heaven were given to us in Jesus. . . . God has resources of power of which we as yet know nothing, and from these He will supply us in our time of need" (*Messages to Young People*, p. 106).

Do you have a dream for your life that seems to be impossible? Something you hardly dare tell anyone? Something that everybody "knows" you couldn't do or that couldn't happen for you? Keep holding on to God. He will make you laugh with joy someday. There is nothing impossible with Him!

Weeping may endure for a night, but joy comes in the morning.
Psalm 30:5.

January **12**

Sarah had been with Abraham, a stranger in a strange land, for many, many years. They'd left Ur, and she was about 65 when they were called out of Haran and God gave her the promise of a son. For 25 years she hoped for a son, and when she sadly gave up hoping, the promised son came. Sarah was 90 when Isaac was born, and for 37 years she was gloriously happy. She died happy in the assurance that all God's promises would be fulfilled. However, it was a sad time for Abraham and Isaac. They mourned as they laid Sarah's body in the cave of Machpelah. This is the first grave mentioned in the Bible, and later Abraham, Isaac, Rebekah, Leah, and Jacob were all buried there. Today a mosque has been built over the traditional spot.

To all of us there come seasons of sorrow when we weep for loved ones who have died. But, thank God, we are able to comfort one another with the words "The dead in Christ will rise first. Then we who are alive and remain shall be caught up together with them in the clouds to meet the Lord in the air. And thus we shall always be with the Lord" (1 Thessalonians 4:16, 17). What a grand and glorious day that will be—when God will wipe away all tears from our eyes.

I think of my old schoolmates Norman and Alma Wiles, missionaries to the Big Nambus tribe in the New Hebrides Islands. There was a threatened tribal war on their island, and even though Norman was sick, he got out of bed and succeeded in bringing peace. He then returned to his bed, but later died of blackwater fever. Alone, Alma dug a shallow grave. Alone, she buried her dead companion. Alone, she mourned. But God had seen those tears! In His plan, tears are like seeds, which in His own time will grow and blossom with joy and gladness. And God not only comforted Alma with the hope of a glorious resurrection but also watered the gospel seed in the hearts of the people. Today there are thousands of Sabbath school members in the New Hebrides Islands.

Are you mourning today for a friend or loved one who has passed away? Take comfort. "Joy comes in the morning."

*The Lord, before whom I walk, will send His angel
with you and prosper your way. Genesis 24:40.*

January 13

The story of how the angel went all the way with Eliezer 500 miles from Beersheba to the city of Nahor in Mesopotamia, and how "it came to pass" (Genesis 24:52) exactly as he prayed, "before he had finished speaking (verse 15)," is one of the loveliest stories in the Bible.

It will keep us happy if we remember that day by day God has commissioned a guardian angel to be with each one of us also.

For several years Pastor Norman Ferris was the Adventist missionary to the people of Pitcairn Island. One day he was repairing the engine in a launch the islanders had purchased. He had to take the engine apart, but neither he nor his helpers could get the flywheel off the main shaft. It had rusted on, and no amount of tapping, pulling, coaxing, or the liberal use of rust removers did any good. After three days two of the workmen gave up and said, "We're going fishing." The island men shook their heads. "It's no good," they said. "Tip it into the sea."

Then Pastor Ferris closed his eyes and prayed: "Dear Lord, I have come to the end of my ability. My unseen companion and watchman, who has been with me and helped me so often in the past, is so much stronger than I am. Just let him take over if this experience will bring honor to Your name." Before he could say "Amen" there was a noise and a bang—and the flywheel lay in the bottom of the boat!

"What's the matter?" shouted his friend, Mr. Anderson, who was not far away.

"We've just had a miracle!" cried Mr. Ferris. And before many days the engine was in operating condition and the launch was running perfectly.

"When you rise in the morning, do you feel your helplessness, and your need of strength from God? and do you humbly, heartily make known your wants to your heavenly Father? If so, angels mark your prayers, and . . . when you are in danger of unconsciously doing wrong, . . . your guardian angel will be by your side, prompting you to a better course, choosing your words for you, and influencing your actions" *(Messages to Young People*, p. 90).

GENESIS 27

Lying lips are an abomination to the Lord, but those who deal truthfully are His delight. Proverbs 12:22.

January 14

Lying produces some of the greatest unhappiness you can ever know. The Bible tells us that Satan "does not stand in the truth, because there is no truth in him. When he speaks a lie, he speaks from his own resources, for he is a liar and the father of it" (John 8:44). Satan told the first recorded lie: "You will not surely die" (Genesis 3:4) Cain told the next. When God asked him where his brother Abel was, he said, "I do not know" (Gen. 4:9). And Sarah lied when she said, "I did not laugh" (Gen. 18:15).

In today's scripture Jacob told lies to his poor old blind father, Isaac. It was not just one little lie, for it was supported by a host of lies. Even his mother lied for him. Jacob told lies not only with his lips but also with his actions and with his clothing.

Satan is going to try to tempt you, too, to tell lies in one way or another. A story in *Guide* some time ago illustrates the way Satan typically tempts us.

Don came rushing into the house after school, and as he slammed the door behind him he heard a splintering crash. A picture on the wall near the door had fallen to the floor. The frame had broken, and shattered glass lay all around it. No one was home, so Don decided to leave it there as if it had fallen down by itself.

When Mom came home an hour later she saw the broken picture and asked, "Don, did you hit that picture when you came in this afternoon?"

"No, I didn't," he said. "I didn't even touch it." It was almost the truth, but (good for Don!) he just couldn't feel right about it. It took a little courage, but at last he said, "Mom, it's my fault anyway. I slammed the door so hard that it fell down. I'm sorry." He felt so good after telling the whole truth that he decided even little "white" lies would be out for him, always.

Fortunately God has made provision for liars to confess their sins, and Jacob, Joseph's brothers, David, and Peter did confess and found their way to happiness again.

If you've told lies, won't you repent too? If you really love the truth, keep in the company of those who "deal truthfully" and are the "delight" of the Lord.

*Behold, I am with you and will keep you
wherever you go, and will bring you back
to this land; for I will not leave you until I
have done what I have spoken to you.
Genesis 28:15.*

January 15

Poor Jacob had made a serious mistake. He had lied and deceived, and as he fled from his home he must have thought that he was a failure. But he repented and confessed his sins, and then, wonder of wonders, in a dream God showed him a staircase that reached from heaven down to earth. And the voice of God assured him that there was still hope, that he was not cast off, that God was still with him, and that it was possible for him to live a successful life pleasing to God.

If we have true faith and courage, failure can be a step toward success.

Elias Howe wrestled with his sewing machine idea for years. Model after model he built and broke, until at last, in 1845, he sewed a suit of clothes for himself on his own machine.

Alexander Graham Bell had to try again and again, until in the 1870s he produced the telephone.

Thomas A. Edison must have failed a thousand times before he succeeded in giving the world the electric lamp in 1879.

So if you have ever failed and made mistakes, don't give up. Make things right and take another step up the stairway toward heaven.

"God has given the youth a ladder to climb, a ladder that reaches from earth to heaven. Above this ladder is God, and on every round fall the bright beams of His glory. He is watching those who are climbing, ready, when the grasp relaxes and the steps falter, to send help. Yes, tell it in words full of cheer, that no one who perseveringly climbs the ladder will fail of gaining an entrance into the heavenly city" (*Messages to Young People*, p. 95).

Peter describes the steps on this ladder when he says, "Add to your faith virtue, to virtue knowledge, to knowledge self-control, to self-control perseverance, to perseverance godliness, to godliness brotherly kindness, and to brotherly kindness love" (2 Peter 1:5-7).

The only true failure is stopping right there. Get up. Figure out what you can learn from the failure, and start over again. God will be with you every step.

GENESIS 29:1-28; 31:2, 3, 17, 18

So Jacob served seven years for Rachel, and they seemed
only a few days to him because of the love he had for her.
Genesis 29:20.

January **16**

'Tis love that makes us happy,
'Tis love that smooths the way;
It helps us mind, it makes us kind
To others every day.
—F. E. Belden

The first love we know in life is the love for our mother and father. After that comes love for brothers and sisters, then boy playmates if we are boys and girl playmates if we're girls. This continues until we are teens; then guys begin to notice girls and the girls begin to notice the guys. In college, young people begin to think of having their own home in the future, and it is natural for a young man to select one special girlfriend, and for a young woman to be especially interested in one special boyfriend. Then, usually when college days are over, comes the glad day when they get married and hope to live happily ever after. Each kind of love leaves its influence on the kind of love that follows it.

Now, it is natural to have plenty of cuddling, hugging, and kissing between children and their parents, not so much between brothers and sisters, and none at all among playmates and young people. Then again, it is natural for husband and wife to hug and kiss each other. But remember, "hands off" is the best advice anybody can give to teens and even older youth, until they are married.

It is natural for us to desire to possess and own things. This desire, when controlled and guided, makes us work and save and become thrifty. But uncontrolled, desire makes some people misers and some people robbers. Love is a wonderful thing. It is the desire that, when controlled, brings us everything in life that is beautiful, lovely, pure, and fine.

But uncontrolled, desire leads to sin and to disappointment. Instead of the happy years seeming as days, the days seem like weary years, and the unhappy people wish they were dead.

So play the game of love cleanly, according to the rules, and you'll be ready for the love that makes us happy, and that makes the years that go by seem like a few short days.

I will not let You go unless You bless me!
Genesis 32:26.

January 17

Jacob made his mistakes. He had his weak points, but he also had some very admirable traits of character. Perseverance was one of them. It took a lot of perseverance to work for his uncle Laban. "I served you fourteen years for your two daughters, and six years for your flock," Jacob told Laban, "and you have changed my wages ten times" (Genesis 31:41). Many other young men would have given up after two disappointments, but not Jacob; he kept on. He stuck at it, and succeeded. When he recognized that he had been wrestling with the Lord all night, he again summoned all the perseverance he had, and said, "I will not let You go unless You bless me!" And God did bless him.

Today is the birthday of another great man who had this trait of perseverance—Benjamin Franklin (1706-1790). This great man was the fifteenth child in a family of 17. His father was only a humble candlemaker in Boston, so there was not much money to clothe and feed the children. Little Ben went to school when he was 8, but had to leave school and go to work when he was 10. But Benjamin had brains, and Benjamin had perseverance. At 12 years of age he began to learn the printing trade. Every odd minute was used for study and research. He discovered a great deal about electricity, and he wrote and published *Poor Richard's Almanac* for 25 years. He was a signer of the Declaration of Independence, and for years he was deputy postmaster general of the Colonies. He put his whole heart and soul into everything he did, and once he said to his wife, "Debbie, I wish the good Lord had seen fit to make each day twice as long as it is."

"Nothing worth having is obtained without earnest, persevering effort. In business, only those who have a will to do see successful results. Without earnest toil we cannot expect to obtain a knowledge of spiritual things. Those who obtain the jewels of truth must dig for them as a miner digs for the precious ore hidden in the earth.

"Those who work indifferently and halfheartedly will never succeed" (*Messages to Young People*, p. 259).

How is your perseverance? What are you doing with your time? Do you put your heart and soul into your studies and the work you do?

GENESIS 33

But Esau ran to meet him, and embraced him,
and fell on his neck and kissed him, and they wept.
Genesis 33:4.

January **18**

Repentance is another of God's ways to happiness. Jacob found this to be true. So also did Ta Wa and Mg Sein. Thara Chit Maung brought them to me for fighting during night study.

I had Ta Wa come in to see me. "Whatever started it?" I asked.

"Well," he replied, "Mg Sein stood up, and his shadow fell on my book. I had a pin in my hand, so I pricked him. Then he hit me on the head. Then I hit him. And—"

"And you're a church member! What an example for Mg Sein, who has just joined the baptismal class!" I said.

"I know, Thara, I know. It's all my fault. I started it."

"Since you started it, Ta Wa, will you say you're sorry first and ask forgiveness first?"

"Yes, Thara. I will, I will."

Then I called in Mg Sein and asked Ta Wa to wait outside.

"Mg Sein," I began, "you've just joined the baptismal class and expect to overcome the devil and all of his temptations, and you couldn't even overcome a little pinprick?"

"I know, Thara, I know," he said. "I'm so ashamed. I started it."

"Then, Mg Sein, since you started it, will you say you're sorry first? And ask forgiveness first?" He agreed.

Then I called in Ta Wa, and gave each boy the chance to say "I'm sorry" first. I saw them swallow hard. I saw them open their mouths. But the words wouldn't come. The perspiration stood out on their foreheads.

At last Ta Wa began, "I'm—"

"No—I'm sorry," interrupted Mg Sein. "I started it."

"But I started it first. Please forgive me."

"No, you forgive me."

Their hearts were softened. They put their arms about each other's shoulders and went back to night study, their hearts filled with joy. Are you truly happy today? If not, maybe there's something of which you should repent!

Put away the foreign gods that are among you, purify yourselves, and change your garments. Genesis 35:2.

January 19

I suppose the gods that Jacob gathered up from his household and buried under the oak near Shechem were made of bronze. But not all gods are made of bronze. Anything that we put before God or allow to take the time of family worship, Sabbath school, church services, and Christian duty could be called an idol or a god.

"By idolatry he meant not only the worship of idols, but self-serving, love of ease, the gratification of appetite and passion" (*The Acts of the Apostles*, p. 317).

Do you have regular family worship? Are you faithful with your homework, your music practice, your chores? If not, why not? Is it because of TV? trashy reading? Or is it just plain indifference, laziness (love of ease), and worldliness? What strange gods are these! Better gather them up and bury them somewhere.

Today is the birthday of a famous Scotchman—James Watt (1736-1819). As a child, he was rather a dreamy, dull student, but when he was 13 he suddenly woke up and began to study in earnest. Soon he was attracting much attention by his ability in mathematics. He is generally given credit for inventing the steam engine, though actually a few crude, impractical steam engines had already been made. But James Watt made the steam engine practical, and to this day the unit of electric power bears his name—watt. So when we talk of a 75-watt lamp we are giving honor to a youth who put away indifference and laziness.

Daniel diligently overcame all temptation to carelessness in prayer. He allowed nothing to prevent his study, and he became a great prophet. David practiced and practiced with his slingshot, and practiced and practiced on his harp. And he became a great deliverer, and he played before the king.

The temptation to put pleasure before duty, to be lazy and indifferent, is the idol of which we must beware. You can become great and successful in God's eyes too. You have enough talents to make you happy and successful. But you must put away all your gods, and be pure and clean.

GENESIS 37

To have respect of persons is not good.
Proverbs 28:21, KJV.

January 20

In our Scripture reading today we have seen the misery and sorrow caused by a father's favoritism and by some brothers' feelings of superiority.

Satan knows the misery and sorrow he can produce if he can only get people to "have respect of persons," and he tries his best to plant this seed in the heart of youth. A child of foreign parentage, or a child from a poor home, or someone a different color from you may be attending your school. How eagerly Satan tries to make you act superior to them, so they will feel inferior to you!

Listen! Down in Macon, Georgia, a little girl named Anna was born. Her mother was a slave who had been sold to a man named Knight. Soon after this the slaves were freed, and Anna's family settled on a farm in Mississippi. Anna saw the White children going to school, but they wouldn't let her go to school, because she was "colored."

Anna was so hungry to learn that she helped the White girls with their work so that they would teach her to read. But they "couldn't be bothered." So she secured an old Webster's speller and mastered every word in it. She subscribed to the *Signs of the Times* and read every word. She taught the younger children to read. She was baptized, and went to one of our Adventist schools, but the students and their parents made such a fuss that she was forced to quit after just one day. One of our workers befriended her and sent her to Mount Vernon Academy. They tolerated her there, though some of the students snubbed her and called her that "green girl from the South." But Anna Knight stayed on.

Then she went to Battle Creek and took the nurse's course. In 1901 she went to India as a missionary. She served the Lord there for eight years with great honor and distinction, and then served 39 more years in the Adventist cause in North America. My guess is that many who shunned her once wished they had been kind. I'd like to be there when Jesus says to Anna, "Well done, thou good and faithful servant."

No favoritism or partiality to anyone, but kindness to all, is the pathway to happiness.

*How then can I do this great wickedness,
and sin against God?*
Genesis 39:9.

January 21

Two or three times during my lifetime I have heard of honorable men who have fallen into sin in a moment of great temptation to impurity. It has made me tremble, for I have wondered whether I could be stronger than they were if some big temptation came to me.

For years and years a great oak tree grew in Takoma Park, Maryland. It was a thing of beauty. It gave cooling shade to passersby and provided food and playground for the chipmunks and squirrels of the vicinity. Then one day there was a terrible storm. The lightning flashed, the thunder roared, the rain came down, and the winds blew. When Elder F. M. Wilcox, the *Review and Herald* editor, walked to work the next morning he found that the great oak tree had fallen to the ground! He couldn't believe it! *Impossible*, he thought, *that such a great strong tree should be overcome by a storm.*

He stood looking on in shocked amazement. Others joined him. Then someone near the broken stump said, "Ah! No wonder! Come and see!"

They went to see, and they found that the heart of the tree was riddled with worms. Its heart was rotten. If that great tree had been able to keep the little worms out of its heart, it could have withstood the storm. It never would have fallen.

That is why men and women here and there fall into sin. Their thoughts are not pure; their hearts are not clean. They give in to little sins—secret sins that others cannot see—then, when the great temptation comes, down they go!

Joseph overcame the little temptations day by day. Joseph kept his thoughts pure and his heart clean. Then when the great temptation came, he did not fall. What an inspiration he is to us!

Never underrate the importance of little things. It is by little things that the soul becomes Christlike or becomes evil.

So heads up! Shoulders back! No one need tremble and fear the day of great temptation. By the grace of God, overcome the little temptations day by day, and in the day of big temptations you will be an overcomer.

GENESIS 40

Now it came to pass on the third day, which was Pharaoh's birthday, that he made a feast for all his servants; and he lifted up the head of the chief butler. . . . Then he restored the chief butler to his butlership again.
Genesis 40:20, 21.

January 22

This is the first mention of a birthday party in the Bible. Did you notice that Pharaoh made the feast and Pharaoh bestowed the honors?

Maybe because the Wise Men brought gifts to Jesus it has become customary for others to give gifts and presents to children when they reach another birthday. But let's remember that when we grow up we should bestow gifts on others on our birthdays. A gift doesn't have to cost a lot. Some of the best gifts cost only your time.

January 19 is Martin Luther King, Jr.'s birthday. February 12 is Abraham Lincoln's, and February 22 is George Washington's. It's good to recognize the birthdays of people who did a lot for their country. April 21 is the birthday of England's Queen Elizabeth II. It is a public holiday, and many honors, favors, and promotions are given by her on that day.

The late Aga Khan, the spiritual leader of the Ismailis, was born on August 10. He celebrated that day by sitting on a scales while his followers matched his weight with diamonds and jewels, which he gave to build and support Muslim schools in many places.

What are you doing to bless others on your birthday? In 1919 the Sabbath School Department suggested that we Sabbath school members match the number of our years with a copper penny for each year to help send the gospel to all the world. The idea was a good one—when a penny was worth something! Today many match their years with dimes, quarters, or dollars. Why don't you do that too?

You and I are indebted to God for life, health, the food we eat, the money we earn, and the clothes we wear. But most of all, we're indebted to God for His gift of eternal life!

Let's grow up a little more. Let's think less of what we will get for our birthdays and more about what we can do and how much we can give to bless others.

It is not in me; God will give Pharaoh an answer of peace. Genesis 41:16.

January 23

In Revelation 14:12 John gives us a picture of the people Jesus is going to take to heaven. "Here is the patience of the saints; here are those who keep the commandments of God and the faith of Jesus." Notice that there are three outstanding characteristics of these redeemed ones. 1. They are patient; they have overcome pride; they have been humble and meek and long-suffering. 2. They keep the commandments; they have learned obedience and self-control. 3. They keep the faith of Jesus; they have overcome doubt, and have believed God and learned to trust Him in every trial.

Two days ago we read how Joseph met a great temptation to break the commandments. But he had learned how to be pure in thought and to hate wrongdoing. Next, although he was innocent, he was thrown into prison. How often he must have been tempted to doubt God and His love! But no, he overcame doubt and trusted God there in the darkness.

Now in today's Scripture reading we see Joseph tested on his feelings of pride and ambition. "I have heard it said of you," said Pharaoh, "that you can understand a dream, to interpret it" (Genesis 41:15). Oh, how easy it would have been for him to swell up with pride and say in his heart, "Of course, he surely means me!" But he didn't. Joseph had learned to keep the commandments; he had kept his faith; and now he easily humbled himself and overcame his pride, saying, "It is not in me; God will give Pharaoh an answer of peace."

Wouldn't it be a happy world if everybody were as humble and patient as Joseph was! How is your ego? Have you learned to overcome selfish pride and worldly ambition? As surely as you are worth anything, God will permit you to be tempted and tried, for "the trials of life are God's workmen, to remove the impurities and roughness from our characters. . . . Upon no useless material does the Master bestow such careful, thorough work. Only His precious stones are polished after the similitude of a palace" (*Messages to Young People*, p. 117).

And in God's tomorrow He must have a people whom He can trust with the glories of eternity.

GENESIS 42

We are all one man's sons; we are honest men.
Genesis 42:11.

January 24

You can think into the words "we are honest men" everything that makes a person "more precious than fine gold" (Isaiah 13:12, KJV). It is interesting to know that it was on this day, January 24, 1848, that James Wilson Marshall discovered gold at Sutter's Mill near Sacramento, California. It is only too bad that men in their greed for the golden metal have often forgotten to cultivate the gold of character. Good-for-nothing men and women and those worth their weight in gold live in the same world. The difference lies in whether they develop character.

Many years ago two German boys, brothers, came to America. The elder brother, being an expert sauerkraut maker, went at once to Eldorado County, California. He staked out a ranch, grew cabbages, and made sauerkraut. It was the best sauerkraut in the country, and the world made a path to his door to buy his kraut.

The younger boy apprenticed himself to a metallurgist for three years, and he soon became expert in assaying metals. After completing his course, he too went west, and stayed the first night there with his older brother. In the morning they went to look at the garden. With pride the elder brother pointed to the rows of the best cabbages one could ever wish to see. But the younger brother kept looking at the ground. Finally he picked up a handful of gravel from a little stream and examined it carefully.

"What are you doing?" asked his brother. "Here I show you the best cabbages in the world, and all you do is pick up a handful of dirt."

"Do you know what this is?" asked the younger brother, pointing to a piece of metal. "This is gold! You have been growing cabbages on a gold mine!" That ranch became one of the richest mines in the gold rush days of 1849.

"A good character is a capital of more value than gold or silver. . . . And in that day when earthly possessions shall be swept away it will bring rich returns. Integrity, firmness, and perseverance are qualities that all should seek earnestly to cultivate" (*Messages to Young People*, p. 416).

And be kind to one another, tenderhearted, forgiving one another. Ephesians 4:32.

January 25

How beautiful it is to see how Joseph loved and respected his dear old father. Surrounded as he was with wealth and honor in Egypt, his thoughts were of the one who had guided and cared for him, and he asked his brothers, "Is your father well?" (Genesis 43:27).

Few of us realize fully how much our parents have done for us, how much they have worried over us, or how much they love us.

Dr. S. Parkes Cadman was one of America's well-known evangelists and authors. When he was a boy, he lived in England and worked in a coal mine. One day he was given the job of driving a mule that hauled a car of coal through one of the long dark tunnels of the mine. On his track was a very dangerous crossing. The track that crossed his track went up a steep incline, and once in a while a car full of coal broke loose and came thundering back to the crossing. Several boys had been killed by crashes at this spot.

As young Cadman approached this dangerous intersection on his very first trip he thought of all the terrible accidents he had heard about, and he was so afraid that cold perspiration broke out all over him. Suddenly his mule turned the last corner, and there, right at the crossing, he saw a light! He was so glad that big happy tears welled up in his eyes and ran down his cheeks. Nearer and nearer he came to the light. A man was holding a lantern in his hands. It looked like—it was—it was his father! His father was a coal miner; he remembered how he had felt the first time he drove a mule through a dark tunnel, and now he was there to hold a light for his boy as he made his first trip.

Dr. Cadman often told that story of his father's care and love, and he always said, "That was the most beautiful light I have ever seen in all my life, and my dirty, coal-smeared father standing there with a grin on his face and the light in his hand was the handsomest man I have ever seen."

I am sure that your father has often held a light for you also at the dangerous places in your life. Thank God for good fathers.

GENESIS 44

For how shall I go up to my father if the lad is not with me?
Genesis 44:34.

January **26**

When Judah asked his father's permission to take Benjamin to Egypt the second time that the brothers went to buy grain, Judah went as security for him. He gave his word of honor that he would bring Benjamin back or bear the blame forever. Now that Joseph was testing his brothers to see whether they were still jealous, Judah begged to be allowed to become a servant in the place of Benjamin, in whose sack the governor's cup had been found. "How shall I go up to my father if the lad is not with me?" he asked. In other words, "How can I break my promise? I must keep my word."

Judah had some unlovely traits of character, but he had dependability, or reliability—the keeping of one's word of honor, one of the most beautiful and most valuable traits.

In A.D. 79 Pompeii, one of the most beautiful cities in Italy, was destroyed by the volcano Vesuvius. Many people were buried by the tons of ashes that fell on the city while they were trying to escape. Others smothered in deep underground basements where they had fled for safety. But there was one person who did not try to escape. He did not flee to safety. He was the Roman soldier stationed at the city gate. He remained at his post of duty and perished in his proper place. There he had been stationed by his captain. There, while the heavens poured fiery hot ashes upon him and lava streamed about him, he stood with his hands grasping his weapons. And there, more than 1,600 years later, scientists discovered his remains, still at his post.

This immortal story has become a symbol of this beautiful thing called reliability or dependability.

It's unlikely that you will be called upon to perish at your post of duty, but keep your word of honor to all people at all times. "Character strength is made up of two things: power of will, and power of self-control." True greatness and nobility are measured by one's power to subdue their feelings, not by the power of feelings to subdue them (see *Messages to Young People*, p. 412).

See that ye fall not out by the way.
Genesis 45:24, KJV.

January 27

The worst way to fall is to fall out, because it is hard to say you're sorry and make friends again. Joseph had given his brothers the secret of how not to fall out, and also its cure. Joseph had forgiven his brothers, and he wanted them to keep a forgiving spirit always in their hearts. There is a story told about a grown-up family of five brothers and sisters, Philip, Roger, Louis, Gertrude, and Ellen.

When their aging father died, Philip ran off with all the inheritance money. He didn't even say goodbye. For years they didn't hear from him, and naturally thought that he had spent all the money he'd taken.

Then one Christmas they each received a Christmas card from Philip. He gave no address, so they could not reply, but they said to one another, "He must be getting hard up. He wants to make friends again. He'll be asking us for help soon." You can only imagine how they felt after all Philip had done, but at last Ellen said, "If he's in trouble, I'll help him all I can. After all, he's our brother."

"I will too," agreed Roger, Gertrude, and Louis, and they started an account at the bank for Philip.

Five more years went by. Five times they each received Christmas cards from Philip, but never an address. Then one night someone knocked on Louis' door. It was Philip!

Louis began to explain, "If you're in need, we have started an account—"

"No! No!" said Philip. "I've come back to ask your forgiveness. How could I ever have wronged you all so much? But one night when all the money was gone I went into a church to get out of the cold. Afterward, all I could remember was one word: "Repent! Repent!" But I couldn't sleep, and that night I decided I would pay back every penny that I had stolen. It has taken a long time to save the money, but here it is." He took out his wallet and gave each of them their share of the full amount. Can you imagine the happiness it brought to them all? Can you imagine who was the happiest?

Keep your heart soft and tender, and full of a forgiving spirit, and you need never worry about falling out with anybody.

GENESIS 46:1-7, 28-34

Do not fear to go down to Egypt. . . . I will go down with you to Egypt, and I will also surely bring you up again. Genesis 46:3, 4.

January **28**

How comforting it was for Jacob to know that God was going with him into Egypt. He knew he would be safe with God, no matter what happened.

This same assurance has comforted God's servants all through the ages.

When Ellen Gould Harmon was only 17 years old, God called her to a very special place in His service. God gave her a vision of the Advent people traveling the straight and narrow path to heaven. In a second vision the angel said: "Make known to others what I have revealed to you." But Ellen was very troubled. She had poor health, and she suffered so much that it looked as if she had only a short time to live. It seemed impossible for her to do the work the angel gave her. She was also afraid that she might become proud if she spoke as God's servant. Then came the promise. The angel told her that the hand of God would be stretched out to save her, and if she delivered the message faithfully and endured to the end, she would eat of the fruit of the tree of life and drink of the water of life.

Ellen grasped the promise, and was faithful to her call. She later became Ellen G. White, and lived to deliver God's messages for 70 years. She wrote more than 80 books, and traveled in many countries all over the world. She could not have done it without God and His protection. In 1854 she and her husband were to take the train from Jackson, Michigan, to Wisconsin. They felt a strange anxiety about the journey and prayed for God's protection. When the train arrived they got aboard a coach toward the front of the train, but it seemed to be full so they walked further back into another coach and there found seats.

The train had gone only three miles when there was an awful crash. The engine was derailed. The front car was raised nearly on end, and the car they had first tried to find seats in was badly damaged. However, the car in which they were sitting was unfastened from the wrecked cars, as though an angel had separated them from the wreck. How comforting it was for them to know that God was with them.

If time lasts, you might be called into God's service. Never be afraid to go. You are always safe for eternity when you go with God.

Honor your father and your mother.
Exodus 20:12.

January 29

What a beautiful example Joseph has given us of honoring our fathers and our mothers. Today godly people everywhere make careful plans to care for their aged, sick, or invalid parents. They bring them into their homes where they can enjoy the companionship of their children and grandchildren, and when they need extra help, they care for them in a nursing home.

Take a pen and figure out how much money it has cost your parents for just your food, clothing, and perhaps tuition from the time you were born till you will be on your own at 18. You will find the total comes to many thousands of dollars, and this does not begin to include the thousands of hours they have given to your care in cooking your meals, washing your clothes, driving you here and there, and looking after you when you are sick. What a privilege it is for us to return some of this love and care when our parents grow old.

Queenie was a little Solomon Islands girl. It was during World War II, and her father was away at work in the mountains. The enemy were landing on her island and had passed the word around that they were going to burn the Adventist village where Queenie lived because the people there were helping the Allies. In their fear and excitement everybody picked up a bundle of food or clothing and fled to the mountains. Everyone, that is, but Queenie, her baby brother only a few hours old, and her dear, sick mother. Queenie was only 8, but she wouldn't leave her mother and little brother to run away to save her life. Not she! She got a little bundle of food and put it on her back. She wrapped up the tiny baby and held him in one arm, then pulled and coaxed her mother to try to walk just a little bit. The mother was very weak, so she went slowly and had to rest often, but Queenie kept pulling and coaxing. Soon after dark they saw the flames from their burning village, but Queenie kept going, carrying the baby and pulling and coaxing her mother, till by midnight they reached safety, and all was well.

What a noble example Queenie has given us all! I met Queenie when I visited our Kambubu College a few years ago. I was so proud of her. Make up your mind now that you too will honor your dear parents and care for them when the need arises.

GENESIS 48, 49

The scepter shall not depart from Judah . . . until Shiloh comes.
Genesis 49:10.

January 30

In spite of the fact that some of the kings of Judah and Israel were bad men, we must always remember that both the good and the bad ruled with the permission of God. And even among the rulers of the nations, Daniel tells us that "the Most High rules in the kingdom of men, and gives it to whomever He chooses" (Daniel 4:25).

Today is the birthday of Franklin D. Roosevelt, president of the United States of America for more than 12 years (1933-1945), longer than any other American president. Born in 1882, he was a member of the New York Senate (1911-1913) and practiced law in New York City (1919-1927). Sad to say, in 1921 he was struck with polio, and for a while it looked as if that would be the end of his career. His friends were anxious and his enemies clapped their hands, but Roosevelt wouldn't give up. To the surprise of the whole world, he made a heroic comeback. In 1928 and again in 1930 he was elected governor of New York, and from 1933 to 1945 he was four times elected president of the United States.

Although he was very busy with the duties that come to a president, he found time to launch a caring successful project to help others. Because he had been paralyzed by polio himself, his heart went out to all the other victims of this awful disease. So he established the National Foundation for Infantile Paralysis to help treat and rehabilitate children who were affected by polio. In connection with this he sponsored the famous March of Dimes for two weeks just before his birthday, to raise funds for this project. In 1962 the March of Dimes raised nearly $25 million and gave assistance to some 22,000 polio patients. Thousands of polio patients learned to walk and lived to thank this courageous president for the helpful birthday idea he had. And now, since the discovery of a polio vaccine, few children in developed countries even know what polio is.

It is our duty to pray for our leaders, and to be subject to them. Let us do our duty faithfully and cheerfully until Jesus comes as King of kings. "For there is no authority except from God, and the authorities that exist are appointed by God. . . . Render therefore to all their due: . . . honor to whom honor" (Romans 13:1-7).

I beg you, please forgive the trespass of your brothers. Genesis 50:17.

The most joyful moments Joseph's brothers ever had were when they knew they were forgiven for their terrible behavior toward their father, Jacob. But now that Jacob was dead, they wanted the assurance of Joseph's forgiveness once more.

It isn't easy to ask someone to forgive you for doing them wrong. Ellen White says: "The warfare against self is the greatest battle that was ever fought. . . . Surrendering all to the will of God [is] a struggle; but the soul must submit to God before it can be renewed in holiness" (*Steps to Christ*, p. 43).

Years ago an elderly Christian woman was walking quietly down a street in New York City, carrying a basket of apples, when along came a mischievous young sailor. He rudely pushed against her and upset her basket, then stood by and laughed as she picked up the apples. Meekly the woman picked them up without saying a word. Then with a look of pity and kindness, she said to the laughing sailor, "God forgive you, son, as I do." Those quiet words did something to him. He stopped his laughing, and then the battle was on. The still small voice inside him said, "You ought to be ashamed of yourself." His bad heart replied, "I was only having fun." The still small voice said, "You ought to say you're sorry—go on." His face went red. "Go on, go on!" His voice choked up, but at last the words came. "Forgive me, and God bless you, kind mother. I'll never do the like again," and he put some money in her hand. Who was happy then? Both the woman and the sailor!

Of course, it isn't easy to ask for forgiveness, and it isn't easy to give forgiveness. You can depend on Satan making it as hard as he possibly can. But it is God's way to happiness. And the measure with which we forgive is the measure with which God forgives us.

A young blind boy was asked to explain forgiveness. He said, "It is the perfume that flowers breathe out when they are trampled upon." That's the kind of forgiveness Joseph gave to his brothers.

Make sure that you, too, give out this perfume of forgiveness.

EXODUS 1; 2

Take this child away and nurse him for me,
and I will give you your wages.
Exodus 2:9.

February **1**

Who gave Jochebed her wages for nursing the baby Moses? No doubt the princess gave her money, but that was not all the wages she received. God gave her better wages than money, for she had the satisfaction of seeing Moses grow up, turn his back on the pleasures of Egypt, and become, under God, the mighty deliverer of His people.

I hope that many of you will choose to be teachers when you're grown, because the wages that God pays teachers are the best in all the world!

Once upon a time two sisters were asked to teach a class of children in Sabbath school. "I can't teach," said the first sister, "and anyway, I'm too busy. I have just decided to embroider a lovely centerpiece for my table." So she didn't teach.

The second sister said, "I don't know how to teach either, but I think I ought to try. At least I will do my best." And so she did.

At night they sat at the table. One sister had a beautiful piece of linen with a pattern marked on it, already with a few inches of colored thread showing on it. The other sister had a headache and was making notes from a book on teaching. A week went by. The pattern on the centerpiece was taking shape, and the first sister smiled with satisfaction. The second sister was struggling through a book on storytelling.

Several weeks went by. The table centerpiece was finished and placed on the living room table, and visitors oohed and aahed as they saw it. The following Sabbath a little boy went home, thrilled and excited. "Mother, those people in the Bible are real! You ought to hear my Sabbath school teacher tell about them."

Several years went by. The centerpiece was faded and worn. "I can't stand the sight of it one more day," said the first sister as she stuffed it in the ragbag. The following Sabbath the other sister had the joy of seeing one of her Sabbath school students baptized—born into the kingdom of God. Oh, what wages!

There is no satisfaction so great as the joy of leading a soul to Christ. What are you going to be when you grow up?

EXODUS 3; 4:1-17, 27-31

I will be with your mouth, and teach you what you shall say. Exodus 4:12.

February 2

It is easy to understand how God could tell Moses what to say. Moses was a grown-up man and well educated. But our pioneer storybooks and our church papers have many stories in them that show how God can fulfill this promise to juniors and teens, and even to younger children.

There are the stories of the young people, and even of a little 5-year-old girl in Sweden who preached "The hour of his judgment is come." And there is another story I like to tell of a little girl who went to camp meeting in Buckston, Maine, when she was just 6 years old. Her greatest treasure was a little pink umbrella that she carried around with her all the time, and even took to bed with her. When she heard the ministers pleading with the people to give up everything and get ready for Jesus, she began to fear that she loved her pink umbrella too much, and thought she should give it up for Jesus too. But how could she do it? She hugged it tightly in her arms, looked at it lovingly, and then burst into tears. "Dear Jesus," she said, "I want to love You and go to heaven too. Take away my sins. I give myself to You, umbrella and all." Her mother threw her arms around her little girl as she said, "Oh, Mother, I'm so happy. Jesus loves me, and I love Him better than any pink umbrella or anything."

Of course, the preacher explained that since she wouldn't let the umbrella take her love from Jesus, she might keep it, and the little one was happy. But she had no idea how much encouragement her few words and tears brought to the people in the big tent that day—and to one girl there, 17 years old, who received a great blessing from this little one's words. This teenager was Ellen Harmon. Do you know who she was and who she became afterward?

You remember that Jesus said to His disciples, "But when they deliver you up, do not worry about how or what you should speak. For it will be given to you in that hour what you should speak; for it is not you who speak, but the Spirit of your Father who speaks in you" (Matthew 10:19, 20). And that promise is for all, old and young, who will keep close to Him.

God wants to teach you what to say too. Won't you keep close to Him and let Him do it?

EXODUS 5; 6

*I will bring you out from under the burdens
of the Egyptians, . . . and I will redeem you
with an outstretched arm.
Exodus 6:6.*

Ever since the days of the martyr Abel, the people of God have had periods of persecution and bad treatment from enemies of God. God has permitted these trials to come so that His people could learn to pray and trust in Him.

The children of Israel suffered a great deal at the hands of the Egyptians, "but the more they afflicted them, the more they multiplied and grew" (Exodus 1:12). The same was true in the days of the early Christian church. They were persecuted and scattered abroad, but "the hand of the Lord was with them, and a great number believed and turned to the Lord" (Acts 11:21).

The same is true in many places today. In a certain country, which better not be named, in 1956 nine Seventh-day Adventists were killed, 49 were beaten and wounded, 89 laypersons were imprisoned, 108 church workers and colporteurs were imprisoned, and 234 believers had to flee from their homes to the mountains. Two of those who were killed were junior boys who were known in their community as "singing Sabatistas." They loved the Lord and were soon to be baptized. They were caught by their enemies, tied back to back, and then ordered to sing. "Sing, you heretics, sing!" the mob shouted angrily, and our juniors sang. And when their songs were finished they were kicked and beaten, then stabbed to death.

We are sure that those dear boys will be given special honor with Stephen and John the Baptist someday. But listen. Before this trouble we had only 2,000 Adventists in that country, but only a few years later the membership was nearly 100,000!

"While the Lord has not promised His people exemption from trials, He has promised that which is far better. He has said, 'As thy days, so shall thy strength be.'. . . If you are called to go through the fiery furnace for His sake, Jesus will be by your side even as He was with the faithful three in Babylon" (*Thoughts From the Mount of Blessing*, p. 30).

Sometimes I think we have things too easy, and our lives are too soft. But our turn at persecution will come someday. Let us learn now how to trust in the Lord, so that we will be faithful.

Today, if you will hear His voice:
"Do not harden your hearts."
Psalm 95:7, 8.

February 4

Many people have misunderstood the third verse of our Scripture reading today (Exodus 7:3), where it says, "I will harden Pharaoh's heart." They have thought that Pharaoh was not to blame for refusing to let God's people go. But in Exodus 8:15 we read: "When Pharaoh saw that there was relief, he hardened his heart." And that is the correct meaning, for God has given everybody the privilege of choosing. Each of us can make our heart like wax or like clay. Put wax in the sunshine, and it becomes soft; put clay in the sun and it becomes hard.

Elder W. A. Spicer used to tell a story about a barrelmaker in Brussels who said he didn't believe there was a God and who never read the Bible or went to church. However, an Adventist evangelist came to this town, and this man's wife and their little 3-year-old daughter went to the meetings. "Don't you ever go there again," said the man angrily, when he found out they were going. "If you do, I will kill you." But his wife softly replied, "Husband, I love God, and as long as I live I will go to worship Him." And she went again. When she came home, the husband was furious. He knocked her down, dragged her over to his chopping block, lifted his sharp ax, and shouted, "Now I'm going to chop your head off." "You could easily do it," said his wife softly. "You are stronger than I am, but you'd never get another woman to love you and cook for you and look after your little girl for you the way I do." Suddenly the man felt ashamed and threw the ax down, but he was too angry to speak to her for a long time.

The mother kept on going to the meetings and was baptized. Then one Sabbath morning the little girl climbed on her father's knee, put her arms around his neck, and said, "Daddy, please come to Sabbath school with Mommy and me. Don't you know Jesus is coming soon to take us to heaven?" Tears came to the father's eyes, and with a choking voice he said, "Do you really want me to come?" "Of course," she answered, giving him a big kiss. "What would Mommy and I do without you in heaven?" So he went to Sabbath school, and he kept on going. At last he was baptized and became a deacon in the church. You see, he himself had hardened his heart. He *chose* to resist the Spirit of God. Then later he *chose* to believe and respond to the Spirit.

See to it that you do not harden your heart.

EXODUS 8

So Moses . . . entreated the Lord. And the Lord
did according to the word of Moses.
Exodus 8:30, 31.

February 5

God gave Moses special training to prepare him to be the leader of His people and to deliver them from the hand of Pharaoh. Today is the birthday of William Miller, another man whom God trained and used to establish the Second Advent message in America.

Miller was born in 1782 and lived most of his life in Low Hampton, New York. He was the oldest of 16 brothers, so there was little time for school. But his mother taught him to read, and he loved to sit by the fireplace at night and read the Bible, the psalmbook, the prayer book, and history books. After he was married, his friends influenced him to read books that denied Christ and ridiculed the Bible, so although he believed in God, he was not a Christian. For two years he was a soldier in the War of 1812, and what he saw there made him wonder whether there really would be a judgment. Now, Mr. Miller's grandfather was a good old Baptist minister, and soon a little company of Baptists was raised up and a little church was built near his house. Just to please his mother, William used to go to church on Sunday. When there was no preacher, one of the deacons would read a sermon, but because he couldn't read very well people liked for William to read instead. So Mr. Miller read sermons to the people—sermons that he did not believe. Before long he was converted and began to study his Bible earnestly. He found the prophecies in Daniel about the judgment and the cleansing of the sanctuary, and he believed they meant that Jesus was coming in 1844.

Then one day the still small voice spoke to him, "Go and tell it to the world." And he did. And because of his preaching, many began to study and to understand the true meaning of the cleansing of the sanctuary. Soon they found what the Bible says about the true Sabbath, and that is how the Seventh-day Adventist message began.

"There is no limit to the usefulness of one who, by putting self aside, makes room for the working of the Holy Spirit upon his heart, and lives a life wholly consecrated to God" (*The Desire of Ages*, pp. 250, 251).

February 6

But indeed for this purpose I have raised you up, that I may show My power in you, and that My name may be declared in all the earth. Exodus 9:16.

Pharaoh hardened his heart, and all the world has heard the story. But if Pharaoh had softened his heart and obeyed God, and allowed the children of Israel to go in the first place, the mercy and greatness of God would have been told around the world just as much and maybe more.

A few years ago I was visiting our Sabbath schools in the land of the pharaohs. At one place I met a strong, muscular young man with a handshake like a grip of iron. "Who is that young man?" I asked. "His name is Adlai Botross," our leader told me. "When I first came here and hired this hall in which to hold meetings, he was the worst man in town. He used to be a prize-fighter, and when he got drunk he was the terror of the town. Of course, we had some enemies in this place, and they promised Adlai some money and some whiskey if he would disturb the meetings. He was glad for the chance. So at the very first meeting, there he was, sitting under the light switch, ready to turn out the lights and shout. Then the others were to come in and beat me up. But the singing touched his heart, and he listened all the way through.

"'What's the matter with you?' said our enemies to him after the meeting. 'Here we promise you money and whiskey, and you just sit.'

"'Oh, I forgot all about it,' said Adlai. 'That man is a good preacher, but I'll do it tomorrow night.'

"The next night he came again, and again sat quietly all through.

"'What's the matter with you?' asked our enemies again after the meeting.

"'Listen,' said Adlai. 'I don't intend to disturb that man tonight or *any* night. He is preaching the truth, and you know it. I'm going to come to every meeting, and if any of you want to disturb that preacher, you'll have to disturb me first.'

"He did come to every meeting. Our enemies were too afraid of him to try disturbing the preacher anymore, and Adlai Botross was the first to be baptized."

God sees in every one of us something worthwhile—something He needs. Won't you let Him show His power in you?

EXODUS 10; 11

We will go with our young and our old; with our sons
and our daughters, . . . for we must hold a feast to the Lord.
Exodus 10:9.

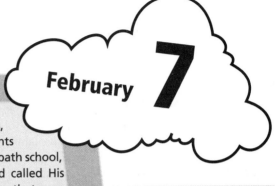

February **7**

God has always had a place for juniors and teens, and even tiny tots, in His great plan of salvation. God wants boys and girls in family worship, in Sabbath school, in church, and in heaven. When God called His people out of Egypt, He wasn't willing that even one be left behind. We are on our way from this wicked old earth to heaven, and if you could hear the hearts of your parents talking, they would be saying, "With our young and our old, with our sons and our daughters, will we go, for we must be together in heaven." God has put these longings in the hearts of parents, for that is part of His plan.

Have you ever read *Pilgrim's Progress?* You know, the first part of that book tells how a man named Christian struggled through this world and into the kingdom of heaven. Then the second part tells how his wife, Christiana, and the children struggled through this world to the kingdom of heaven also. Well, one day a grandmother finished reading this book to her 5-year-old grandson, Johnny. As she closed the book, Johnny looked into her face and said, "Grandma, in all the book, which person did you like the best?" Grandma thought quickly, then replied, "I think I liked Christian the best."

"You did?" asked Johnny, a little surprised.

"Yes," replied Grandma. "Didn't you?"

"No," said Johnny, "I didn't."

"Well, which one did you like the best?" asked Grandma.

"I liked Christiana the best, I did," said Johnny.

"And why did you like Christiana the best?" asked Grandma.

"Because Christiana took the children with her. That's why," said Johnny.

"I think you're right," agreed Grandma thoughtfully.

I know that your parents' greatest hope is to take you with them into the kingdom of heaven. See that you make it as easy for them as is possible. Come willingly to family worship. Go willingly to Sabbath school, and sit willingly with them when they go to church to worship the Lord.

When I see the blood, I will pass over you; and the plague shall not be on you to destroy you when I strike the land of Egypt.
Exodus 12:13.

February 8

There is a story that I love to tell. It is about a firstborn son in a Hebrew home on that first Passover night. The lamb had been slain. Jared, the faithful servant, had been told to sprinkle the blood upon the doorposts. The lamb had been roasted and eaten with bitter herbs, and now while the older members of the family all waited the fateful midnight hour, the little son was told to sleep. He tried and tried to go to sleep, but he couldn't. "Father, I've named the patriarchs and all the animals that Noah took into the ark, but still I cannot sleep. Father, are you sure the blood is on the doorposts?"

"Yes, yes, my firstborn," said the father soothingly. "I gave the word. You have nothing to fear. The angel will see the sign and pass over you."

He tried again, but he could not sleep. "Oh, Father," he cried, "I seem to see the angel pausing sadly at our door. What if the blood has been washed off or if Jared forgot?"

"Rest, rest, little one," said the father. "Jared is faithful, and even if some hungry dog licked the blood from the side posts, the blood would still be on the top, and the angel would see it. Sleep, sleep, my little one."

The night wore on. Sleep came at last, but with it a frightful dream. "Father, oh, Father," the boy cried out, "my heart is filled with fear of coming danger. Take me, please, take me to the door and let me see the blood."

The father lit a torch, tenderly lifted his little son in his arms, and took him to the door. The blood had not been sprinkled! It was still in the bowl. Trembling, the father took the hyssop and, in eager haste, he himself applied the blood. A sigh of relief escaped the boy's lips, and he was asleep before he was put on his bed. And when the great cry arose and the children of Israel went out of Egypt, he didn't even wake up. His father carried him in his arms, still sleeping peacefully.

Have you been baptized? Are you careful to take part in the ordinance of humility and of the Lord's Supper at church each quarter? This is one way we apply the blood of Jesus to the doorposts of our hearts. Jesus has shed His blood for us—but *we* must apply it.

EXODUS 13:17-22; 14

*"Do not be afraid. Stand still and see the salvation
of the Lord." . . . And the Lord said to Moses . . . ,
"Tell the children of Israel to go forward."
Exodus 14:13-15.*

February 9

I can never forget how God enabled five of us missionaries to cross the Irrawaddy River with two motor cars when we were escaping from the war in Burma. No more boats ran across the wide river, and it looked impossible to get to the other side. At last we hired two large country boats and tied them together, but we could not find any big long planks to place across the boats on which to put the cars. There was a sawmill in the town of Myingyan, three miles away, but it was locked up. The owner and the workmen had fled into the country, and no one knew where they were. We were stuck. I heard the boatmen laughing at our trouble.

"They will have to leave their cars and go across the river in canoes!" said one.

"I'm going to have a wheel!" "I'm going to have a suitcase!" said others.

Sick and weary, I turned to God in prayer: "O God, it is not as hard to get only five of us across the river as it was to get the children of Israel across the Red Sea." But no answer came. I prayed again and again. Midnight came, but no answer. One o'clock . . . two . . . three . . . four o'clock, and then the answer came. The still small voice seemed to say in my heart, "Go to the sawmill in the town. Go now!" I woke up the boatman and said, "My God has just told me to go now to the sawmill."

"All right," he said, "I'll go with you." We got a bullock wagon and went into the town, and we found the gates of the sawmill open. The son of the mill owner had come for some important papers and had just opened the gates as we arrived. He sold us four big long planks, and we loaded them onto the cart and drove out of the gate. The mill owner's son came out after us, closed the gate, and went back to his father's hiding place.

The old boatman and I walked in silence for a while behind the planks my God had provided for us; then he touched my hand and said, "Your God did talk to you, didn't He?"

God did talk to me that night—but what if I had not obeyed?

*If you diligently heed the voice of the Lord your God . . . ,
I will put none of the diseases on you which I have
brought on the Egyptians. For I am the Lord
who heals you. Exodus 15:26.*

February 10

Our great God is still changing bitter experiences into sweet ones. It was the middle of winter in New York City. Elder and Mrs. W. A. Fagal (founders of the TV program *Faith for Today*) had gone to bed. Their daughter was attending a program, and her mother sat in bed reading till she would return. Suddenly Mrs. Fagal smelled smoke. Jumping out of bed, she found fire in the basement. She rushed next door and telephoned, and soon firefighters came and put the fire out. It had damaged only the basement, but the Fagals were told not to sleep in their house that night. Kind neighbors took them in. Early in the morning they heard the sirens of fire trucks, and, looking out, they found their house was on fire again! This time the upstairs was burning.

"Never mind the clothes and the furniture," Mrs. Fagal told the firefighters who were trying to save some of their belongings. "Only try to get the letters on the desk. They're the *Faith for Today* letters. Some have checks in them, some have lessons, and some have application cards in them. Please try to get them." Soon one of the firefighters came out with the briefcase. Some of the letters were in it, but others were on the desk. "I couldn't get anything else," he said.

Still Mrs. Fagal kept praying, "Dear Lord, please keep the letters safe. Don't let them burn up. The people need this truth. Please, Lord." In a few hours there was nothing left of their home but a heap of ashes. It was so cold that in the gutters and on the street the water from the fire hoses had become sheets of ice. Even the water at the bottom of the ashes was solid ice. Later on the Fagals poked around in the ashes, looking to see whether there was anything not burned. They dug down through the ashes till they came to the ice at the bottom, and there, frozen in the ice, were the *Faith for Today* letters that had been washed off the desk by the water used to fight the fire. The ice was melted off; the letters were dried; and although they were smudgy, they were still readable and the checks still cashable.

When some great disappointment comes to you, remember that God can change the bitter into sweet.

EXODUS 16

*[Do not] complain, as some of them also
complained, and were destroyed by the destroyer.
1 Corinthians 10:10.*

February **11**

God had delivered His chosen people. But before He could bring them into the Promised Land it was necessary for Him to prove them, to see whether they would obey His commands. He tested them at the bitter waters of Marah; they failed and complained. He tested them with a 15-day journey through the wilderness; they failed and complained. Again and again they failed and complained, and the complainers never did get into the Promised Land.

Today is the birthday of one of the world's greatest inventors, Thomas Alva Edison. One of his outstanding qualities was that he never acknowledged failure or defeat. He never quit. He is credited with making nearly 1,100 inventions in 60 years. After completing 10,000 experiments with a project in his electrical laboratory, some friends told him not to be discouraged about his failures. But Edison replied, "I have not failed. I've found 10,000 ways that won't work!" He has given the world the well-known saying "Success is 1 percent inspiration and 99 percent perspiration."

When Edison was 9 years old, his mother bought him a chemistry book. Young Tom proved every experiment to make sure it worked. He had 100 bottles marked "poison" to keep others from touching them. When he was 12 years old, he got a job selling newspapers, candy, and peanuts on a train. Between his trips through the train, he kept on experimenting in the baggage car, till one day there was an explosion that set the car on fire. At age 16 he got a job as a telegrapher. He had to report train activities every hour to Toronto, Ontario, Canada. Soon he invented a device that would do the reporting automatically. In 1877 he invented the phonograph; in 1879 the incandescent electric lamp; and in 1888 his motion picture machine, called the kinetoscope. He was called the Wizard of Menlo Park.

Yet in his greatness he was humble. "I can invent," he said, "but I cannot create." God has given you talents also. You may make some mistakes. You may encounter some failures. But never complain, and never quit.

And when you have returned to Me, strengthen your brethren. Luke 22:32.

February 12

I love to think of Aaron and Hur holding up, or strengthening, the hands of Moses as he prayed for Israel to be victorious over the Amalekites. It is so easy to criticize our leaders, our teachers, and our workers, but Aaron and Hur left us a beautiful example of being kind and helpful. You know that today is the birthday of Abraham Lincoln. He was born in a log cabin in Kentucky, on February 12, 1809. Maybe more than any other president of the United States he is loved for his kindness and helpfulness to all. Many books have been written of how this great man lifted, strengthened, and supported others, but here is a paragraph from one of my favorite books—an imaginary story of how God made Abraham Lincoln.

"He took a little babe and called to his side, His favorite angel, the angel of sorrow. Stooping, he whispered, 'O Sorrow, thou well-beloved teacher, take thou this child of mine and make him great. Take him to yonder cabin in the wilderness; make his home a poor man's home; plant his narrow path thick with thorns; cut his little feet with sharp rocks as he climbs the hill of difficulty. Make each footprint red with his own lifeblood; load his little back with burdens; give him days of toil and nights of study and sleeplessness. Wrest from his arms whatever he loves, make his heart, through sorrow, as sensitive to the sigh of a slave as a thread of silk in a window is sensitive to the slightest wind that blows; and when you have digged lines of pain in his cheek and made his face more marred than the face of any man of his time, bring him back to me, and with him I will free four million slaves'" (E. V. Odle, *Quest and Conquest*).

What a man was Lincoln! He was called names, criticized, and made fun of. But when his personal papers were opened and classified, there was not found one unkind word about anyone in all of his letters.

"Kind words, looks of sympathy, expressions of appreciation, would be to many a struggling and lonely one as the cup of cold water to a thirsty soul. A word of sympathy, an act of kindness, would lift burdens that rest heavily upon weary shoulders" (*Thoughts From the Mount of Blessing*, p. 23).

God expects you to be kind, and to strengthen the weak.

EXODUS 18

But in the multitude of counselors there is safety.
Proverbs 11:14.

February **13**

In our story today Moses has given us a splendid example of taking advice. If there is one thing we all need, it is to realize that we do not know everything yet. We can always learn from others, and it pays to take advice. Solomon said that in the multitude of counselors there is safety. In his delightful little book *University of Hard Knocks,* Ralph Parlette tells a pathetic little story about himself that illustrates the point excellently.

Little Ralph was 3 years old, and he thought he knew everything about what was good for him. One day he sat at the table in his high chair, and there on the table before him, within reaching distance, was the coffeepot. At once he knew that was just what he wanted. He needed that coffeepot in his business. He reached out for it, but his mother, sitting right beside him, said, "No, don't touch that coffeepot!" The idea! That mother of his was always spoiling his fun and meddling in his business. He did want that coffeepot. And the longer he thought about it, the more determined he was to have it—and the more angry he became with his unsympathetic mother. Always giving advice! What did she know about it, anyway? He decided emphatically not to take her advice, and while Mother was looking elsewhere he reached out and got the coffeepot. He also got about a quart of the hottest coffee a boy ever spilled over himself. He felt the pain for weeks afterward. They put apple butter all over him, and coal oil and egg white and starch and anything else the neighbors could think of that might help. (Today we know that cold water is the best emergency treatment for hot water burns, and that he should have been taken to a doctor.)

As time went by, little Ralph learned that his mother really did know more than he did, and that if he did not take her advice a pot of boiling-hot coffee might spill on him.

Paul tells us that in the last days perilous times shall come and people will be lovers of their own selves, boasters, disobedient to parents, unthankful, unholy, despisers of those that are good. (See 2 Timothy 3:1-3.) This is the Bible way of saying that people of the world rebel against taking advice, and that's why so many get into hot water.

Learn to take advice from your parents and teachers. You may miss many a spilled quart of boiling-hot coffee if you do.

If you will indeed obey My voice and keep My covenant, then you shall be a special treasure to Me above all people.
Exodus 19:5.

February 14

Obedience must be very important, because so much is said about it in the Bible. Disobedience results in death, but obedience is rewarded with life.

I found this happy-ending story in the Washington *Star*, February 20, 1961: Seven-year-old Harry Stage went from his home in Phoenix, Arizona, with his father to a farm about 25 miles away. While his father was talking to Mr. Faubion, the ranch owner, Harry was playing near a little platform. Soon he climbed onto the platform, and there on the ground at one side of it he saw a piece of plywood. Without thinking, he jumped down onto it. It was the cover to an irrigation well 16 inches wide and 250 feet deep, with water at the bottom! As Harry jumped on it, it gave way, and down went Harry feet first. Down, down, down till he hit the water. Most of the plywood went with him, and no doubt this slowed his fall a little. When he hit the water, he was able to push against the sides of the well with his hands and keep himself from going under. "Daddy, get me out of here," he shouted.

"Don't worry, son, and don't be scared," replied his father calmly. "We'll get you out. Just push against the sides of the pipe so you don't sink."

"OK, Daddy," Harry shouted back, "I will."

Mr. Faubion drove seven miles to a neighbor's ranch and got many cowboy lariats. He tied them together, and they made a rope 300 feet long. The father put a strong loop on the end of it and let it carefully down the well. "I've got it, Daddy," called Harry. "I can hold on while you pull me up."

"No, no, son," said his father. "Put that loop over your head and under your arms." "OK," called back Harry. "I'll try." He tried and he did it, and soon called out, "OK, I'm ready." In minutes Harry was out of the well and in an ambulance. He had two broken legs, but was very much alive. "You're the bravest and luckiest boy in Arizona," Mr. Faubion said. Then his father added proudly, "He's always been an obedient boy."

Do you always obey, or do you sometimes think you're too old to be told what to do? Be careful. Obedience really pays.

EXODUS 20

If you love Me, keep My commandments.
John 14:15.

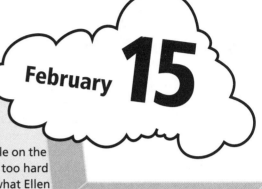
February 15

In Exodus 20 are written down the Ten Commandments of God—the great rules of life for men and women and boys and girls since there were people on the earth. Some say the commandments are too hard to keep, so they don't try. But listen to what Ellen White says: "The church of God is made up of vessels large and small. The Lord does not ask for anything unreasonable. He does not expect the smaller vessels to hold the contents of the larger ones. . . . Do your best, and God will accept your efforts" (*Messages to Young People,* p. 96).

One day when my son Leonard was just a little 4-year-old, he came walking into my office. "Daddy, Daddy! I love you," he said.

"You do?" I asked kindly.

"Yes, Daddy, I love you. You made me a toy car, didn't you, Daddy?"

"Yes, son," I replied. "I do lots of things for you because I love you too, don't I? But you don't do very much for me, do you?"

"But, Daddy, I want to. Tell me what to do, and I'll do it."

I thought quickly, then said, "Son, I'll tell you what to do. See that big green box in the other room? I need it right here by my desk. Will you bring it in for me?"

"Yes, Daddy, I'll bring it," he said, and off he went. He caught hold of the handle and pulled and grunted, but he couldn't move it. I knew he couldn't do it. But then he called, "Daddy, come and help me." I smiled as I went over and took the other handle, and together we pulled that big box into my office just where I wanted it.

"I did it, Daddy. Didn't I, Daddy? I did it," he said triumphantly. And I took him on my knee and hugged him tight.

"Of course you did it, son," I whispered. And from my little boy I leaned how we could keep the commandments of God.

I want you to notice that Lenny tried to carry the box, not because he had to, but because he wanted to. In doing his best to carry the box, he showed that he really did love me.

Do you really love God for all He has done for you? Then you can easily find a way to keep His commandments. He will help you as I helped Leonard.

All the words which the Lord has said we will do.
Exodus 24:3.

February 16

A very solemn promise is called a vow. God does not force anyone to make a vow, but if a vow is made, He does require that it be fulfilled. People who do not fulfill a vow are called traitors, betrayers, deserters, or deceivers, and they are despised by everyone.

On the battlefield of Saratoga, New York, stands a fine monument to commemorate the winning of the great battle. In the base of the tall shaft are four niches that were designed to hold the marble likenesses of the heads of the four American generals who fought in this battle. The marble heads of Generals Schuyler, Morgan, and Gates are there, but the fourth niche is empty and will always remain so. It was designed for General Benedict Arnold, who became a traitor to his country before it was finished.

Arnold took the oath of loyalty at the age of 15 and became a soldier, but before long he deserted. He ran a bookstore and drugstore for a while, but became tired of that and returned to the army. He served gallantly in several encounters against the British and was made a brigadier general. A year later he became a major general. In 1778 he was put in command of the forces at Philadelphia, but soon got into trouble and was court-martialed. Two years later he was sent to take command of the American forces at West Point. But he had kept his anger for the superior officers who had reprimanded him. In July 1780 Arnold entered into negotiations to betray the fort to the British for $30,000. The plot was foiled because the British agent was caught. Arnold escaped to the British lines, and was given a commission in the British Army, but he was despised and scorned even by the British. He died alone and friendless in a little upstairs room in London, June 14, 1801. It is said that the doctor who was attending him at the time of his death asked, "Is there anything else you need?"

"Yes," replied Arnold feebly. "I need a friend."

EXODUS 32

You shall not make for yourself a carved image; . . .
you shall not bow down to them nor serve them.
Exodus 20:4, 5.

February **17**

We can't help feeling a little dis-gusted with the children of Israel for falling into the sin of idol worship so soon after seeing their mavelous deliverance by the mighty, living God. But listen! Images are not all golden calves. What about the idols of self, popularity, money, and fashion? Were you ever tempted to bow down to them and serve them?

Two sisters, Jan and Kathy, once took a vacation in Miami. They had been working very hard in college, and so they decided that while they were away they might not live by the standards they usually followed. Near their hotel was a movie theater, and since they knew no one in town they decided to go see a movie they normally wouldn't have viewed. But it so happened that some other nice young people staying at the same hotel saw them leaving the theater and invited them to a beach party the next day. Both girls played guitars, and they all had a good time.

Then one of the young men said, "Anyone want to play poker?"

"Oh, yes, let's," said some of the others.

Jan looked at Kathy and whispered, "Just once won't hurt us." So they let themselves be taught the game, and each lost just a little money. Then Friday afternoon one of the young men said, "I've hired a launch to take us all for an outing and a beach picnic tonight."

"And you'll bring your guitars, girls, won't you?" asked Mrs. Marshall, the young man's mother.

But that evening Jan and Kathy talked things over. "I wish we hadn't tried to cover up who we really are," Jan sighed. "I don't feel right going to a party on a Friday night."

"Why can't one of us get a sick headache?" Kathy moaned.

"I wish!" Jan said. "But I've decided to go to Mrs. Marshall and tell her we're Seventh-day Adventists and this is our Sabbath—even if we did make some mistakes." And she did. And Mrs. Marshall understood perfectly and admired the girls all the more for their courage and their convictions.

Just be sure that you don't bow down to some golden calf someday and worship it.

*I will be gracious to whom I will be gracious,
and I will have compassion on whom
I will have compassion.
Exodus 33:19.*

February 18

Israel had sinned against the Lord so terribly that they deserved to be consumed. But in response to Moses' pleading, God extended His gracious mercy toward all who would repent. Remember, there is always hope and happiness ahead for those who are truly sorry for their sins and repent.

Once upon a time, according to an oft-told story, two brothers moved out to California and started a sheep ranch. They were dishonest young men, and after being suspected for some time, they were caught actually stealing their neighbors' sheep. In those days in the "wild and woolly" West it was just too much trouble to have the men arrested, taken to court, and put in jail, so the neighbors took the law into their own hands. With a red-hot branding iron they branded both men on the forehead—ST for sheep thief—then let them go. One of the brothers was so utterly ashamed that he moved away, built a tiny cabin high up in the hills, and, afraid that the story would follow him, became a hermit and kept away from people as much as he could.

The other brother said, "I can't run forever. I'll stay right here and make things right." And he did. He gave back the sheep that he'd stolen, lived an honest life, and in time was looked up to as one of the leading citizens of the community. One day one of the neighbor boys was helping him shear some sheep, and when he took his hat off to wipe the perspiration from his brow the boy was surprised to see scars on his forehead that looked like ST. That night he asked his father, "Did you ever see those scars on that man's forehead? What does ST stand for?" The father didn't want to tell his boy of the man's sin and punishment of so long ago, so he thought for a moment, then said, "Let me see. In the Bible don't we have S-T Matthew and S-T Mark and S-T Luke and S-T John?"

"Well, Dad," replied the boy, "that could be it. If there's a saint around here, he's the one!"

I hope you never fall, but if you do, get right back up. Receive God's gracious mercy, and become an S-T.

EXODUS 34:1-14, 21-35

Six days you shall work, but on the seventh day you shall rest.
Exodus 34:21.

February 19

The first lesson Israel had to learn was how to live successfully. That's why God gave them the Ten Commandments. Obedience to those commandments would make them different from all other people in the world. And the commandment that would make them most different would be the keeping of the seventh-day Sabbath.

Very early in my ministry in Burma I set out one day with an evangelist to visit one of our church members. We knew his name—Aung Baw—and we knew he lived in the Doyin district. We also knew that he was cross-eyed and that when he was young he had been a prizefighter. But we did not know in which of the 30 or more villages in that district he lived. We hired a bullock wagon and went to the nearest village in the Doyin district and asked the headman if he could direct us to the Aung Baw who used to be a prizefighter and was cross-eyed.

"Aung Baw? Aung Baw?" said the headman. "Used to be a prizefighter, and you say he's cross-eyed? No, I'm sorry. I've never heard of him, but try the next village."

We tried the next village and the next, with always the same result. At last I became desperate. "Somebody must know him," I said. "He belongs to our mission and he keeps the seventh-day—"

"Oh, you mean that seventh-day man?" blurted out one of the seven headmen we had asked. "Why, yes! Everybody knows him, but we didn't know his name and we didn't know he had been a prizefighter. But we all know he keeps the Sabbath. He's different. Look! See that mountain with the little pagoda on top of it? Well, straight down at the bottom of that mountain you'll find that seventh-day man."

And sure enough, within an hour we had found Brother Aung Baw. We could have looked for a cross-eyed prizefighter for days, and might never have found him.

Someday the angels are going to be looking for people to take to heaven. If you love Jesus and are following His commands, they will have no trouble finding you.

Take from among you an offering to the Lord. Whoever is of a willing heart, let him bring it . . . : gold, silver, and bronze.
Exodus 35:5.

February 20

When the hearts of the children of Israel were right with God, they loved to bring offerings to help along the Lord's work. And it has always been the same. We had only two organized Sabbath schools 133 years ago. Twenty-six years later we had 177 Sabbath schools, with 5,851 members. Then the Advent people began to bring their offerings, at first for their Sabbath school supplies. After eight more years they began to bring offerings for the Lord's work in the mission fields. In 25 more years they had brought in $1 million for missions! And there were more than 4,000 Sabbath schools, with nearly 103,000 members. By the end of 1984, members had brought in $628 million for the Lord's work, and there were more than 50,000 Sabbath schools and more than 5,340,000 members. In 1984 the Sabbath school offering totaled more than $30,212,000, or an average of nearly $1 every second! That is the way God blesses when His people bring a willing offering.

In Puerto Rico there lived a small widow who had quite a large family. Everyone called her Mother Borrilla. One day she went to Sabbath school, and when she heard the appeal for an offering she felt that she ought to give $2. Now, $2 was just about all she had, but she loved the Lord, and she knew He would give her strength to wash clothes and earn some more money. So she willingly gave her $2 for an offering. Soon after going home she went out into the backyard, and what do you think? Two mina birds flew overhead, and each one had a $1 bill in its beak. They must have found them somewhere and thought they would make a nice lining for their nest. But a mysterious thing happened. They opened their beaks, and the two $1 bills floated right down to Mother Borrilla's feet. She knew God would bless her for her willing sacrifice in some way or another, but she hardly expected a miracle like this.

Do you bring a willing, loving offering to the Lord every Sabbath? And does God bless you for it?

EXODUS 40

You shall keep My Sabbaths and reverence
My sanctuary: I am the Lord.
Leviticus 19:30.

February **21**

When the tabernacle was finished, it was filled with the glory
of the Lord. Every time the priest entered the tabernacle, and every time the children
of Israel came near it, they were quiet and reverent, because they could see the cloud and almost
feel the presence of God. When you go to church,
do you feel God's presence there? An astronomer once said, "I have swept the
heavens with my telescope, and nowhere have I found God." But another astronomer by the name of Kepler, after discovering the planetary motions, said,
"God, these are Thy thoughts I am thinking after Thee." What made the difference? Just going to church won't make you a Christian any more than going to a
garage makes you a mechanic. It is your being quiet and reverent in church that
enables you to find the glory of God there, and once you have found God, He can
do anything He wants to with you.

Once upon a time, when our first missionaries were going to India, a little
baby boy was born in Seattle, Washington. His father was not an Adventist, but
his mother was, and she began taking her baby boy to Sabbath school and
church soon after he was born. She taught him to sit quietly in church, and
when he was big enough, she taught him that church is God's house. Every
Sabbath he looked forward to putting on his Sabbath clothes so that he could
go to God's house. When he grew bigger, he heard the Word of God read and
preached there; he heard about the missionaries who were doing God's work
all over the world. And when he was 12, he said, "Mother, God needs more
than nickels and quarters. I think He needs me for a missionary too." He was
baptized, and eventually he went to Walla Walla College. After he graduated, he went to the Philippine islands as a missionary and was there for 19
years. Then the Lord's work organized in South America needed a president,
so he served there for 10 years. In 1954 our denomination needed a new
General Conference president, and Reuben R. Figuhr was ready for the responsibility. The baby boy who'd loved Sabbath school and who had felt
God's call to the mission fields became the president of a world church.

Don't just go to church. Go to see the glory of God and to feel His
presence, and let God have His way with you.

Now Moses said to Hobab, ". . . Come with us, and we will treat you well." "And you can be our eyes."
Numbers 10:29, 31.

February 22

Hobab, the brother-in-law of Moses, had an outstanding talent. He knew the country through which the children of Israel were to pass, and he was needed. But he was reluctant to accept the responsibility of being a guide. But he did, for later we read of his inheritance being with the children of Judah.

Today is the birthday of another man with an outstanding talent who also was needed for a great responsibility—George Washington. He was born in 1732. As a boy he was quiet and shy, but as a soldier and a leader of soldiers he showed great wisdom and skill. He took the side of the British against the French in the dispute over the Ohio Valley. Later he took the part of the Americans against the British in their struggle for independence. In 1789 he was elected as the first president of the United States, and was elected again "against his will" in 1793. The people would have gladly elected him a third time, but he refused. Of him it is said that he was "first in war, first in peace, and first in the hearts of his countrymen."

There are many stories told of his boyhood, but here is the one that I like the best. When he was 14 years old, he wanted to join the Navy. His father was dead, and his Navy idea broke his mother's heart. But he teased and coaxed until she unwillingly gave her consent. Then he packed his things in a trunk and put it on board the warship he was to join. However, at the last minute his mother couldn't go through with it, and withdrew her consent. No doubt young George was disappointed. He might even have felt angry, but he was obedient and went back to school. He had skill in mathematics and specialized in surveying, and his first job was as a surveyor for Lord Fairfax. Then he became a public surveyor for the colony of Virginia. Yes, George Washington had a special talent that his country needed. When he died, December 14, 1799, at the age of 67, he was mourned as one of the great men of his time.

No matter who you are, you have a special talent. God needs you. Let obedience to your parents anchor you in your days of preparation, and you will be ready when responsibility calls you.

NUMBERS 11

Has the Lord's arm been shortened? Now you shall see whether what I say will happen to you or not. Numbers 11:23.

We feel sorry that the children of Israel grumbled and complained about the manna God provided for them in the wilderness. Nobody but a mighty God with a mighty hand could have supplied the tons of manna necessary to feed that great multitude every day. And God had to punish them for their grumbling and complaining. Remember that the next time you're tempted to grumble about having to eat spinach or squash or anything else you don't particularly like. Also remember that we have the same mighty God with the same mighty hand today, and when we are in need He can provide us food as easily as He provided food for the Israelites.

Once upon a time there lived on the Isle of Wight a sea captain by the name of Sargent. He was the first Seventh-day Adventist on the island. His wife and 12 children dreaded the many long days he was away sailing the seven seas. Once Captain Sargent was delayed because of a terrible storm. At home Mrs. Sargent used up the last shilling and saw the last food in the pantry disappear, and still the captain did not come home. What could they do? There was only one thing left to do—they prayed. "Give us this day our daily bread" was their prayer.

While they were praying the woman from the next house knocked on the door. "You know," she said, "I am one of the servants at the king's summer palace on the island here. He was supposed to arrive yesterday, and we had prepared a lot of food for him and his company. But he did not come. We hate to waste the food. Would you mind accepting this basketful? And if you will let the children come with me, there is lots more." So they had food from the king's table until their father came home. One of those 12 children, Alfred, was one of our missionaries in Burma for many years. He loved to tell that story.

During the time of trouble you may wonder sometimes where your food is coming from. Remember, God has promised, "Bread will be given him, his water will be sure" (Isaiah 33:16). "The poor and needy seek water, and there is none. . . . I, the God of Israel, will not forsake them. I will open rivers in desolate heights, and fountains in the midst of the valleys" (Isaiah 41:17, 18).

Jealousy [is] as cruel as the grave; its flames are flames of fire, a most vehement flame.
Song of Solomon 8:6.

February 24

It is so hard for some people to glory in the success of others. God has placed within each heart the desire to succeed, and without this desire we would be a sorry lot. It is a wonderful thing to be an honest winner, but it is also a wonderful thing to be an honest loser. Covetousness, jealousy, envy, revenge, and hate all belong to the same family, and if we are not careful they will lead us to belittle our classmates, our teachers, and even our leaders. Covetousness and jealousy have been at the root of all the wars and all the killings in the world.

History is full of examples of people who rebelled against their leaders, exactly as did Aaron and Miriam.

Southern radicals did not like President Lincoln. One of the reasons was that he was against slavery. And one week after he was elected, seven Southern states formed their own government and rebelled against the Union. They bombarded Fort Sumter, in the harbor at Charleston, South Carolina, April 12, 1861. This started the Civil War, often called the War of the Rebellion. In January 1863 Lincoln issued his Emancipation Proclamation, which freed 4 million slaves. The South hated him all the more, and fought on for two more years. Finally, on April 9, 1865, the war was over. All the slaves were free. Around 204,000 soldiers had been killed on the battlefields; some 414,000 died of disease. Thus, about 618,000 soldiers lost their lives, compared with some 405,000 U.S. servicemen who died in World War II. But it was hard for the spirit of rebellion to die out of some people's hearts. Only six days after peace was proclaimed, on April 15, 1865, John Wilkes Booth, a Confederate supporter, with his heart burning for revenge, shot President Lincoln.

I like the spirit of people who say the day after a president is elected, "Yesterday I was against him; today I am for him. He is my president, and I am proud of what he is and what he stands for." And when a new president is elected, I love to see the outgoing president congratulate him.

That is the spirit we all need. See to it that you are an honest winner *and* an honest loser.

NUMBERS 13

Let us go up at once and take possession,
for we are well able to overcome it.
Numbers 13:30.

February 25

What was it that made Joshua and Caleb different from the other eight spies? It was faith. All 10 spies saw a goodly land flowing with milk and honey. But eight of them mainly saw the giants. Joshua and Caleb saw a mighty God driving out the wicked nations before them.

One of the greatest men I have ever known was Captain G. F. Jones, although he was only five feet four inches tall. He was born in 1864, became a certified sea captain when only 26 years old, and accepted the Seventh-day Adventist message a few years later after picking up a page from a *Present Truth* paper on the deck of his ship. In 1902 he became a missionary to the Pacific Islands, and in 1921 he was asked to spend a little time in New Guinea to help those who had been faithfully sowing the seeds of truth there for 13 years. The situation seemed hopeless, but as he prayed about it, God impressed his heart with the words of Judges 18:9 and 10: "Arise, let us go up against them. For we have seen the land, and indeed it is very good. Would you do nothing? Do not hesitate to go, that you may enter to possess the land. . . . For God has given it into your hands." Captain Jones took this for a command to go into the interior. He went to see the British commissioner in Port Moresby to obtain permission to go over the mountain.

"You're too small," said the commissioner. "Why, those savages in the interior would eat you." Drawing himself to the utmost of his five foot four inches, he replied, "Mr. Commissioner, I may be only a very little man, but I am plenty big enough for God to save New Guinea with if He wants to."

What can you do with a man like that? Nobody could stop him! Up over the mountains he went, and soon the younger men were following along with schools and churches. And that's where those wonderful carriers came from who made a whole contingent of American soldiers keep at least one Sabbath by putting down their bundles as the sun set Friday night and saying, "Sun he go down. God's day he come. We stop." Captain Jones belonged to the tribe of Caleb. It's a good tribe to belong to. Do you belong to it?

NUMBERS 14

Children, obey your parents in the Lord.
Ephesians 6:1.

February 26

How hard it was for the children of Israel to learn to obey God! Caleb and Joshua did their best to tell them to go up and possess the land as God had told them to do. But they would not, and they even wanted to stone Caleb and Joshua!

Then the Lord said, "All right, you must wander around in the wilderness for 40 years till all the grumblers have died."

"Oh, no!" they said. "We are so close now. We'll go up after all."

"You'd better not go," said Moses. "God won't go with you now."

"We'll go anyway," they said.

So they went, and the Amalekites smote them.

Josephine Cunnington Edwards tells a story about an African boy named Watford whose father was one of our schoolteachers in what is now Malawi. "You cannot go swimming in the river, my son!" said his mother. "There are crocodiles in it. Only last year two boys were eaten."

Watford scowled. In the distance he could hear the happy shouts of other children swimming. "Mother and Father don't want me to have any fun," he whined. Then while Mother wasn't looking he darted off to the river. "I'll just look on," he said to himself. But on the way he met another boy. "Didn't your father tell you not to go swimming?" he asked.

"Yes."

"Well, mine did too, but I'm just going to slip in and out—just to cool off."

"I am too. There are no crocodiles there. Our fathers just don't want us to have any fun, that's all." So pulling off their clothes, they slipped into the water.

But the other lad didn't slip out again. There was a crocodile there. The boy let out a horrible scream and disappeared. Watford and everybody else jumped out in an awful hurry and scrambled up the riverbank to safety. But Watford could never forget the fleeting glimpse of his friend's horror-filled face and clutching hands—the boy who helped him disobey.

When God and your parents tell you to obey, do it. You may save yourself a lot of sadness.

NUMBERS 16

Tomorrow morning the Lord will show who is His and who is holy, and will cause him to come near to Him. Numbers 16:5.

February **27**

It is easy to tell who are the workers God has chosen to be leaders. Like Moses and Aaron, they are humble and reluctant to accept the responsibility. It is also easy to tell which workers choose themselves. Like Korah, Dathan, and Abiram, they are proud and ambitious, and they "lift up" themselves above the congregation.

"Each has his place in the eternal plan of heaven. . . . Not more surely is the place prepared for us in the heavenly mansions than is the special place designated on earth where we are to work for God" (*Messages to Young People*, p. 219).

The history of the Advent message is full of accounts of humble young people who have found their special place in the service of God. James White was only 21 years old when he began to preach, and he won 1,000 people to the Lord in six weeks. Ellen Harmon was only 17 when she humbly became a mouthpiece for God. Uriah Smith was 21, J. N. Loughborough was 20, and S. N. Haskell was 19 when they each began to preach.

Another of the pioneers—Luther Warren—was only a boy of 14 when his heart burned within him to do something for God. But he didn't go to the conference president and say, "Are you the only one who can lead out in this work? Let me have a turn now." Oh, no. Luther humbly began to influence his companions for Christ. One day he was walking down the road with Harry Fenner, 17 years old, and they were talking about what they could do to further the Advent cause. "Harry, let's go over the fence and pray about it," said Luther. So they climbed over the rail fence, found a quiet place among the bushes, and prayed. Soon they had a little band of boys praying with them, and doing helpful work for the sick and needy.

Do you wonder that when Luther Warren had graduated God chose him to be a preacher and a leader? He looked for ways to do God's work, and in 1894 he organized the first Missionary Volunteer Sunshine Band, which idea in a few more years had spread around the world.

God has a special place for you, too. Keep humble, and He will lead you to it.

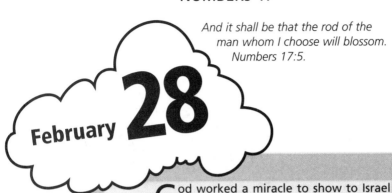

*And it shall be that the rod of the man whom I choose will blossom.
Numbers 17:5.*

February 28

God worked a miracle to show to Israel that Aaron and his family had been chosen among the tribe of Levi for the priesthood. And there was no mistaking it, for Aaron's rod not only blossomed but also grew almonds. When God calls you to higher responsibility He will make it very plain, even if He has to work a miracle that all may know He has chosen you.

In the middle of the eighteenth century, David Brainerd heard about a savage tribe of Indians living in the New Jersey forests. He felt called of God to go and preach Christ to them. The more he prayed about it, the more burdened he became, and feeling sure that God was indeed calling him, he made his plans and journeyed through the wilderness until he found himself near their village. There he camped awhile to rest, and to pray that angels would attend him on this dangerous undertaking.

When he at last reached their wigwams, he was astonished to find the whole village out to meet him, as though he were a long-looked-for friend. He had expected to find hostile enemies, but led by their chief, they welcomed him and reverenced him as if he were a prophet. He stayed with them and preached. It was years later that he found out the secret of their early friendship. Their scouts had discovered him as he traveled toward them and had decided to kill him when he retired in his tent. Peering between the folds of the canvas, they found him kneeling in prayer. And as they watched they saw a rattlesnake crawl over his feet, pause beside him, then glide out of the tent on the opposite side. The scouts hurried back to their village and told with great exicitement that a man under the protection of the Great Spirit was coming to them. Even the Indians knew that Brainerd's "rod had blossomed."

Keep close to God. God alone knows the places He has prepared for you, the skills He'll help you learn, and the doors He'll open for you to walk through. You need never be in doubt. God can make your "rod" blossom and bear almonds too.

NUMBERS 20

He will dwell on high; his place of defense will be the fortress of rocks; bread will be given him, his water will be sure.
Isaiah 33:16.

March 1

Five of us missionaries were fleeing from the war in Burma in March 1942. We were in a group of about 200 evacuees. One afternoon as we came down the hillside to the camp, the captain shouted out, "There's only water enough here for 80 people. Drink only a half cup of water each, and no face washing and no tooth brushing." It made us feel more thirsty than ever, but when we got to camp the good people formed lines by the five-gallon cans of chlorinated water, each waiting patiently to get a drink. But when the selfish ones came, they pushed and shoved and snatched water from others, and soon the water was all gone. "There's a spring coming out of a rock not far away," someone shouted. So over to the spring we all went, but the line was too long. I decided to wait until after the evening soup and campfire worship. At this time there were only six men standing in line, so I took my place at the end of the line and waited with our three waterpots.

"Push up to the spring," said the first man to leave. "You're a White man. They're only coolies."

"Not tonight," I replied. "I'll wait my turn like a Christian."

Then the five men in front of me began to talk. "Ta-ta-ta-ta-ta-tata-ta," said the man in front of me as he wriggled his fingers up and down in front of his mouth, and I knew he recognized me as the man who'd played the trumpet at campfire. It felt wonderful to be recognized as a Christian there. Just then the next man moved away, and we all took one step nearer to the spring. The next thing I knew, this man had filled my waterpots from his can of water. Then pointing to my heart, he lisped in broken English, "You Clistian." Then pointing to *his* heart, he lisped, "Me Clistian."

I tried to talk to him in English, in Hindustani, in Burmese, in Karen, but it was no use. So I just threw my arm over his shoulder and patted his back, and he threw his arm over my shoulder and patted my back, and together we said again and again, "You Clistian; me Clistian."

God's wonderful "Clistian" water was the sweetest I ever drank.

NUMBERS 21

Make a fiery serpent, and set it on a pole; and . . .
everyone who is bitten, when he looks at it, shall live.
Numbers 21:8.

March 2

There was no healing power in the bronze figure of the fiery serpent on that pole. The power was with God, and it required an act of faith and obedience on the part of the sufferers to receive that healing power. Israel already had been taught a severe lesson about worshipping graven images, and this time they did not worship the image of the serpent. But they did preserve it, and a later generation did worship it and burn incense before it, so King Hezekiah destroyed it. It is interesting to see how some of the Bible stories have been changed and carried over into the legends of other nations. The Greeks and Romans worshipped the sun, and called the god of light, who drove the chariot of the sun, Apollo. They said Apollo had a son called Aesculapius, who was taught the art of medicine and became so skilled that he could restore life to the dead. In art Aesculapius is represented as a strong, earnest youth bearing a knotted staff around which a serpent is entwined. The staff is called a caduceus.

Have you ever seen a caduceus anywhere? If you look at the insignia of the United States Army Medical Corps, there you will find it—a staff with two serpents entwining it and surmounted by wings. If you ever become a medical doctor, the caduceus will be on your insignia also. But remember, there is no charm in that caduceus. It has no power to protect you or to heal. It is used only as a symbol of healing. Your protection, as well as all healing power, is still in the hands of God. Keep your eyes on Him and have faith in Him.

Through His servant, God has given us much instruction, which, if we will only look upon it and heed it, will mean life to us. "Health is a blessing of which few appreciate the value; yet upon it the efficiency of our mental and physical powers largely depends. . . . By allowing ourselves to form wrong habits, by keeping late hours, by gratifying appetite at the expense of health, we lay the foundation for feebleness." "Without health, no one can . . . fulfill his obligations to himself, to his fellow-beings, or to his Creator. Therefore the health should be as faithfully guarded as the character" (*Messages to Young People*, pp. 235, 232).

NUMBERS 22

Then the Lord opened Balaam's eyes, and he saw the Angel of the Lord standing in the way. Numbers 22:31.

When Balaam's eyes were opened he not only saw the angel but also realized that the Lord had opened the mouth of a dumb animal, and he had actually seen it and heard it speak.

Today is the birthday of another man whose eyes were opened, and who under the blessing of God was able to make a wire talk. Alexander Graham Bell was born in Scotland in 1847. It was time for the third angel's message to go to all the world. It was time for knowledge to be increased. Bell's father was a teacher of speech in Edinburgh University and had specialized in the technique of lip movements, so that students could be taught to speak correctly. With his system of "visible speech" he also succeeded in teaching people who had been born deaf to speak. Young Alexander was intensely interested in his father's work, and he carried on some experiments of his own at home. By manipulating the lower jaw of his pet dog, he actually succeeded in teaching it the sounds "Ow-ah-oo, ga-ma-ma," which he interpreted to mean "How are you, Grandmamma?" His friends were delighted with his demonstrations.

By the time Bell was 17 he was teaching in a small academy. He soon went to London to attend the university there. While there he experimented in teaching deaf-born children, and he was successful. Soon after this the family moved to Canada, and before long he was teaching in a school for deaf mutes in Boston. He was so successful that he won a professorship in Boston University. By 1844 the telegraph had been invented, and with a friend, Thomas Watson, he began his experiments in carrying the human voice over a wire. Many people laughed at him, but he kept at it and at it, until on March 10, 1876, Watson heard Bell calling clearly over the wire, "Watson, come here; I want you."

Of course, in the more than 130 years since then technology has skyrocketed. Now satellites almost instantly beam not only our voices but pictures and video around the world. Only eternity will show how much this invention is helping to speed the work of God.

Keep close to God. He will show you how to speak for Him too.

NUMBERS 23

*For there is no scorcery against Jacob, nor is there any
divination against Israel. It now must be said
of Jacob and of Israel, "Oh, what God has done!"
Numbers 23:23.*

March 4

As the message of the third angel has been taken to country after country around the world, Satan has stirred up many Balaks to try to curse God's work. Religious leaders, devil doctors, bandits, and apostates—all have tried, but the work of God goes on.

Our first mission among the Quechua Indians was established by Pedro Kalbermatter and his brave wife. The people wanted our missionaries and had already built a house for them, but the landowners and the religious leaders did not want them. They knew that missions meant education and gospel light, and they wanted to keep the people in darkness and ignorance. So they told Pedro to get out of the country by a certain date and threatened his life if he did not.

Pedro stayed on, and one morning while he was working on a schoolhouse he saw a mob of angry White men riding toward him. His first thought was to protect himself with his rifle, but he thought, *No! Jesus wouldn't do that*, so he quickly buried his gun. Then committing himself to God, he went out to meet the mob. Cursing and threatening, they ordered him to go away. He answered kindly that the Lord had brought him there and that he would stay till the Lord should send him away. They tried to ride him down, but not a horse would ride over him or even strike him with its hoofs.

At last, baffled and still cursing, the mob rode away, and Pedro Kalbermatter and his brave wife stayed. Today we have more than 2,000 churches and about 850,000 church members in Peru and Bolivia! And although our enemies laughed when the early Sabbathkeepers began to proclaim the third angel's message, and prophesied it would soon come to naught, today there are about 20 million Sabbath school members in all the world. With Balaam we say, "Oh, what God has done!"

Someday enemies may try to bewitch or curse *you*. Never fear. The words of Balaam are still true: "He has blessed, and I cannot reverse it" (Numbers 23:20). Make God first, and you will find that "those who are with us are more than those who are with them" (2 Kings 6:16). And you can say, "If God is for us, who can be against us?" (Romans 8:31).

NUMBERS 24

A Star shall come out of Jacob; a Scepter shall rise out of Israel.
Numbers 24:17.

Balaam's prophecy of the Star that would rise out of Jacob was remembered down through the ages for 1,400 years. Then King Jesus was born, and a host of shining angels praised God and took up their abode over Bethlehem. Then the Wise Men in the East saw the glory of this distant company of angels as a great and glorious star. They followed it and found Jesus. All the stars are the handiwork of God, and if we will but take time to look at them, and think of their greatness, their brightness, and their dependability, they will help us find our way out of the darkness of discouragement and despair and into the light of the presence of God.

In China there is an old legend of two surveyors who were crossing a trackless desert. They had a rough map they had made from information other travelers had given them. There was a tree marked on it here and there, and it showed a dry stream bed and a hill or two.

But one night a terrible storm arose. They hid in a cave while the lightning flashed, the thunder roared, and the rain pelted down. When morning came, all the landmarks had been swept away, and they realized that they were lost. Their map was useless. All day long they tried to figure out some way to safety, but there seemed to be no way out. They were desperate. Night came again, and with the night came the stars. "We're saved! We're saved!" cried one of the men. "The stars are stll there." The stars were still there, and the men took their direction from the stars and found their way back home again.

David spoke truly when he said, "The heavens declare the glory of God; and the firmament shows His handiwork. Day unto day utters speech, and night unto night reveals knowledge. There is no speech nor language where their voice is not heard. Their line has gone out through all the earth, and their words to the end of the world" (Psalm 19:1-4).

If you ever get lost in discouragement or despair, look up at the stars and find your way back to God.

The name of the Lord is a strong tower;
the righteous run to it and are safe.
Proverbs 18:10.

March 6

Did you ever hear our Seventh-day Adventist schools and colleges called cities of refuge for Seventh-day Adventist young people? Well, they certainly are. In this great battle of life the devil is seeking the life of every one of us, and thousands of people can bear testimony that our schools and our colleges have saved them from certain destruction.

Dick was the youngest son in a family of six. His mother died when he was only 9 years old, but his big sister Lottie took charge. Lottie was a Seventh-day Adventist, so Dick and his brother went to Sabbath school and church with her, and after a few years Dick was baptized. But Dick had to attend public grade school and high school. He was very popular, and it grew easy to hang out with a crowd that didn't share the goals and standards he'd been taught. He played football, and it became an idol to him. He played on Sabbath in spite of the pleadings of his father and his sister. It looked as if the world just about had him when one Sabbath, while playing in the last test game of the season, Dick broke his leg. As he was carried from the field he remembered Lottie's last words to him before the game. They came to him again and again: "I'll be praying for you."

Dick's leg healed, but there was a change in him, too. One thing after another happened to remind him of God. Then one day he found his Bible in his suitcase. He picked it up and read "My son, give me thine heart" (Proverbs 23:26, KJV). He went to an Adventist youth meeting, reconsecrated himself to God, and finally went to Walla Walla College. Now no organized sports were scheduled for Sabbath. His goals changed. Now what he found the most fun were things that helped others, and he came back to his first love—serving God. He was possessed by an intense burden to become a missionary to the Peruvian Indians. A book was published about Richard Hayden's life, *From Football Field to Mission Field*. Had it not been for our Adventist city of refuge in Walla Walla, the cause of God would have been robbed of a valuable missionary. Make sure you go to your Adventist church school, then to your Adventist academy, and then to your Adventist college—and you too will be safe.

DEUTERONOMY 32

As an eagle stirs up its nest, . . . spreading out its
wings, taking them up, . . . so the Lord alone led him.
Deuteronomy 32:11, 12.

March **7**

The eagle has become a symbol of courage, swiftness, and strength. When the United States became a nation, the bald eagle was selected as its emblem.

A little more than 150 years ago an Indian traded a bald eagle to a farmer for a bushel of corn. The eagle became a great pet, and when the farmer joined the Army and went to take part in the Civil War, the eagle went too. The farmer soldier was in the Eighth Wisconsin Regiment, and the eagle became the regiment's mascot. They called it Old Baldy. When the regiment was moved up to the front lines during the battle of Atlanta, Old Baldy went with them, and as you can imagine, when the guns were booming and the bullets were flying, it was very encouraging to the soldiers to see Old Baldy flying around above them and to hear him screaming defiantly.

One day Old Baldy was nowhere to be seen, and when the eagle regiment went into battle, the men were discouraged and blue. If Old Baldy had deserted them, it must mean bad luck. As the first shots were fired, however, with a scream and a screech Old Baldy came zooming down from the sky. A great cheer went up, their weariness and their troubles were forgotten, and the eagle regiment rushed on to win the battle. When at last Old Baldy died, he was stuffed, and placed in the Wisconsin capitol.

Sometimes an eagle finds itself in a dark valley, surrounded with storm and clouds, but it won't stay there. With its mighty wings it shoots upward, pierces the clouds, and is once more in the clear sunshine above.

The darkness and the tempest are now below it, and the eagle rejoices to be in its own beloved nest. It took a great deal of effort and faith to go through the darkness, but what a satisfying reward was gained!

So we may be surrounded by difficulties, discouragement, and darkness; but we need not stay there. With a will and a prayer, on the wings of faith, we can rise into the sunlight of the presence of God.

The eternal God is your refuge, and underneath are the everlasting arms. Deuteronomy 33:27.

March 8

Moses was the man of God who led and counseled and blessed the children of Israel. We are the spiritual children of Israel, and the man of God who led and counseled and blessed the early Adventists was James White.

James was the fifth child in a family of nine, and as a child he was not very strong. But by the time he was 16 his health began to improve. He made rapid strides in his schoolwork, and at 19 years of age he was teaching school. The family were all members of the Christian church, and when they heard William Miller, Joshua Himes, and T. M. Preble preach about the second coming of Christ, one by one they believed. Young James was a dynamic leader, and he felt impelled to preach, but who would support him? There was no Adventist Church yet, he couldn't expect his Christian church to support him, and he had no funds of his own. Still, he felt he must go. So one day his father said, "Well, James, if you must go, I'll give you the use of a horse for the winter. And may the God of our fathers support and bless you." Then a neighbor said, "I have a saddle and some straps you can make a bridle of. You may have them for your horse." So, taking his prophetic chart and his books, and buttoning them under his heavy winter coat, off James went.

One night while preaching in a schoolhouse a group of rough men, urged on by some angry Universalists, began to disturb the meeting with catcalls, howls, and snowballs. It became impossible for James's voice to be heard. But rather than stopping, he closed his Bible and, lifting up his voice, cried, "Repent and call on God for mercy and pardon." The noise quieted down, and 100 people arose for prayer that night. But the mob was not through yet. They gathered around outside the entrance, but just then a man of "noble countenance" came up to James White and, taking him by the arm, led him through the mob. As soon as they were free of the mob, James turned to thank the man, but he was not there.

Who was he? Can you guess? That's what Moses meant when he said, "The eternal God is your refuge." Someday you may need help. Remember that His everlasting arms are around you, too.

DEUTERONOMY 34

But since then there has not arisen in Israel a prophet like Moses, whom the Lord knew face to face. Deuteronomy 34:10.

March 9

Let me tell you some more about James White, who was the "Moses" of the early Adventists. In the summer of 1844 James met a lovely young woman, nearly 17 years old, whose name was Ellen Harmon. They, with many others, waited for October 22, the day the early Adventists thought Jesus would come the second time. Their disappointment was terrible, but God brought comfort to them through young Ellen. He sent a vision of His children on a path to heaven, and God gave light to the Advent leaders about the true meaning of the cleansing of the sanctuary. Then God brought the Sabbath truth to the little Adventist group in Washington, New Hampshire. One by one some of the Adventists accepted the Sabbath. One by one they were disfellowshipped from the other churches, or they left of their own desire. James and Ellen were married in 1846, and the third angel's message was on its way. It was a small group. The people were poor, but they had a Moses in James White and they had a prophet in Ellen.

Soon the publishing work began, and in 1863 the General Conference was organized and the name Seventh-day Adventist chosen. The next year James White was elected the second General Conference president, and, during three separate periods, he held this office for more than 10 years. During this time Sabbath schools were organized and the tithing system was adopted. By 1880 James White had seen the Seventh-day Adventist believers grow in number from a mere handful to more than 15,000 church members. The following year he was stricken with a malignant form of malaria, and on August 6, 1881, he passed away.

"Is Jesus precious to you?" Ellen whispered to James, when she saw death was near.

"Yes, oh, yes," he answered faintly.

"Have you no desire to live?"

"No," he replied weakly.

"Jesus loves you. The everlasting arms are beneath you."

"Yes, yes," he said. And so another Moses passed to his rest.

Pray that God will give you confidence in the leaders of this great cause and keep you always loyal to them.

JOSHUA 1

Be strong and of good courage; do not be afraid, . . .
for the Lord your God is with you wherever you go.
Joshua 1:9.

March 10

Strong faith and courage were always prominent in the life of Joshua, the second pioneer leader in Israel. Strong faith and courage have always been prominent in the lives of the pioneers of the Advent movement. Perhaps one of the most courageous was J. N. Loughborough. He was only a boy of 12 at the time of the Disappointment. But he was on fire with love for the Lord. When he was just 17, he began to preach. People called him the boy preacher, and his genial, youthful, dependable nature, with the blessing of God, brought him success. When he was 20 years old, he attended some meetings held by J. N. Andrews, and soon accepted the Sabbath. He kept on preaching, but at that time the Seventh-day Adventist Church was not yet organized, and so there was no pay. Every man with a message had to preach at his own expense, relying on the gratitude and generosity of his hearers.

But it was not easy, and four years later, in addition to preaching on Sabbath and Sunday, John had to work in the hayfields and do harvesting to make ends meet. "This is too much," said Mrs. Loughborough. "We can't live any longer in this way." And in a moment of discouragement John said, "Mary, let us go to Waukon. I'll make a living at carpentry, and as I can, I will preach the message." They went to Waukon, Iowa, but not for long. A few weeks later James and Ellen White came to visit them, and their courage revived. They came back to the work and stayed with it through thick and thin.

At the General Conference session in 1868 John learned that Adventist leaders were needed to build up the believers in San Francisco. Go to California? Why, in those days going to California was like going to the farthest parts of the earth. But J. N. Loughborough and D. T. Bourdeau volunteered to go. It took them 24 days to go by boat to Panama, then by train across the isthmus to the Pacific coast, and by boat again to San Francisco. But they had come to a new land and were filled with faith and courage.

Sometimes into your life will come days when things go wrong and disappointments threaten to discourage you. Think then of the examples of these pioneers and be strong and of good courage.

JOSHUA 2

We have heard how the Lord dried up the water
of the Red Sea for you. . . . The Lord your God,
He is God in heaven above and on earth beneath.
Joshua 2:10, 11.

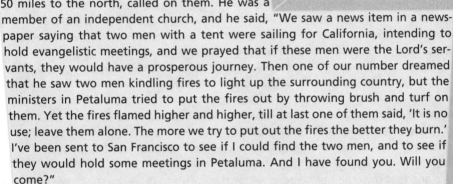

March 11

The Lord has many ways of letting the people hear in advance about His power and about the coming of His messengers. The very next day after Elders Loughborough and Bourdeau arrived in San Francisco a stranger from Petaluma, a town about 50 miles to the north, called on them. He was a member of an independent church, and he said, "We saw a news item in a newspaper saying that two men with a tent were sailing for California, intending to hold evangelistic meetings, and we prayed that if these men were the Lord's servants, they would have a prosperous journey. Then one of our number dreamed that he saw two men kindling fires to light up the surrounding country, but the ministers in Petaluma tried to put the fires out by throwing brush and turf on them. Yet the fires flamed higher and higher, till at last one of them said, 'It is no use; leave them alone. The more we try to put out the fires the better they burn.' I've been sent to San Francisco to see if I could find the two men, and to see if they would hold some meetings in Petaluma. And I have found you. Will you come?"

The evangelists saw the leading of their mighty God in all this, and in less than a month they opened meetings in the tent in Petaluma.

The ministers in that town began their opposition, just as the dream had shown, but nothing could put the fires out. After raising up a church in Petaluma, they went to Windsor, then Piner, then Santa Rosa, then Healdsburg, and soon there were churches in these five towns. There was opposition in each place, till at last the ministers got together and said, "Let the Adventists alone. The more we oppose them, the more their doctrine spreads."

Several years later, in December 1884, Elder Loughborough was back in California again, holding some revival meetings in the little church in Ferndale. Among those who were baptized at that time was a young woman named Henrietta Johnson. And a few years later she became my mother!

Learn to trust this great God, and let Him go before you and select your school, your place of abode, and your work for Him.

73

Sanctify yourselves, for tomorrow the Lord will do wonders among you. Joshua 3:5.

The next day after Joshua said these words, all the Israelites passed over the Jordan River on dry ground. It was a miracle, and thereby everybody who heard about it knew that the living God was among His people.

The same living God still works miracles for His servants. It was November 1856. Elder and Mrs. White were visiting the churches in Illinois, holding meetings and strengthening and encouraging the church leaders, when a definite burden came to Ellen that a company in Iowa, 200 miles away, needed help. It was good sleighing weather, and Brother Hart and Brother Everts prepared to take the Whites to this place in a two-horse sleigh. Then it rained for 24 hours! "We must give up the journey," said James, but Ellen said, "We shall go."

"Yes," her husband said, "if the Lord works a miracle."

The next day it turned colder and began to snow. At 5:00 p.m. they began their journey and got as far as Green Vale. It snowed for days, and they were snowbound for a week. Then they started again and got to a hotel a few miles from the great Mississippi River. The river was frozen over, but again it began to rain. There was danger that the rain would melt the ice and that it would not be possible for the horses to draw the sleigh over it.

"Can we cross the river?" they asked everyone they met.

They were stunned by the answers: "No." "It's risky." "I'd never try it." "Some have already broken though the ice." "You can't make it."

"We have come to the Red Sea," said Brother Hart. "Shall we cross?"

"Go forward, trusting in Israel's God," said Ellen White.

And they went on. The sound of the horses' hooves on the ice was fearful. But on they went. Men gathered on the opposite bank to watch them. They prayed and kept going, and at last they reached the Iowa riverbank! The God who had parted the waters of the Jordan River for the ancient Israelites had frozen the waters of this much greater river to let these servants pass safely over.

The living God is your God. Sanctify yourself every day. Who can tell? Maybe tomorrow you will need a miracle.

JOSHUA 4

When your children ask their fathers in time to come, saying, "What are these stones?" then you shall let your children know, saying, "Israel crossed over this Jordan on dry land."
Joshua 4:21, 22.

March 13

I'm so glad we have memorials that remind us of God's mighty works. I would love to have seen that stone memorial in Gilgal that reminded everybody about the way God brought His people into the land of Canaan. We have a memorial in Washington, New Hampshire, that reminds us of the way God brought into being His remnant church. It is a little white church in the valley not far from Millen Pond. In 1844 it was one of the Christian churches. One Sunday the district elder, Frederick Wheeler, who was a Methodist Adventist, was conducting the Communion service. In the congregation that morning was a visitor, Mrs. Rachel Oakes, the mother of their schoolteacher. In his sermon Elder Wheeler said, "All who confess communion with Christ in such a service as this should be ready to obey God and keep His commandments in all things."

He noticed that the visitor was quite agitated, and after the service he went to visit her in her daughter's home. "I came near getting up in the meeting and saying something," she said.

"What did you have in mind to say?" asked Brother Wheeler kindly.

"I wanted to tell you that you had better set that Communion table back and put the cloth over it until you begin to keep the commandments of God," said Mrs. Preston. Then he remembered that this good woman was a Seventh Day Baptist who believed that Christians should keep Saturday for Sunday. They talked and visited together, and not many weeks later Elder Wheeler kept his first Sabbath. This was in March 1844. Several of the members of that little church joined him, and that was the first group of Sabbathkeeping Adventists. That little church still stands. It is only a memorial now, but one of the greatest thrills I have ever had was to knock on the door of the Farnsworth home one day and get the key and go into the little white church. I stood in the pulpit where Frederick Wheeler spoke those words. Then I told my children the story I have just told you.

Keep your eyes open for memorials that will remind you of the certainty of the Advent message.

By faith the walls of Jericho fell down after they were encircled for seven days.
Hebrews 11:30.

March 14

God is still able to make walls fall down flat if He can find the right kind of faith in the hearts of His servants. Many years ago missionary L. B. Halliwell told a wonderful story about one of our colporteurs, Brother Andre, who made his headquarters in Fortaleza, in northeast Brazil. One day a man from a distant town bought a copy of *Bible Readings*. On his way back home he read and studied, and by the time he arrived he was keeping the seventh-day Sabbath. He began at once to tell his friends, and soon a little group was keeping the Sabbath with him. Some months later a minister from another church in this distant town happened to meet Brother Andre while he was in Fortaleza on business.

"Quite a group of people are keeping your Sabbath in our town," he said. "You'd better go up there and preach to them."

Brother Andre started off at once on the long trip. At last he came to a village 25 miles from the place. He began to inquire around for a mule that he could hire to make this last part of the journey. Soon a police officer appeared and took him to the mayor.

"What are you going to do out there?" asked the mayor.

"I'm going to visit my friends and preach to them," answered Brother Andre.

"No, you're not!" said the mayor. "You can visit them all you want, but it is against the law to preach, and if you try to preach, I'll have the police arrest you and put you in the brand-new jail there."

"Then you had better arrest me now and put me in jail now," said Brother Andre, "for I am going there and I am going to preach."

"But we can't arrest you before you break the law," said the mayor.

"Well, I'm going," said Brother Andre, and he did. But while he was preaching and the police officer was ready to arrest him, the Lord sent a great storm and wind. It blew upon the brand-new jail— and its walls fell down flat! Brother Andre kept on preaching, and a few months later, when Mr. Halliwell and some others went to baptize the group, the jail was still in ruins.

Remember that there is nothing too hard for the living God to do for you if you have the right kind of faith.

JOSHUA 7

The love of money is a root of all kinds of evil.
1 Timothy 6:10.

March 15

The temptation to see, then covet, then take, comes to everyone, rich and poor alike. When it came to Achan, he failed and bore the penalty. It came to a certain millionaire who I once heard about. This rich man failed to overcome the temptation to dishonestly make even more money, and he went to jail for a long prison sentence. One day an old friend visited him and found him in the prison workshop with needle and twine, sewing bags.

"Hello," said the friend. "I see you're sewing."

"No," replied the once-rich man. "I'm reaping!"

Just so surely will everyone reap who covets and steals. But most Seventh-day Adventist young people are so strictly honest that a temptation to covet and take has no appeal to them. One such young man was Bill. He went into a bank to cash a check for $20. The cashier counted out two fives and a ten. "That makes twenty dollars," he said.

Bill took the money in his hand and turned to go. But before leaving the bank, he paused to count it. There were two fives, but there were also two tens. The two tens must have been stuck together. For the briefest second the temptation came to keep it, but Bill was just too honest. He went right back and very quietly explained it to the cashier and gave the extra $10 back.

Do you think he was foolish? Listen! A few months later the bank manager needed a chauffeur to drive his car. Bill was looking for work, and the cashier recommended Bill to the bank manager for the job.

"I'd trust that chap with a truckload of diamonds," he said. "He's as honest as a spotlight! He's a Seventh-day Adventist."

Bill got the job and kept it for a while; then the bank manager made him his private secretary. Not so foolish, was he?

"Never underrate the importance of little things. . . . It is by them that the soul is trained that it may grow into the likeness of Christ, or bear the likeness of evil. God helps us to cultivate habits of thought, word, look, and action that will testify to all about us that we have been with Jesus and learned of Him!" (*Messages to Young People*, p. 202).

*"Do not be afraid, nor be dismayed; . . .
arise, go up to Ai." "For the Lord your
God will deliver it into your hand."
Joshua 8:1, 7.*

March 16

In the great Christian warfare against Satan and the powers of darkness there have been many Ai's, where it has been humanly impossible to establish a mission and where only the Lord our God could deliver these places into our hands.

Take the island of Mussau, for instance. It was one of the bloodiest of all the islands in the Matthias group. No White man had ever landed on that island and lived. One day in 1931 missionary Gilbert McLaren, with a group of Seventh-day Adventist young men from the Solomon Islands, anchored near one of the large villages on the island, hoping to go ashore and visit. In a very short time a dozen war canoes filled with angry, gesturing warriors circled the mission launch *Veilomani I*. They shook their spears, beat their war clubs on the sides of their canoes, and shouted, "Go! Go! Go!" The more they shouted, the more menacing they became, and missionary McLaren didn't know what to do. Even the men from the Solomon Islands were afraid. Then God told the missionary what to do, and, turning to his friends, McLaren said, "Sing!" And sing they did! Their voices blended harmoniously in the beautiful song and words "Anywhere with Jesus I can safely go."

As they sang, the fierce warriors stopped their blood-curdling shouts and stopped banging their clubs against the sides of their canoes. The young men kept on singing. They sang every hymn they knew, then began all over again. And as the sun set, the war canoes silently paddled back to the village. Early the next morning the chief himself came out to the missionaries. "Could you teach my people to sing like that?" he asked.

"Of course we could," said McLaren, "but it would take time. We would have to have a school. They would have to learn to read and write."

The chief nodded his head. "We want! We want!" he said.

In a few weeks the *Veilomani I* returned with two Solomon Islands missionaries, Salau and Oti, and before too long Mussau was a Christian island.

Is there an Ai in your life? Don't be discouraged. The Lord our God can give you the victory over it, too. And He will.

JOSHUA 24

Choose for yourselves this day whom you will serve. . . .
But as for me and my house, we will serve the Lord.
Joshua 24:15.

March 17

This beautiful invitation has helped many a young person to make a decision for Christ, and in turn it has been used by thousands of them to invite others to come to Christ. Today is the day set aside to honor the first missionary to Ireland—known to the world as Saint Patrick. He was born in southern Scotland and was taken prisoner by a band of Irish pirates in A.D. 411. He was only 16 years old at the time, and although his parents were Christians, he had not yet made his decision for Christ. He was set to herding his pagan master's swine and cattle on the hills of Antrim, and there in his loneliness he felt the need of God to help him forsake his sins. He gave his whole heart to God.

After six years of slavery he managed to escape and find his way back to his home in Scotland. As he studied to become a worker for God, he seemed to hear a voice from Ireland constantly calling, "We beseech thee, child of God, come and again walk with us." Early in his middle life he went back to Ireland and entered upon his lifework. He knew the language. He knew the needs of the people. He preached the Word and pleaded with people to receive it. Many legends have been connected with Patrick's name. The Catholics claimed he was one of their bishops and made him a saint. But there is much evidence that shows he believed in the supreme word of God and had no allegiance to human authority. He reduced the Irish language to writing and established schools, and there are definite indications that the early Irish church kept the seventh-day Sabbath. He lived to see Christianity triumph over the Irish pagan religion of druidism.

On the hill of Tara, where once the fires blazed on the druids' altars, there now stands a great statue of Patrick. It shows him with crook and miter, dressed like a Catholic bishop. But to us a far better memorial is the green hill of Slemish, where as a slave, Patrick first made his choice to serve God. He little realized what great results the blessing of God would bring because of that humble decision. In every land young people are making similar decisions.

Have you made your decision to serve God yet? If not, why not choose to do it today?

If there is dew on the fleece only, and it is dry on all the ground, then I shall know that You will save Israel by my hand, as You have said. Judges 6:37.

March 18

The Lord often has been pleased to give His servants signs that they might know that He is leading and guiding them. It was in November 1846, about two years after the Great Disappointment, that the early Advent believers were called to a meeting in Topsham, Maine. Although they were strong workers for God, James and Ellen White had not yet seen the importance of keeping the seventh-day Sabbath. They were at this meeting, as was Captain Joseph Bates. He already had accepted the seventh-day Sabbath, but he was not so sure that Sister White was a messenger of God and that her visions were from God. You may be sure that Joseph Bates did his best to persuade the Whites of the truth of the Sabbath. Talking with them, he often referred to the stars and other heavenly bodies, for as a sea captain he was a great lover of astronomy. Ellen White, however, couldn't talk very knowledgeably about the stars, "for," she confessed, "I have never looked into a book on astronomy."

Nevertheless, one day during a meeting Mrs. White was taken off in vision and began describing the stars. Captain Bates was thrilled. "Now she is describing Jupiter," he said. "Now Saturn, and now the nebula in Orion. And she is telling more than the astronomers know," he exclaimed. That was all the sign he needed that God truly spoke through her. From that time on he was a firm believer in the Lord's messenger. A few weeks after this experience Ellen White had another vision. She saw the ark of the covenant in the heavenly sanctuary. In the ark were the Ten Commandments—with a halo of light around the fourth. And that was all the sign she and James needed. They began at once to keep the seventh-day Sabbath.

Thus it was that each helped the other, and the early remnant church was strengthened and blessed.

"The leader whom God chose to overthrow the Midianites occupied no prominent position in Israel. He was not a ruler, a priest, or a Levite. He thought himself the least in his father's house. But God saw in him a man of courage and integrity. He was distrustful of himself and willing to follow the guidance of the Lord" (*Patriarchs and Prophets*, p. 553).

Keep close to God. Maybe one day your "fleece" will be "wet."

JUDGES 7

*When I blow the trumpet, I and all who are with with me,
then you also blow the trumpets on every side of the whole
camp, and say, "The sword of the Lord and of Gideon."
Judges 7:18.*

March 19

The blowing of trumpets is connected with victory for the cause of
God on several occasions related in the
Bible. And in our modern missions the blowing of
trumpets has brought success a number of times
too. During the early years of our ministry among
the Karens of Burma I used to take 10 to 15 of my
biggest schoolboys on a tour each summer vacation, to teach them how to preach.
We carried a supply of simple medicines, as well as a complete stereopticon outfit
to show pictures on the life of Christ; and I always took my trumpet. In the summer of 1921 Brother L. W. Melendy, the Burma Union secretary, and Brother
Harold Baird, my associate missionary, accompanied us on our tour and brought
their trumpets—so we had three trumpets!

One afternoon we came to the tumbledown village of Parkete. The boys
took one look at it and said, "Nobody lives here anymore." Looking around,
however, we found about a dozen people, so we got ready for our evening program. A half hour before sunset the three trumpets began to play; a half hour
before sunset the people began to come. They came from the village; they came
from their nearby gardens and fields where they were camping. There came
mothers and fathers, aunts and uncles, grandpas and grandmas, and lots of little children, till there were more than 50 at our meeting that night. "We know
what did it," said the boys as they expressed their surprise at the good attendance. "It was the trumpets!" Then they added, "Wouldn't it be wonderful if
every one of us had a trumpet!" And right then there was born in my heart
a determination to have a brass band in the jungle someday.

The next year we went home to Australia on furlough, and I came back
with 23 brass horns. Before long we were "blowing our trumpets" from village to village. It was a new day for our preaching. Now everybody came to
our meetings; nothing could keep them away. For 20 years the brass band
was used by God to overcome fear and superstition. Then, sad to say, it was
totally destroyed during World War II.

Do you blow a trumpet or play some other musical instrument? Do
your very best. Dedicate your talent to God, and He will use you to put
Satan to flight.

The Spirit of the Lord came mightily upon him.
Judges 14:6.

March 20

It was the Spirit of God coming mightily upon Samson who made him strong. What a pity Samson didn't always realize this and keep on walking with God in the path of obedience! The Spirit of God often has come upon His servants mightily and made them strong.

When Ellen White was a young woman, she weighed only 80 pounds, and she was not very strong physically. But when the Spirit of God came upon her and took her off in vision, she was phenomenally strong. Strong men tried to move her hands or arms while she was in vision, but could not. One morning in 1845, before she was married and while she was still living with her father and mother in Portland, she was taken off in vision. She walked over to a bureau on which rested the Harmons' big family Bible that weighed 18½ pounds. She picked it up and held it at arm's length in one hand for a half hour while walking around the room. All this time she was not breathing. Yet when the vision ended, she felt no fatigue. Under ordinary circumstances she could hardly have lifted that big Bible with both hands.

If you ever visit the office of the Ellen G. White Publications in the General Conference office building, you will be able to see that very Bible. And if you try to hold it at arm's length, you will know that only the Spirit of God could have enabled her to do such a thing.

In writing to young people, Ellen White says: "God has made ample provision for His people; and if they rely upon His strength, they will never become the sport of circumstances. The strongest temptation cannot excuse sin. However great the pressure brought to bear upon the soul, transgression is our own act. It is not in the power of earth or hell to compel anyone to do evil. Satan attacks us at our weak points, but we need not be overcome. However severe or unexpected the assault, God has provided help for us, and in His strength we may conquer" (*Messages to Young People*, p. 62).

We all need this kind of strength. Only the Spirit of God can give it to us. Let us always walk humbly with God in the path of obedience and be strong.

JUDGES 16:4-31

But he did not know that the Lord had departed from him.
Judges 16:20.

March 21

There was no excuse for Samson. He knew that worldly pleasures "destroy all relish for serious thought and for religious services" (*Messages to Young People,* p. 399). He knew that marriage with an unbeliever would give him a home "where the shadows are never lifted" (*ibid.,* p. 440) and that connecting with unbelievers would "grieve the Spirit of God and forfeit His protection" (*ibid.,* p. 441). Yes, he knew it all. His godly parents had told him many times, but the saddest thing about it all is that he didn't know "that the Lord had departed from him." He thought he was still all right and that everything was fine.

Some time ago, so the story goes, there was a lonely sheepherder on a lonely ranch in the West. His only comforts, above the barest necessities of life, were his old violin and a little radio, and in the evening when his work was done he would listen to the news, then tune up his violin and play the tunes that made his heart happy. One evening he realized that there was something wrong. His pitch was too low and the tunes seemed dull, but what could he do? He had no tuning fork. Then he got an idea. He dropped a card to the radio station and said, "Will you please strike an A during your evening broadcast? I'm far away from a piano, and the only comfort I have is my old fiddle. It's all out of tune, so will you please strike A so I can get my fiddle in tune again?"

The radio announcer granted the unusual request, and a few days later he received a letter of appreciation from the lonely man, saying, "Now I am in tune again."

Is your life in tune with God? Are you sure? Have you been walking with dangerous companions in dangerous places? Send up a little prayer and ask God whether everything is really all right. He will surely let you know.

That is what David was doing when he prayed, "Create in me a clean heart, O God; and renew a right spirit within me" (Psalm 51:10, KJV). And I think that is why David was a man after God's own heart (see 1 Samuel 13:14).

Entreat me not to leave you . . . ; for wherever you go, I will go; and wherever you lodge, I will lodge; your people shall be my people, and your God, my God. Ruth 1:16.

March 22

These beautiful words spoken by Ruth show that she had given her heart to God. All heaven rejoices when a sinner is born again. Some boys and girls are "born into this message." Some young people go to college and accept the truth there. Some attend evangelistic meetings, and give their hearts to God there.

Ruth, however, was not born into a family that believed in God. She was from Moab, and her people worshipped idols. She never attended an evangelist meeting or went to a godly school. But she had the privilege of living in a God-fearing home. Then God permitted sorrow to come to her, and in her sorrow she turned for comfort to the living God. She found what she needed and gave her heart to Him. God still uses sorrow to turn people toward Him, and it often has been said, "God sometimes has to make a man lie on his back in order to make him look up."

There is a parable that tells of two godly old men who planted olive trees so that someday they could have olives to eat and have a supply of oil. As the first one planted his tree, he prayed: "Lord, it needs rain, that its tender roots may drink and swell. Please send gentle showers." And the Lord sent gentle showers. "Lord," he prayed again, "my tree needs warmth. Please send sunshine." And the Lord sent sunshine. "Now send frost, Lord, to make its fibers tough." And behold, the little tree stood sparkling with frost.

But one evening it died. The next day the old man went to see his friend and found his tree growing well. "I prayed for rain and sun and frost," he said, "and my tree died."

Then his friend said, "I entrusted my tree to God. God made it, and He knows better than I what it needs. So I make no conditions, but simply pray, 'Lord, send what it needs. Storm or sunshine, wind, rain, or as You know what is best.' And behold, it grows well."

So whatever God permits to come into your life, easy experiences or hard ones, joy or sorrow, you can be sure that God is permitting it so that you can grow up as Jesus did, "in favor with God and men" (Luke 2:52).

Do not fear. I will do for you all that you request,
for all the people of my town know that
you are a virtuous woman.
Ruth 3:11.

March **23**

Boaz was a rich relative of Ruth's, and the story of his kindness to Ruth, and the way he redeemed the property of her deceased husband and married her warms everybody's heart.

We too have a rich relative and elder brother, Jesus, who has redeemed us; and we have a heavenly Father who has promised to supply all our needs.

In a clipping from one of our old Adventist periodicals I found a lovely story about a dear old Scotchman who was well acquainted with his heavenly Father. An evangelist had pitched a tent in a town some distance from where he lived, and he very much wanted to go and stay in that town while the meetings were being held so that he could attend every one of them. He started off, and on the way another Christian brother who was bound on the same errand caught up with him. When they were nearly there, the Scotchman suggested that they pause for a moment behind the hedge for a short prayer. So they did, and the younger man was astonished to hear the old man say, "Lord, You know that I'm deaf and need a seat right up in the front. Please, let me have one, so I can hear Your Word. And, Lord, my toes are poking out of my shoes, and I am not much credit to You, so I wish You could get me a pair of new shoes. And, Lord, You know I have no silver, and I want to stay for all the meetings, so I want You to get me a place to stay."

When they got to the meetings, the old man stood at the rear for a while, cupping his hand to his ear. But soon someone noticed him and gave him a seat right up front. After the meeting a woman whispered, "Are those the best shoes you have?"

"Yes," he said, "but I expect my Father to get me a new pair soon."

"Come with me," she said, "and I'll get you a new pair. Where are you staying?"

"I have no silver and I'm a stranger here, but my Father will find me a place to stay, for He knows I want to attend the meetings."

"Then you are welcome to stay at my house," she said.

And that night the dear old man thanked his Father in heaven for sending him the three things he had asked for.

Are you well acquainted with your heavenly Father?

Go in peace, and the God of Israel grant your petition which you have asked of him.
1 Samuel 1:17.

March 24

God answered the earnest prayer of Hannah and gave her a baby boy. She called him Samuel, which means "asked of God." If you only knew how many earnest prayers have ascended for you, and how many times God has answered those earnest prayers, and healed your sicknesses and saved your life, and helped you overcome temptation, you would feel like calling yourself "Samuel" also.

A few years ago an Adventist soldier found himself in the U.S. Army in one of the European countries. He was a strong Adventist Christian, and had quite an ability in dealing with children. With the aid of a little chewing gum he managed to gather a small group of children together as he came off duty every afternoon. He told them Bible stories, and soon they were his friends.

One afternoon he missed one of his regular little visitors. He asked the others about him and learned that the boy was sick in bed. He went at once to visit him, but the little boy's mother said, "It's no use to see my son. He is unconscious, and the doctor says there's nothing anyone can do. He will soon die."

"I'm sorry to hear that he is so ill," said the soldier. "You know, he is one of my little friends. I tell the children stories every day. I wish you would let me go in and offer a prayer for him." Nobody could refuse such a request, so into the room went our soldier and fell on his knees and prayed. The mother felt so helpless that she could not stand being in the room, so she quietly went out. When she thought the prayer was finished, she came back, but our soldier was still on his knees. She went away again, and came back again and again, but our soldier was still praying. When at last she found the soldier standing, he turned and said, "Your son will not die, but will recover."

Then the mother began to cry. "Who are you?" she asked. "What church do you go to?" Our soldier gave her the address of the nearby Seventh-day Adventist church. The next Sabbath the mother and her son were in church, and they kept on coming.

Are you really earnest when you pray? Our God still answers earnest prayers.

1 SAMUEL 2

But Samuel ministered before the Lord,
even as a child, wearing a linen ephod.
1 Samuel 2:18.

March 25

Many, many times in Bible days, and also in our modern days, children have ministered for God. In the January 12, 1961, *Review and Herald* there was a beautiful story about a little blind girl who brought comfort to a sorrowing woman. They met on a transcontinental train going west when a kindhearted woman found a fellow passenger in the lounge weeping her heart away.

"Is there something I can do?" asked the woman. "Are you ill?"

"No, no, I'm not ill," replied the one weeping, "but I have more trouble than I can bear. My husband died some years ago. My only son is in the Air Force in Europe, and my daughter in California is dying. I am hoping I can reach her before it is too late."

No wonder she wept as if her heart would break. Back to the coach went the would-be good Samaritan, and waking up the sleeping passengers one after another, she asked, "Is there a minister in this car? Or a priest? Or a rabbi?" But no one responded. Then in desperation she asked, "Well, isn't there someone who can pray? There's someone in the lounge who needs help badly."

Now, among the passengers there was a young blind girl, maybe 10 or 12 years old, and when no one offered to help, she touched the arm of the woman and said, "Will I do? I know the Bible a little, and I can pray a little, too."

"Oh, yes, dear, you'll do," said the kind lady. "Come with me." And she led her into the lounge. The little girl felt for the hands of the weeping woman, then in a soft, tender voice began, "Our Father which art in heaven . . ." Then she repeated the twenty-third psalm and the Beatitudes, including "Blessed are they that mourn: for they shall be comforted." The sobbing stopped, and the heartbroken woman sat up.

"Thank you for bringing this girl," she said to the kind woman. "She helped such a lot." Then turning to the girl, she patted her cheek and suddenly saw that she was blind. For a moment or two the words wouldn't come. Then she said, "Thank you, dear. You have not only brought me comfort; you have restored my faith."

Remember that God has a special place where you can minister for Him.

Speak, Lord; for Your servant hears.
1 Samuel 3:9.

March 26

Samuel heard a voice speaking to him, but he didn't know it was God's voice until after he said, "Speak, for Your servant hears." Do you know that God is speaking to every one of us? But too often we don't recognize the voice of God. In *Christ's Object Lessons* Ellen White says: "God's holy, educating Spirit is in His Word. A light, a new and precious light, shines forth from every page. Truth is there revealed, and words and sentences are made *bright* and *appropriate for the occasion*, as the voice of God speaking to the soul" (p. 132; italics supplied). Just think! The voice of God is speaking to you as you read the Bible, as you study your Sabbath school lesson, and as you read the daily devotional book. But does a sentence ever stand out as though it was written specially for you? I'm going to recommend a little formula that has worked for me for many years, and I am sure it will work for you, too. Here it is. As you take up your Bible to study your lesson or to read the devotional, breathe this little prayer—"Speak, Lord, for Your servant hears," and words and sentences will surely be made bright and appropriate for you.

During the Battle of Rangoon in December 1941 thousands of people were fleeing overland into India. No food stations had been prepared, no proper paths had been made, and hundreds of poor people died for lack of food and from the ravages of wild animals. We missionaries began to wonder whether we should flee also. Then one morning one of the missionaries reading the daily portion of the Bible Year read, "You shall not go out with haste, nor go by flight; for the Lord will go before you, and the God of Israel will be your rear guard" (Isaiah 52:12).

As he read, the words were "made bright." We all knew it was the voice of God speaking to us. We obeyed. We stayed a little longer—till the paths were made and the food stations established, and we all got out safely.

Someday you will need to have God speak to you. Learn now to hear His voice by saying, "Speak, Lord, for Your servant hears," as you read and study His Sacred Word.

1 SAMUEL 4

The wages of sin is death, but the gift of
God is eternal life in Christ Jesus our Lord.
Romans 6:23.

March **27**

Hophni and Phinehas did very bad things. They were disobedient to their parents and to God. They were selfish. They desecrated the sacrifices of people, and the Bible says they were vile. The first time they sinned it most likely was only a little sin, but they did it again and again. They added sin to sin till at last they took the sacred ark of God into battle, with the result that the ark was taken by the enemy and they were both slain. That is often what happens to people who play with sin and do not forsake it.

Alice was brought up in a Christian home, attending both church school and academy. After graduation she took a job to earn enough money and go to college in a year or two. Her work was in a large Christian office, but Alice fell in with a group of worldly friends who didn't care what the church taught or what anyone said. Alice began going out with them. She went to parties and local bars. It was there that she met a wonderful young man. No, he wasn't a Christian, but he was so pleasant and fun. No one had ever made her feel so happy. There was just one problem: she was making even more compromises in her personal standards and spiritual life. Now and then she wondered whether she was slipping. What would her mother say if she knew? Her boyfriend teased her to try cigarettes. "Oh, no! Never! No one with any sense smokes." But social drinking? A little wine? What could be so bad about it? Then came the New Year's party, and the crowd decided to see the old year out in a nightclub. She remembered a rather strong cocktail—but nothing else till she woke up in a hospital, the only survivor in an automobile accident that took the lives of the other merrymakers. During the four months Alice spent in the hospital she had plenty of time to think. Fortunately, she made an about-face and rededicated her life to God.

It is not safe for anyone to play with sin. No, it doesn't usually end in tragedy, but it surely separates you from God. In the end it replaces your joy with guilt and provides no comfort in pain. It really pays to walk in the path of obedience toward eternal life.

I am the First and I am the Last;
Beside Me there is no God.
Isaiah 44:6.

March 28

God worked miracle after miracle to prove that Dagon the stone god, half man and half fish, which the Philistines worshipped, had no power to help them, and that He alone was God. And God still works miracles to bless and help His people prove that He alone is God.

I recently read a lovely story about a miracle that God performed for the Brown family. Mrs. Brown had been sick, and all their money was gone. Mr. Brown had nothing in the bank, there was nothing in his pocket, and he still owed a big doctor bill. Things looked very blue for them all, and to make matters worse, Mrs. Brown needed to go to the doctor again. What could they do? They just had to see the doctor, bill or no bill. So Mr. Brown got his old Ford ready, bundled up Mrs. Brown, and after telling the Lord all about their embarrassing situation, they started off down the rutted country road. They had gone only a few miles when the car stopped and Mr. Brown couldn't start it again. He checked the gas and the oil and everything else he could think of, but couldn't find any problem. At last he got under the car to see if something had broken there. Sure enough, he saw something on the road just under the engine. Had it dropped off the engine? He picked it up, but it wasn't metal and it wasn't rubber or plastic. It was paper. A roll of paper. Why, it looked like money! It was money. It was a roll of bills! There was enough to pay the doctor bill and then some. What a miracle! But that wasn't all. Mr. Brown got in the car again, turned the key, and off the car went, just as though nothing had been the matter with it at all.

For a long time Mr. Brown could hardly believe it had happened. "Mother," he said, "is the money real?"

"Yes, dear," she replied. "And God is real too."

"Then it's not a dream?"

"No indeed! You're very wide awake, and so am I."

Young people, things like that don't just happen. No "Dagon" or "Baal" could ever do anything like that. Only the living God could stop a car right over a roll of money. And that living God is your God. Keep close to Him. You need Him every moment of every day.

1 SAMUEL 6; 7:1, 2

Then the cows headed straight for the road to Beth Shemesh, . . . and did not turn aside to the right hand or the left.
1 Samuel 6:12.

Today we've read about another miracle the living God performed, this time with cattle. Who ever heard of two cows going away from their calves and taking the right road to Beth Shemesh? Yet I read a story by Elder R. S. Watts, of another miracle our living God performed with an animal, this time a water buffalo. A certain farmer had been planting rice all day in his paddy field on the island of Lubang in the Philippines. Just as he was ready to go home, three water buffalo came wandering into his paddy field. He tried to drive them away. Two of them left, but one refused to go. You can believe it or not, but this one turned right toward the farmer, opened its mouth, and spoke! "Prepare to meet God. He is coming soon. You must keep the Sabbath to be ready." After this the buffalo plodded away, and the farmer, astonished beyond description, ran back to his village and excitedly told his family and his neighbors about this strange experience with a talking buffalo.

Soon after this experience a relative of the farmer, Brother Faustino Tardeo, who was a Seventh-day Adventist, came to this village to spend his vacation, for this was his former home. He was soon giving Bible studies, and when they studied about the Sabbath, the farmer told again about this experience with the talking buffalo who told him he must keep the Sabbath to get ready for Christ's soon coming. It was such a striking coincidence that they believed God's hand was in it all, and the farmer and a number of his neighbors began to keep the Sabbath. And soon there was quite a company of people there studying the Bible and learning what God had for their lives. No wonder Isaiah says God's name is "Wonderful."

Paul declares that this wonderful God "chose the foolish things of the world to shame the wise; God chose the weak things of the world to shame the strong. He chose the lowly things of this world and the despised things—and the things that are not—to nullify the things that are" (1 Corinthians 1:27, 28, NIV).

This God—your God—may do something wonderful for you or some of your friends someday to bring them into the truth of His love and mercy.

Come out from among them and be separate, says the Lord. . . . And I will receive you. I will be a Father to you, and you shall be My sons and daughters.
2 Corinthians 6:17, 18.

March 30

The poor children of Israel! They weren't satisfied to have God lead them and speak to them through His prophets. No! They were going to have a king at any price—"like all the nations" (1 Samual 8:5). They wanted to do what everyone else was doing. They wanted to be like the world. This is the strongest temptation that comes to any of us, and Satan makes it his business to try to make us believe that we cannot be happy unless we look like the world, talk like the world, sing like the world, and do everything else like the world.

If only you could be old before you were young! If only you could see, before the temptation comes to you, the tears and broken hearts of those who have been deceived by old Satan, then you could easily believe that God never says "Thou shalt not" to rob us of any pleasure. He never says "Come out and be separate" to keep us from having a good time, but only to save us from sorrow, from tears, from shame, and from disappointment.

A few years ago I was talking like this to the students in one of our large colleges. After one of the meetings a young woman put this little note into my hands:

"Dear Elder,

"I want you to know that I never found happiness until Jesus came into my life. Life in show business is most unhappy to those who are in it. I know this is true, for I was in it from when I was 4½ years old till I was 20. How fortunate I was to find God, and I am growing closer to Him all the time here at college. I love my Lord so much and I have put Him first, above all things. If anyone in show business ever asks how happy one can be, think of me.

"Sincerely

"Nonajane."

And if you could have seen her happy face you would have known she was telling the truth. If you want to be really happy, "Come out from among them and be separate. . . . I will be a Father to you, and you shall be my sons and daughters," says the Lord.

1 SAMUEL 9

And what does the Lord require of you, but to do justly, to love mercy, and to walk humbly with your God? Micah 6:8.

March 31

The children of Israel were determined to have a king so that they could be like all the nations around them, so the Lord directed in choosing the best man they had. Saul was a tall, impressive young man, but above all, he was humble. "Am I not a Benjamite, of the smallest of the tribes of Israel, and my family the least of all the families of the tribe of Benjamin?" (1 Samuel 9:21). Humility is a trait of character that pleases not only God but also others.

Several years ago the young people from Newbold College in England were collecting money for humanitarian work. One humble, earnest young man called at a home where he expected to receive only the usual small donation. But he loved the Lord and loved to help do the Lord's work, and it showed in his face. The woman in this house was well to do, and she was impressed. "Yes," she said, "I will be glad to help in a work like this. I will give you $500." The young man was almost speechless, but he managed to thank her, and went on showing her how much her donation would do. "I'll make it $1,000," she said. "That is a wonderful work." The young man kept on sharing, and the woman's interest still grew. "I'll make it $1,500," she said. Then looking the young man straight in the face, she added, "Wouldn't you like to be a missionary yourself?"

"Yes indeed," he replied, "but I don't have enough education yet."

"Then listen! If you will go to Africa as a missionary, I will pay your way through college and give your missionary society $3,500!" she said.

And the young man replied, "I certainly will be glad to do it." And she did; and he did. Roy Warland was in Africa for years, and later was one of our conference Sabbath school secretaries in England, still the same lovable, humble man.

"Let this mind be in you which was also in Christ Jesus," says Paul, "who, being in the form of God, . . . made Himself of no reputation, taking the form of a bondservant, and coming in the likeness of men. . . . Therefore God also has highly exalted Him and given Him the name which is above every name" (Philippians 2:5-7, 9).

What a pity Saul did not remain humble. And say, how do *you* rate for humility?

Then the Spirit of the Lord will come upon you, and you will . . . be turned into another man. 1 Samuel 10:6.

April 1

Saul has not been the only young man turned into another man by the Spirit of God. Consider Eugene Farnsworth. His father was the first one in that little company of Adventists in Washington, New Hampshire, to take his stand for the seventh-day Sabbath. In 1855 Eugene was in his teens, and not too interested in religion, so when Elder J. N. Andrews arrived at his home for a visit, Eugene took a hoe and went out to work in the field. But John Andrews was a lover of young people and knew what a power they could be for God when they were definitely on His side. So Elder Andrews got another hoe and went out to help Eugene in the field. "Well, Eugene," said the elder, "what are you going to make of yourself?"

"I intend to get an education first," said Eugene.

"Good! That will be the best thing you can do. And what then?"

"I think I shall study law."

"You might do worse," replied the elder. "And what then?"

"I intend to be the best lawyer in the state."

"And what then?"

"I hope to make a lot of money and may visit other countries."

"And what then?"

"I suppose I shall get married and have a nice home."

"And what then?" The questioning was becoming a little unpleasant.

"Oh, I suppose I shall grow old and die, like other men," said Eugene.

"And what then?" said the good elder as he fixed his eye on the young man and put his hand on his shoulder. "Eugene, what then?"

Eugene couldn't get away from that searching question. It followed him to bed, to work—everywhere—and in a meeting a little later on, when Elder and Mrs. White were also present, Elder Andrews whispered, "Eugene, isn't it time for you to make your decision now?" And he did, and the Spirit of God came upon him and turned him into one of our mighty pioneer preachers! The Spirit of God wants to turn you, too, into the best you can be. Won't you let Him?

1 SAMUEL 12

Do not turn aside from following the Lord,
but serve the Lord with all your heart.
1 Samuel 12:20.

April 2

Samuel was getting old, and although Israel had displeased the Lord by asking for a king, he pleaded with them not to turn aside from following the Lord. "Only fear the Lord," he begged, "and serve Him in truth with all your heart" (1 Samuel 12:24). The story of the Advent movement is filled with the experiences of men and women who served God with all their hearts and did not turn aside in spite of trouble or hardship.

In 1944 Mr. Soans, an expert welder, accepted the Sabbath during a series of meetings in Bombay, India. Although he had worked at the largest electrical shop in the city for 20 years, at once he was let go from his job. Up and down the streets of Bombay he walked, looking for work. Up and down the streets Satan followed him, with his devilish insinuations: "Your God doesn't hear your prayers. He's going to let your wife and children starve."

Two weeks went by. Mr. Soans was still looking for work. Then into the harbor came a ship filled with bales of cotton and ammunition. While the ship was being unloaded, one of the workers dropped a cigarette into the hold among the bales of cotton. By the time the fire was discovered it was impossible to put it out. "Our only hope is to sink the ship," said the officials, so four expert welders were called from the biggest electrical shop in Bombay to burn four holes under the waterline to sink the ship. While they were working, the fire reached the ammunition, causing a powerful explosion. It killed the four welders and hundreds of others. Mr. Soans was still looking for work! When he heard the explosion and pieced the story together, he said, "I'm the happiest man in the world! If I hadn't lost my job because of the Sabbath, I would have been one of those welders who lost their lives." Soon after this, Brother Soans opened his own welding shop, and the last I had heard of him, he was making three times as much money as when on the job he lost.

It will pay you in every way to serve the Lord with all your heart too. Ellen White says, "Be faithful. Put heart into your work" (*Messages to Young People,* p. 148). "Those who learn to put thought into everything they undertake, however small the work may appear, will be of use in the world" (*ibid.,* p. 149).

*To obey is better than sacrifice,
and to heed than the fat of rams.
1 Samuel 15:22.*

April 3

How hard it was for Saul to learn to obey the voice of God! Because he didn't know all the reasons God had told him to destroy the Amalekites, he pleased himself. We must all learn to obey, whether we understand the reason for the command or not.

An Eastern king needed a faithful servant, and two men applied for the position. The king paid both men the day's wage in advance, then took them to a well and put a basket down beside it. "Now, men," he said, "try your best to fill this basket with well water. I'll be back this evening to see how you have gotten on." So saying, he went away; and the men began to work. It wasn't long before one man said, "What a silly business—trying to fill a basket with water!"

"But we've been paid our wages," said the other. "He knows why he told us to do it. That is not our business."

"Well, I'm not going to keep on doing such foolish work," said the first man, and throwing down his bucket, he went away. The other man worked on faithfully, lowering his bucket, drawing up water, and pouring it into the basket. And just before sunset the well was dry. Looking down into the well, he saw something shiny. He let down his bucket, moved it carefully this way and that, and drew up a beautiful diamond ring! "Ah, now I see why the king wanted us to pour water into the basket," he said. "If we had brought up the ring before the well was dry, it would have been found in the basket!" Just then the king came back. The man showed him the ring he had just drawn up. The king smiled and said, "It's yours. You have been faithful in a little thing; now I see I can trust you in great things. Henceforth you will stand at my right hand."

Life is just like that. Often we're told to do something that doesn't make sense to us, but that doesn't mean it's wrong. For example, thousands of people have died because they thought it was silly to keep to the speed limit when they drove. And even today, despite all the evidence of its dangers, people still start smoking.

You may be tempted to think that some commands your parents and teachers give you are foolish. But be wise! To obey *is* better than sacrifice.

1 SAMUEL 16

The Lord does not see as man sees;
for man looks at the outward appearance,
but the Lord looks at the heart.
1 Samuel 16:7.

April 4

No doubt Eliab thought he was bigger and better and stronger than his smallest brother, David. His father, Jesse, may have thought so too. Samuel certainly did, for when he saw Eliab he said to himself: "Surely the Lord's anointed is before Him" (1 Samuel 16:6). But the Lord wasn't looking at the outward appearance. He was looking at the heart, and the Lord chose David, the youngest of eight brothers. God's choices are often big surprises to grown-up men and women.

Once upon a time, away over in a little church in Scotland, was a discouraged preacher. He had tried for an entire year to invite people to unite with the church, but the only person to accept and openly confess Jesus as his Savior was a little lad. The church officers weren't happy. One morning one of them went to the pastor and said, "There must be something wrong with your preaching, for only one person has taken his stand all year long, and he is *only a boy*." The poor preacher felt so discouraged, and after everybody had left the church, he stayed there, wondering why he had failed. He didn't notice the door open. The first thing he knew, the boy—the only one who had responded to his preaching—was standing beside him. The boy put his hand on the preacher's hand, and said, "Do you think that if I am willing to work hard I could become a preacher?"

"A preacher!" said the minister.

"Yes, and perhaps a missionary," said the boy. Tears came to the pastor's eyes as he said, "May God bless you, my boy. Yes, I think you can become a preacher."

That little lad was Robert Moffat, who became one of God's great missionaries to South Africa. God used him mightily in Africa, but not only there. Once when he was back in England he was telling of the land where he saw "in the morning sun the smoke of a thousand villages where no missionary has ever been," and David Livingstone responded to the call! But once Robert Moffat was only a boy, a boy who responded to God's call.

Never mind *your* looks—whether you are tall or short, fat or thin. Keep your heart right, for "the Lord looks at the heart."

I come to you in the name of the Lord of hosts. . . .
This day the Lord will deliver you into my hand. . . .
And . . . all the earth may know that there is a
God in Israel.
1 Samuel 17:45, 46.

April 5

Did it ever occur to you that not all giants have two legs? Well, they don't! Anything beyond your strength or ability, anything that makes you call on God for help to overcome, is a giant. It might be a bad habit; it might be a hard job; it could even be a tough math problem or history question. That's what Cory's father said one evening after they had studied about the 10 spies who felt like grasshoppers before the giants in Canaan. It made Cory think as he sat down to do his homework, for he soon realized he had a tough problem. An hour later Howard called, "Hey, Cory, aren't you coming down to Tim's?"

"I almost forgot," Cory replied. "But I've got a tough problem that I'm stuck on."

"Aw, that old problem! I tried it once or twice too, and I couldn't do it. I'm sure no one will get it. Anyway, I heard Miss Andrews tell Professor Bowen that she was only giving us that problem to try our patience. I'm sure not going to waste any more time on it." Just then Cory's cousin walked through the room. She was staying in Cory's home, and she just seemed to be saying to herself in a sweet voice, "And there we saw the giants." Cory's face burned, and he said, "Look, Howard, you may as well go on. Tell Tim I can't come. I'm going to lick that problem. I'm no grasshopper."

The next morning when they went to school, to their surprise they found Judge Dennison from Buffalo visiting the school he attended as a boy. He stayed and stayed, until time for math class. "Howard, come to the board and do the thirty-ninth problem," said Miss Andrews.

"Sorry, Miss Andrews. I couldn't do it," Howard said as his face went red. "I couldn't do it either," said the next boy and the next. Then it was Cory's turn. He went right up to the board, worked it out, and explained it perfectly. The whole room, including the judge, applauded.

"Did anyone help you?" asked Miss Andrews.

"Yes, my cousin Carol! She said, 'And there we saw giants!' And I said to myself, 'I'm no grasshopper!' And I stuck at it till 11:00 and got it!" Then everybody applauded again.

Say, have you got giants? You can lick them with God's help.

1 SAMUEL 18:1-16; 19

So Saul eyed David from that day forward. . . .
Now Saul was afraid of David, because the Lord
was with him, but had departed from Saul.
1 Samuel 18:9-12.

April 6

In today's Scripture reading we have pictured one of the loveliest things in life—friendship. The friendship of David and Jonathan. We also have one of the ugliest things we can see in life—jealousy. Saul's jealousy of David. It is good for us all to examine our hearts now and then to see whether there's anyone in our life that we give a cold shoulder to, or anyone of whom we are envious. Jealousy is like having a poisonous viper fastened to the heart—to your heart. And honestly, there is nothing a friend might do or say that makes them deserve to be put in "cold storage." Jealousy hurts. But it hurts the one who is jealous the most.

Some time ago I came across a fable about an eagle who was jealous of another eagle because it could fly swifter and higher than he could. The more he saw the rival eagle, the more jealous he felt, till he wished he could find some way to kill him. One day the jealous eagle saw a hunter and said to him, "I wish you would shoot that other eagle so I would never have to see him again."

"If I had some feathers to put into the end of my arrow," said the hunter, "I would try."

The jealous eagle gladly pulled some feathers out of his wing and gave them to the hunter. The hunter put the feathers into his arrow and shot, but the arrow didn't quite reach the rival eagle. The jealous eagle gave him some more feathers and said, "Try again." The hunter tried again, but missed. The jealous eagle gave him more feathers and more feathers, and the hunter shot again and again. At last the jealous eagle had lost so many feathers that he couldn't fly at all! Then the hunter turned around and killed him. And that was the end of the jealous eagle, and it pretty much sums up what jealousy will do to you.

"Grief, anxiety, discontent, remorse, guilt, distrust, all tend to break down the life forces and to invite decay and death. . . . Courage, hope, faith, sympathy, love, promote health and prolong life" (*The Ministry of Healing*, p. 241).

So look out! Practice getting along with everybody and being kind to everybody. Rejoice with others when they win and succeed, and you will be loved and have many real friends.

1 SAMUEL 20

Teach me to do Your will, for You are my God.
Psalm 143:10.

April 7

Have you ever lost your kalar? Oh, you say, you don't know what your kalar is. I'll tell you. When the sun is shining and you walk along the path, your kalar is there. If you run, it runs. If you walk, it walks. If you lift your hand, it lifts its hand. What do you call it? A shadow, of course. But the Karens don't call it a shadow. They call it a kalar, and they live in mortal fear that the spirits will catch their kalars. Around every corner, in the shade of every bunch of bamboo, they believe that the spirits are waiting to catch their kalar. And if they do they'll wake up feeling miserable, cross, and out of sorts, and if they don't get their kalar back they can even die.

When a Karen wakes up feeling out of sorts, he decides at once that evil spirits have caught his kalar. So he makes a little basket and puts an egg in it, then takes it to the place where he thinks he last saw his kalar. Hanging the basket on a twig, he walks backwards . . . all the way home. As he walks he calls out, "Kalar, Kalar! Heh Kay Kaler! Kalar, Kalar, Kalar!" And if he comes to a stream he cuts three bamboos and puts them across the water so the kalar won't get his feet wet. When he gets home, he cuts a little branch and puts it by the steps to the house so the kalar will know which house is his. It's surprising how well he feels when he's done all this, so he decides the spirits have accepted his offering and let his kalar go.

I think you'd feel good too if, after waking up out of sorts, you went for a nice walk in the sunshine. Maybe you'd meet a friend or two and stop to talk. Maybe you'd see bright-colored birds or hear the soft call of a deer. You couldn't help feeling better.

I can't tell you all the different ways the jungle folk hunt for their kalars. But I have a prescription I always give them so that they won't lose their kalars: Live in the sunshine! This is a good prescription for everyone, adults included. True sunshine means obedience to God's laws, for that will keep us truly happy. True sunshine means thinking of others, and cheerfully helping wherever you can—in your home, your school, or your neighborhood.

If you and I and our friends stay with God all the time, even a rainy day can't take our kalar away.

1 SAMUEL 24

I will not stretch out my hand against my lord,
for he is the Lord's anointed.
1 Samuel 24:10.

April 8

David has given us all a shining example of reverence and respect for our rulers and our elders and all who are ordained of God. How careful we should be never to criticize them or do anything against them.

You know the story of how John Wilkes Booth "stretched out his hand" against President Lincoln and shot him, but did you ever hear the story about John Wilkes Booth's brother Edwin, and what he unknowingly did to bring great happiness to President Lincoln? Well, as the story was told in *Reader's Digest*, Edwin Booth, who was a famous American actor, had just finished his evening performance in New York one night during the Civil War. He crossed over on the ferry to Jersey City and hurried to the Pennsylvania Railway station to catch the train for Philadelphia. The train was already at the station when he got there, and just as he boarded the rear platform of one of the cars, the train started with a jolt that threw him off balance for a moment. That same jolt caused a well-dressed young man who was getting on behind him to lose his footing, and he fell between the train and the platform. Edwin Booth saw it happen, and, holding on to the handrail for all he was worth, he reached down and grabbed the young man by the collar, and pulled him up onto the moving train. The young man was scared but not hurt. He recognized the actor and thanked him profusely. "That was a narrow one, Mr. Booth," he said. Edwin Booth smiled and went on. He did not even ask the name of the young man. In a few weeks, however, he received a letter from General Adam Badeau, military secretary to General Grant, thanking him for his heroic act and telling him the young man whose life he saved was Robert Todd Lincoln—the president's son. Booth kept that letter, and later, when he heard that his brother had shot the president, it was the only consolation he had in those days of family shame.

"It is dangerous to utter a word of doubt, dangerous to question and criticize divine light. The habit of careless and irreverent criticism reacts upon the character" (*The Desire of Ages*, p. 323).

Won't you make up your mind to do all you possibly can to support your teachers, your church leaders, and your rulers, and to bring them happiness?

*So David took the spear and the jug of water . . . ;
and no man saw or knew it; . . . For . . . a
deep sleep from the Lord had fallen on them.
1 Samuel 26:12.*

April 9

God delights in mercy, and He worked miracle after miracle to help David when he showed mercy to King Saul, who was trying to take his life.

Here is a story about another person who showed mercy, and a miracle that happened to a young Union Army sentinel who was found asleep at his post.

Eighteen-year-old William Scott was in Company K of the Third Vermont Regiment during the Civil War. One night he volunteered to go on guard duty in the place of a sick comrade. All went well that night, but the next night his own turn came to be on guard duty. Overtired, the next morning the relief guard found him asleep at his post. Scott was court-martialed, found guilty, and condemned to be shot within 24 hours. His comrades felt terrible. His captain said it was his fault, that he should have known better than to let a soldier do all-night guard duty two nights running. They appointed a committee that went to L. E. Chittenden, a Vermont lawyer and a friend of President Lincoln's. "There must be some way to save him, Judge!" said the captain. "He's a good boy. He's not to blame. If anyone is to be shot, I am the one. I'm the guilty one. Won't you help us?"

There was only one who could help—President Lincoln, and to Lincoln they went. The captain told the story. Lincoln understood, and his heart was moved with mercy. He thought of all the possible complications and said, "I'll have to do it myself, and I'll have to do it today." And down to the camp he went.

He had a long talk with William Scott, and finally said, "William, you are not going to be shot. I am going to send you back to your regiment. But how are you going to pay my bill?" The lad hardly knew what to answer. Then putting his hand on William's shoulder, the president said, "William, if from this day you will do your duty, so that if you suddenly came to the time to die you could look me in the face and say, 'I have kept my promise. I have done my duty as a soldier,' then my bill will be paid."

What a beautiful thing is mercy! How do you rate?

"Vengeance is Mine, I will repay," says the Lord.
Romans 12:19.

April 10

David had been anointed to be king before Saul began to persecute him. How easy it would have been for David to put Saul out of the way! Opportunity after opportunity presented itself, but David said, "I will not stretch out my hand against the Lord's anointed," and he patiently waited for God to work it out in His own way and in His own time. When you have problems, remember that God can still do the "repaying" if only we will let Him.

Elder A. V. Olson told a story of the way God took a hand in affairs in one of the European countries in the early 1930s while he was president of the Southern European Division. In this country the Greek Orthodox Church was the state church, and Adventists were always persecuted. Only when the ruling cabinet was made up of men educated in Western countries did the Adventists enjoy a degree of freedom.

Then the king made the metropolitan of the state church the prime minister, and he called in a number of bishops and priests to make up his cabinet. Immediately they made a decree that on a certain date all Seventh-day Adventist churches and schools would be closed. The publishing house would be taken away, and all ministers and colporteurs would be imprisoned. The Adventists would not be permitted to visit one another in their homes or on the streets. The men were determined to destroy our work. In vain our leaders went to see some of the cabinet members. They even went to the prime minister himself, but he said, "I have tried to destroy the Adventists for a long time. Now this is the time, and we are going to do it."

Our leaders sent word to the General Conference officers. They designated a day of prayer and fasting, and the word was sent to Adventists and others all around the world. On that special Sabbath Adventists everywhere, with prayer and fasting, pleaded with God to keep His work from being destroyed. God answered that prayer. Just a few nights before the decree was to be enforced, the prime minister went to bed as usual, and to sleep—and *never woke up!* God had poured out His vengeance upon him and removed him from power. The new prime minister called a new cabinet, and the first thing they did was to rescind the decree to destroy the Adventists. God still has power. I wish we had more days of fasting and prayer for our workers in lands where liberties are restricted. Don't you?

2 SAMUEL 1

Love your enemies, bless those who curse you, do good to those who hate you, and pray for those who spitefully use you and persecute you. Matthew 5:44.

April 11

Saul was dead at last, and David "mourned and wept and fasted until evening" (2 Samuel 1:12). Only a person who loves God with all his heart and soul and strength could love an enemy like that. And there are many people all over the world who have loved their enemies and done good to those who hated them. I think of one of our ministers in one of those countries of southeastern Europe who was persecuted, arrested, brought into court, and falsely accused by the priest in the village in which he was working. The priest knew that our minister was innocent. So did the lawyer who prosecuted him, and so did the judge. But they were determined to stop his work if possible, and he was sentenced to one year in prison. It was winter, and there were 16 prisoners in the cell in which he was placed. Each prisoner had a narrow bunk and one blanket. At first our brother was tempted to be discouraged, but soon he decided that God had a work for him to do there, so he did his best to be cheerful. Then one day the police opened the cell door and shoved in another prisoner. Who do you think it was? It was the lawyer who had prosecuted our pastor. They recognized each other, and the lawyer was so ashamed that he went over to a corner and stayed there.

Soon it came time to go to sleep. But the lawyer had no bunk and no blanket. No one offered to share with him, so our brother went over and said, "Friend, you can't sit here all night. You'll get pneumonia. My bunk is small, but if we are real good friends, I think we can make it." The lawyer hesitated, but finally went over and shared the bunk with our brother.

"Are you ill?" our brother asked.

"Oh, no" was the reply. "I'm troubled and perplexed. There are 15 men here who belong to my church, but not one of them offered me any help, only you, the man I prosecuted falsely."

"Jesus, my Master, has told us to love our enemies," said our pastor. And when they were released from prison, the lawyer was ever our pastor's friend.

There truly is Christian power in loving our enemies and in doing good to those who hate us. You try it.

2 SAMUEL 5

When you hear the sound of marching in the tops
of the mulberry trees, then you shall advance quickly.
For then the Lord will go out before you.
2 Samuel 5:24.

Do you know what I think made the sound of "marching" in the tops of the mulberry trees? I think it was the Spirit of God going before them like a mighty wind. You see, David depended on the Spirit of God for every victory, and that is something we must all learn to do. Listen to another chapter in the story of the minister who was imprisoned and who did good to the lawyer who had prosecuted him. The Holy Spirit turned him into a friend. But that's not all the Holy Spirit did.

You can hardly believe it, but some time later two big police officers opened the prison door and put in another prisoner. And who do you think this one was? It was the priest himself! And when the priest saw our pastor he was even more ashamed than the lawyer had been. He turned his back, and like the lawyer he went over into the corner and sat on the floor. When it came time to sleep, just as before, nobody offered to help the poor priest. So our brother went over and invited him to come and share his bunk and his blanket. At first the priest would not move or say a word, but our brother pulled him up and led him over to his bunk, and they lay down together. It was after midnight when our brother heard the priest sobbing.

"Are you sick?" he asked.

"No," replied the priest, "I'm not sick, but I'm troubled. Right here in this cell are 15 men who belong to my church, and not one of them has offered me any help but you, the man I falsely accused. How could you do it?"

"It is because Jesus lives in my heart, and I try to do what Jesus would do," said our minister. The priest then asked for our brother's forgiveness and asked him to pray for him.

"If I ever get out of this place," said the priest, "remember that Adventists will always find a friend in this priest." And he was true to his word.

Who but the Spirit of God could change the heart of a man like that! That's what I need. That's what you need. We all need to be filled with the Spirit of God always.

When he does wrong, I will punish him with the rod of men. . . . But my love will never be taken away from him."
2 Samuel 7:14, 15, NIV.

April 13

God had to punish David. God had to punish Solomon. God has to punish every one of us. But what a joyful thought—God's love does not depart from us! Let me tell you another chapter in the story about our minister who was falsely accused and put in prison. The past two mornings I have told you how the lawyer and the priest were each brought into the prison and how the Spirit of God, through the Christlike kindness of the minister, changed them into friends of the Seventh-day Adventists. Well, that's not the end of the story.

Some time later the prison door opened, and the two policemen came in and said to our brother, "Take your few belongings and come with us." It was night. Where were they taking him? Home? To another prison? To the place of execution? He was soon to find out, for as they drove along, one of the officers said, "I'm so sorry. We have learned to know you and respect you. You are a Christian, but now we are taking you to the worst prison in the country." And it was true. As soon as he was put in the new prison cell, the prisoners asked, "Why are you here?"

"For preaching the gospel," replied our brother kindly. "Why are you here?"

"I killed my wife," shouted one. "I killed my neighbor," shouted another. That was the kind of men they were. When the lights went out, they began to scream and howl. The noise spread from cell to cell until it made our poor brother's blood run cold. Then the Spirit of God whispered in his heart, *Sing.* So he lifted up his voice and sang.

"Sing again," the men called when he finished, and he sang again.

"How can you sing such songs in a place like this?" they asked as they crowded around him.

"Because of my religion. I have Jesus in my heart," he replied.

"What does that mean?" they asked. And he told them.

"Does God still love us?" "Will God still have mercy on us?" "Won't you pray for us?" And our brother explained the love and mercy of God and prayed for those poor men, and by the time his year of imprisonment was up, 17 of those criminals had given their hearts to God and had been baptized.

2 SAMUEL 15

*"For rebellion is as the sin of witchcraft,
and stubbornness is as iniquity and idolatry."*
1 Samuel 15:23.

April 14

We mustn't be surprised that rebellion and stubbornness are often the most common temptations that come to all of us. That's the way Satan got started. And he knows he can ruin and destroy anyone if only he can make them rebellious. God regards rebellion and stubbornness as very serious sins, and He longs to help us overcome them.

Once there was a stubborn and rebellious junior boy whom we shall call Charles. When his teacher corrected him, he skipped school for three days. Then his parents found out, and they were heartbroken. They wanted more than anything else to help him make things right.

"Son," said his father, "you have not been honest with us. I have always said that I can trust my boy. But evidently I can't, for you have been living a lie for three whole days. I can't tell you how bad I feel about what you've done." Charles felt ashamed and angry. He would rather have had a whipping than to see his father's sorrow like this. After talking with his son and praying, the father said, "You will be housebound for three days. We will make you a bed in the attic, and we will bring your food and your books to you. You can study and make up your schoolwork. You will be there for three days and three nights to make up for the three days you were away from school." So Charles moved into the attic. He had his books, he had his food, and he had time to think. Downstairs, his father tried to read, but he couldn't. Mother tried to sew, but nothing went right. Nine o'clock came, then 10:00. "Aren't you going to bed?" asked Mother.

"Not just yet; I'm not sleepy," said Father.

"I think I'll wait a little longer too," Mother said. The minutes passed. Eleven o'clock!

"I can't stand this another minute," said Father at last. "I'm going upstairs with Charles." Upstairs he went. Charles was wide awake. The father lay down beside him. He didn't need to talk. He just put his arm around his son. Charles sobbed, "I'm sorry," and put his arm around his father. They wept together for a little while, then went peacefully to sleep. The second night and the third night Father went upstairs with Charles, and the rebellion was over.

Search your heart for the tiniest seed of rebellion and root it out.

O my son Absalom—my son, my son Absalom—if only I had died in your place! O Absalom my son, my son!
2 Samuel 18:33.

April 15

Absalom was not only rebellious but wicked and quite deserving of the judgment of God that came upon him. But how his father loved him!

In spite of his son's rebellion, David would gladly have died in his place. That's the kind of love God has for us.

Several years ago a man named Joe Hunt wrote a beautiful story about his father's love. Joe was just a little fellow when his family lived on a farm, and more than anything else he loved to drive the big team while his father filled the wagon with hay. It made him feel truly grown-up. One day as he guided the team from one pile of hay to another he dropped one of the horses' reins. Trying to grab the rein again, Joe lost his balance and fell onto the steel tongue of the wagon, right between the horses. The frightened animals lunged forward and dashed wildly across the field. For a while Joe held on to the tongue of the wagon. He heard his father shout "Whoa! whoa!" but the horses wouldn't stop. In a moment or two Joe figured out that if he dropped straight down to the ground, the wagon wheels wouldn't go over him. So he let go.

There was a thud, an awful noise as the wagon rolled on overhead of him, but that was all. A moment more, and Joe sat up, spat the dirt out of his mouth, then got up and ran back to tell his dad that he was all right. He found his father hunched over, groaning with pain. Trying to reach the reins to stop the horses, he had jumped fearlessly between the wagon and the horses. But the wagon had struck him with tremendous force, knocking him down, and two big wheels had run over his body, almost crushing out his life. As Joe came near, his father looked up and with great effort asked, "Are . . . you . . . all right, . . . Joe?" Joe said, "Yes," but could say no more, for he realized his dad had been badly hurt while trying to save him. Then someone who'd seen the accident from the highway came running, and soon the man took his dad to the hospital.

The next morning when Joe went to see him, he saw a satisfied smile on his father's face. "How did you manage to escape?" Father asked. Joe told him all about it. Father smiled with satisfaction, but he was very seriously hurt and a few hours later he died. Joe's father had given his life for him.

2 SAMUEL 22

The Lord is my rock and my fortress
and my deliverer; . . . in whom I will trust.
2 Samuel 22:2, 3.

April 16

In his battles with the enemies of Israel, David was always victorious because he trusted in the Lord. He found in God a rock and a fortress. All through the ages, in their battles against sin and self, the children of God have always been victorious when they made the Lord their rock and their fortress.

Once I had the privilege of taking a guided tour through New Mexico's Carlsbad Caverns with my son Leonard. We walked down a winding trail that quickly became darker and deeper until we were 750 feet below the surface of the earth. We went through the King's Room and the Queen's Room and saw the many fantastic formations through Fairyland and the Cave of the Totem Pole. We went through the Big Room—a mile and a half long and 348 feet high—and then into a room that had a huge stalagmite in the center of it. Our guide told us to be seated, and at once we noticed the name of the huge stalagmite, Rock of Ages. There must have been 500 people in our group, and as we sat down on the stone seats that had been carved out in rows, our guide said, "We are far away from the hustle and bustle and the noise of life. I want you to see how quiet it can be and how dark it can be down here 750 feet from the earth's surface." With that he turned out the lights.

How can I describe the darkness? It seemed that we could feel it! And the quietness? It was like the grave. For a few seconds we sat there wondering what would happen if the lights never came on again. Then far off in the distance we heard a quartet begin to sing, "Rock of Ages, cleft for me, let me hide myself in Thee." It was the most beautiful singing I have ever heard. There was no need to fear; we had a living Rock. "Let the water and the blood, from Thy riven side which flowed, be of sin the double cure, cleanse me from its guilt and power." All around me people were sobbing. As the singing stopped I blew my nose and wiped my eyes, and breathed a little prayer of thankfulness that God was my rock and my fortress. Right then I reconsecrated myself to His loving service.

Have you made Christ your rock of ages? your fortress? Have you learned to put your trust in Him? Do it now, just for today. Then do it every day for the rest of your life.

To Him who loved us . . . and has made us kings and priests to His God and Father, to Him be glory and dominion forever and ever.
Revelation 1:5, 6.

April 17

Davd had made a promise that his son Solomon would someday be king. So as he neared death he commanded Zadok the priest to anoint Solomon and proclaim him king. And all the people said, "God save King Solomon." Many times as Solomon grew up he must have said to himself, "Someday I'll be king," and that thought must often have helped him do what was right.

In *Messages to Young People* we read: "Higher than the highest human thought can reach is God's ideal for His children" (p. 40). Think of it, if you can. God plans that we are to be kings and priests for Him! If we keep this thought in mind, how often we will say, "What manner of persons ought we to be!"

The story is told that in the days of the French Revolution the people were sick and tired of the tyranny of their kings. So one day the mob surrounded the palace and dragged out Louis XVI and beheaded him. Again they went to the palace and dragged out Queen Marie Antoinette and beheaded her. Then they laid hands on Prince Louis, who would have been King Louis XVII someday. "To the guillotine! To the guillotine!" shouted the mob. "Make an end of royalty."

But one man shouted, "Don't do that! That will only send him to heaven! I'll tell you what to do. Hand him over to Old Meg, the vilest woman in Paris. Let her clothe him in rags, feed him filth, and teach him to lie and steal and swear. Let Old Meg curse his little soul and send him to hell!" The idea pleased the mob; so, according to some historians, Prince Louis was handed over to Old Meg. She clothed him in rags, fed him garbage, and tried to teach him to lie and swear and steal. But it is said that every time Old Meg tried to teach him a new swearword, he would clench his little royal fists and stamp his little royal foot and say, "I will not say it! I will not say it! I was born to be a king and will not say it!"

What a boy! What a prince! And what a lovely example! For God has planned that you shall be a king or queen unto God someday. Keep the thought always in mind, and when you are tempted to do wrong, clench your fists and stamp your feet and say, "I will not! I was born to be royalty, and I will not do it!"

1 KINGS 3; 4:20-34

Therefore give to Your servant an understanding heart . . . ,
that I may discern between good and evil.
1 Kings 3:9.

April 18

Today is a good day for everyone to pray for an understanding heart that will help to "discern between good and evil," a good day to resurrect your faith in God if it has died. Dr. A. J. Cronin tells the story of how his faith in God was resurrected after being dead for many years. After graduating from the University of Glasgow, in Scotland, he went to practice medicine in a mining community in southern Wales. At first he felt somewhat superior to the deeply religious Welsh people, and almost pitied their simple faith and reliance on God. But as he lived among them, and saw them live and worship and suffer and die, he realized that they had something that all his university knowledge had not given him. Then one day there was a terrible explosion in one of the mines, and 14 miners were entombed. For five days the men remained buried in the mine. For five days the village prayed while the rescuers worked day and night to open up the caved-in tunnel. Then, on the fifth day, as the men got near the victims of the accident, they heard them singing! It was the good old hymn "O God, Our Help in Ages Past." The miners had no food, no water, and no light, but they had faith, and they had chosen to keep their faith alive by singing. Dr. Cronin was there to look after those who might be injured. But they came out unharmed. And as they came up to the surface the great crowd of more than 1,000 people joined in singing "O God, Our Help in Ages Past." Dr. Cronin was never the same again. His dead faith came to life and remained that way the rest of his life.

Say, how is your faith? Today is a good day for you to take it out, and shine it up, and keep it alive. Remember: "By faith he who has been renewed lives day by day the life of Christ. Day by day he shows that he realizes that he is God's property. . . . He has bought us, and He desires us to remember that our physical, mental, and moral powers belong to Him" (*Messages to Young People*, pp. 68, 69).

I dwell in the high and holy place, with him who has a contrite and humble spirit.
Isaiah 57:15.

April 19

In 1791 there was born in New York City a man by the name of John Howard Payne. He became quite a famous actor, not only in America but also in England and in France. From 1842 to 1845 and again from 1851 to 1852 he was the United States consul in Tunis, in North Africa. He died at his post in 1852 and was buried there in Tunis. Thirty years later his body was exhumed, brought back to America, and buried among America's famous dead in the cemetery at Dumbarton Oaks, near the heart of the capital city. On the day of his burial in Washington, D.C., Congress and the Supreme Court adjourned in honor of the occasion, and the president, the vice president, and the members of the cabinet led the funeral procession down Pennsylvania Avenue. Can you imagine why they paid him all this honor? Was it because he was a famous actor? Oh, no! Was it because he was an honorable U.S. consul? Oh, no! You couldn't guess. It was because he was the author of that beautiful, much-loved song "Home, Sweet Home!" At his graveside a choir of 1,000 voices sang:

"'Mid pleasures and palaces though we may roam,
Be it ever so humble, there's no place like home!
A charm from the skies seems to hallow us there,
Which, seek through the world, is ne'er met with elsewhere."

Every language on earth has a word for "house," but only the languages of Christian peoples have a word for "home." Home is a house where people live who love God and love one another. Solomon purposed to "build a house for the name of the Lord" (1 Kings 5:5), and no doubt God was pleased to bless that house with His presence. But Isaiah tells us that God will dwell "with him who has a contrite and humble spirit." What a lovely thought! We can make our hearts beautiful homes in which God will be pleased to dwell.

Is *your* heart contrite? Do you acknowledge your mistakes and quickly say you are sorry? And are you humble? If you are, you will know the joy of the presence of God.

1 KINGS 6

He shall give His angels charge over you,
to keep you in all your ways.
Psalm 91:11.

April **20**

The rain, the rain! My wife and I were still new in Kamamaung, and we lived in a little mat hut with a leaf roof. With the fury of the wind and the pounding of the rain, the house soon became wet inside. So I lighted the lantern and discovered four places where the rain was falling right over our bed. By the time I had stopped the leak the bed was wet. "We must get some more blankets and sheets," my wife said, kneeling by the bureau. Then I heard, "Oh! Come quick! Bring the light!" Our chest of drawers was filled with ants. Now, ants are nice things to preach sermons about to lazy people, but they're nothing you want among your things. They'd ruthlessly destroyed sheets, shirts, and almost everything else in the bureau. It took days of warfare with fire and kerosene to persuade them they were not welcome in our house.

One Sabbath morning we were just off to church when we opened a box and found our hats in the hands of white ants. Even more, our nice tablecloths, table covers, and curtains were riddled with holes. I found that the ants owned my cornet. They were eating my boots, the babies' toys, and even the electric battery. It took us a week of warfare to get rid of them all. You may think it our fault for not looking after our things better, but if you lived where we lived you would feel that the half has never been told. Then there are the snakes in the jungle, and the tigers that come right to the house. I remember the night my wife awoke me, saying there was something in the cattle shed. "It must be tigers," she said, but I went back to sleep. The next morning we found two of our cattle dead. Now, I'm no hunter, but the next night found me in a tree with a gun, waiting for Mr. Stripes. He came, all right, and I shot, I did. Twice. The first time I missed him, and the second time I hit him in just the same place!

But with all this, I must tell you that I've never been really frightened. Has not God promised to take care of us? For more than 11 years I tramped through the jungles, visiting and preaching. We couldn't carry guns, for they were too heavy. By the time we carried a change of clothing, medicines, pictures, and our Bibles, all there was to do was walk by faith. So we did. Don't you ever be afraid to put God to the test. He means what He says. When you're doing His work, He'll care for you.

113

The end of a thing is better than its beginning.
Ecclesiastes 7:8.

April 21

It took Solomon 13 years to build his house, and when it was finished it was beautiful. That is the way it ought to be done. If you started school at age 6, what should you be doing about 13 years after that? You should be graduating from high school or trade school, or beginning your college work. Here's another question. If you start smoking as a teen (not that you would), how will it affect your life? Most teens who take up smoking think it won't much affect them. Only three out of 100 think they'll still be smoking five years later. But the American Cancer Society knows that five years after starting, 60 out of 100 will still be smoking. And the cost? Cigarettes cost at least $4.50 a pack. That may not sound like much, but smoking is addictive! Smoke through a pack a day, and you spend $31.50 a week or $135.00 a month—for something that goes up in smoke. That's $1,650 a year! Think of all the things you could buy, or do, with that much money.

A friend of mine went to a wedding recently. The bride was truly beautiful in her simple cream gown. The groom and groomsmen were handsome in their tuxedos, and the bridesmaids looked lovely in pale blue. But about an hour into the reception almost the whole wedding party disappeared. Where could they have gone? Music was still playing. People were still eating. The cake had not yet been cut. My friend went to look for them and found them clustered outside in the cold—smoking. No smoking was allowed in the building, and every one of them was "dying" for a smoke. How very, very sad.

What do cigarettes contain besides nicotine? Well, here are a few of their ingredients: cyanide (used in rat poison), benzene (found in gasoline), acetone (the main ingredient in nail polish remover), and ammonia (found in many disinfectants). With all these poisons and more, no wonder secondhand smoke is almost as harmful as firsthand.

Today's text tells us that the end of a thing can be even better than its beginning. That reminds me of graduation. Surely holding your diploma is even better than your first few days of high school. Getting paid for what you enjoy doing is even better than the training you took so you could get the job you love. And heaven is going to be way, way, way better than anything we can imagine here on earth.

1 KINGS 8

When Your people Israel are defeated before an enemy because
they have sinned against You, and when they turn back to
You and confess Your name, and pray and make supplication
to You in this temple, then hear in heaven, and
forgive the sin of Your people Israel.
1 Kings 8:33, 34.

April **22**

At last the Temple was dedicated. The people had promised to obey God's commandments so that they could be assured of His presence with them. Yet Solomon realized there was always a danger that the people would be tempted and would sin. So he prayed earnestly that when the people confessed their sins, God would hear and forgive.

No matter who we are, no matter how long our body temples have been given to God, temptation to defile our bodies in one way or another is sure to come. Most of you reading this book aren't going to take up smoking or chewing tobacco—both very dangerous habits. You have sense enough not to try them even "just once." But what about wine coolers, those fruity alcoholic drinks on a hot day? You might think *What harm could there be in that?*

It's so simple it seems foolish, but it is the pure truth. If you never take the first drink, you'll never take the second or third or tenth or the hundredth.

One day Abraham Lincoln was riding in a stagecoach with a Kentucky colonel. "Mr. Lincoln, will you have a cigar?" the colonel asked. "I have some of Kentucky's finest cigars with me."

"Well, now, Colonel," Lincoln replied, "seeing you are so kind and generous, maybe I should have a smoke with you. But first, let me tell you a story. When I was about 9, my mother called me to her bedside and said, 'Abe, I'm very, very sick, and the doc says I'm not going to get well. Before I die I want you to promise me that as long as you live, you will never use whiskey or tobacco.' Colonel, I promised my mother I never would, and up to this hour I've kept that promise. Now would you advise me to break that promise and smoke with you?"

The colonel put his hand on Lincoln's shoulder and said, "No, Mr. Lincoln, I wouldn't do it for the world. And I would give $1,000 today if I'd made my mother a promise like that and kept it as you have."

What a promise! Why don't you make a promise like that to your mom or dad right now!

It was a true report which I heard. . . . However I did not believe the words until I came and saw with my own eyes; and indeed the half was not told me.
1 Kings 10:6, 7.

April 23

We are not told who gave the queen of Sheba the first report about the wisdom and glory of Solomon. No doubt she asked every traveler she saw about it, and everyone told her a little more, but when she came and saw for herself she realized that the half had not been told. This has been the experience of many of our church members who have the privilege of attending a General Conference session for the first time. Take Pastor Kalee Paw, for example, who was Burma's delegate to the General Conference session in Cleveland in 1958. From his fascinating book *Jungle Flower*, let me quote a few sentences. "[On our way to the General Conference session] we walked through Jerusalem, Bethlehem, Jericho, and Bethany in the footsteps of Jesus. . . . We paused in the Garden of Gethsemane and breathed a prayer of reconsecration. Suddenly the Bible story became real and living. There was the Mount of Olives. There was Calvary. There was Golgotha, the place of the skull, and right beside it, the Garden tomb where perhaps my Savior's body was laid.

"I have not words to describe our feelings as we saw the real Statue of Liberty, and the real skyscrapers as we steamed slowly into the New York harbor. We had seen pictures of them before. Now it seemed as if we were in a dream. . . . Toward evening we went 102 stories up by elevator to the top of the Empire State Building. We stayed there till the great city's lights came on. I just cannot describe the rivers of light and the fountains of light we saw. . . . Then we tried to think that even this great city of New York cannot begin to compare with the New Jerusalem that God is preparing for His children. . . . The next day dear Brother S. A. Wellman . . . took us all around the [General Conference] building and also around the Review and Herald. . . . I cannot describe how we felt. . . . Then came the General Conference session in . . . Cleveland. . . . And on Sabbath there were 15,000 present. And all of them Seventh-day Adventists. I think it's going to be like that in heaven, only better."

Indeed it is going to be better. Paul says, "Eye has not seen, nor ear heard . . . the things which God has prepared for those who love Him" (1 Corinthians 2:9). Make sure that you are there.

*Because the Preacher was wise, he still taught the
people knowledge; yes, he pondered and sought
out and set in order many proverbs.
Ecclesiastes 12:9.*

April 24

The story of Solomon's turning away from God is a sad one. It is hard to think that one who was so humble and so wise to begin with could ever fall. Solomon gives the sad reasons in Ecclesiastes 2:4-18: "I made my works great; I built myself houses. . . . I acquired male and female servants. . . . I also gathered for myself silver and gold. . . . Whatever my eyes desired I did not keep from them. I did not withhold my heart from any pleasure. . . . Then I looked on all the works that my hands had done. . . . Then I turned myself to consider wisdom and madness and folly. . . . I hated life. . . . I hated all my labor in which I had toiled under the sun."

In time Soloman became fed up with the world, with pleasure, and with himself. God was fed up with him too, and sent him a message: "Because you have done this, and have not kept My covenant and My statutes, which I have commanded you, I will surely tear the kingdom away from you and give it to your servant" (1 Kings 11:11). The message woke him up as from a dream, and we read in the book *Prophets and Kings:* "Chastened in spirit, with mind and body enfeebled, he turned wearied and thirsting from earth's broken cisterns, to drink once more at the fountain of life. . . . In penitence he began to retrace his steps toward the exalted plane of purity and holiness from whence he had fallen so far" (pp. 77, 78).

It was after he repented that Solomon recorded his many proverbs. It was the forgiven Solomon who wrote, "Remember now thy Creator in the days of thy youth" (Ecclesiastes 12:1, KJV). "Solomon's repentance was sincere; but the harm that his example of evildoing had wrought could not be undone" (*ibid.*, p. 84). As long as he lived, the thought of meeting the results of his example and influence in the judgment would haunt him like an eerie ghost from the past. The story of Solomon proves to us that self-indulgence is not the pathway to happiness. It also proves that no one has fallen too low; that all those who repent can be forgiven and be saved.

If you would be really happy, and escape the regret and remorse that is sure to come to those who lead others astray by their example, then search your heart now, and if you need forgiveness, repent right now.

Blessed is the man who walks not in the counsel of the ungodly.
Psalm 1:1.

April **25**

We cannot help feeling a little bit disgusted with Rehoboam for refusing the advice of the old men, and following the advice of the young guys who had grown up with him. But this business of not taking advice didn't begin when Rehoboam was made king. It began when he was just a little boy. That's when it always begins, and if you want to miss all kinds of trouble when you grow up, you had better begin taking advice now.

Several years ago in my jungle school there were six little girls—Sleep-sweet, Clear-gold, Clever Queen, Diamond, Brave, and Golden-bead. It was the rainy season. The river was in flood, and its angry, muddy waters were tearing out trees and gardens as they swirled along. "There will be no swimming in the river today," I announced in chapel. "The river is angry and it is too dangerous." But by afternoon these six little girls forgot, and when the stop-work bell rang they got their *longyis* and started for the river. As they passed the schoolhouse the teacher saw them and said, "Where are you little girls going? Remember, Thara said there was to be no swimming in the river today." But the six little girls just put their noses up in the air and went right on. As they passed the girls' house the matron said, "Hey, where are you girls going? Remember, Thara said, 'No swimming today.'" But they put their noses a little higher and went right on. At the river's edge they saw a man fishing from a canoe, and he said, "Hey, girls, it's dangerous to swim when the river is angry."

"Oh, we're not scared. We can swim," they said. And they jumped right in, and the man went away.

They could swim, and all went well for a while, until Diamond got out too far and was caught in a whirlpool. Around and around she went. Five frightened girls scrambled out and began to scream for help. Around and around went Diamond, and down, down the raging river while five frightened little girls followed along screaming and crying. Fortunately, the whirlpool brought her in near a jutting rock, and Golden-bead jumped in and pulled her out.

"I wish we hadn't come," said Golden-bead, and they all agreed.

"I don't feel good inside," said Clever Queen. And they all promised to be good and take advice and obey after that.

1 KINGS 13

Because you have disobeyed the word of the Lord, and
have not kept the commandment which the Lord your
God commanded you, . . . your body shall not
come to the tomb of your fathers.
1 Kings 13:21, 22, RSV.

What a lot of disobedient people we read about in the Scripture reading for today! A disobedient king, a disobedient prophet, and a deceitful old false prophet. It must be that God knew that disobedience would be one of the greatest sins in these last days. Perhaps that's why He had the men of old record so many examples of its punishment. Not long ago I came across this story of disobedience and its terrible result.

A party of young men hired a guide and hiked up to the crater of a semiactive volcano. Then they climbed down among the lava rocks to the lowest ledge that was considered safe. "I'm going farther down," said one adventurous young man.

"No, you're not," said the guide. "It's too steep, and it isn't safe."

"But I brought a rope for this very purpose, and I'm going," the young man persisted.

"No, you're not," said the guide. "Those ashes and lumps of lava look cold, but you can never tell. Maybe some of them were erupted just before we got here."

But in spite of all that the guide and his friends could say, the young climber tied one end of his rope around a good strong rock, the other end around his waist, and lowered himself carefully and slowly down the steep side of the crater. His friends held their breath as they watched him go down, down, farther and farther. It looked so thrilling. But some of the lava pieces were recent, and they were hot, and soon a tiny spark started eating into the rope. The climber below the rope couldn't see it, and his friends up above couldn't see it. But all of a sudden the fire burned through and the rope broke—instantly hurling the young man into the boiling depths. What a price to pay for disregarding counsel! As you can imagine, the terrible experience haunted the dreams and the waking hours of his friends for a long time afterward.

But why must we learn these lessons the hard way? Disobedience never pays. Learn to obey and take the advice of your teachers and parents in the little things now, and save yourself the sorrow and disgrace that are sure to catch up with the rebellious ones someday.

1 KINGS 17

*And it will be that you shall drink from the brook, and
I have commanded the ravens to feed you there.*
1 Kings 17:4.

April 27

What a loving heavenly Father we have. He is patient with us when we are discouraged and weak, and He has promised that our bread shall be given us, even if He has to tell the ravens to bring it to us. Pastor R. A. Anderson brought a wonderful story back from Greece after attending a meeting there many years ago. Our worker there at that time was Pastor C. A. Christoforides, and he and his family went through a very trying time while civil war raged all around them. For weeks they were cut off from supplies. At last their food was almost gone. They could not get milk for their 8-month-old baby, and they were about at their wits' end when one day there was a knock on the door.

In those days a knock could mean anything, so saying goodbye to his family, Pastor Christoforides fearfully opened the door. "Are you Mr. Christoforides?" a soldier asked.

"Yes," replied our brother timidly. The soldier stepped inside, closed the door, put a pack on the floor, and, handing him a note, turned and left. Trembling, Mr. Christoforides opened the note and read, "These things are for you." It was not signed. Eagerly they opened the pack. There were bread, butter, chocolate, and milk! Could it be true? Who could have sent them? It must have been God in some way or other. In a few days the soldier came again. In fact, every few days he came. He came just when they needed those things the most. Mrs. Christoforides soon got to recognize the knock, and she would say, "Did you hear that? Our raven is still alive! He has come again!" Later they learned that the provisions were being sent by an army officer who knew Pastor Christoforides. Although the officer was not a Christian, he felt impressed that if Mr. Christoforides was still alive, he would need food. So you see it was God sending the food after all.

Learn to cast all your care upon the God of Elijah. He is your God, too, and He can bring you help just when you need it most.

Remember, God has ten thousand times ten thousand, and thousands of thousands, of angels (see Revelation 5:11), and they are all His ministering spirits (Hebrews 1:14).

1 KINGS 18

Then Elijah said to all the people, "Come near to me." . . .
And He repaired the altar of the Lord that was broken down.
1 Kings 18:30.

April 28

In answer to faithful Elijah's prayer, the living God—the Creator of heaven and earth—sent down fire from heaven to consume the sacrifice, and then sent rain to end the severe drought. Thus He demonstrated that the gods of the surrounding nations were powerless.

Again and again our living God has revealed His power on behalf of His faithful followers before the eyes of the people. I remember reading about a severe drought in Bombay state, India. The condition of the gardens, and of the people themselves, was so pitiful that the municipal officers called upon all the citizens of the town to pray to Varuna, the goddess of rain, to send rain and relieve their suffering.

Now, we had a good church in that town, and when the members heard about the call to pray to Varuna, they hurried to the officers and said, "We will pray, sirs. But we can pray only to the living God in heaven, the Creator of all things." The poor officers were so desperate that they quickly agreed that the Hindus should pray to Varuna on Wednesday and Thursday, and the Adventists would pray to their God on Friday and Saturday. During Wednesday and Thursday the worshippers of Varuna burned incense, blew trumpets, beat drums, and offered sacrifices; but no rain came. On Friday our church members began fasting and praying. They prayed for themselves. They prayed that the people of the town would see the salvation of the living God. All day Friday no rain came. Sabbath morning no rain came. But our people kept on praying. Sabbath afternoon, clouds began to appear. The people in the town gathered in excited groups and discussed the test of power. Our members kept on praying, and while they were still praying, before the sun set, it began to rain—and it rained for four days.

Thank God, He has unlimited power! He is the same yesterday, today, and forever. He longs to show forth His power for you, too. Is there anything wrong with your altar—the one at your bedside, the one in your home? Why not repair the altar of the Lord now?

*Suddenly a voice came to him, and said,
"What are you doing here, Elijah?"
1 Kings 19:13.*

April 29

In discouragement Elijah fled to Mount Horeb. And, behold, the Lord passed by and there was a great wind, then an earthquake, then a fire, and after the fire a still small voice saying, "What are you doing here, Elijah?"

We have all heard that still small voice. We call it the voice of conscience. It is the little voice by which God speaks to us. Many people hear it saying only, "Don't do that!" "It's not right!" "Do this!" But if we obey it, and train our heart to listen to it, God will lead us and guide us and comfort us with that still small voice.

I can still remember the embarrassment I had when I came to America after 20 years of service in Burma and tried to carry on a conversation over a telephone. There had been no telephones in the jungle where my mission station was, and my ears were not accustomed to hearing the little voice in the telephone. It would talk and talk and talk, and I'd say, "I beg your pardon. Say it again." And it would talk and talk and talk, and I would say, "I can't understand." Then I would have to ask my secretary to take the message and tell me what it said. They all laughed at me because I couldn't hear the words of the little voice in the telephone. But they didn't laugh long, for I kept on trying and listening, and in a few weeks I could understand everything it said.

If you ask God to speak to you by the still small voice, He will. One of the first things you will hear God asking is "What are you doing here?" Think now. What *are* you doing?

Once, so the story goes, three men were cutting stone in a Vermont quarry. A stranger approached them and said, "What are you doing?" The first man replied carelessly, "I'm cutting stone." The second man said, "I'm earning my living—$7.50 a day!" The third man said, "I'm helping to build a cathedral!" There they were—three men doing the same work, but what a difference.

Now, what are you doing? Just going to school, working for a diploma, or are you building a character that will be worth taking to heaven? There is a big difference between *having* to go to school and wanting to go to school, and between *having* to obey and *loving to* obey.

1 KINGS 21

Let no one seek his own, but each one the other's well-being.
1 Corinthians 10:24.

April 30

We cannot help despising Ahab's actions. What a selfish man he was! He wanted his neighbor's vineyard, and when he couldn't get it he threw a tantrum. Then he arranged for his neighbor's murder and took possession of the vineyard anyhow. He deserved all the judgment that finally came to him.

We need to be constantly aware lest selfishness overwhelm us, for we read that in the last days people will be lovers of their own selves—covetous, boastful, and proud. And you know, if you leaf through magazines featuring stars of TV, music, and other media, you might get the idea that the above description applies to some of them. Years ago a proud old nobleman lived in Sweden when people did their traveling by stagecoach. It was the custom to stop now and then at an inn to change horses during a long journey. Well, this proud, rich man came to an inn one day and shouted, "Horses, landlord. Horses at once!"

"I'm sorry, sir," said the landlord, "but you'll have to wait till your horses are rested. I have no more fresh horses." Just then two lovely horses were brought out of the stable and hitched to a carriage in which a quiet little gentleman was sitting.

"I thought you said you had no fresh horses," shouted the selfish man.

"These were ordered by that gentleman before you came," the landlord said quietly.

But the selfish man called toward the carriage, "Say, my man, let me have those horses, and I will pay you well for them."

"I'm sorry," he replied. "I need them myself, and I am ready to start."

"Perhaps you don't know who I am," the other man boasted. "I am Field Marshal Baron George Sparre, the last and only one of my race."

"That's good," said the quiet gentleman. "It would be terrible to think there might be more like you." And he drove off.

Then the landlord turned to the haughty man and said, "There goes the king of Sweden."

And the story ends there. I'm sorry, for I'd like to know how the selfish old man felt after that. But never mind. We can imagine it easily enough. Just be sure you are never selfish and demanding like that.

And when they say to you, "Seek those who are mediums and wizards, who whisper and mutter," should not a people seek their God? Isaiah 8:19.

May 1

Ahaziah knew better. During the reign of his father, Ahab, he had seen many wonderful works of God. He well knew that God could help, and he well knew that severe judgments were often meted out upon transgressors. He should have gone humbly to Elijah and had him inquire of God. But no! Baalzebub, the Philistine god who was supposed to be able to foretell the future, was much more appealing to him. So he sent his servants off to Ekron to get his fortune told. It is a dangerous business to associate with fortunetellers and spirit mediums. God and evil spirits can never get along together.

I learned of an interesting experience that a woman named Mary Jane had with a spirit medium. Mary Jane lived in Minnesota several decades ago, at a time when modern medicine was not able to prevent childhood diseases as it does now. Of her and her husband's nine children, four of them had died. Then little 3-year-old Robbie got sick and died. Mary Jane was heartbroken. At Robbie's funeral the minister said that her little dead children were rejoicing in heaven, but even though she was deeply religious, that thought brought her no comfort. Then one day a neighbor asked, "Wouldn't you like to talk with your little children who are in heaven?"

"Oh, yes," said Mary Jane. "How can I do it?"

"I'll take you to our spirit medium in town, and he'll get you in touch with them," said the neighbor. Mary Jane was delighted. Now she could find out if they were truly happy, and maybe it would help her heartache. However, before she went she felt she should have some spiritual preparation, so she read her Bible and prayed. Then she went to see the medium, but nothing happened. He could not "reach" the children. She went again and again—but nothing ever happened. At last the medium said, "Something's wrong. What do you do before you come to me?"

"Why, I pray and—" Mary Jane began, but she got no further. "You pray!" the man shouted. "No wonder they won't come!" Soon after that, Mary Jane met some Adventists and learned that the dead are sleeping until Christ's return. It is true. No one can serve two masters. If you always read your Bible and seek God, you will be safe.

2 KINGS 2

"Please let a double portion of your spirit be upon me." . . .
Now when the sons of the prophets . . . saw him,
they said, "The spirit of Elijah rests on Elisha."
2 Kings 2:9-15.

May 2

It's a strange thing, isn't it! You can't see the Spirit of God and you can't take hold of Him, but when He rests upon a person, you know it. For He fills us with faith and makes us fearless, courageous, kind, and patient. That's what He did for Elijah; that's what He did for Elisha; and that's what He can do for every one of us. It reminds me of a letter I read from Kyaw Balay, a leader of our work in Burma.

Away up in the Chin Hills a school in a certain village was opened. The children were very happy to come, and soon they were attending Sabbath school and singing our Sabbath school songs all around the village. But the old people did not like it. "We don't want our children to become Seven-days," they said. And they took their children out of school. But still they came to Sabbath school, and the old folks were alarmed. They threatened some children and whipped some, but still the children came to Sabbath school. Then one of the chief opposers, Uncle Tha Doo, became curious and said to himself, "What is it that makes these children want to go to Sabbath school?" He began to ask, he began to listen, and he began to read his Bible. Then he had Bible studies with the teacher and was baptized.

At that, his wife, Aunty Tha Doo, got angry. She called him names. She cooked only unclean meats and fish for him, but Uncle Tha Doo never got angry. He was always patient and kind. When she put the unclean foods before him, he just ate rice and salt; and when she called him names, he just smiled and said, "Please read your Bible carefully, and you will find it is true." Soon Aunty Tha Doo got curious and said to herself, "What's the matter with him? What makes him so kind and patient? It must be what he reads in his Bible. I believe I'll read it a little bit and see." And now *she* is different!

She is kind and patient, and she is taking Bible studies. And the village people are becoming curious. They are wondering what has happened to Aunty Tha Doo.

It's true. When the Spirit of God rests on someone, they are different, and everyone knows it. Is the Spirit of God resting upon you? Does anyone know it?

2 KINGS 4

He who receives a prophet in the name of a prophet shall receive a prophet's reward. Matthew 10:41.

May 3

Throughout the experiences of Elijah and Elisha we can see that God pours out His blessing upon those who are hospitable. The widow woman who shared her last measure of meal with Elijah, and the Shunammite woman who prepared a little room where Elisha could stay when he was in that district were both doubly blessed. Hospitality still brings blessings to all who practice it.

Listen! Two days after Hurricane Carla left a path of wreckage for miles along the coast near Galveston, Texas, Mrs. Kirke and her two children, Danny and Betty, stood in front of their little cabin, wondering what to do. The morning before the storm Dad had gone to work in Galveston, 75 miles away. They had no radio, and they heard no warning. Suddenly the storm was on top of them. Great ocean waves from a half mile away rolled over and over the land. The road was broken and impassable. The neighbors had all fled before the storm, and now the Kirkes were alone with just a little food to eat and very little water to drink. Danny put up a flag and made a fire, but it was no use. The dense fog and heavy clouds made it impossible for any passing plane to see them. On the third day after the storm Mrs. Kirke had to ration their food. Just one bowl of corn grits twice a day—no gravy, no butter. Danny and Betty were desperate. They gathered sticks and arranged them to spell the word *help* on the white sand. Then suddenly they saw people coming. It was a Mexican family—a father, a mother, and three children, one a baby, ragged, hungry, and desolate. "We've lost everything," said the father. "We've had no food for three days. I ask a little food—just for the little ones."

"We too have only a little food, but you shall all have a share of it while it lasts," said Mrs. Kirke as she led them into the cabin. I'm sorry to say that Danny was sulking a little bit. He was hungry too, and tomorrow would be worse. But hardly had Mrs. Kirke finished asking a blessing when Danny left the table and rushed outside. "I hear something!" he shouted. He saw something too! He saw the clouds part. He saw the sunshine. He saw a plane swing low and drop a parachute with a great big bundle of food attached to it

You see, a blessing often comes with hospitality, doesn't it?

2 KINGS 5

Bondservants, obey in all things your masters according to the flesh, not with eyeservice, as men-pleasers. . . . And whatever you do, do it heartily, as to the Lord.
Colossians 3:22, 23.

May **4**

The little captive maid didn't realize that every time she appeared clean and neat and was truthful and honest, kind and polite, she was witnessing for God. But she was, and Naaman and his wife talked about her and her religion and her God. It made such an impression on him that this great general did what the little servant girl suggested he do—and Naaman was healed.

What wonderful things can also happen when Seventh-day Adventists are clean and neat, truthful and honest, and kind and polite in the places in which they work. Dear Elder Spicer told about a Seventh-day Adventist farmer way up in the Northwest who wanted to buy some cows. Because he couldn't pay cash, the man with cows for sale asked him what security he could furnish. The farmer showed him the papers of ownership for his car and his farm machinery. The man looked them over and said, "All right, but this is only enough security for you to buy six cows. Come tomorrow morning at 10:00, and we will sign the papers."

"But tomorrow is Saturday," said our brother. "I'm sorry, but I can't come then. I'm a Seventh-day Adventist, and that is our day of worship. I do not do business on the Sabbath."

"You are a Seventh-day Adventist?"

"Yes."

"Oh, well, that's different! You know, I have had Seventh-day Adventist girls working for me for the past five years. And if you are a Seventh-day Adventist, you can have the whole lot of cows if you want them. It will be quite all right."

Those young women working away faithfully at their daily tasks little knew that their boss was measuring their religion and their church by the way they lived and did their work. But he was! And he felt confident that he could trust this Seventh-day Adventist man who wanted to buy the cows because he could trust those Seventh-day Adventist girls who were working for him.

When your neighbors and friends see you at work, at study, and at play, what do they think of your religion and your church and your God?

"Lord, I pray, open his eyes that he may see." . . .
And behold, the mountain was full of horses
and chariots of fire all around Elisha.
2 Kings 6:17.

May 5

There are three ways in which the Lord reveals His will to us, to guide us. . . . God reveals His will to us in His Word, the Holy Scriptures. His voice is also revealed in His providential workings. . . . Another way in which God's voice is heard is through the appeals of His Holy Spirit, making impressions upon the heart" (*Messages to Young People,* p. 156).

We all have heard God's voice speaking to us as we read the Bible and as the Holy Spirit makes impressions on our heart or speaks with the still small voice. But it is not so easy to understand God's voice when He closes a door in front of us or surrounds us with some disappointment.

Here was Elisha's servant surrounded by enemy soldiers. He couldn't understand God's leading in that. Then Elisha prayed, "Lord, open his eyes," and *then* he saw the angels! Elder C. L. Paddock tells a good story that illustrates the way God's voice is revealed in providential workings. A ship was wrecked in the Pacific Ocean, and the one survivor was washed ashore on a small uninhabited island. He made a little hut out of the wreckage he found on the beach and put a blanket on a tall pole, hoping to attract some passing ship. Every day he prayed that God would send a ship to deliver him.

The days dragged on into weeks. He still prayed and hoped. Then one day as he returned from hunting for sea birds' eggs and wild yams, he was filled with horror to find his little hut going up in flames! You can only imagine his discouragement, praying every day and hoping for deliverance, and now his only comfort was gone. But a few hours later a ship appeared on the horizion. It came closer and closer! A dinghy was put to shore, and sailors took him aboard. The captain said, "We saw your smoke signal and figured it must be someone in distress after the recent wreck." Of course, *then* his eyes were opened, and he thanked God many times for burning up his little hut.

When disappointment comes to you, and the day looks blue and discouraging, just pray, "Lord, open my eyes." And you too will be able to see the voice of God "revealed in His providential workings."

2 KINGS 7

*"We are not doing right. This day is a day of good news,
and we remain silent. If we wait until morning light,
some punishment will come upon us. Now therefore,
come, let us go and tell the king's household."*
2 Kings 7:9.

May **6**

I like this story about the four lepers, don't you? I like the urgency they felt to tell the good news to others. They couldn't even wait till morning light! It's just like this with people everywhere who hear the good news of the gospel of salvation. They can't wait to tell others about the joy they have found; they have to begin right away.

Pastor F. G. Clifford tells about a 10-year-old boy in New Guinea. He lived in a little section called Papus, and he went down to the seacoast with his big brother to work on a coconut plantation. While there he heard about the seven-day mission school not far away, and one day he slipped over to see what the school was like. He went again and again, and he decided he would rather go to school than pick up coconuts. So he joined up as a day student and got a slate and a songbook. He loved school. He loved learning to read and write, he loved singing, and he loved Sabbath school. In fact, he loved everything on that seven-day mission. On the back cover of his songbook were printed the Ten Commandments, one column in English and one in his own language. He memorized them and listened intently as the teachers explained them. Then a little fire began to burn in his heart.

"How the boys and girls back in my village would love to know these things and sing these songs," he said to himself again and again. Of course, he wasn't baptized yet, and he didn't know anything about graduating or about committees that appoint people to the work. He could read and write and sing, and he knew the Ten Commandments, and the fire burned in his heart till he couldn't wait any longer. So off he went, back to his village, and the teacher just crossed his name off the class book! Several months later missionary C. E. Mitchell found this 10-year-old boy working as the schoolteacher and preacher for that village. All he had was a hymnbook and the Ten Commandments, but the people could sing and were having Sabbath school, and they were all ready for a big teacher to come.

I hope the fire burns in your heart too. Don't wait till "morning light." Begin now to help someone to be obedient, pure, and true.

S-5

And he did what was right in the sight of the Lord. . . .
The Lord was with him; he prospered wherever he went.
2 Kings 18:3-7.

May 7

It is simply marvelous how God prospers kings and teachers, salespeople and preachers, farmers and nurses, and young people who do that which is "right in the sight of the Lord." Many years ago one of our young men was selling books in Naples and was invited to attend a meeting of other sellers of Christian books in Florence. He had a train ticket, but there was no room in the train. So he had to stand on the outside of the coach and hang on for dear life. As the train stopped at a station another young man climbed up and hung on right next to him.

"How far are you going?" asked the new hanger-on.

"To Florence," replied our colporteur. "And you?"

"To Bologna. And what takes you to Florence?"

"Oh, I'm going to attend a meeting of the Seventh-day Adventists. Ever hear of them?"

"Indeed I have. I know one who lives in Bologna. I was there during the war, and one day a bomb shattered a whole section of the city. When the rescue squads got to work, they found only one corner of one of the buildings still standing, and in the kitchen, still intact, was a little old lady reading her Bible. She was a Seventh-day Adventist. They must have lots of faith."

"They surely do," answered our colporteur. "I am a Seventh-day Adventist, and in my work I must have lots of faith too.

"What do you do?"

"I sell books."

"What kind of books?"

"I'll show you," said our colporteur, and, holding on with one hand, he showed his book with the other.

"That *is* a good book. I'll take one," said his newfound friend. As he signed on the dotted line he added, "Seventh-day Adventists do have a lot of faith, all right."

Yes, that is faith, but it is also an excellent example of a young man doing what is right in the sight of the Lord, and of the Lord prospering him wherever he goes. God will prosper you, too.

2 KINGS 19

*Do not be afraid of the words which you
have heard. . . . Surely I will send a spirit upon
him, and he shall . . . return to his own land.*
2 Kings 19:6, 7

May **8**

The threatening letter that Senna-
cherib sent to Hezekiah was enough
to frighten anyone. Then the Lord sent
just one angel, and there was nothing to fear anymore. At a General Conference session I heard
Pastor R. E. Adams from Brazil tell a wonderful
story about two men, Peter and Paul, who started
out to hold some meetings. They went by train to a little town. They knew no one
there, and hardly knew how to get started. But while they were still at the railway
station a man came up to them and said, "Gentlemen, could I help you?" He was
the mayor of the town, and he owned a theater, which he gladly offered to them
to use on Sunday nights. They hardly knew how they would advertise, but while
they were setting up their projector, many curious children crowded around.
"What are you going to do, mister?" they asked.

"Show pictures on the life of Christ," Paul replied. "Tell everybody to come."

"Everybody?" asked the children, and off they went to tell everybody! They
did a good job, for the theater was well filled. The next Sunday night Paul and
Peter came again and held another good meeting.

But the third Sunday night, just as Paul was about to start the pictures, an
angry priest walked right up to him, beamed his flashlight in his eyes, and demanded, "Who gave you authority to hold these meetings? Turn the lights
on!" Someone turned the lights on, and the priest began to scold the people.
"You have no business coming here. Now when I go out, everybody follow
me." The priest went out, but nobody followed. He came back the second
time, more angry than before. "Follow me out!" he shouted. Still nobody
did.

Coming back a third time, he ordered Paul and Peter to follow him out,
but just then a giant of a man stepped up and said to Peter and Paul, "You
keep on with your meeting." Then, turning to the priest, he said, "You go
out, yourself, and don't come to interrupt these meetings anymore." The
priest did leave, and he never came back. Today we have many members
in that city.

You have nothing to fear if you are on God's side.

Then he turned his face toward the wall, and prayed to the Lord. . . . And Hezekiah wept bitterly.
2 Kings 20:2, 3.

May **9**

How much better it would have been if Hezekiah had accepted God's plan for him. But no, Hezekiah was determined to have his own way. He wouldn't pray ". . . if it be Thy will." And so God let him have his way. He lived 15 years longer, but those 15 extra years brought him only shame and trouble. The temptation to have our own way at any cost comes to all of us in one form or another.

A boy named Byron begged his mother to get him an air rifle. His mother tried to show him that it was not good for him to have an air gun, but Byron begged and begged, and "wept bitterly" until, very much against her good judgment, his mom bought him one. Then the trouble began, and the neighbors complained about cracked windows and their dogs and cats being hurt till at last Mother took the gun away and hid it. "I wish I had never bought it for you," she said. "I knew it would be this way. Now I shall keep it till you have learned to be more careful."

Byron begged and pleaded to have it again, but Mother said, "No! I've had enough trouble over this gun to last me a long time." Still, Byron was determined to have it. When Mom wouldn't give it to him, he began to look for its hiding place. He looked in the attic and the basement, with no success. Then one day he looked in the garage, and saw the end of the barrel poking over the edge of one of the rafters. Yes! It was his gun. He was going to do what he wanted with it. He sneaked off behind a tree and, holding the gun under his arm, began loading the lead pellets into the muzzle with his right forefinger. He was so absorbed in what he was doing that he did not notice his little brother Jock sneaking up behind him. Suddenly there was a *pift* and a scream.

You guessed it. Little Jock had pulled the trigger just for fun, and now Byron's finger was bleeding terribly. He didn't dare tell Mother. He just put the gun back and tied a rag around his finger, and you can imagine the rest, but that wasn't the end of his punishment. Later his hand swelled and his finger developed an abscess. When the doctor lanced the abcess, he found the rifle pellet.

We all must learn to take no for an answer sometimes. Not everything is good for us.

132

2 KINGS 22

"Because your heart was tender and you humbled yourself before the Lord . . . , I also have heard you," says the Lord. 2 Kings 22:19.

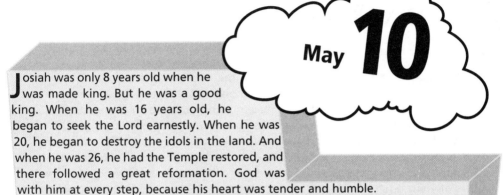

May 10

Josiah was only 8 years old when he was made king. But he was a good king. When he was 16 years old, he began to seek the Lord earnestly. When he was 20, he began to destroy the idols in the land. And when he was 26, he had the Temple restored, and there followed a great reformation. God was with him at every step, because his heart was tender and humble.

Here is another story of a boy with a tender, humble heart. Little William was going to bed, and Mother said, "Be sure to say your prayers, William." So William knelt at his bedside and prayed, "Now I lay me down to sleep" (you know that little prayer), and then he added a few words of his own. "Bless Mama and Papa and bless Willie and make him a good boy, for Jesus' sake. Amen." Then he looked into his mother's face and said, "Mama, do you and Papa pray?"

"No, darling," she said.

"Well, why do I have to pray?"

"So you will be a good boy."

"Don't you and Papa want to be good, Mama?" he asked.

"Oh, yes, we want to be good."

"Then why don't you and Papa pray too?" asked William.

Mother didn't have an answer to the last question, so William went on talking. "Well, Mama," he said, "I guess God will hear the prayer of a little boy like me, but don't you think you and Papa expect too much of a little fellow like me? Do you think that God wants me to do all the praying for this whole family? It seems to me that you and Papa might help me a little." His eyes were heavy, and in a moment he was fast asleep. He didn't even know that Mother had wiped her eyes and that Father had heard his little speech as he sat reading the paper. He didn't know that Father and Mother held hands for a long time, then tiptoed back into his room and knelt by his bed as they prayed and gave their hearts to God. After that both Mother and Father helped do the praying for the whole family.

Keep your heart tender and humble, and God will hear you, too.

Let your father and your mother be glad,
and let her who bore you rejoice.
Proverbs 23:25.

May 11

Almost hidden in the record of the last days of King Jehoiakim's wicked reign is the sad statement that when he was taken captive by the servants of Nebuchadnezzar his mother was taken captive too. How true are the words of Solomon: "The rod and rebuke give wisdom, but a child left to himself brings shame to his mother" (Proverbs 29:15). However, I am glad that Solomon also said that a wise son would make his mother "rejoice," and in the lives of many good wise people we have many examples of this. When James A. Garfield was elected president of the United States in 1880, he wrote to his mother and said, "I want you to go to Washington, D.C., with me for the inauguration."

"Oh, no," she said. "I could not go. I would feel out of place with all those great people. I'll stay at home and pray for you."

But James Garfield wrote back, "Mother, I will not go without you." So they traveled to Washington together and stayed in the same hotel, and when he went to the Capitol for the ceremony his mother was leaning on his arm. When he got on the platform, he put his mother in the chair that had been provided for him, and he sat in a seat beside her. Then, after he had delivered his address and taken the oath to be true to his high office, he turned around, put his arms around his mother, and kissed her. At that, the more than 100,000 people watching cheered and applauded. They all thought it was one of the most beautiful acts they had ever seen.

I wish that today youth everywhere would throw their arms around their mother and kiss her. Ellen White wrote: "When the judgment shall sit, and the books shall be opened; when the 'well done' of the great Judge is pronounced, and the crown of immortal glory is placed upon the brow of the victor, many will raise their crowns in sight of the assembled universe and, pointing to their mother, say, 'She made me all I am through the grace of God. Her instruction, her prayers, have been blessed to my eternal salvation'" (*Messages to Young People*, p. 330).

I wish that every young person might do this in that glad day. Then every mother would rejoice. But for now, plan to make your mom happy today and every day.

2 KINGS 25

Happy is the man whom God corrects. . . . For He bruises,
but He binds up; He wounds, But His hands make whole.
Job 5:17, 18.

May **12**

At last punishment had come. The people of Judah were carried away captive. Still, God promised, "'I am with you' . . . 'to save you; though I make a full end of all nations where I have scattered you, yet I will not make a complete end of you'" (Jeremiah 30:11).

God permitted great trouble to come to our people in many countries during World War II, but always God's saving power could be seen protecting His work from a "complete end." Korea was taken over by the Japanese in 1905, and although many restrictions were placed upon our workers, by 1941 we had almost 4,000 church members there. Then World War II broke out, and the Japanese government determined to destroy the Christian faith. Our churches were closed, our leaders arrested, our members forbidden to worship. One of our Sabbath school superintendents, Lee Tuk Hoe, was summoned by the chief of police. The officer lectured about national affairs to the men brought there that day, then announced that they must all make obeisance at a Shinto shrine to show their loyalty. They were all afraid to speak, but Lee stood and asked to be excused because such worship was contrary to the law of Jehovah. The chief of police seemed to take no notice of him, and led them all to the shrine. Everyone else bowed and burned incense, but Lee refused. The guard grew very angry, but the chief of police said nothing. So they were all marched back again, and the chief of police made another speech. He talked about loyalty and commended Lee for his courage, but said that he would have to suffer the consequences. Dismissing the others, he took Lee into another room and commanded him to kneel. This was the customary way for a criminal to receive a beating, so Lee knelt down and began to quietly pray. The officer left the room and didn't come back for a half hour. Lee was still kneeling. Then the police chief said, "I hate to punish a man who is loyal to the Majesty of heaven, but as an officer I am obliged to punish you for breaking the law. Your punishment has been to kneel for a half hour. You may go now."

No matter how much trouble God permits to come to you, remain faithful to Him and see how He will bind up your "wounds."

May 13

Come, and let us return to the Lord; for He has torn, but He will heal us; He has stricken, but He will bind us up. Hosea 6:1.

Today we have read one of the saddest chapters in the story of Israel and Judah. Because of their persistent sinning, their land was to be desolate, and they were to be captives of the king of Babylon for 70 years. Just before Israel was taken captive, however, Hosea reminded them of the long-suffering and mercy of God. "Come," he said, "and let us return to the Lord; for He has torn, but He will heal us; He has stricken, but He will bind us up." Let me give you another example of how God binds up and heals after trouble has "stricken."

After World War II, Korea had only a few years of rest, for in 1950 the Communists invaded the country, and for the next two years poor Korea was torn and bruised. The capital city, Seoul, was overrun four times, and 75 percent of it was destroyed. Our college just outside the city was a shambles, and our dear people were scattered all over the country. But everywhere our believers went the people wanted to know what this suffering meant, and our people had the answers. God's Holy Spirit was poured out upon them, and they began branch Sabbath schools and held Bible studies everywhere. In 1952, when peace again came to the land, they began to rebuild, and soon our presses were printing again and our school was full again. The Spirit of God moved mightily on both the old and the young—and even on the children. In a few years some of our churches had to hold two worship sessions. One group had Sabbath school and church in the morning and another had Sabbath school and church in the afternoon. One church had to have five worship sessions each Sabbath day! Ten years later, in 1962, the baptized church membership had grown from about 2,000 to 20,000! The Sabbath school membership had grown from about 5,000 to 82,000! There were 600 young people enrolled in our junior academy. Our publishing house, our sanitarium, and our nurse's training school were working to capacity, and our elementary schools were overflowing.

That is the way God binds up and heals. That is what God wanted to do for Israel and Judah. When trouble and sorrow come to you, remember that God wants to do that for you, too.

EZRA 1

I am the Lord . . . who says of Cyrus, "He is My shepherd, and he shall perform all My pleasure, saying to Jerusalem, 'You shall be built,' and to the temple, 'Your foundation shall be laid.'"
Isaiah 44:24-28.

May 14

God Himself named Cyrus, through Isaiah, about 100 years before he was born, and foretold that he would make the decree that Jerusalem should be rebuilt and the foundations of the Temple should be laid. As the 70 years of captivity came near the close, there can be no question that Daniel showed Cyrus the prophecy in Isaiah, and in this way the Lord stirred up the spirit of Cyrus to do His pleasure.

Herodotus, the famous Greek historian, tells this story about the early boyhood of Cyrus. Astyages, king of Media, had a dream in which he saw a great river flowing over Asia. "It means that the children of your daughter Mandane will someday conquer the world," said his wise men. Eager for the neighboring Persians to be always friendly, old Astyages married his daughter to the Persian prince Cambyses. In time a baby boy was born to Mandane and was named Cyrus. When old Astyages saw the babe, he said to himself, "I'll have him killed; *then* he can never conquer me." So he called Harpagus, a trusted servant, and told him to take the baby and kill it, then to bring back its little body so he'd know it was dead. Harpagus asked a poor herdsman to kill the child.

As the herdsman took Baby Cyrus into his small home, he found his wife crying. Their own newborn baby had just died. "Here," said the herdsman, "let's change the babies' clothes. We'll keep this baby and give the wicked old king our dead baby." So they did, and no one knew till Cyrus was about 12 years old. Then one day while the children were playing soldier, Cyrus, who was playing a general, punished a nobleman's son for not obeying. The nobleman's son told his father, and the nobleman told the king. The king scolded the herdsman's boy, but was so impressed with the boy's dignity that he became suspicious. At last the whole story came out. The king sent Cyrus back to his parents, hoping to keep Persia friendly. It did for a while, but when Cyrus grew up he became the general of the Persian army.

Our wonderful God knows your future and has a plan for you, too. Don't be afraid to trust Him with your life.

So shall My word be that goes forth from My mouth; it shall not return to Me void, but it shall accomplish what I please, and it shall prosper in the thing for which I sent it. Isaiah 55:11.

May 15

God foretold through Isaiah that Cyrus would make the decree to rebuild the Temple. And although Isaiah did not live long enough to see it fulfilled, he was certain that it would be accomplished. This same living God foretold that the three angels' messages of Revelation 14 would be preached "to every nation, tribe, tongue, and people" (Revelation 14:6), and today God's Word "prospers" in all the world.

In 1885 the first group of Seventh-day Adventist missionaries to Australia was led by S. N. Haskell. They settled in Melbourne and immediately began to plan for the work there. In November of that same year, while waiting for some printing machinery to arrive, Elder Haskell went to New Zealand to spy out the land. "Can you recommend a boardinghouse in Auckland run by a religious person?" he inquired of one of the seamen during the trip. "Yes," said the seaman. "Go to the house of Edward Hare. He has rooms."

So Elder Haskell went to Edward Hare's house as soon as he arrived. "Yes, I have a room you may have," said Mr. Hare. It wasn't long, however, before the man in the room next to Mr. Haskell came downstairs and said, "That new man is crazy! He's talking to himself all the time. You either get rid of him or I will go."

Mr. Hare went upstairs and listened. Sure enough, the new boarder did seem to be talking to himself, but as he listened a little more carefully, he realized that Mr. Haskell was praying! "O God, help me to win this good man to the message. Help me to—"

Edward Hare waited to hear no more. He went downstairs and said to his wife, "That man's not crazy. That man is praying for us!" And it was only a few days until Edward Hare had accepted the Adventist message. He took Elder Haskell 200 miles north to Kaeo, where Edward's father, Joseph Hare, and five of his brothers lived. In a few more days they all had accepted the third angel's message and were keeping the Sabbath.

Edward Hare was *my* uncle, and my father was one of his brothers who accepted this message in Kaeo. That's the way God's Word began to prosper in New Zealand. You can put your faith in every promise and in every prophecy foretold in the Word of God.

EZRA 4

For we can do nothing against the truth, but for the truth.
2 Corinthians 13:8.

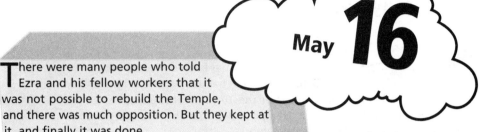

May **16**

There were many people who told Ezra and his fellow workers that it was not possible to rebuild the Temple, and there was much opposition. But they kept at it, and finally it was done.

Associated with Elder S. N. Haskell at the beginning of the work in Australia were J. O. Corliss and M. C. Israel, both preachers; Henry L. Scott, a printer; and William Arnold, a colporteur. They hoped to be invited to speak on the second coming of Christ in some of the other Protestant churches, but the churches were closed to them. They tried to hire halls, but the rent was too high. They pitched a tent, but the clergy of the city threatened to discipline any of their church members who attended the meetings or admitted the strangers to their homes to hold Bible studies. And sometimes Bible studies in private homes were actually broken up by disturbers. Even William Arnold went for six weeks without selling a single book! But the dear workers clung to the promise that "my word . . . shall not return to Me void" (Isaiah 55:11), and they kept on.

Then one Sabbath afternoon Elder Haskell knocked on a door and introduced himself to the good woman of the house. "Father," she called to her husband, who was a coach builder, "there are some Americans at the door to see you." John Henry Stockton was heating a dashboard at the time, preparing to mold it. He came to the door and talked with the Americans so long that the dashboard was spoiled. But in spite of the ruined dashboard, he invited the Americans to come again and again, and John Henry Stockton was the first one to accept this truth in Australia. It wasn't long before the first church was organized there, and John Henry Stockton was the first ordained local elder of that church. And William Arnold, who hadn't been able to sell a single book for six weeks, sold more than 1,000 copies of *Daniel and the Revelation* in less than a year. After 99 years there were in all the South Pacific Division 1,220 churches, with 163,825 members.

So when people tell you it can't be done, when worldly people try to entice you to join with them, just keep on doing what God has given you to do, and it will be done!

So Zerubbabel . . . and Jeshua . . . rose up and began to build the house of God . . . ; and the prophets of God were with them, helping them. Ezra 5:2.

May 17

Whenever there has been difficult work to do, God has had His prophets right there to help the leaders. After the 70 years of captivity, when the Temple was to be rebuilt, Haggai and Zechariah were there encouraging Zerubbabel and Jeshua in the work.

In the beginning of the Advent movement God also had a prophet—a humble little woman, Ellen White—and God used her mightily to counsel, inspire, and encourage the early workers. In 1875, just after our first foreign missionary, J. N. Andrews, had been sent to Europe, God revealed to Ellen White that publishing houses in various countries would be sending out literature filled with the Advent message. She especially mentioned Australia. Ten years went by, however, before the first group of missionaries was ready to go there. When at last they arrived, one of their first decisions was to print, and in January 1886, only a few months after their arrival, they rented a shed and began to print a paper called *The Bible Echo and Signs of the Times*. Its light began to shine at once, and before long they were doing business in a fine building in North Fitzroy.

Ellen White found them there when she went to Australia in 1891, and as she looked over the pressroom she recognized it as one of the places she had seen in vision 16 years before! With her encouragement the work increased, and in 1905 the publishing house moved to Warburton, 40 miles from the city. If you could see the lovely building and its surroundings and the earnest group of workers there today, your heart would rejoice. They have sold millions of subscription books since they began! But just think of it: 10 years before it started, the prophet was shown the publishing house in Australia.

EZRA 6

So the elders of the Jews built, and they prospered
through the prophesying of Haggai . . . and Zechariah.
Ezra 6:14.

What would Zerubbabel and Jeshua have done without the prophets? They took their counse and, encouraged by their words of inspiration, finished the Temple at last.

There were only about 450 church members in Australia when God's messenger, Ellen White, arrived to help with the work. Seeing that the publishing house was doing good work, she began to urge the church members to open a training school. Two large houses in one of the suburbs of the city of Melbourne were rented, and 24 young people came to school. But Mrs. White kept advising them to look for land in the country, far from the influence of city life. So the church leaders looked and looked, and finally they found a tract of 1,500 acres about 70 miles north of Sydney that could be bought for $4,500. The price was wonderfully low, but many said the land was very poor. In fact, government experts said the land was worthless: "It wouldn't support a bandicoot." A bandicoot is a bush rat.

On May 23, 1894, Mrs. White visited the site. As she walked here and there she seemed to be looking for something. Soon they came to a place where the land had been cleared, and there before them was a furrow nine inches deep and six feet long. She spoke to Elder Starr, who was with her. "There it is," she said in effect. "There it is, just as I saw in my dream! And in my dream I heard one man say, 'This is not good land. The soil is not favorable!' But One who has often spoken in counsel was present also, and He said, 'False witness has been borne of this land.' He then described the land and said that if it was well worked it would produce an abundance of fruit and vegetables."

The land was bought. The school was started in the country, and graduates from that school have gone to the Pacific Islands, to India, Burma, China, and to all the countries of eastern Asia—and all over the world. I attended that school for six years. I ate oranges, grapes, apples, vegetables, and corn that grew on that land. I have never ceased to be thankful for the prophet that God gave to the Adventist people for the building up of His work.

Are you thankful for God's messenger too?

From the going forth of the command to restore and build Jerusalem until Messiah the Prince, there shall be seven weeks and sixty-two weeks.
Daniel 9:25.

The decree to restore and to build Jerusalem began with Cyrus. It was renewed by Darius, maybe 19 years later, and completed by Artaxerxes 80 years after the first decree by Cyrus. The completion of the decree in 457 B.C. is very important, for it is the beginning of a time prophecy in Daniel that foretells the date of Christ's ministry, A.D. 27 to A.D. 31, and the date for the opening of the day of the judgment in 1844. Jesus Himself told His disciples about two great signs of the end of the world and of His second coming—signs that were fulfilled within this time prophecy. One was the darkening of the sun, and the other was the falling of the stars.

Today, May 19, is the anniversary of the day in 1780 when the sun darkened across New England and into Canada, an area where the Revolutionary War was being fought and many people were studying Bible prophecy. You can read about it in history books or on the Internet. The darkness lasted about 14 hours. It began about 10:00 or 11:00 in the morning and continued until the middle of the following night. It was so dark at noontime that no one could read without a candle. Birds sang their evening songs and went to bed. Fowls went to roost. Cattle went into their barns, and candles were lighted in the houses. People were filled with alarm. Many thought the end of the world had come. Others thought it was the day of judgment, and they hurried to their neighbors to confess their wrongs and ask for forgiveness. Others rushed into the meetinghouses and called on God to preserve them.

In the Connecticut legislature, as the darkness settled on the assembly, some believed that the day of judgment had come and said they ought to adjourn. But Abraham Davenport, the speaker, said, "No! If it is the day of judgment, I want to be found doing my duty." So he ordered candles to be lit, and they went on with their business. That night people prayed around their family altars as they never had prayed before. Many sat up all night to see whether the sun would ever shine again.

How would you have felt if you'd been in the New England states on that dark day? If you keep your heart right with God, you need never fear, for these things simply say Jesus is coming soon.

EZRA 8

The hand of our God was upon us, and He delivered us from the hand of the enemy and from ambush along the road.
Ezra 8:31.

May 20

It took Ezra four months to make the trip from Babylon to Jerusalem. *The Seventh-day Adventist Bible Commentary* estimates there were about 8,000 men, women, and children in the group that accompanied him, and they were carrying a fortune in silver and gold and brass. Ezra wanted God to have all the glory for their safe journey, so he did not ask for any soldiers to go with them. What an opportunity for hostile Samaritans or others to attack and plunder their caravan! But God in His own way brought them safely through.

God still has a way to protect His workers as they travel through dangers, both seen and unseen. Elder W. H. Anderson was one of our pioneer missionaries in central Africa. He was with the group that established the Solusi Mission station in 1894. Eight months after they arrived, the Matabeles rose in rebellion, and the lives of all foreigners were in danger. The missionaries fled to the city of Bulawayo, 25 miles from the mission. Now and then when there was a lull in the fighting the missionaries went back to the mission for supplies from the farm. It was a very hazardous undertaking, and they made these trips by night for added safety.

On one occasion when Elder Anderson was going for supplies he came to a shortcut that led to the station. It was a rough path and especially difficult in the darkness, so he decided to stay on the wagon road, which was much easier to follow. He had gone but a few yards when he heard a voice clearly say, "Go back! Get out of here quickly. Take the footpath." The voice was so urgent that he obeyed it at once and went back to the rough shortcut. No sooner was he well out of sight of the road than he heard a war party of hostile Matabeles hurrying along the road toward Bulawayo. If he had kept on the road, he would surely have run right into them. But by obeying the voice, he reached the mission safely, and in a day or two was able to bring back the needed food supplies from the garden for the other missionaries in Bulawayo.

Wherever you go, whenever you travel, be sure to put yourself in the hands of God. He can bring *you* through safely, too.

NEHEMIAH 1

If you return to Me, and keep My commandments and do them, . . . yet I will gather them . . . , and bring them to the place which I have chosen as a dwelling for My name.
Nehemiah 1:9.

May 21

Thirteen years after Artaxerxes had sent Ezra with the final decree to complete the building of Jerusalem, God began to work out His plans to have Nehemiah, the king's cupbearer, sent to Jerusalem as governor of Judah. Nehemiah became an excellent organizer.

Today is the anniversary of an important day in the history of the Advent Movement, for on May 21, 1863, just three years after our name Seventh-day Adventist was chosen, the General Conference was organized in Battle Creek, Michigan. There were just 20 delegates at that meeting, and John Byington was elected the first president. One hundred twenty-two years later, in 1985, the fifty-fourth session of the General Conference was held in New Orleans. There were 2,110 delegates, and Neal C. Wilson was reelected president.

In 1863 we had 3,500 church members; by 2007 there were more than 15 million church members. In 1863 we had 22 ministers; in 2007 we had nearly 16,000 ordained and licensed ministers. In 1863 our church members spoke only one language; by 2007 our message was being given in almost 900 languages. We now speak of reaching people groups, the unique tribes and languages used within many different countries.

Maybe some of you were in St. Louis on the first Sabbath of the General Conference session in 2005. In 1985 I was at the opening meeting—at that time, the largest Sabbath school ever held in one city. I was thrilled to watch the Parade of Nations, 130 nations represented by nationals and missionaries wearing the traditional dress of each country. What a glorious sight it was! There they were—from the Bible lands, from India, from eastern Asia, from Africa, from Europe, from South America, from Inter-America, from Alaska, and from the islands of the sea. You couldn't help realizing that the amazing progress reported at this meeting was not the work of human beings but of the living God. All of us had felt that we had had a preview of the great multitude which no one can number, who will someday stand before the throne, praising God. May God help every one of us to be there.

NEHEMIAH 2

The God of heaven Himself will prosper us;
therefore we His servants will arise and build.
Nehemiah 2:20.

May 22

Nehemiah had all the faith in God, all the wisdom, and all the determination needed to make a success of rebuilding the walls of Jerusalem. Do you know that building a successful life requires those very same factors?

Once upon a time a man built a three-story hotel in a small town. For a number of years it was all the town needed, but one day oil was found nearby, and overnight the little town bustled with life. Day after day the three-story hotel was filled to capacity. The hotel owner saw his chance to make a fortune, so he called a contractor and asked him to add a fourth story to the hotel. "All right," said the contractor, "but first I want to see the basement."

"The basement?" said the hotel owner. "I don't want the fourth story built down there. Let us go up to the roof."

"We'll get to the roof," said the contractor, "but before I think of adding the fourth story, I must see if the foundations are strong enough to stand the extra weight." And down to the basement he went. He measured the thickness and the depth of the foundations, then sadly shook his head. "I'm sorry," he said, "but that foundation is not strong enough to bear the weight of another story."

The hotel owner stood there for a long time without saying a word, and no wonder. He'd suddenly remembered that when he first planned the hotel the contractor had urged him to have the foundation made strong enough for an addition sometime in the future. "There might be a boom," he had said. "You can never tell."

The hotel owner also remembered his own reply: "There's not one chance in a thousand. Why should I put extra money into a foundation for something that will never come?" But something had come, and he needed that fourth story. "Can you make the foundation strong enough now?" he asked the contractor. "Of course I can, but it will cost you a lot more to do it now than if you had done it at first," he replied.

You are laying the foundations of your life now. Be sure you take the advice of your parents and teachers, and build your foundations firm and strong.

"Do not be afraid of them. Remember the Lord, great and awesome. . . ." And it happened . . . that all of us returned to the wall, everyone to his work.
Nehemiah 4:14, 15.

May 23

I love to read this chapter telling how Nehemiah closed his ears to the invitations and threatenings of Sanballat and Tobiah, and kept right on with his building until at last the wall was finished.

We all have our Sanballats and our Tobiahs who are trying to stop us from building our lives and making them successful—but they don't have two legs! Our Sanballats and Tobiahs are *laziness* and *indifference.* "It's too much bother!" "It's too hard." "You'll never need that anyway!" That reminds me of the story of a girl named Ruth.

Ruth was talented, but she disliked anything like hard work. She didn't see any sense in having a program for study as long as she could "get by." That was good enough for her. When she got into geometry, that was the end. She just shrugged her dainty little shoulders and said she simply "couldn't be bothered," and dropped out of school.

Parents, friends, and teachers did their best to urge and coax her to keep on with her studies, but it was no use. She got a clerical job. Someone suggested that she could do well as a secretary. She didn't mind typing; that was fun. But shorthand! That was too hard, so she was contented to be a not-too-good typist.

Then she got married. "You see," she said triumphantly to those who had advised her to get more education, "I don't need an education to keep house for Ray." But after a few happy years passed, and two little children had joined their family, Ruth suddenly found herself a widow. It took her some time to get her bearings when she was overwhelmed with tragedy and sorrow. Then what do you think she did? She went right back to school and began again where she had been silly enough to stop. But it would have been so much easier if she had taken no notice of her Sanballats and her Tobiahs and had kept right on building her walls. It wouldn't have cost her nearly so much to have done it then.

Sanballat and Tobiah are after you, too. You had better watch out! And do keep on building your wall.

NEHEMIAH 5

To a foreigner you may charge interest, but to your brother you shall not charge interest, that the Lord your God may bless you in all to which you set your hand in the land which you are entering to possess.
Deuteronomy 23:20.

What a lot of trouble the people of our Bible text got into just because some of their "big" men were too "little" to realize that love and mercy and kindness are more important than business. So when the poor people to whom they had lent money couldn't pay the interest on it, the big men took their land and even made their children slaves. Here is a beautiful old legend told in India.

Long, long ago there lived a powerful king who had lots and lots of money. He called a builder by the name of Jakoob and told him to build him the most beautiful palace he had ever made, in a beautiful place way up in the hills. So Jakoob set off with all the king's money, and he traveled till he came to the most beautiful place way up in the hills. But when he got there, he found the people without food. Many were sick, and many were dying. Now, Jakoob had a very kind heart, so he took all his own money and all the money the king had given him to build the most beautiful palace and used it to feed the hungry and care for the sick.

After a long, long time the king came to see his palace, and he found that not one stone had been laid for the building. The king was furious, and demanded that Jakoob give him the reason for this strange conduct. Jakoob told him about the poor and the sick and the hungry, and how he had fed them and cared for them until all the money was gone. The king was more angry than ever. He put Jakoob in prison and said, "Tomorrow you will die." But that night the king dreamed that he went to heaven and was shown the most beautiful palace he had ever seen.

"Whose palace is this?" he asked the angel.

"This is the palace of beautiful deeds, built for you by Jakoob, the wise builder," the angel said. "After all the buildings of earth have been destroyed, this one shall still be beautiful."

Then the king woke up. Shaken by his dream, he took Jakoob out of prison and made him the most honored builder in all his kingdom.

When you grow up, always remember that love, mercy, and kindness are more important than worldly gain in business.

*I am doing a great work, so that I cannot
come down. Why should the work cease
while I leave it and go down to you?
Nehemiah 6:3.*

May 25

Good for Nehemiah! I like to hear people talk like that. He was determined
to build those walls, and no one could talk him out of it. Nothing
could turn him away from it. He stuck at it till the walls were finished. Too many people start to do something, then give up when it gets hard or
discouraging. And there's no telling how many wonderful things never happened
because someone stopped in discouragement.

During the California gold rush a young prospector laid out his claim and
began digging for gold. It was hard work, for with only a pick and shovel he
began to dig a tunnel toward the center of a mountain. It was slow going. With
a drill and with dynamite he worked his way foot by foot through rock, lime-
stone, and earth, hoping every day that he would find the precious yellow
metal. The weeks wore on into long months of hard, strenuous work, and he
never saw even a grain of gold. Finally he'd spent his last cent. His supplies
were all gone. Overcome with discouragement, leaving behind his pick and
shovel and all of his equipment, he went back home. He never came back
to the mine. What was the use? It held no gold.

Years went by. A large mining company bought the property and re-
opened the deserted mine. They cleared away the fallen rock and debris.
They found the place where the discouraged prospector had left his tools
and quit. With their modern equipment they began to dig farther into
the heart of the mountain, and *just six inches* farther on they struck a
rich vein of gold. The prospector had been only six inches away from
success and a fortune!

"In perfecting a Christian character, it is essential to persevere in
right doing. I would impress upon our youth the importance of perseverance and energy in the work of character building. From the ear-
liest years it is necessary to weave into the character principles of
stern integrity, that the youth may reach the highest standard"
(*Messages to Young People*, p. 45).

Have you set out to get an education? Never give up! Get it!
Sickness or misfortune may make your goal seem impossible or a
long, long way off, but don't lay down your tools and quit. Keep
going on. There may be a rich vein of gold only six inches farther
on!

NEHEMIAH 8

*All who are . . . Israelites shall dwell in booths, that your
generations may know that I made the children of Israel
dwell in booths when I brought them out of the land of Egypt.
Leviticus 23:42, 43.*

May 26

When at last the walls of Jerusalem were finished, the first
thing the people did was to have a camp
meeting. It was a joyous occasion. The people
gathered branches and built shelters to sleep in
on the flat roofs of their houses. During the day
they had meetings during which teachers read
and explained the Law of Moses. And oh, yes, accompanied by flutes, trumpets,
tamborines, and many other instruments, there was a lot of singing.

Have you attended modern camp meetings? Do you know about the first
Seventh-day Adventist camp meeting? It was in 1868, just eight years after our
name, Seventh-day Adventist, was chosen. Our first camp meeting was held in a
maple grove on the farm of E. H. Root, in the township of Wright, Michigan—and
the people met among the trees. A platform was made for the ministers to
preach from and rough boards placed on stumps and rocks for the people to sit
on. There were two large circular tents. One contained straw for the campers to
put in their own tents to cushion the ground for sleeping, and one tent was to
use in case of rain. Seventeen smaller tents for sleeping were pitched in a circle
around the meeting place. Of course, many other campers rented rooms or
slept in the barns of the nearby farmhouses. The camp had no electricity, but
campfires built here and there served very well for light.

There were enough children in attendance to have their own meetings.
Elder James White was their favorite storyteller, and Elder J. N. Andrews their
favorite "good-night sayer." Every night he walked around to each tent and
said in his pleasant voice, "Are you comfortable for the night? Good night.
Good night." Then those who had kerosene lamps or candles put out their
lights and went to sleep.

It was very primitive, but about 300 regular campers attended, and
about 2,000 came during the weekend. Many gave their hearts to Jesus
while there. On the way home they told and retold the stories they had
heard, and began looking forward to going to camp meeting again the
next year. Camp meeting does something to you. You really do get closer
to God there.

I hope you can go to camp meeting this year.

Charm is deceitful and beauty is passing, but a woman who fears the Lord, she shall be praised.
Proverbs 31:30.

May 27

Queen Esther was the most beautiful of all the maidens in the land, but her beauty was more than skin deep. Esther also feared the Lord, and that is really why she "obtained favor in the sight of all who saw her" (Esther 2:15).

This reminds me of another old legend. Nobody seems to know where it came from, but it illustrates our text very well. Once upon a time there were three girls who were always quarreling about which one had the most beautiful hands. The first one dipped her hands in the clear, sparkling water of a running brook and said, "See how beautiful my hands are! My hands are the most beautiful!"

The second girl gathered berries till her hands were pink, just as though an artist had painted them. "See how pink my hands are!" she said. "My hands are the most beautiful."

The third girl walked among the flowers and picked the roses till her hands smelled like perfume. "See how fragrant my hands smell," she said. "My hands are the most beautiful." Now, there was another girl with them, but she never argued with the others, because she didn't think her hands were beautiful at all. Well, one day a wrinkled old woman came along. She looked like a beggar. She asked the girls for something to eat. The three girls who were always quarreling about their beautiful hands put their hands behind their backs and said they had nothing to give her. But the fourth girl gave the woman a chair, then ran inside and brought her some bread and milk. Then a wonderful thing happened. The poor old woman smiled and changed into an angel! Turning to the other girls, the angel said, "It is not the hands that are dipped into the brook, nor the hands that are painted with berries, nor the hands that are fragrant with perfume that are the most beautiful, but the kind hands that give to the poor."

The story may be only a legend, but what the angel said is true. That was the secret of Esther's beauty. Her heart was filled with sweetness, goodness, kindness, and love. Would you like to be beautiful? truly beautiful? Try filling your heart with sweetness, goodness, kindness, and love for God and others; then see what happens!

ESTHER 3; 4

Yet who knows whether you have come
to the kingdom for such a time as this?
Esther 4:14.

May 28

When the Lord needed someone with the right influence, someone He could use to save His scattered people, there was Esther—the right person in the right place at the right time.

But listen while I tell you of another young woman in the land of Queen Esther, who was also in the right place at just the right time.

In 1959 the Iraq government took over our lovely Dar es Salaam hospital in Baghdad. All the foreign doctors and nurses were sent away. The only Seventh-day Adventist left in the hospital was Sohila, a national nurse. When she saw all the non-Christian workers come in to staff the hospital, Sohila said to herself, "Remember that you are a Seventh-day Adventist. You must be faithful and always do your best." And she did. A few months later there was an attempted counterrevolution, and an attempt was made to kill Premier Abdul Kassem. He and several of his bodyguards were badly wounded and rushed to the hospital, where Sohila was assigned to special duty for the premier. She did her very best to be kind, helpful, and cheerful. On Sabbath she was off duty as usual. The next morning when she came on duty the premier looked at her and said, "I know where you were yesterday. You went to church. Did you pray for me?"

"Oh, yes, sir. We did," she said. "And, sir, if you would like, our pastor and some of our young people would be glad to come and sing for you and pray for you here." The wounded premier thought for a moment and said, "Tell them to come." Three days later Pastor Behnam Arshat and a group of young people came. They sang. Dr. Fargo read the ninety-first psalm, and the pastor prayed. "Please go and sing and pray like that for my wounded men in the ward," said the premier, and they went. In due time the wounded men were well.

As a result of this experience, Seventh-day Adventists were granted full denominational rights! And today there is a fine church in the center of the city.* Sohila was just the right person in the right place at the right time.

God wants *you* to be the right person just where you are today.

_____
*Today, in the twenty-first century, some things have changed, but Adventists enjoyed relative freedom there for many years.

*The thoughts of the wicked are an abomination to
the Lord, but the words of the pure are pleasant.
Proverbs 15:26.*

May **29**

What a thrilling story is told in today's scripture! I just love to imagine how Haman looked and felt as he led Mordecai around town on the king's horse. Haman had come to ask permission to hang Mordecai on his 75-foot gallows. Then, thinking that he was the one the king wanted to honor, Haman suggested the greatest possible honor he could imagine. And then, after all that, to have to give this honor to Mordecai! Oh, it is just too, too good! But do you know, the wicked still plan evil on the servants of God, and often they do reap it back upon themselves.

At the General Conference I heard a story that thrilled me through and through. In an Inter-American country one of our evangelists went to hold some meetings. He rented the town hall, but when his enemies heard about it they stirred up a lot of opposition, and the use of the town hall was denied him. Then he found a privately owned hall on the edge of town, and advertised that his meetings would be held there. His enemies were furious, but they could not influence the owner to break the contract, so they decided to hold open-air meetings themselves near the hall. They planned to have loudspeakers and lots of music and noise so they could drown out the speaking of our evangelist.

On the first night of the meetings a large crowd gathered, shouting and making a terrible racket. You can imagine how they gloated because the evangelist's meetings would be spoiled. But just about the time for the meeting to begin, a thunderstorm came up, and down came the rain—and the crowd dashed for shelter. The evangelist's hall was so near and so handy that many of them crowded in and stayed for the meeting. He'd never had such good attendance! The enemies were furious over their defeat, but there was nothing they could do about it. And many of the people who had not planned on going to all the meetings now kept on going.

How hard it is for people to learn that those who lay a snare for their neighbor's feet are in grave danger of getting caught in the snare themselves. Just make sure that you plan no evil for your neighbors.

ESTHER 7; 8

*Those who plow iniquity and sow trouble reap the same.
Job 4:8.*

So Haman was hanged on the gallows he had made for Mordecai! Haman had surely plowed iniquity and sowed wickedness, and just as surely he reaped the same. And even today, the judgment of God upon those who have threatened the lives of His workers has been seen again and again.

Soon after 1911 Elder Fernando and Ana Stahl went to live in Plateria on the western shore of Lake Titicaca, Peru. The government had laws granting religious freedom, but there were many priests who hated the Protestants and did all they could to stir up mobs against them. On one occasion while the Stahls were visiting in the little town of Quenuani, two priests got together a mob, armed them with rifles, shotguns, clubs, whips, and stones, and marched toward the house where the Stahls were staying. When they were about a block away the priests passed around liquor to each man and told them what an honor it would be to them if they killed the foreign heretics. Then the priests fired off a rocket, and the mob advanced. They cut loose the horses and sent them plunging wildly down the hill. When Elder Stahl went out to try to catch the horses, the men hurled stones at him. One stone hit him on the head, and the blood ran down his face. Mrs. Stahl ran out and pulled him inside. They piled the furniture against the door, but a barrage of stones soon broke the door. "Set fire to the thatch roof!" yelled one of the priests, but the house's owner snatched the torch and threw it away. Someone brought another torch— but suddenly the mob turned and ran.

"Why are they running away?" Elder Stahl asked a friendly Indian.

"Don't you see that great company of armed Indians coming to defend you?" he asked, pointing across the plain. The Stahls looked and looked, but they could see nothing. Then they realized that God must have sent angels to deliver them. But wait a minute, the story is not yet finished. Not long after this, one of those priests died of a terrible fever, and only those who were paid to bury him went to the funeral. Then the other priest became sick. He called Elder Stahl to care for him, but in spite of all Elder Stahl could do, he too died.

If you ever are persecuted for righteousness' sake, just leave the punishment of the persecutors to God.

153

Be sure of this: The wicked will not go unpunished,
but those who are righteous will go free.
Proverbs 11:21, NIV.

May 31

In spite of the law of the Medes and the Persians, which everyone knows could not be changed, God made a way for the wicked to be punished and the righteous to be delivered. Let me tell you another experience in the ministry of Fernando and Ana Stahl that illustrates this truth very well. Again and again the priests tried to stir up a mob to attack their mission station at Plateria. The first night they came to attack, they heard drums and saw a company of soldiers running from boats at the lake shore toward the mission. The second time the mob came they saw soldiers standing all around the mission. The third time they came it was just the same, so they gave up and wouldn't come anymore. The priests were furious, but there was nothing they could do. The people were afraid of the soldiers. Months afterward the Indians asked Elder Stahl where his soldiers were hidden. He let them look everywhere, and when they found none, they told him about the soldiers they had seen when they came to attack the mission. Then Elder Stahl knew that God had sent the angels to protect him again.

But that's not the end of the story. One night a messenger from an unfriendly village came and asked Elder Stahl to please come and help a prominent man who was very ill. "Of course! That's what I came for," said Elder Stahl. "Who is the sick man?"

One of them said, "He is the priest." He was the one who had tried to destroy the mission station. Elder Stahl found the man in great agony, and he was able to give him immediate relief. However, the priest needed surgery, so Elder Stahl advised him to go to a large hospital on the coast, "Then," said the priest, "please take me to the train." So Elder Stahl gathered 40 carriers and rode his horse beside the patient all the way to the railway station. And he heard the people say, "What is this we see? Has the *evangelista* taken the *padre* prisoner?" On the train Elder Stahl had the pleasure of putting the sick man to bed and tucking the blankets around him. And the power of the enemy was broken. That man never made any more attempts to destroy our mission.

That's the way God does it. Make God first in your life, and He will do things like that for you, too.

JOB 1; 2

Does Job fear God for nothing? Have you not made
a hedge around him, around his household, and
around all that he has on every side?
Job 1:9, 10.

June 1

God certainly did have a "hedge" around Job, but in order to prove that Job served God because he loved Him, and not only for what he could get out of it, God gave Satan permission to "touch" all that Job had. And in a short time Job had lost everything. But listen to what Job said then: "The Lord gave, and the Lord has taken away; blessed be the name of the Lord" (Job 1:21).

This test will come to every child of God in some form or other. It came to me. I know what it feels like. Mrs. Hare and I, with our 12-year-old Verna May and 8-year-old Peter, were in Rangoon, Burma, when World War II broke upon us. We saw the "terror by night," "the arrow that flies by day," and "the destruction that lays waste at noonday" (Psalm 91:5, 6). More than "a thousand" (verse 7) fell around us, and the U.S. consul urged us to get our women and children across to India. But there were no boats running, and thousands of people were on the waiting list ahead of us. Then suddenly on January 20, 1942, the consul telephoned us and said, "We have a little freighter going to Calcutta. It is not listed with the steamship agents, but if you can get some of your women and children to the wharf by 3:00, we'll take them across for you." That gave us just an hour and a half to pack a suitcase and roll up a bundle of bedding for each. But three of us missionary men waved goodbye to our families, and I can't tell you how desolate we felt. You will have to try to imagine it.

"They'll never get across," said a stranger beside me. "The bay is full of submarines." For more than a week our hearts were as heavy as lead. Then came a letter from Mrs. Hare: "As our little freighter sailed out of the Rangoon River into the Bay of Bengal a thick, heavy fog settled down around us, and we couldn't see the sun for four days. Not until we were in the Hooghly River, on our way up to Calcutta, did the sun shine again. Then when we landed and bought a newspaper we read that two boats had been torpedoed and sunk while we were covered with the cloud."

Trouble, loss of possessions, and destruction all around you may be your lot someday. But remember that God still has His "hedge" around you, or His "cloud" covering you, or His "wings" over you under which you can hide.

And the Lord restoreod Job's losses when he prayed for his friends. Indeed the Lord gave Job twice as much as he had before. Job 42:10.

June 2

I think I know how happy Job was when the trial was all over and God gave him seven more sons and three more daughters and twice as much livestock as he had before. Yes, I think I know a little bit, because I can still remember how I felt when I found my family again after we men escaped from the war in Burma. That one letter telling how they were covered with a cloud of fog for four days, and telling of their safe arrival in Calcutta, was the last word we received for six weeks. Those six weeks were the darkest, most discouraging, and loneliest six weeks through which I have ever lived. The tempo of the war increased. The city of Rangoon was taken, and the enemy moved northward. We men had to walk across the border mountains into India, but when we got to Calcutta Mr. Wyman, Mr. Baird, and I learned that our wives and children were waiting for us in the hill station of Mussoorie. We couldn't send them a telegram, for the government had taken over all telegraph lines, so we got on the train and journeyed toward them without their knowing that we were alive and had escaped into India.

As we neared the house where our families were staying, we heard the children playing in the yard. Then we heard a great shout. I knew what it was. They had seen Mr. Wyman coming through the gate. Then there was another shout. That was when Mr. Baird came through the gate. The mothers, hearing the shouting, came running out to see what it was all about. By this time I had come through the gate, and there was more shouting! Oh, glad day! I can never forget it. There we all were, the Wymans, the Bairds, and the Hares, with our arms around our loved ones, all laughing and crying with joy! At last I shouted into my wife's ear. "Dear, we've lost everything—our furniture, our books, our dishes. All I could bring out was this one suitcase."

And she shouted back, "Oh, no. We haven't lost everything. Here's Peter. Here's Verna May, and now that we have you, nothing else matters."

I think that was the way Job felt after his trial was over.

Keep close to God always. He will comfort you when trials come. He is the only one who can restore your happiness.

PSALMS 1; 15; 19

*He [shall abide with God] who walks uprightly, and works
righteousness, and speaks the truth in his heart; . . .
He who does these things shall never be moved.
Psalm 15:2-5.*

June 3

Many of David's psalms were written after God had delivered him from his enemies, so I am going to bring you a few stories that happened during World War II, to show that today the same loving, merciful God still delivers His children. After getting our families on the freighter to Calcutta, we began evacuating our church members from Rangoon. Some went by train to upper Burma; some went by riverboat to the delta district. Then the enemy crossed the great Salween River, and we knew we had only a few days before they'd take Rangoon. We five men could go only as far as the gas in Elder Christensen's car would take us, then we'd have to walk. "Only one suitcase and one blanket each!" said Elder Meleen. "Store the rest of your stuff in the schoolroom." I think it would be easier to lose everything at once than a few items at a time. As I packed my wife's lovely dishes, Peter's train, Verna May's doll, my books, files, and new band instruments, it was like a long drawn-out funeral.

With a heavy heart and many tears I stored the belongings in the mission headquarters, together with the personal belongings of the other missionary families. I had just finished my sad task when the next-door neighbor called. "Mr. Hare, I've just got a way to go overland to India, but can only take one suitcase and one rug. I have to leave everything behind. But worst of all, I can't take my car. I have to leave it, and I don't want the enemy to get it. So Mr. Hare, please take it and use it if you can. But if you have to abandon it, pour some gasoline over it and burn it." She turned quickly to hide her sorrow, leaving me too bewildered for words.

The next day a group of workers from the delta arrived with the news that they had found a way to go by boat upriver to the border, and Dr. Walker couldn't take his car. So now there were three cars for the five of us who were evacuating the church members, and this meant that we could take some of the office equipment and perhaps be able to set up headquarters in upper Burma! Little by little it was plain that "the Lord knows the way of the righteous" (Psalm 1:6), and that He was caring for us, too. Someday you may need one of God's special miracles. Walk uprightly before Him every day, and He will always be near.

157

You prepare a table before me in the presence of my enemies.
Psalm 23:5.

June 4

We saw government headquarters and military headquarters move out of the city. We saw the last riverboat leave the wharf. We saw the last train leave the station. And the next morning we five men left the mission headquarters to take to the road with the thousands of people who were also fleeing for their lives. Mile after mile we picked our way through scenes of suffering and woe. We passed burning cars. We passed hundreds of crying babies and little children dragging at their parents' clothes. We passed hundreds of people lying on the roadside, and hundreds being carried in blankets hanging from bamboo poles, riding piggyback, or being carried on someone's shoulder. We saw suffering until our hearts were wrung dry with sympathy. It was with relief on the second day that we neared the town of Taungdwingyi, 300 miles away from the bursting bombs in Rangoon. But it was dark, and we were thirsty. Our waterpots had been empty since that afternoon. We'd pushed on to this town, and the police sent us to the high school grounds to camp. We were welcomed there, and while we were unpacking Mr. Baldwin took our waterpots to get some water. He was back a few moments later. "No water till morning," he announced. "There are so many people here that there is not enough water, so they turn off the town water supply from sunset till sunrise." No water! But we must have water. Every other comfort was forgotten, and we prayed, "Lord, You have promised that our bread and water shall be sure. Never mind the bread, Lord, but we must have water."

We were still praying when we heard, "If it isn't Pastor Christensen!" It was Mr. Hem, a young man who had attended our meetings in the city. "And what are you doing here?" he asked.

"Fleeing for our lives," said Brother Christensen, and I added, "But at this moment we are dying of thirst. We can't get water till morning."

"Well!" said Mr. Hem. "We knew the water was to be turned off, so I filled two cans. I'll have one here in just a moment." And as he turned to go he added, "Don't bother cooking anything. We have plenty of rice and curry. In a few moments our "table" was prepared, and I wish you could have heard us give thanks that night—especially for the water!

The Lord is a good shepherd. He does prepare a table before His children.

PSALM 37

Commit your way to the Lord, trust also in Him, and He shall bring it to pass. Psalm 37:5.

June 5

If ever anyone committed their way to the Lord, we five missionaries certainly did. God let us have enough trouble so that we had to trust in Him, but He miraculously brought us through. Fifty miles out of Taungdwingyi Mr. Christensen waved for us to stop. "There's a horrible noise in my left rear wheel. Listen while I start up."

We listened, but the car didn't start; the wheel flange had broken off from the hub. We were all quiet. Nobody wanted to say, "You'll have to burn your car." Then Pastor Meleen said, "I've got it! The two good cars will drive on to Yenangyaung, just 32 miles away. We'll find a place to camp, unload one car, and come back after Mr. Christensen and take him to Yenangyaung. He can get on a bus there for Mandalay."

We drove on, found the place to camp, unloaded one car, and Mr. Baldwin left to get Mr. Christensen. "I'll be back in the morning," he said. But he wasn't! Ten o'clock a.m., and still no sign of him. "Let's go see what happened," we said. We found them in a little town three miles off the highway. Mr. Baldwin had burned out his clutch trying to get his car out of deep sand. "I can leave my broken car here," Mr. Christensen said, "so I won't have to burn it. And a bicycle repairman said he can repair Baldwin's clutch. We can be on the road again by morning."

"Then give me the broken wheel," I said. "I saw two garages in Yenangyaung. I'll get the wheel welded." Back I went and stopped at the first garage.

"Sorry," said the man, "my welder has left me." I went to the second garage.

"Sorry, there are no welders in town." How hopeless it all seemed. Just then I saw the English manager of the Nat Sing Oil Company. I told him of our predicament.

"They're right," he said. "There *are* no welders in town, but come explain this to the boss." The boss! I needed a welder, but to be polite, I knocked on the door and went in. Mr. Nat Sing, a pleasant Indian gentleman, listened kindly to my story, then rang a bell, and Mr. Lawson came in.

"Mr. Lawson," he said, "these men are in a tight place. Please take Mr. Hare out to our workshop. It's only 20 miles out. Have our boys weld that hub!" And inside of an hour the hub was mended! "Thank you so much, Mr. Lawson," I said. "What is the bill?"

"There's no bill," he replied. "Just drop in and thank the boss." I did, and also took time to thank God. And that's the way God "brought it to pass" for us. He'll do it for you, too.

Blessed is he who considers the poor; the Lord will deliver him in time of trouble. Psalm 41:1.

June 6

"It's fixed! It's fixed!" I shouted as I pulled up suddenly beside the men in Magwe. Pastor Christensen could hardly believe his eyes. He took the hub, turned it over and over, then raced off to his car, and in a half hour we heard him purring around the block.

"It's better than ever it was before," he cried as he finally drove up to us. "It's just like getting the old car back from the grave." The work on the burned-out clutch took a little longer, but by 2:00 the next day three good, strong cars drove onto the highway and again headed for Yenangyaung. We slept there that night, then early in the morning packed carefully and were ready to leave on the next stage of our journey,

"Let's call in and thank Mr. Lawson again," I suggested. He was glad to see us and gave us the latest news that had come over the radio. While we were chatting together I whispered in his ear. "Of course, Mr. Lawson, the government has commandeered all the gasoline, but I was just wondering if you might know of some private supply where we could get a drop or two."

His eyes twinkled. "Quite right, Mr. Hare," he whispered back. "Just come along with me." And he took us down a little road to his own private garage. He filled our tanks and every empty can we had. And when we pulled out of Yenangyaung we had more gasoline than when we had left Rangoon five days before!

During that day we had 10 unbridged rivers to cross. Because it was the dry season the rivers had only a little water in them, but the descent into each riverbed and the ascent on the other side were so steep and perilous that we held our breath as we labored down one bank and up the other. After every crossing Brother Christensen would say, "I'm so glad that hub broke down near Magwe. If it had broken halfway up this riverbank, what would we have done?"

And after every crossing Pastor Meleen would say, "I'm so glad the clutch burned out down yonder in the sand. It never could have pulled me out of this river." And can you believe it? By the time we reached Meiktila that evening, we had actually been praising God all day long for the broken hub and the burned-out clutch. Truly "all things work together for good" (Romans 8:28) in God's way of delivering His children from trouble. Remember that when trouble and trials come to you.

PSALMS 46; 47

God is our refuge and strength, a very present help in trouble.
Psalm 46:1.

June 7

We reached our mission station at Maymyo in northern Burma without any more trouble, and waited there for 10 days, hoping that the enemy would be content with taking Rangoon and that we could establish temporary headquarters where we were. But the enemy turned northward and was traveling 30 to 75 miles a day. We had to get out, or we'd be made prisoners of war. So we reorganized. My car was too small for the rough roads to the border, so it was left behind, and the five of us, in two cars, started for the border pass. After being helped again and again by our loving God, we crossed the Irrawaddy River and found ourselves in Pakokku, at the beginning of the cart track to Tamu, 300 miles away.

After cleaning ourselves up, we went to the district magistrate for a permit to travel that road. "Gentlemen," he replied solemnly, "the road has been closed, and I have been forbidden to issue any more permits for people to go that way. You see, cholera and plague have broken out, and the poor evacuees are dying like flies. So no permits will be issued until the camps have been cleared up. The road is very rough, but cars and buses have been getting through in about five days."

Pastor Meleen looked into the magistrate's face and said, "Sir, just what might happen if we chose to proceed without a permit?" We gasped at such unbelievable frankness, and anxiously awaited the magistrate's reply.

"You would have no difficulty with my policeman at this end. Of course, at Tamu they could make you come back, but I hardly think they would." Then he lowered his voice and added, "Gentlemen, if I were in your position, I think I would go without delay." We couldn't believe our ears. It must be a dream. Real people just wouldn't talk like that.

Brother Baird asked, "Sir, how many gallons of gasoline does a car need for the trip?"

"About 40," he replied. "We have only 30 gallons each," said Brother Baird. The magistrate took his pen and wrote an order for 22 gallons of gas, and handing it over, he said, "Would that help?" It did, and in five days we were at Tamu at the end of the road and the beginning of the foot trail to India. We never ceased to praise God for very present help in our day of trouble. When your day of trouble comes, God will be your help, just as He was ours.

161

For I was envious . . . when I saw the prosperity of the wicked. . . . It was too painful for me—until I went into the sanctuary of God; then I understood their end.
Psalm 73:3-17.

June 8

No doubt many of us have been surprised at the prosperity of the wicked. But David is not the only one who was shown what their end was to be.

God gave me a preview of the punishment of the wicked too. Let me tell you about it.

While we were walking across the mountain pass into India when escaping from Burma, there were always two distinct groups of people at every place we camped. There were the good and the bad, the selfless and the selfish. And every day the selfish ones pushed and shoved; they wanted the best; they wanted to be first. At last we came to the town of Imphal at the beginning of the Indian road. There were big bamboo barracks for the evacuees, and the captain came in at breakfast time and called out, "Everybody be ready at 8:30! Buses and trucks will come and take you to the Dimapur railway station, There you'll get free tickets to any part of India you want to go to." We clapped and we cheered, and everybody was ready by 7:30, because it doesn't take long to close one suitcase and tie a string around one blanket. Soon two trucks came rattling into the camp. They had canvas roofs and half walls, but no seats of any kind.

"These are ours! These are ours!" shouted the selfish ones. "We were ready first."

"OK, OK," we called back. "We can wait for the next ones."

We watched them load up, yelling, shouting, shoving, cursing. And no sooner were they out of sight than three elegant passenger buses came into camp—with padded seats and backrests. We put the women in the front near the windows, stacked the suitcases carefully, and made sure everyone was comfortable, and off we went. Five miles down the road we passed the two trucks, and *that's* when I had a preview of the punishment of the wicked. "Stop!" they shouted. "Put the luggage in the trucks and let us on the buses." But our driver wouldn't stop, and as we looked back through the clouds of dust, it looked like smoke ascending up and up. Then I remembered the text "The last will be first, and the first last" (Matthew 20:16). That is exactly how it turned out, for we arrived at the railway station two hours before they did, and got all the best seats in the train. Don't worry if you often have to be last in this old world. Someday the wicked will come to their end, and you can be among the first to go through the pearly gates into the heavenly city.

PSALM 78

Marvelous things He did in the sight of their fathers. . . .
He divided the sea and caused them to pass through.
Psalm 78:12, 13.

June 9

Psalm 78 is one of the national songs of Israel, and recounts God's marvelous works in delivering His people from Egypt. We also saw God do marvelous things when we were trying to evacuate our church members from Rangoon during World War II. I remember how God opened up the way for our last two families and "caused them to pass through." With a great deal of difficulty we had gotten them aboard a riverboat headed for the delta. But hardly had they settled down when the military took over the boat and ordered all passengers off. We felt terrible. However, that evening Mr. Baldwin heard that the military had arranged for two evacuation trains to go north and two to go west the next morning for the people to use. So after a little conference we all thought it best for our last two families to go to the station at midnight and sleep there so that they could board the train in the morning.

Ordinarily Grand Central Station was a beautiful place. It was surrounded with gardens, lawns, and parking places, but as we neared it at this midnight hour our hearts sank. For acres and acres the lawns, gardens, sidewalks, and parking places were covered with the sleeping forms of thousands of people who were hoping to get on the evacuee trains the next day. How could we hope to get through this mass of people and through the gates onto the platform? As we stepped in and out and around the sleeping forms, we caught sight of the soldiers with bayonets set, guarding the gates. We had no authority. We had no passes, no tickets, and no permits! But we had God. We prayed as we had never prayed before, and that night we saw God work a miracle. As we drew nearer to the gates the English guard recognized the ambulance uniforms and helmets that Mr. Baldwin and I were wearing, and we heard him call to his partner on the other side of the gate. "Hello, buddy! 'Ere come the marines. Open up!" he said, and the gates opened and we all passed through! Once inside, we explained everything, and the guard said, "OK, buddy, now y'er in. We'll see your people get on the train all right!" And they did.

Sometimes you may be able to get along without authority, without passes, or without permits, but you'll never be able to get along without God. Keep close to Him today and every day.

I would rather be a doorkeeper in the house of my God than dwell in the tents of wickedness. . . . No good thing will He withhold from those who walk uprightly.
Psalm 84:10, 11.

June 10

God takes notice of all the volunteer work we do for His sanctuary. You may be a junior deacon, a song leader, or an usher at the doors. You may pass out the songbooks, or take up the offerings. God sees it all, and someday everyone who works for God will receive their reward.

One day while we were waiting in Maymyo, in northern Burma, to see what turn the war would take, Pastor Wyman and I met a stranger as we were walking along. He shook hands with us, but we didn't recognize him until he spoke. It was Deacon Johns from the Rangoon church. "Oh, brethren," he said, "I've been praying that I would meet some of the workers. You know, I was in government work, and I couldn't leave the city till just the day before the enemy came in." He pulled out his pocketbook as he spoke. "I was paid my last money two days before I left. It may be the last money I will have on this earth, but I folded away my tithe, for I wanted the Lord to have His share." He took out some folded bank notes and handed them to me.

But I didn't feel worthy to accept what might be his last money, so I said, "No, no. Mr. Wyman is the church elder. Give him the tithe." But Brother Wyman said, "No, no. Mr. Hare is the union secretary. Give him the tithe."

Seeing our embarrassment, Deacon Johns took Pastor Wyman's hand, put the tithe in it, and said, "Friends, don't worry about me. I have known the Lord too long to fear that He will forget me now." Then he put another folded note in my hand and said, "This is my Sabbath school offering. I want the Lord to have some of what may be my last money." Then he asked, "Have you any idea where my wife and children are? The government promised to fly them out three weeks ago, but I can't find a trace of them anywhere." We did know!

Just then the train whistled as it came into the station, and we said, "Deacon Johns, run for your life, and catch that train! Your wife and children are at Lashio, 70 miles away, and they are going out on the next plane." He never even said goodbye! He took to his heels, caught the train, found his wife and children a half hour before the next plane came in, and flew out to India with them! God does reward those who faithfully help out in church and Sabbath school and personal witnessing. Are you doing your part faithfully and well?

PSALMS 91; 92

He shall cover you with His feathers, and under His wings
you shall take refuge; . . . you shall not be afraid of the
terror by night, nor of the arrow that flies by day.
Psalm 91:4, 5.

June 11

The ninety-first psalm has brought comfort to thousands of God's children who have gone through the terrors of war or storm, from the days of the children of Israel down to these present days. I am sure that everyone who has ever experienced an air raid, with screaming sirens giving warning of its approach, will agree that it is indeed a "terror by night"—or day. During World War II there lived in Rangoon a piano tuner by the name of Mr. Ward. He had lost his wife two years before, but his 12-year-old boy, Stanley, helped him keep the home together for his two little girls, ages 8 and 9. One morning as Mr. Ward went to work he said, "If an air raid comes today, Stanley, take your little sisters to the trench. I'll come running home as soon as the all-clear sounds.

At 10:30 a.m. the sirens began to scream the air-raid warning. Calmly Stanley locked the apartment and took his little sisters downstairs, across the street, and into the big covered storm drain. It was big enough—two feet wide and four feet deep. It was safe enough—covered with thick concrete slabs. But it was smelly, and it was dark. Soon they heard the bombers overhead, and when the bombs began to burst, the little girls began to cry. Stanley put his arms around them and said, "Girls, don't be frightened. Listen! Hear how my voice echoes! This gutter is just like a cave. Come, girls, let's sing! Then our voices will echo so loud that we won't be able to hear the bombs." And there in that dark smelly gutter they sang, "Jesus loves me, this I know, for the Bible tells me so." And their voices echoed and echoed so much that they couldn't hear the bombs bursting overhead. When the all-clear sounded, they crawled back to the road. But what an awful sight! One bomb had burst right in front of their house. It had blown the front steps away and killed a half dozen people. Their bodies lay right there among the broken pieces of the nearby houses. "Children, we can't stay here," said their neighbor.

"Let's run! Father will find us somehow," Stanley said. They ran for four miles, till they found a small, empty bamboo house. And there Father found them, without a scratch or a bruise on them. I think you should memorize all of the ninety-first psalm. Someday you may need the comfort of its precious promises.

*Oh, sing to the Lord a new song! For He has
done marvelous things; His right hand and
His holy arm have gained Him the victory.
Psalm 98:1.*

June 12

Some songs are new because they have never been sung before. But I know some old songs that have become new because of an experience that people have gone through. One Friday night we had five air raids. They came at 2:30, 3:15, 4:00, 5:00, and 6:00 a.m. Nobody had slept since 2:30. Everyone had been in the gutters and trenches all that time, so I hardly expected to see anyone at Sabbath school. But can you believe it? There were 37 people there and on time! Every Sabbath school member who was still in the city was at Sabbath school! I'll never forget the song we sang to open our service—"A Shelter in the Time of Storm." And I wish you could have heard us sing. Everyone had found God a shelter during some narrow escape, and it is wonderful how different that made the words sound. Mr. Ward and Stanley and the two little girls were singing with all their hearts. I wish you could have heard them.

Brother and Sister Martin were there too. He was a customs official. One day he came home for lunch. He'd just parked his car under the porch when the air-raid signal sounded. Down into the trench they went, and just as they got under cover a bomb dropped right on their house. Everything burned to ashes. All they had left were the clothes they were wearing, but they were at Sabbath school that morning. Now, ordinarily Brother Martin can't carry a tune, but tune or no tune, he was singing "A Shelter in the Time of Storm." I wish you could have heard him.

Brother Ross, an electrician, was there too. He'd been baptized only recently. One day he was at the top of a telegraph pole, repairing some wires, when the air-raid signal sounded. He shouted to his four assistants to run for cover. Down the pole he came as fast as he could, and just had time to throw himself facedown into the curbside gutter. A bomb burst so close that his four assistants, still running, were instantly killed. But he escaped without a scratch, and he was there that morning singing "A Shelter in the Time of Storm." I wish you could have heard him sing. It was a song of experience. That's what made it sound like a new song.

If you are faithful, you'll be singing a "new song" in heaven someday, and it will be a song of experience. Get that experience with God now.

166

PSALM 103

As a father pities his children, so the Lord pities those who fear Him.
Psalm 103:13.

June 13

What a beautiful psalm we have just read! All the goodness and mercy and love and care of God are summed up in this portion of Scripture.

Some years ago I read a story that beautifully describes a father's love for his child. Nina was only 4 when her mother died, leaving her and her father, Jim, alone. They were heartbroken, but Jim did his best to comfort Nina. He got a kitten for her. He cooked and swept, he washed and mended, and at night he heard her say her prayers. And every night he prayed that God would help him do what was right for his little girl.

Two years later Jim became ill with tuberculosis, and was told he wouldn't live more than six months! That night when Nina came to kiss him good night he held her at arm's length and said, "Daddy doesn't want you to get his cold, sweetheart. Anyway, you're a big girl now." Nina's eyes filled with tears, and her little lips trembled. So Jim saw another doctor—who made the same terrible diagnosis. Jim had one thought: *What can I do for Nina?*

At last he put an ad in the city paper: *A man with just a few months to live seeks nice couple to adopt his 6-year-old daughter. References required.* Soon a couple drove up in a limousine. Jim talked to them, then said he had other plans for his little girl. Jim's neighbor sneered, "You've done her out of a fortune!" Other cars came and went. Jim said no. The neighbor said, "You ought to be reported to the authorities."

Then one day another car came. "We've just lost our little girl," said the man sorrowfully, "and we thought—"

"You are the ones," said Jim. "But give me one more day." He spent the entire day with Nina. He listened to her sing to her doll and her kitten. He told her about the lovely visit she was going to have with the loveliest people. He heard her say her prayers and tucked her into bed.

The good people came the next morning, and Nina went on her trip, leaving her father with a breaking heart full of loving memories.

Your heavenly Father loves you just like that—and even more. And even when you are bad He can't bear the thought of ever giving you up. He pleads for just one more day, and one more day. Won't you promise God that you will never go away from Him?

PSALM 106

Remember me, O Lord, . . . that I may rejoice in the gladness of Your nation.
Psalm 106:4, 5.

June 14

Today is Flag Day in the United States. It is the anniversary of the adoption, in 1777, of the good old Stars and Stripes. It is a pleasing coincidence that the psalm we read for today is one of the national hymns of Israel. It is fitting for Christians to be good citizens and to rejoice in the gladness of their nation on earth, as well as to be good citizens and rejoice in the kingdom of heaven that is to come.

Ira Dutton was born in Vermont in the 1840s. He served with the Union forces in the Civil War, then after an unhappy marriage tried to find peace for his troubled heart by becoming a priest in a Trappist monastery. But nothing gave him peace, so he left the monastery, and one day in 1887 he picked up a magazine and read the story of Father Damien and his heroic work among the lepers on Molokai in the Hawaiian Islands. "He's getting old," said Ira. "Someone needs to take his place. I will be that man." So he went to Molokai. In those days leprosy was feared much more than it is today, and Ira knew he would never see his own country again.

In Molokai they called him Brother Joseph. He nursed Father Damien through his last illness and then took his place as a missionary to the lepers. Among the few things he had brought with him was an American flag. He erected a flagpole near the beach, and every morning he ran up his flag, and every evening he took it down. It was the only touch he had with his country except for the few letters and papers that came now and then. In 1908 he saw in the papers that the American fleet was going around the world on a goodwill tour, and would be sailing around the Hawaiian Islands. "They might come past Molokai," he said to himself excitedly. "I might be able to see them!" And every morning as he ran up his flag he scanned the horizon in hope. Someone told President Theodore Roosevelt about Brother Joseph and his deep desire, and President Roosevelt got in touch with the admiral of the fleet that was then in Honolulu. He was told to sail by Molokai so that Brother Joseph could see the fleet. One morning as Brother Joseph ran up his flag he saw a great gray ship coming nearer and nearer. Then another and another came, till at last he saw the long file of battleships all go by. And as each ship passed by, it dipped its own flag in salute to the flag of the loyal hero of Molokai.

Make up your mind to be a good citizen and rejoice in the gladness of your nation.

PSALM 119:1-56

Your word I have hidden in my heart, that I might not sin against You.
Psalm 119:11.

June 15

The Bible is different from every other book in the world. There is power in the dear old Book of God, and our only hope of standing true and faithful through the temptations of the last days is in getting that power down into our hearts by reading the Bible every day. When I was a missionary in Burma, an old man came to my dispensary with a severe attack of malaria. I gave him a bottle of the best medicine we knew of, and told him to take three doses each day. I even marked it on the outside of the bottle, and said, "Uncle, if you take this medicine you will be well again in three or four days." But after four days his eldest son came to me and said, "Father is much worse. Please come and see him."

"Worse?" I asked. To myself I said, "Everybody who takes that medicine gets better. Could I have given him the wrong medicine?" As soon as our clinic treatments were over I put a few things into my medicine bag and went with the young man to his father's house about four miles away. I climbed the bamboo ladder and looked at the poor old man lying on his mat, and saw at once that he was worse.

"I can't understand it, Uncle," I said. "You should be better by this time. Let me see the medicine bottle. Let me see if I gave you the right medicine."

"It's over there, on the shelf," he said weakly, pointing with a trembling hand toward the fireplace. I went over to the shelf, and sure enough, there was the medicine bottle, and all at once I understood. The medicine was still in the bottle!

"Uncle, Uncle," I said, "this medicine is not like a charm. It has no power over malaria when it is in the bottle. You must get the medicine down inside of you where the malaria is. Come now, open your mouth. Let me give you a dose." He opened his mouth, and I gave him a big spoonful of medicine. "There now," I said, "that's the way. Take another dose tonight, and three more tomorrow, and three more the next day, and see if it doesn't make you better." Sure enough, soon he was better, and he came down to get another bottle of medicine. "I want to keep it in my house so that if ever the fever comes again I can take it and get better," he said joyfully.

Many of us are like that poor old jungle man. We keep our lovely new Bibles in the bookcase or on the table or maybe under our pillows but seldom read them.

Make up your mind now to hide the Word of God in your heart, and read it every day.

Forever, O Lord, Your word is settled in heaven. . . .
[By] Your precepts . . . You have given me life. . . .
You, through Your commandments, make
me wiser than my enemies.
Psalm 119:89-98.

June 16

How the men of old loved the words of God! What beautiful things they said about it. "Your law is better than gold and silver! Your words are sweeter than honey! Your commandments make me wiser than my enemies" (see Psalm 119:72, 103, 98). It is so easy to see the difference in the lives of people who read the dear old Book of God and believe it and the lives of those who don't.

A man who didn't believe in the Bible was talking with a Christian doctor who did love and believe in it. "I'm surprised that you put any faith in the Bible," said the unbeliever. "An educated man like you! Why, no one knows for sure who wrote many of the books in it."

"Couldn't you have faith in something even though you didn't know who wrote it?" asked the doctor calmly.

"Certainly not, my good man!" replied the unbeliever.

"Do you know who wrote the multiplication table?" asked the doctor.

"Well—no."

"Yet you believe in it and use it, don't you?"

"Well . . . yes," the man replied, feeling uncomfortable. Then a gleam of hope came to him. "Well, the multiplication table works so well that no one needs to know who wrote it."

"The same is true of the Bible," said the believer. "It works well too! Did you ever hear a man say, 'I was a thief and a drunkard and a disgrace to my family. Then I began to study mathematics and geology, and it made a new man out of me'?"

"Uh . . . no," stuttered the unbeliever.

"Well," answered the doctor, "I can show you not one or two, but thousands of people who became new creatures because they loved and studied and believed the Word of God."

Do you love the Bible? Do you read and believe it? Then the words will give you life and make you wiser than your enemies.

PSALM 119:105-176

Your word is a lamp to my feet and a light to my path.
Psalm 119:105.

June **17**

The darker the night, the brighter shines the light. The Bible does become a light to our paths, as shown in this story from New Guinea. In the 1870s a baby boy was born among the cannibals in the mountains. His mother named him Faole (fa-o-le), and litttle dreamed how evil he would become. He killed his first man at 15, simply because it was "fashion belong headhunters." This murder seemed to awaken an unquenchable thirst for blood, and soon he had killed another man, two women, and a baby. By now he had a bad reputation and was greatly feared. When his mother died a few years later, he became angry and so killed two more men. At last police were ordered to track Faole down and capture him, and eventually he landed in jail.

By the time he'd served his sentence, there was a new Adventist mission at Efogi, in his mountain district. Though he now was about 50 years old, he came to the missionary and said he wanted to go to school. It was there that he found the Bible, and soon had learned to read it. Then the light began to shine, and a great change came over him. He cleaned his body, his clothes, and his house. He became friendly. Anyone who had trouble went to Faole for comfort. It was this Faole who befriended the Allied soldiers during World War II, and who was responsible for the heroic first-aiders who carried so many wounded soldiers to their base hospital.

On one occasion he was trying to lead a company of Australian soldiers back through the enemy lines to their own platoon, but they became hopelessly lost. Faole gathered those soldiers about him and said, "Me sorry too much. Me lose 'im way altogether." The men were hungry, tired, and in despair, but Faole had them kneel down while he prayed to the "big fella Master, stop along top" to ask which way to go. Faole finished praying, then turned in the opposite direction, as God impressed him to do. Within an hour the soldiers were safe behind their own lines! Oh, what a difference! What a change! All because the man in darkness followed the "light to [his] path."

You will need this light and the God of the light in your life, too. Read it, study it now, and it will be a light to your path, too.

I will lift up my eyes to the hills—from whence comes my help? My help comes from the Lord, who made heaven and earth.
Psalm 121:1, 2.

June 18

Here's another story about Faole and the way God helped him. By the time Faole was baptized, there was a call to open a new mission in the village of Maibikee, a two-day journey from Port Moresby on the coast. They sent Faole and his wife and little children there. He built a new village and new church and a new school, and the people just loved their teacher and the new way of life he brought them.

Now, just over the mountain was a heathen village. The village chief was very angry when he saw the change that had come to Maibikee. The people in that village didn't want their old heathen customs changed! So when the heathen chief suddenly died, the witch doctor decided that Faole was to blame and that he and his family must die. So 50 warriors in the heathen village tightened their bows, sharpened their spears, tipped their arrows in poison, and put on their war paint—ready to attack when night came The news of the coming attack reached Maibikee. The village people fled to the jungle and begged Faole and his family to come too. Faole knew the danger, but he would not flee. He picked up his Bible and read, "The angel of the Lord encamps all around those who fear Him, and delivers them" (Psalm 34:7). Then he said to his wife and children, "Don't be afraid. Just go to sleep. God will help us." They slept peacefully all night. Nothing happened that night or the next or the next.

When the news of the heathen threat reached the missionary in Port Moresby, he came up to Maibikee to see what had happened, but found everyone well and happy. He went to the heathen village over the mountain and found the men sullen and angry, and the women were laughing at them. At last the new chief explained, "You know why I did not do it? How could I kill Faole when you and a lot of other men dressed in white stood in a ring around his house all night?" That was the secret! Faole's God had sent help just when he needed it most.

When you need help, lift your eyes to the God of the hills. He has promised to send you help too.

PSALMS 148; 149; 150

Sing to the Lord a new song. . . . For the Lord takes pleasure in His people; He will beautify the humble with salvation. Psalm 149:1-4.

June **19**

The book of Psalms closes with this exhortation: "Let everything that has breath praise the Lord." Singing is one form of praise, and all the reasons for praising God with singing can be summed up in the words "For the Lord takes pleasure in His people." It is a pleasure for God to send His angels to help and protect His people, and it is a pleasure for God to receive their thanks and praise in prayer and in singing. Here is another story about old Faole and the way he praised the Lord.

When Faole was an old man, he wanted to live in the mountains where he had grown up. So a new mission was opened up in the village of Enevologo, and Faole was put in charge. He built a new church, and it was about ready for dedication when the enemy during World War II came over the mountains. They killed everyone they suspected of being friends of the Allies, and burned their villages. So as they came nearer, Faole told his people to flee to the mountains. By this time Faole's children were grown, but in the bigness of his heart he had taken several orphan children into his home, so these children all went with Faole. He wanted to be near enough to keep an eye on the village, so he crossed the river and built a little hut in the jungle.

One Sabbath afternoon Faole dreamed that danger was near, so before morning dawned he took all the children into the jungle to hide. A few minutes later enemy planes dropped bombs on the village, and it was entirely destroyed. Soon after that some Allied soldiers came creeping through the jungle looking for enemy hideouts. "There's one!" whispered one of the soldiers, pointing through the undergrowth at a neat grass hut in a small clearing. The soldiers froze. They could hear the sound of voices. "It must be an enemy officer and his staff," whispered another, and they trained their guns on the door so they could pick them off as they came out. But the next minute they heard the voices singing, "Anywhere with Jesus I can safely go."

"It's OK, fellows," said the officer in charge. "There are no enemies there!" And there certainly were not! It was Faole and his family of orphans praising God for His goodness at morning worship. Make it a habit to sing at family worship.

PROVERBS 1

The fear of the Lord is the beginning of knowledge.
Proverbs 1:7.

June 20

When knowledge is based upon "the fear of the Lord" (or reverence for the Lord) its results are limitless. In 1856, in a little windowless, mud-floored cabin, was born a little boy. His mother was a slave. She named this son Booker, and one of the first things he remembered was his mother earnestly praying, "Dear God, here I am with my children. Look on us with pity and give us freedom, dear God. Please give us freedom." There was no school for the slaves. There was nothing Booker could do except grow up and wait for God to answer his mother's prayers.

The Civil War began when Booker was 4, and by the time he was 6 or 7, Lincoln had proclaimed freedom for all the slaves. Soon Booker was working in a salt factory with his stepfather. One day he saw a young man reading a newspaper to a group of people. "If I could only read," he said to himself, "wouldn't that be wonderful!" He told his mother of his great desire, and she managed to buy him a spelling book. He took it with him to work and asked everyone and anyone to explain the letters and the words. Finally his stepfather agreed to let him go to school half a day if he would get up at 4:00 a.m. and put in his work hours. The first day at school was the happiest day in his life, but it brought a little embarrassment, too. Booker noticed that all the other children had two names, while he had only one. So when the teacher asked for his full name, he stammered, "Booker Washington." The name stuck with him all his life. With his school days came the new experience of attending Sunday school. A few years later he traveled 500 miles to Hampton Institute in Virginia, where he worked his way through school. Returning home, he taught for two years, spent a year in the Wayland Seminary, in Washington, D.C., then went back to Hampton Institute as one of the instructors.

In less than 20 years a young ex-slave, with a great thirst for knowledge and a heart full of love for God and people, became a college instructor! Two years later he opened the now-famous Tuskegee Institute. It began with a rented church, a shanty, and 30 students, but it grew into a magnificent group of buildings with thousands enrolled.

"There is no limit to the usefulness of one who, by putting self aside, makes room for the working of the Holy Spirit upon his heart, and lives a life wholly consecrated to God" (*The Desire of Ages*, pp. 250, 251). And that means you!

PROVERBS 3

In all your ways acknowledge Him, and He shall direct your paths.
Proverbs 3:6.

June 21

The writer of Proverbs identified simple trust in God's leading as the secret of much happiness in the Christian life. Let me tell you how this worked in the life of Booker T. Washington. After the emancipation of the slaves, and little Booker's work in a salt factory, his stepfather tried him in the coal mines. But since this kind of work gave no opportunity for Booker to study, his mother kept looking around, and finally got him a job as houseboy for a well-to-do Southern woman. The job sounded good and opportunities for study were splendid, but think of poor Booker! He had lived his life in a windowless mud-floored cabin and knew absolutely nothing about neatness, cleanliness, or order—and was his boss strict! She made him do his work over and over till she was satisfied. At first it was very discouraging, but Booker decided to do his very best and learn all he could about housework while he was at it.

After four years as a houseboy Booker applied for admission to the Hampton Institute in Virginia. He didn't have enough money to pay his railroad fare all the way, so he had to walk part of the way. When he presented himself to the woman who was principal and asked whether he could work his way through school, she looked at him a moment, then said, "The classroom next door needs sweeping. Take this broom and sweep it." Booker realized that this was his entrance exam. But if he knew how to do anything at all, it was how to sweep and clean a room. God had directed his preparation to this end! He swept the room three times, then dusted it four times, not missing a nook or a corner. When he had finished, the principal came in. She took a clean white handkerchief and rubbed it over the table and some of the woodwork. Not finding one particle of dust or dirt, she quietly said, "I guess you will do to enter this institution." These were the happiest words Booker had ever heard. He had passed his college entrance exam! Do you see how God had directed his ways?

What do you want to be when you grow up? Tell God about it every day, then do your very best at your chores, your homework, your music, your job—at everything—and just see how God will direct your ways, too.

PROVERBS 4

But the path of the just is like the shining sun,
that shines ever brighter unto the perfect day.
Proverbs 4:18.

June 22

In Proverbs 4 Solomon compares the path of the just and the path of the wicked. The path of the just is the path of obedience, of obtaining an education, and of self-control. He closes the chapter with the words "Let your eyes look straight ahead" (verse 25), and right in the center of the chapter is the promise "But the path of the just is like the shining sun, that shines ever brighter unto the perfect day" (verse 18). The light on the pathway of the just never goes out.

Many years ago the New York newspapers carried a story about a lighthouse keeper, Tom Jones, and his brave wife, Mary. They were stationed on a lonely point of rock off Staten Island called Robin's Ledge. When they arrived there and discovered how lonely and rocky and bleak it was, it took Mary a whole week before she could make up her mind to unpack her trunk and household things. She didn't like it there, but at last they made up their minds to make the best of it. Then Tom got sick with pneumonia. She called the coast guard on Staten Island and they came for him in a boat to take him to the hospital. As they were carrying him out of the lighthouse Tom looked up and weakly said, "Mary, mind the light." So Mary stayed and kept the light burning. Two nights later the coast guard came back, and one of the men said, "Mrs. Jones, we have bad news for you. Your husband is worse."

"You mean my husband is dead," said Mary. "I know. I have felt it in my bones."

"Yes, you're right," said the man. "Tom is dead. Mrs. Jones, we have a relief man for the light if you want to leave. But if you want to, you can stay on as lighthouse keeper. Take a little time to think it over. There's no hurry."

"Tom's words to me were 'Mary, mind the light! Mind the light,'" she told them, then added, "I'll stay." Mary Jones stayed for 18 years on that barren, lonely rock. And for all those 18 years the light never went out.

"The bright beams of heaven's light are shining upon your pathway, dear youth, and I pray that you may make the most of your opportunities. Receive and cherish every heaven-sent ray, and your path will grow brighter and brighter unto the perfect day" (*Messages to Young People*, p. 32).

PROVERBS 10

*The fear of the Lord prolongs days, but
the years of the wicked will be shortened.
Proverbs 10:27.*

June 23

In Proverbs 10 Solomon compares the lives of the righteous and the wicked, the wise and the foolish, and the obedient and the disobedient. "He who keeps instruction is in the way of life, but he who refuses correction goes astray," verse 17 says. And in chapter 14, verse 12, Solomon says, "There is a way that seems right to a man, but its end is the way of death." How careful we need be to make sure we take the counsel and advice of our teachers and parents, even if our own way does look all right to us.

I can never, never forget a certain weekend I spent at one of our hospitals. I will not tell you where, nor will I give you the real names of the people, for it was too, too sad. But I was there. I saw the tears. I heard the story personally from the doctor and the girls' dean.

Carrie grew up in the country. Her father died when she was just a little girl, and her mother had quite a struggle rearing her. Money was tight, and Carrie was not well. She had a heart problem and tired easily. When she was 17, she was fortunate to get a job at a hospital so she could work and attend the nearby academy. The doctor examined her carefully and said that if she was careful, she could work 20 hours a week and go to school. In time her heart would grow stronger, he said, but she must get her full sleep. There must be no strenuous activities or late hours. All went well for a while. Carrie was a lovely girl, and was doing well at both work and school. Then one night her roommate, Lucia, said, "Oh, I wish we could go skating tonight."

"So do I," said Carrie. "I'm feeling fine. I don't think it would hurt."

"Come on, then," said Lucia. "We can get out of the dorm, and back in, and no one will ever know." So they went to the rink and skated around until midnight. Then they crept back to their room, and nobody knew they'd been out. But at 3:00 a.m. Carrie was dead. The doctors did all they could, but her poor little heart was so swollen it just couldn't beat any longer.

And Lucia? Poor Lucia! "It's all my fault," she cried. "I killed her." She was kept sedated for two days. I was there. I saw the nurses and teachers crying and wishing. I will never forget it. No matter how *right* your plans seem, listen to your parents and teachers. The end of the seemingly right path could be death.

A soft answer turns away wrath,
but a harsh word stirs up anger.
Proverbs 15:1.

June 24

In today's chapter Solomon has had quite a bit to say about words. Maybe the best known verse is the one we have chosen for this morning: "A soft answer turns away wrath."

Mr. and Mrs. Mantusea lived in central Java, where Mr. Mantusea was a teacher in the government school. Mrs. Mantusea became an Adventist, but her husband, although convinced he should keep the Sabbath, was afraid he would lose his job. Every Sabbath Mrs. Mantusea took her two younger children, baby Peter and little Patricia, to Sabbath school. In that country children went to school six days a week, so Christine and her brothers had to be in school on Saturday.

Now, Christine was the oldest child in the family. She had listened carefully to all her mother was learning from the Bible, and in her heart she believed as her mother did. She longed to go to Sabbath school and church, but her father wouldn't hear of it. Then one Sabbath Christine just couldn't stand it any longer. She went to school as usual, but soon after answering the roll call she jumped out of the window and ran to the church. Her mother was surprised to see her, and hoped and prayed that Christine would not get into trouble. Sabbath after Sabbath Christine did this. Then her father heard about it, and gave her a hard beating. "Now will you go to school or go to Sabbath school?" he shouted.

"I'm going to go to Sabbath school, Father," Christine said softly. "Jesus will help me." Enraged, the father left the house.

Next Sabbath he beat her again. "If my own daughter won't obey me they will take my job away," he said angrily. "Now will you go to school?"

"Father, I cannot go, whatever may happen," Christine replied softly. "Jesus would be sad if I did not obey Him."

"Then go to your Sabbath school! Go all your life! But don't tell me anything about it," he screamed. And Christine went to Sabbath school. And what do you think? We heard the good news that her father has been baptized. Her three brothers have been going to Sabbath school for some time, and the oldest brother plans to be baptized too.

You see, it's true. The power of God goes with a soft, gentle answer. Remember this whenever you are tempted to answer back impatiently.

PROVERBS 20

Wine is a mocker, strong drink is a brawler,
and whoever is led astray by it is not wise.
Proverbs 20:1.

June **25**

The proverbs of Solomon contain many good verses warning us against the use of strong drink. This morning's text is one, and there are several others in chapter 23, such as verses 31 and 32: "Do not look on the wine when it is red, when it sparkles in the cup, when it swirls around smoothly; at the last it bites like a serpent, and stings like a viper."

The words "do not look" remind me of the pictures of the three wise monkeys. One has its hands over its eyes, so it cannot see any evil; one has its hands over its mouth, so it cannot speak (nor taste) any evil; and one has its hands over its ears, so it cannot hear any evil. This comes from a sculpture of the three wise monkeys made on the wall of a temple in Japan. If you ever see models of these wise monkeys for sale, buy one and keep it in your room. It will remind you of Solomon's advice about wine and liquor. Don't talk about it or taste it. Don't even look at it. You'll notice that TV commercials for beer only show rugged, handsome men and young beautiful women. They never show someone throwing up or passed out from the alcohol. They say "drink responsibly," but don't show wrecked cars and broken bodies. If you take the advice of the three wise monkeys, you will never be deceived by liquor.

Vance, a friend of mine, worked in a repair shop. Everyone in the shop drank except him. They teased him and called him names, but Vance didn't mind. One day, however, a guy by the name of Johnson began to sing, "Vance is a fraidy cat! Vance is a fraidy cat!"

"What am I afraid of?" asked Vance.

"You're scared to take a drink," he said, and everybody laughed. Then Vance had an idea, and he sang, "Johnson is a fraidy cat! Johnson is a fraidy cat!"

"What am I afraid of?" shouted Johnson.

"You're scared to eat a plate of barnyard fertilizer," said Vance, and everybody roared.

"Oh," said Johnson afterward, "you mean liquor is disgusting to you?" And no one ever taunted Vance about not drinking again.

Liquor *is* disgusting. Never taste it. And don't be tricked by the beer commercials.

Whoever has no rule over his own spirit is like a city broken down, without walls. Proverbs 25:28.

June 26

In today's chapter Solomon refers to several things that are signs of true greatness. One of them is *humility*, and in verses 6 and 7 he writes: "Do not stand in the place of the great; for it is better that he say to you, 'Come up here,' than that you should be put lower." Another sign of greatness is *kindness*. Only a great person can give his enemy food and drink (verses 21, 22). Another sign of greatness is *self-control*, and this morning's text means that a person without self-control is like a city without walls. Put these three things together—humility, kindness, and self-control—and they present a picture of a truly great person.

Some time ago a teacher asked her students to write an essay on true greatness. This is what one 12-year-old girl wrote: "A person can never get true greatness by trying for it. You can get it when you are not looking for it. It is nice to have good clothes. It makes it a lot easier to act decent, but it is a sign of true greatness to act decent when you have not got them, to act just as good as if you had.

"One time when Ma was a little girl, they had a bird at their house, named Bill, that broke his leg. They thought they would have to kill him, but next morning they found him propped up sort of sideways on his good leg, singing. That was true greatness.

"Once there was a woman that had done a big washing and hung it on a line. The line broke and let it all down in the mud, but she didn't say a word. She did it all over again, and this time she spread it on the grass, where it couldn't fall. But that night a dog with dirty feet ran over it. When she saw what was done, she sat down and didn't cry a bit. All she said was 'Ain't it queer that he didn't miss nothing?' That was true greatness but it is only people that have washing that know it" (Vincent Edwards, in *Children's Friend*).

I think that junior girl had the right idea of true greatness, don't you? Now, just how great are you? Are you humble? Are you kind? Do you have self-control?

ECCLESIASTES 1; 3

The eye is not satisfied with seeing, nor the ear filled with hearing.
Ecclesiastes 1:8.

Solomon set his heart upon seeing all the works that were done under the sun. He saw the works of people, the sorrows, the pleasures, the vanities, and was bored with them all. Poor Solomon. With so much to see and hear, he was still unsatisfied.

Today is the birthday of one of the world's most remarkable women—Helen Keller. Helen Keller was totally blind, yet she read far more books than most people who can see. She wrote seven books herself. She was totally deaf, yet she enjoyed music far more than do many people who can hear. For nine years she couldn't speak. Yet she learned to talk and lectured in every state in America, as well as in many countries all over the world. Helen Keller could put Solomon with all of his wisdom, as well as eyes and ears, to shame.

Helen was born in 1880, a perfectly normal child. For the first 18 months of her life she could see and hear and had begun to talk. Then suddenly she was struck down with a high fever that left her deaf, dumb, and blind. When she was 6 years old, Anne Sullivan, a specialized teacher, came into Helen's life, and little by little the path of communication with the outside world was opened. Helen's sense of touch became so acute that she could understand what her friends were saying by placing her fingers lightly over their lips. And if she shook hands with you, she could remember you by your handshake five years later. Her life brought inspiration and courage and hope to thousands of people with disabilities. On one occasion a celebrated lecturer asked her what was her favorite book. "The Bible," she replied vigorously. "It is the most wonderful book in the world. The Bible! It is beautiful."

"And why does the Bible mean so much to you?" he asked.

"It is because in my darkness the Bible makes me see the great light," she replied.

Thank God for your eyes and your ears this morning, and set your heart to seek out only those things that are pure and kind and true, that *your* life may be a blessing to others too.

It is good and fitting for one to eat and drink, and to enjoy the good of all his labor in which he toils under the sun all the days of his life which God gives him. Ecclesiastes 5:18.

June 28

In the beginning God gave us work to do. This work was intended to be a great blessing and a source of great happiness. God intended that we should enjoy the good of all our labor. He gave us a body, a mind, and a soul. In order for us to be happy and healthy we must exercise all three parts of our being.

A number of years ago a discouraged, despondent man came to see Dr. Henry Link, a famous New York doctor. This man had lost his job, and he felt that nobody cared about him anymore. He wanted to commit suicide and end all his troubles. Dr. Link explained that because his work was sedentary, he had exercised only his mind, and not his body. "I will give you a program of manual work," he said, "and soon you will be feeling better."

"I don't like manual work," said the man. "I don't want to work. I want to die." The doctor did his best to persuade him that his life was still worth living, but it was no use. At last, in exasperation he said, "All right, then, commit suicide. But if you do, do something out of the ordinary, something heroic. Get into the headlines when you die." The man liked the idea.

"What do you suggest, Doctor?" he asked. Dr. Link said, "I have never heard of a man running himself to death. If you want to get into the headlines, run around the block until you drop dead, and every newspaper will have it on the front page."

"That's what I'm going to do," said the man, and off he went. He went home, wrote his letter of farewell, then started running. He ran and he ran, but he couldn't drop dead. He got so tired that he said, "I'll have to finish it tomorrow night." He went back home and slept better than he had for a long time. The next night he ran again, around and around, but he couldn't drop dead, and—you've guessed it—he didn't drop dead at all! He literally ran himself back to health and strength.

I hope you have physical work to do—a lawn to mow, floors to sweep, packages to deliver, or something. I even hope you have to walk to school, for that body of yours needs good, healthy exercise.

ECCLESIASTES 7

A good name is better than precious ointment.
Ecclesiastes 7:1.

June 29

Solomon has said a lot about having a good name. In Proverbs 22:1 he says that "a good name is to be chosen rather than great riches." And in Ecclesiastes 9:10 he gives us the secret of having a good name: "Whatever your hand finds to do, do it with your might."

Once there was a young man just out of college who got a job facing stone blocks in a quarry. "You have to face 10 blocks a day," said the foreman as he handed Joel a chisel and a hammer. Joel was eager to make good, so he did his work carefully and well, but by noon he had finished only four blocks. "You are being too careful," said the foreman. "They're only foundation stones and don't have to be so correct."

Joel finished his 10 blocks by the time the whistle blew, but he was not satisfied with them. "May I stay a little longer and smooth them up some more?" he asked the foreman.

"Well, all right; but there's no extra pay, mind you," the foreman said. This went on for several days. Then one evening when Joel got home he found a letter from the quarry manager.

"Your services are no longer needed at the quarry," it said. "Report at the main office at 9:00 tomorrow morning." At that, Joel felt discouraged. He had done more than his best, and he simply couldn't understand why he should lose his job.

At 9:00 he was at the manager's office. There was the big manager, Mr. Johnson, and his son, the chief executive. "My son saw your blocks of stone and says you're taking too much pains with your work," the manager said. "If we finished all the foundation blocks like that, they'd be too expensive. The foreman says he's told you not to be so exact, but you stay after hours to finish your required number. Do you have anything to say for yourself?"

"Yes, sir," said Joe. "I have taken as my motto 'As thou hast meted out to man, so t'will come again to thee.' I love to do them well, sir, and I'd like to have my job back."

Then Mr. Johnson smiled and said, "No, Joel, we can't use you in the quarry anymore. We have a place here in the office for you."

"I'll do my best, sir," said Joel happily. And are you surprised to know that the day came when Joel Prince was himself a great architect? Why don't you decide to do a little better than your best, and see what a good name it will bring to you?

*Cast your bread upon the waters,
for you will find it after many days.*
Ecclesiastes 11:1.

June 30

There were so many inspirational texts in today's reading that it was hard to decide which was the best one, so I chose the first. The promise "You will find it after many days" could apply to farming, to hospitality, to missionary work, and to many other things that do not show immediate results for the effort put forth.

Among America's stories of ordinary people is one whose life was a shining example of the practice and fulfillment of this morning's text. This person is John Chapman, more commonly known as Johnny Appleseed. He was born in New England and settled in the great Ohio River valley. He loved the outdoors, and as a young man he built himself a home and started a nursery. He lived in the days when settlers were moving west, and his heart's desire was to help the settlers get established. Near him were many apple orchards, and the apples were made into cider. He noticed that after crushing the apples the pulp and the seeds were thrown out, so he gathered bags and bags of seeds, washed and dried them, and then gave small deerskin bags of apple seeds to the settlers as they went west.

Not satisfied with this, he finally gave his home to a widow and her children, tied two Indian dugouts together, loaded them with watertight bags of seed, and set off on a lifelong selfless mission. He planted orchards for the settlers everywhere he went. He even came back from time to time to care for the young apple trees. His greatest joy was to see little children eating the luscious fruit that his love and care had made possible. He wore no fine clothes, often went barefoot, and slept in the open, but everywhere Johnny Appleseed went he was welcome. For 40 years he labored unselfishly. He established more than 100 nurseries and helped thousands of settlers plant apple orchards. And when he finally fell asleep, the whole country mourned the passing of a good, kind, generous man. Today there are monuments to this man's labor of love on practically every farm in the Ohio Valley—not monuments of stone, but apple orchards.

Would you like to have loving monuments left to your memory after you have passed away? Find some kind of "bread" or "apple seeds" to "cast upon the waters."

ISAIAH 5

Woe to those who rise early in the morning,
that they may follow intoxicating drink.
Isaiah 5:11.

July 1

I'm so glad that we find so many warnings against strong drink in the Bible, for it is one of the greatest curses to humanity. Benjamin Franklin once said, "Some of the domestic evils of drunkenness are houses without windows, gardens without fences, . . . children without clothing, principles, morals, or manners."

These are but some of the woes that can come to drinkers and their children. Here is a story that tells of another. Jack grew up with a single mother, and understood that his dad had died when he was a baby. Now he was in high school, and his mother warned him more and more never to touch beer at any of the parties. "But why?" Jack asked. "Beer isn't really alcohol."

"I know it is, son," she replied.

"Oh, Mom, you're just old-fashioned."

As the months passed, they had this conversation again and again. At last his mother said, "Maybe I am old-fashioned, but I *know* beer is the devil's own brew. Let me see. Next Monday is your sixteenth birthday. Let's spend the day together." Monday came, and they took a train for the city not too far away. Arriving there, they took a taxi and got out in front of the penitentiary. They rang for admittance, entered the lobby, followed an attendant down a long corridor, and waited in a large room. A prisoner came and sat by a telephone behind a glass window. "I've brought our son to see you, dear," she said to the man. "Jack, this is your father."

"Why did you bring him, Kathryn?" the prisoner demanded. "You know I wanted him to think I was dead." Then looking at Jack, he said, "It was drink that broke up our home, Jack. Just a social glass of beer at first. But it's the devil's own brew, son. The devil is in it, and one night at a party I got drunk and killed a man. Now I'm here for life."

"Oh, Mom," cried Jack on his way home. "I wish I had never known!"

"But you needed something more than my words to show you where drink can lead you," said his mother. "And the tendency toward alcoholism can be passed from parent to child."

Woe? Yes indeed. The drinker and the drinker's children know what woe is. You need never know if you leave the stuff absolutely alone.

185

They shall not hurt nor destroy in all My holy mountain, for the earth shall be full of the knowledge of the Lord as the waters cover the sea.
Isaiah 11:9.

July 2

The beautiful description of happiness and peace between people and animals given in today's reading could have been fulfilled on this earth for the children of Israel if they had been true and faithful to God. Now it can be fulfilled only in the new earth. However, even now we can find many instances of love and kindness between people and animals that help us understand what it will be like when "the wolf also shall dwell with the lamb, . . . and a little child shall lead them" (Isaiah 11:6).

As Tom was playing in a field one day he saw Bob going toward the river, carrying a sack. Something in the sack seemed to be moving, so Tom asked Bob what he had. "Aw, it's just a mongrel pup. We got too many, so I'm going to drown it."

"Oh, don't drown it," pleaded Tom. "Let me have him."

"OK, but ya better make sure it doesn't get back to our place," Bob warned.

"I'll make sure!" said Tom as he raced home. Soon he opened the sack and lifted out a little black puppy. "You're beautiful! And if I hadn't seen Bob, you would've been cold and wet and dead by now." The little pup yipped and yipped and licked Tom's hands, just as if he understood and was trying to say thank you. "I'm going to call you Soot," said Tom, "because you are so very black." And from that moment Tom and Soot were fast friends, and everywhere that Tommy went, Soot was sure to go.

Two years went by. By now Soot was a quite a big dog. One day when Tom was crossing the river on a footbridge, he tripped and fell into the water. Tom couldn't swim, but Soot could—and into the river he jumped. He grabbed Tom by his coat collar and swam with him to the nearest bank. Tom was a bit frightened and very wet, but he hugged Soot and said, "Well, Soot, that makes us even. I saved your life once, and now you've saved mine. You shall have a new collar; I'll build you a new house; and what else would you like?" Soot just said *Bow-wow-BOW-WOW,* which, everyone knows, means "I just want to stay with you forever."

Are you looking forward to the time all the animals and people will be kind to one another? Then remember to be kind to your pets and to everyone you meet today and every day.

ISAIAH 26

Trust in the Lord forever, for in Yah, the Lord, is everlasting strength.
Isaiah 26:4.

July **3**

At least 25 times in the Bible God is called a "rock," "my rock, and my fortress," my "rock, for an house of defense," and "rock of my salvation." In the margin of our text today God is called the "rock of ages," and I think this is one of the most loved of all the names for God. It includes the meaning of all the other names and adds the assurance that God's defense and salvation are everlasting. The name has been made more dear to our hearts by the immortal and almost universal hymn "Rock of Ages." The words of this hymn were written by Augustus Montague Toplady, a Church of England minister who lived in the eighteenth century. When he was still a young man he contracted tuberculosis and died at age 37.

One day while taking a walk on the banks of the Severn River, Augustus was overtaken by a sudden thunderstorm. To escape the downpour, he took cover under a nearby overhanging rock. When the storm was over, he returned to his study and wrote:

"Rock of Ages, cleft for me,
Let me hide myself in Thee."

This beautiful hymn has been translated into many languages and has been sung on many different occasions. It was sung for Queen Victoria at her Golden Jubilee; and when the steamer *London* was wrecked in the Bay of Biscay, in 1866, the last sounds heard by the few who were saved were the voices of the helpless passengers singing "Rock of Ages" as the ship went down. In Constantinople when a company of Armenian Christians were being massacred they sang "Rock of Ages" in their own language. And so throughout the world this beautiful hymn containing this wonderful name of God has brought comfort, hope, and assurance to all who put their trust in Him.

The Rock of Ages was cleft for you, too. In Him you can find forgiveness, peace, and salvation.

Strengthen the weak hands, and make firm the feeble knees. Say to those who are fearful-hearted, "Be strong, do not fear! Behold, your God . . . will come and save you." Isaiah 35:3, 4.

July 4

There are many ways of giving encouragement to those who are weak, tired, sick, or discouraged. Today is Independence Day in the United States, and no doubt speeches will be made reminding Americans how the very first Americans took their first steps toward becoming a nation. The flag with its 13 stripes and stars had a great deal to do with this encouragement. Here is a story I read in the Oakland *Tribune* some years ago about a brave little Chinese girl and a new flag.

During the battle of Shanghai the enemy was slowly driving the gallant but under-armed Chinese forces back to the other side of Soochow Creek. One by one their forces had to retreat or surrender, till at last there was only one company of 150 men left, strongly entrenched in a concrete warehouse. At the top of the flagpole above them still waved the Chinese flag—tattered and torn by flying bullets and bursting shells. From the roofs of the tall buildings in the international section of the city, people looked anxiously on. Among them was a 12-year-old Chinese girl who timidly approached the chair of the chamber of commerce and said, "Just look at their poor torn flag! If you'd give me a new one, I'd take it to them. I know they're tired and hungry, but I think they could fight better if they had a new flag."

"But the enemy would shoot you, my dear," said the man.

"But I'm so little, maybe they wouldn't," she replied. So he gave her a new flag. She folded it and put it near to her heart, under her little dress, and disappeared. The people looking on knew nothing of what was happening. Suddenly they heard a shout from the side of the enemy, and looking over, they saw the torn Chinese flag slowly being pulled down. *They are going to surrender,* thought everyone. But just then there was a thunderous roar from the Chinese side, and looking again, the people saw a brand-new flag being pulled swiftly to the top of the flagpole. Cheer after cheer rolled across the battlefield, and hearts were brave and arms were strong again. And when at last General Chaing Kai-shek ordered their retreat, the little girl and her brand-new flag led them to safety. Do you know anyone who is having a hard time and needs a little encouragement? How about your taking that person a new flag!

ISAIAH 36

But they held their peace and answered him not a word;
for the king's commandment was, "Do not answer him."
Isaiah 36:21.

July 5

There is a wonderful power in silence. Solomon says there is "a time to keep silence, and a time to speak" (Ecclesiastes 3:7), and Amos says "the prudent keep silent at that time" (Amos 5:13). In today's reading the Rabshakeh (chief officer) tried to make the Jews afraid with great blasphemous words, but they wisely "held their peace." And before long, God answered him with total destruction.

Here is the story of a heathen chief in the Solomon Islands who held his peace and was greatly blessed by God. For some time old Chief Tatagu had been dissatisfied with some of the heathen customs of his people. He had been the leader of many a head-hunting raid, but a feeling that there was some better way of life grew steadily upon him. His wife was about to give birth, and ordinarily there would be the usual "devil string" ceremony in which strings were trailed through the fishing grounds and—with the aid of evil spirits—many fish caught. A devil feast then followed, but this time Tatagu said, "No, there will be no devil strings or devil feast."

"Then we will take our own devil strings and we will have our own devil feast," the village men said angrily. And off they went trailing their devil strings to the fishing grounds. Chief Tatagu "held [his] peace," but he also went to the fishing grounds for a supply of fish. On the way evil spirits seized his canoe and rocked it as though he had run into a great storm. Ordinarily he would have been filled with fear and would have gone home and gotten his devil strings, but this time he would not give in. Then with one tremendous shake that almost upset his canoe the spirits left him. Tatagu went on to the fishing ground and had good success. He came home with a full load of fish! The others came home with almost nothing. When his son was born, Chief Tatagu triumphantly named him Kata Ragoso, which means "without devil strings." Don't you think God was leading this heathen chief toward the light? Soon after this, Captain G. F. Jones arrived and opened a mission school. Little Kata Ragoso was one of the brightest in the school. He learned to speak good English and to use a typewriter. Before long he was secretary to the missionary in charge, and in due time he was ordained to the gospel ministry! I'll tell you some more about Kata Ragoso tomorrow. Always remember that God is on the side of those who can hold their peace and be silent when others are trying to pick a quarrel.

Now therefore, O Lord our God, save us from his hand, that all the kingdoms of the earth may know that You are the Lord, You alone. Isaiah 37:20.

July 6

God saved Hezekiah and the children of Israel in such a way that all the world knew it was the work of a mighty God. God still works that way. Listen!

As World War II extended southward the Japanese invaded the Solomon Islands, as a stepping-stone to Australia. The Australian missionaries were ordered to the homeland, and Kata Ragoso (Without Devil Strings) was placed in charge of our work in the Solomons. He did a noble work. He selected and trained spotting units, first-aid parties, and rescue squads. With their drums information was forwarded, and the records show that more than 200 men owe their lives to the skill and efficiency of those wonderful men. Now, there was a detachment of allied soldiers on the same island where Kata Ragoso had his home, and Ragoso and his first-aiders cooperated with them in a wonderful way. But unfortunately, one day the chief officer commanded Ragoso to do certain things that his conscience would not allow. When he courteously refused, he was placed under arrest. "Don't you know there is a war on?" thundered the chief officer.

"I am sorry, sir, but I must obey God first," replied Ragoso quietly. But the officer was angry. He took out his revolver and, using it as a club, beat him over the head with it until he fell to the ground unconscious.

"Sir," said a police boy nearby, "if he is worthy of death, there is a firing squad." And when Ragoso regained consciousness, they tied his hands behind his back and stood him up near a tree in front of the firing squad. "Now then," roared the officer, "when I count to three, shoot! One, two, —" but he could not say three. "I'll try again," he said. "One, two, —" but the angel of God must have put his hand over that wicked man's mouth, for he couldn't say "three." In fact, he couldn't talk at all for almost two days, and Ragoso was saved "from his hand." However, with Ludi, one of his faithful assistants, he was taken back to the prison.

Who but a mighty God could close a man's mouth so he couldn't say that final word?

That mighty God is your God too. Make Him first in your life and in your obedience, and He will care for you, too.

ISAIAH 38

The Lord was ready to save me; therefore we will sing . . .
all the days of our life, in the house of the Lord.
Isaiah 38:20.

July 7

The Lord was indeed ready to save Hezekiah, and someday in the new earth the Lord will tell us how often He sent the angels to save us. Listen to how the Lord saved Kata Ragoso. With Kata Ragoso and Ludi in prison the drums beat out a message over the hills and valleys: Pray—pray—for Ragoso and Ludi. And on the given night more than 300 Solomon Island Seventh-day Adventists got down on their knees and prayed and prayed that God would release His servants. And that night as the moon rose over the mountain a tall man with a bunch of keys walked to the gate of the prison. He unlocked the padlock, opened the gate, and called, "Ragoso! Ludi! Come here!" So they came.

"Come outside," the man said. They stepped outside. The tall man locked the gate and said, "Follow me." He took them down to the beach and pointed to a canoe with two paddles in it. "Take that canoe, boys, and go home," he said. Ragoso and Ludi looked to make sure the canoe was there, then turned to thank the man who had taken them out of the jail, but there was no one there! The moon was shining bright. They could see for 100 yards or more, but the man had vanished. They never found the man who opened the prison gate, and the guard says the keys never left the peg on which they were hung all night.

I visited the Solomon Islands a few years ago and met Kata Ragoso. I saw the scars on his forehead where he was so cruelly beaten. "Who let you out of prison that night, Ragoso?" I asked, and without a second's hesitation he replied, "An angel! The same angel that took Peter out of prison." I looked again at his beaming face. His nose was still a little crooked where it had been broken. I thought again of the terrible blows that had knocked him unconscious, and I asked, "What if the officer had killed you that day?"

"I would rather have died than disobey God" was his calm reply. (The officer who had so cruelly mistreated him was later dishonorably discharged from the service.) No matter where you are or what you are doing, if you make sure your guardian angel is by your side, you will be perfectly safe, for the Lord is ready to save you.

Then Isaiah the prophet went to King Hezekiah, and said to him. . . . "What have they seen in your house?" Isaiah 39:3, 4.

July 8

What an opportunity Hezekiah had to tell the visitors from Babylon about the living God. But poor Hezekiah made the mistake of showing them all his earthly treasures—with the terrible result that the king of Babylon sent soldiers to carry away all the *things* in his house.

Today is the birthday of one of our great Adventist pioneers—Joseph Bates. Let's take a look into his house to see what we may see. He was born in Rochester, Massachusetts, in 1792, and went to sea when he was only 15. For the next 21 years he lived the most exciting but wicked life that you can imagine. Twice he was a prisoner of war. He cursed, smoked, chewed tobacco, and drank. Still he eventually became captain and part owner of a ship. In 1824 his wife placed a New Testament on top of some novels in his trunk. There at sea he read the New Testament, then stopped reading novels. Next he gave up tobacco and liquor. In 1826 he gave his heart to God. In 1828 he left the sea and settled down with quite a fortune. In a few years he heard William Miller preach about the Second Coming. He believed it with all his heart, so sold his property and used up his fortune in giving the message. Then he heard of the seventh-day Sabbath. He studied it, believed it, and accepted it with all his heart. He felt impressed to write a book about the Sabbath, but his money was gone. He had only one York shilling in his pocket—it was worth 12 ½ cents—but he sat down and began to write. "Joseph," called his wife, "I need some flour to finish the baking. Get me about four pounds."

A short while later Joseph brought his wife just four pounds of flour. She looked at it in amazement and said, "You, Captain Bates, a man who has sailed vessels out of New Bedford to all parts of the world—you have been out and bought only four pounds of flour!"

"Wife," said the captain, "I spent for that flour the last money I have on earth."

With that Mrs. Bates began to weep. "What are we going to do?" she asked.

Let us leave the story there until tomorrow. But now, tell me, what did you see in Joseph Bates's house? Great treasures? Grand furniture? What kind of magazines were on his table? What kind of books were in his bookcase? When your friends come to visit you, what do they see in *your* house?

ISAIAH 40

But those who wait on the Lord shall renew their strength;
they shall mount up with wings like eagles, they shall run
and not be weary, they shall walk and not faint.
Isaiah 40:31.

July 9

Let me tell you some more about Joseph Bates and his good wife, who felt embarrassed because the captain had bought only four pounds of flour and they had no more money. In tears she asked, "What are we going to do?" Joseph Bates stood up and said, "I'm going to write a book about the Sabbath, and I am going to circulate it."

"But what are we going to live on?" asked his wife.

"The Lord will open the way," answered the captain.

"That's what you always say," she said, bursting into tears again as she left the room. Joseph Bates kept writing, but he must had been praying, for in about a half hour he felt impressed that he had a letter at the post office, so he walked down to the post office to see.

"Yes, there is a letter," said the postmaster, "but there's five cents to pay on it."

"Mr. Drew," Bates said, "I'm out of money. I don't even have five cents to pay that postage. But I feel impressed that there is money in this letter. Will you please open it and see?"

The letter was opened. In it was a $10 bill! Joseph paid the postage, then hurried to buy a barrel of flour, potatoes, sugar, and other things they needed and asked that they be delivered to his wife. "Mrs. Bates will probably tell you that the supplies don't belong to her," he said, "but don't pay any attention. Just unload them on the front porch anyway."

After going to a printer to arrange for printing his book, he went back home. Mrs. Bates met him at the door. "Just look out there," she exclaimed. "I told the man it didn't belong here. But he said this was the address he'd been given. Where do you suppose it all came from?"

"Why, the Lord sent it," said the captain, and we can imagine the smile on his face.

"Oh, yes, the Lord sent it. That's what you always say," she teased, for she could hardly believe it was true. "Then read this letter and see," he said. She read it, then had another cry! But this time it was a happy cry, because it was plain as could be that the Lord had not forgotten them and that His promises are sure.

Someday you will need your strength renewed. Make God first in your life; He will come through for you, too.

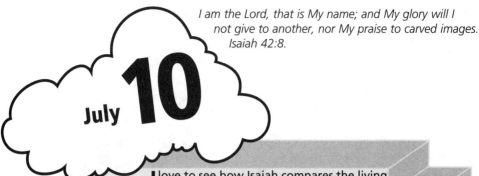

I am the Lord, that is My name; and My glory will I not give to another, nor My praise to carved images. Isaiah 42:8.

July 10

I love to see how Isaiah compares the living God with human-made idols, and I love to collect stories of what only the living God could do for His children.

When the Advent cause was young, some of the members took up a collection to buy James and Ellen White a horse and buggy. It was arranged that several men who had horses for sale would bring them to a certain place on Monday morning for Elder and Mrs. White to choose the one they wanted. Now, you wouldn't expect the God of the universe to be interested in choosing a horse, but He was, and Sunday night He gave Mrs. White a vision. She saw three men holding three horses. As she looked at the first one the angel said, "Not that one." As she looked at the second the angel said, "Not that one." Then she saw a beautiful dappled chestnut. The angel said, "This is the one for you." The next morning everything happened just as Ellen White had seen in the vision. The name of the dappled horse was Old Charlie, and he did much to make their traveling pleasant and comfortable.

Today we cannot realize what traveling was like in horse-and-buggy times. There were no paved highways. The dirt roads were often muddy, rutted, and rocky. You could not travel more than 20 or 25, or, at best, 30 miles in an entire day. One day Elder John Loughborough and another minister borrowed Old Charlie and the buggy to go to a meeting some distance away. There had been a heavy rain, and they came to a place where a bridge had washed out. The creek looked deep, but people said others had crossed over OK, so Elder Loughborough decided to try. (His friend used a small footbridge.) Old Charlie went carefully into the water, but soon the buggy and Old Charlie were floating downstream. Brother Loughborough cried out to God, and just then the buggy wheels struck a rock. Old Charlie looked around as if to make sure it was still right side up. Then he gave two or three lunges, gained a footing, and drew the buggy up out of the creek. Several people had gathered when they saw that the buggy was going to go into the water, and when they saw Old Charlie get safely across, they gave a shout and a cheer.

Isaiah must have seen many providential acts that only the living God could perform. What a wonderful God we have! Take even your little problems to Him.

ISAIAH 43

When you pass through the waters, I will be with you;
and through the rivers, they shall not overflow you.
Isaiah 43:2.

July **11**

God's promise of deliverance has been fulfilled again and again to many people in many places, but I will tell you about the time Captain Joseph Bates fell into the river. James and Ellen White and Joseph Bates were in New York visiting one company of believers after another. They planned to finish their meeting in Port Gibson in time to catch the riverboat for New York City, where they had a Sabbath appointment. However, the meeting lasted longer than expected, and by the time they got to the river landing, the big riverboat had gone.

A smaller riverboat was there, one that stopped at some of the smaller towns on the way. So instead of waiting for the next big boat, they decided to start off on the smaller one, then transfer to the next big boat when it overtook them. All went well, and in due time a big riverboat came near. They called to the captain, but he would not stop. So they decided to pull alongside and jump onto the deck of the bigger boat while it was moving. It seemed easy to do. Brother White jumped aboard; then they helped Mrs. White aboard. With his money for their fares in one hand and his wallet in the other, Joseph Bates jumped from the smaller boat to the larger one. And just then it moved slightly. He missed his footing and fell into the muddy water of the river.

He was a good swimmer, but as he fell into the water his hat came off. And as he grabbed for his hat, he lost the money in his hand. Seeing what had happened, the captain of the riverboat slowed down, and Captain Bates, dripping wet, was pulled up on deck. However, he couldn't go to New York sopping wet like that, so they got off at the next stop and spent the weekend with some believers in that town. It was a surprise visit, all right, but it was such a blessing to one good sister who was healed in answer to prayer and to the others with whom they spent the Sabbath that Bates felt sure the Lord had overruled his misfortune and made it a blessing.

The precious promise of our text for today was written for you, too. Memorize it and keep it in your heart.

ISAIAH 58

Then your light shall break forth like the morning,
your healing shall spring forth speedily.
Isaiah 58:8.

July 12

Isaiah 58 contains one of the many strange yet undeniable truths of the Bible, such as the truth Jesus taught when He said, "Whoever loses his life for My sake will find it" (Matthew 16:25). One thing this chapter teaches is that when we work for others—giving food and clothing to the poor, visiting the sick, comforting the discouraged, helping people to overcome bad habits—we gain an inner joy and improved health! If you look around, you will find that those who think of others and put others first are the nicest and happiest people you know.

A well-educated woman who had worked in a bank for years became despondent. She was so miserable that she feared she was going to have a nervous breakdown. "Who do you work with?" her doctor asked.

"A girl named Dot, but I don't know anything about her." More questions, and soon the doctor realized that her patient had no friends. She lived just for herself. Simple selfishness was robbing the woman of her joy and health. The doctor said that he could help her if she promised to do exactly as he said.

"All right," said the doctor. "First, get acquainted with Dot. Invite her to your home. Find out her goals, and do something to help her. Second, get acquainted with your mechanic and his family. See if there's something you can do to help them. Third, get acquainted with the kid who delivers your newspaper. Then come see me in two months."

At the end of two months she didn't go back, but she wrote her doctor a 10-page letter—10 pages of joy! She had helped Dot with Latin, and Dot had passed her college exam with honors. One of the mechanic's children was recovering from an illness, and she'd stayed with the girl so her mother could get some rest. Now they were good friends. "Where have I been all my life?" she wrote her doctor. "I didn't know there was a joy like this!"

It's as true as it can be. Selfishness leads only to unhappiness, but helping others gives you an inner peace and improved health.

ISAIAH 60

Arise, shine; for your light has come!
And the glory of the Lord is risen upon you.
Isaiah 60:1.

Jesus is the light of the world. All who believe on Him and accept Him receive the light, and in turn become lights. There is nothing more useless in the dark than a lamp that won't shine. There is nothing more disappointing to God than to see a junior youth whose light has gone out. The words of Isaiah are for all of us: "Arise, shine; for your light has come!"

Several years ago I heard an evangelist tell this story. A flagman was stationed at a certain railway crossing. By day he waved a red flag to warn automobiles of approaching trains, and by night he waved a red lantern. He was a faithful man and was always at his post of duty. One night, however, there was an accident. An automobile started across the tracks, and a train crashed into the back end of it. Fortunately, no one was killed. As soon as the car owner recovered he sued the railway company for damages, claiming that he had not been warned of the approaching train. When the case came to court, the flagman was called to the witness box.

"Were you there on the night of the accident?" asked the judge.

"Yes, sir," answered the flagman.

"Did you see this man coming down the road in his car?"

"Yes, sir."

"Did you wave your lantern?"

"Yes, sir," again answered the flagman. Because of this man's testimony the case was dismissed. As they left the courtroom, one of the railway officials thanked the flagman for his testimony. "You answered your questions so well that our company does not have to pay damages," he said.

"Yes," answered the flagman, "but you cannot imagine how scared I was that the judge would ask me if my lantern was lighted."

Oh, no! I wonder what happened after that. The fact is that all of us, juniors and adults, are all in danger of letting our light go out.

God forbid that anyone should lose their way or lose eternal life because your light has gone out! You have the light. "Arise, shine!"

In all their affliction He was afflicted, and the Angel of His Presence saved them; in His love and in His pity He redeemed them; and He bore them and carried them all the days of old."
Isaiah 63:9.

July 14

The sixty-third chapter of Isaiah gives a striking description of the coming Messiah— "mighty to save," with His bloodstained garments, as of one who had "trodden the winepress alone." No one else could help, so His "own arm brought salvation." We talk of salvation being free, but what a price in suffering it cost the Savior!

One day, way over in China, a little girl was brought to a missionary doctor. Her leg had been badly burned, and because she had not had any medical care, scar tissue on her leg now kept her from straightening it out, so she couldn't walk.

"Can you do anything for her?" asked her anxious parents.

"Yes," said the doctor, "I can cut away that scar tissue, but I will have to graft some skin to the raw surfaces so it can heal properly. Will you let me take some skin for her from your arm?" the doctor asked the father.

"Very well," said the man, and he offered his arm for the operation. But when the doctor had washed and scraped the arm and had picked up his knife, the man drew back in fear. "No, no!" he gasped. "I cannot bear it."

So the doctor asked the mother, "May I take some of your skin for your little girl?"

She began to cry. "No," she said, looking away from her daughter. "I couldn't bear it."

So the doctor turned to his assistant and said, "Then you must cut some skin from *my* arm. We must do something for this little girl."

"No!" said the assistant. "I couldn't bear to hurt anyone as kind as you."

"Then I will have to do it myself," said the doctor. And with a small instrument he cut a piece of skin from his own arm, divided it into five pieces, and grafted it onto the raw surface of the little girl's leg. In time her leg healed, and she was able to go home and run about like other children. But she always carried with her the marks of the missionary doctor's great love—five little patches of white skin on her brown leg. Always remember that Christ suffered and was afflicted for *your* salvation. And His body bears the scars.

JEREMIAH 9

"I am the Lord, exercising lovingkindness, judgment, and righteousness in the earth. For in these I delight," says the Lord. Jeremiah 9:24.

July 15

Jeremiah was called to be a mouthpiece for God in the most difficult time in the history of Judah. Again and again other prophets had been sent to warn the people of their sins, but they hardened their hearts. Jeremiah, a young man when God called him (maybe 19 or 20 years old), was called just at the time the people of Judah were to be taken away captive for their many years of rebellion. How earnestly he pictures God exercising "lovingkindness, judgment, and righteousness." Yet in spite of it all, when it is too late he hears them cry, "The harvest is past, the summer is ended, and we are not saved" (Jeremiah 8:20). No wonder his heart was crushed with sadness (verse 18).

I also know how it feels to hear people crying, "Too late! Too late!" During the early months of World War II five of us missionaries were fleeing to the border of India in two cars. As we left the town of Pakokku, Pastor Christensen waved us to a stop at the side of the road. We pulled up behind him and went to see what was the trouble. We found him talking with a well-to-do Indian woman and her family. She was saying, "Oh, Pastor, this is the way you said the end of the world would be. No one can tell whether he will live to see another day. Won't you take me to the river and baptize me now? Then I would feel that all is well with my soul."

And I heard Pastor Christensen say, "It's too late now, dear lady. It's too late now. Can't you remember? Six weeks ago I was kneeling in your home with you and your children, pleading that the Spirit of God would help you make your decision then. You had been coming to the meetings. You knew our message is right, but you wanted to wait for others to take their stand. Now we are fleeing for our lives. We will pray that God will bring you safely into India, so that we can study and get ready for baptism then."

And I saw that well-to-do Indian woman sink to the ground and cover her face with her sari, as she sobbed, "Too late! Why didn't I get baptized six weeks ago? Now it's too late." It is impossible to forget things like that. Is God's Spirit speaking to your heart now? Do you hear Him warning you of some sin or pleading for you to make some important decision? Do it now. Someday the harvest will be past and the summer ended. It will be too late.

The way of man is not in himself; it is not in man who walks to direct his own steps.
Jeremiah 10:23.

July 16

How much we human beings need directing! The best time to ask God for direction is at the beginning of the day, and the best place is at the family altar. Satan knows this, and he does his best to crowd out time for family worship. "The family that prays together stays together" is a true saying. What happens to the families that don't pray together is told in verse 25.

Fifteen-year-old Albert lived in a small Newfoundland settlement overlooking the vast Atlantic Ocean. One fine morning he readied his rowboat for a day of fishing some distance away. The fish were really biting, and for some hours he kept busy pulling in the codfish and stowing them in the stern of his boat. Then, glancing to windward, he noticed a bank of fog coming his way, and in minutes he was completely enveloped. He could barely see the prow of his boat, and all directions looked the same. He was alone on the great ocean, and it was frightening!

He felt for his compass, but it was not in his pocket! He'd forgotten to bring it! "Don't forget your compass," his mother always said. "A body has no business out on the sea without a compass." Of course, he *intended* to bring it. But this time intentions were not enough. He was alone, without his compass, just when he needed it most. He dropped anchor. There was nothing to do but sit it out, hoping that no storm would spring up before the fog lifted. It might be two hours; it might be 10 or longer. How he needed a guide to point him homeward *now*. He knew that his mother would see the fog and be praying. Albert prayed too. He had plenty of time to pray. He prayed again. Then—could it be true? He could see the prow of his boat! The fog was lifting! Soon he could see the coastline, and it was still day. He rowed and rowed, and made it safe and sound before night. Do I need to say that he never forgot his compass again? The *first* thing he thought of when starting on a fishing trip was his compass. And *before* pushing off from the jetty he checked again to make sure it was safely in his pocket.

Good intentions are not enough. Make sure you commit your way unto the Lord and get your directions from Him every morning. It may be dangerous to put off your decision until tomorrow.

JEREMIAH 24

I will give them a heart to know Me, that I am the Lord; and they shall be My people, and I will be their God. Jeremiah 24:7.

July **17**

In the reading for today the Lord gave Jeremiah a vision of two baskets. One was filled with good figs; the other was filled with bad figs. In this way the Lord assured Jeremiah that not all the people of Judah were bad, and He promised to give them a heart to know God, and to bring them back into their own land again. This is what we all need—a heart to know God.

James and Ellen White always had a great interest in boys and girls. They believed that kids, as well as adults, needed to be saved. Once they were holding meetings at Monterey, Michigan, and a number of boys and girls were at the meeting. Elder and Mrs. White both knew that in the Christian life everyone has fears to overcome. So when Elder White made the call, he invited those juniors who wanted to be Christians, and who desired the prayers of God's people, to come and sit in the front seats. This was not easy for many of them to do. But Elder White knew that their overcoming one fear would help them overcome other fears, and he also knew that God could give them a heart to know Him and obey Him.

One by one the juniors went forward until nearly all in the Sabbath school were sitting on the front seats. Later Elder White talked with the juniors about baptism, and in a few days arrangements were made to hold a baptism in a nearby stream. Now, among the 10 girls who were to be baptized first was one very timid girl. She had been afraid of water all her life. She couldn't even watch her friends being baptized, but stood there with her face turned away. Mrs. White spoke to her and tried to encourage her to follow the example of her Savior. Then Elder White came over and stood beside her. He prayed that God would take away her fear of the water. "In the name of the Lord, move forward," encouraged Elder White. And the girl calmly entered the water and was baptized. The next morning that girl was the happiest girl you can imagine. "I'm so happy you didn't leave me alone just because I was afraid," she said. Soon after this five junior boys were baptized, and they were the happiest juniors in Monterey.

Has God given you a heart to know Him? Pray for it, and He will surely give you one, and He will cast out all your timidity, too.

Now therefore, amend your ways and your doings, and obey the voice of the Lord your God.
Jeremiah 26:13.

July 18

The priests and the false prophets didn't like Jeremiah's preaching. They hated being called sinners, and they didn't like that he prophesied that Jerusalem would be destroyed. So they arrested him and decided to kill him (Jeremiah 26:8, 11). But even in the court Jeremiah lifted up his voice, and called them to repentance. That there are sinners among God's people is sad but true.

On one occasion Elder and Mrs. White were holding some meetings in the little church at Washington, New Hampshire. Again they made a special appeal to the juniors and young people. There was one young man there who didn't respond. The real reason was that he knew his father chewed tobacco, even though he was the church choir leader. The father had managed to keep this habit a secret from the church people, but as the boy worked with his father he knew very well what made those brown spots on the snow where his father spat. At the Sabbath morning service Mrs. White was appealing to church members to mend their ways and obey the voice of the Lord. "Oh," said the young man to himself, "I wish she would speak to my father and tell him about his sin. I am sure no one has told her."

Just then Mrs. White turned to the boy's father and said in effect, "Brother, I was shown your case. You are a slave of tobacco." Then she went on to describe how he had tried to hide his sin.

The face of the young man lit up. "Only an angel could have told her that," he said to himself. "Indeed, this message is from God!" God was with them. Many of the older ones confessed their sins, and 13 young people took their stand for Christ. To show you how earnest they were about it, they wanted to be baptized right then—in the middle of winter. The river was frozen. They had to cut through two feet of ice to get to the water. The temperature was minus 10° F, but 12 of those young people were baptized and suffered no ill effects. Most of them became workers in God's cause.

As God looks at you does He see some secret sin that is spoiling *your* Christian life? something nobody knows about but you? Mend your ways and your doings right now. You will then know the joy of obeying the voice of the Lord your God.

JEREMIAH 32

Behold, I am the Lord, the God of all flesh.
Is there anything too hard for Me?
Jeremiah 32:27.

The Lord spoke encouragement to Jeremiah when the future seemed discouraging and altogether impossible. It was hard for the people to see how God could permit them to be carried into captivity, then bring them back again into their land to dwell safely. But it was not too hard for God to do, and we know that He did it.

Ever since the world began God has been doing that which seemed impossible to human beings. Also, throughout the history of the Advent movement God has continually done the "impossible." When Ellen Harmon was just a young woman, before she married James White, one night God gave her a vision in which she was shown that she must go to Portsmouth, New Hampshire, and bear her testimony there.

It was hard for a young woman to have to stand before older people and point out their weaknesses and shortcomings, but Ellen did not hesitate. She had no money to pay her fare on the train, but she believed that God had told her to go and that He would open up the way somehow. So she and her sister got ready. Their home was not far from the railway station. They heard the first bell ring, giving the passengers only 15 minutes to board the train. Ellen put on her hat and walked to her window. Just then a man drove up to their house in a great hurry. As he ran to the house he called out, "Is there anyone here who needs money? I was impressed that someone here needed money." Ellen and her sister explained that they had to go to Portsmouth, but didn't have the money for the fare. "I have come 12 miles to bring you this money. I could not hold my horse back. He seemed driven to go faster and faster." The man put enough for two round-trip tickets in their hands. "Here, jump into my wagon, and I'll take you to the station." They arrived just in time to board the train and find seats before the train started! Impossible? No! Not for God.

Someday God will impress *you* to go to an Adventist academy and perhaps later to college. You may have no money, but don't sit down and say it can't be done. Get your hat on and go to the window, for God opens the windows of heaven for those who make Him first in their life. Nothing is ever too hard for Him.

The Lord is merciful and gracious, slow
to anger, and abounding in mercy.
Psalm 103:8.

July 20

The Lord had been very long-suffering with the people of Judah, but at last their punishment had to come. In today's Scripture reading we learn of the fall of Jerusalem, the burning of the Temple, the capture of King Zedekiah, and the taking of the last group of the children of Judah into captivity. In order to be really happy, we all have to learn to make God first, and to make obedience to God the most important thing in our life. To measure our obedience, God gives us home rules and school rules.

It was wintertime at one of our colleges. The little lake nearby was frozen over, and the students were looking forward to the time that the ice would be thick enough for skating. Finally one Saturday evening the principal announced, "All students who wish to skate please meet at the gymnasium. We will go down to the lake as a group, and when the whistle blows we shall return as a group. Flares have been placed at the limits of the safe ice—beyond the flares the ice is not safe. Do not go beyond the flares. Your skating privileges in the future depend upon your observing this rule."

When they gathered in the gym, the dean of men again gave the warning: "Do not go beyond the flares. It's not safe."

For two hours 120 or more young people had a wonderfully happy time skating in the moonlight. Then a shrill call of "Help! Help! Help!" sent a chill to every heart. Two of the teachers hurried in the direction of the cry and quickly rescued a young woman who had broken through the ice just beyond the flares. It took longer to reach and recover the young man who'd been with her. And in spite of efforts to revive him, the doctor at last pronounced him dead.

Just then one of the girls called, "I can't find my roommate!" They telephoned the boys' dorm to see whether the roommate's skating partner was there; but no, he too was missing. It took the rescuers 45 minutes to find their bodies. They worked and worked to restore them to consciousness, but it was hopeless. Three lives were lost because of carelessness. Careful obedience of safety guidelines can truly save your life.

How do you measure up? Do you cheerfully obey?

DANIEL 1

Daniel purposed in his heart that he would not defile
himself with the portion of the king's delicacies,
nor with the wine which he drank.
Daniel 1:8.

Daniel stands out as one of the greatest examples given us in Bible history. Only 18 years old when taken captive, he was filled, nevertheless, with a holy determination to be a vegetarian and to abstain from strong drink. His three companions did like-wise, and after a 10-day test they were "better" and "fatter" than the other young people who ate and drank from the king's table. They were also "10 times better" mentally than the king's wise men!

This kind of record has been achieved by Seventh-day Adventist youth many times in many countries. I'm thinking of Calvin Hansen. I had the pleasure of meeting him in Colorado. At the time he was a 25-year-old Seventh-day Adventist—a vegetarian, a nonsmoker, and a nondrinker. For three years running he had carried off the championship of the annual Pike's Peak race. In 1959 his record was 26 miles up and back in four hours and 15 minutes. Well, on September 7, 1961, Cal was one of 16 runners who entered the Mount Whitney, California, race. The summit of Whitney is 14,505 feet, and the course up and down was a rugged 21 miles. Of the 16, Cal was the only Seventh-day Adventist, but there were two other vegetarians—Katherine Heard, 59 years old, and Leslie Milson, a 34-year-old carpenter. There also were two boys, ages 12 and 13. The rest were experienced athletes but not vegetarians. Only two of them smoked. Cigarette smokers don't usually specialize in races of this kind. Well, I hardly need to finish the story. You've guessed already. Cal Hansen came in first, covering the entire 21 miles in four hours, nine minutes, and 22 and a half seconds. And Les Milson came in second! Many of the ones who ate meat had cramps in their leg muscles, but the vegetarians had none. Coach Rudy Fahl says that meat leaves poisons in the system and causes muscles to ache. He also warns against smoking and the use of alcoholic beverages, white sugar, and white flour products. This instruction also sounds familiar to Adventists, doesn't it?

Have you heard the song "Dare to Be a Daniel"? I hope that you will sing it, but that you'll do even more than that. Imitate Daniel, and you too can be stronger and healthier, and 10 times better than the king's wise men.

DANIEL 2

In the days of these kings the God of heaven will set up a kingdom which shall never be destroyed. Daniel 2:44.

July 22

The promise of the kingdom Jesus would establish has been the hope of prophets, apostles, and all the faithful for centuries. Today is the birthday of one of the founders of the modern Advent message—John Nevins Andrews. He was born July 22, 1829, in the little town of Poland, Maine. In the early days of 1844, when the Adventists believed and preached that Christ was coming in October of that year, John Andrews was only a lad, 14 years of age. One day he accompanied a Mr. Davis, who was going to hold a meeting somewhere in Maine.

Of course, it sometimes happens that people will ridicule and mock anyone who is religious, and a mob of angry men gathered at this meeting place, determined to stop the preaching. When jeers and shouts could not make Mr. Davis stop preaching, one man rushed forward with a big black snake whip to beat him. Now, young John Andrews was of a timid, retiring nature, but he wasn't going to let his friend suffer alone. John jumped in front of Mr. Davis and said to the man with the whip, "You know it says in the Bible we are to bear one another's burdens. If you whip Mr. Davis, you will have to whip me too."

The man with the whip was taken aback with this little speech. He hesitated a moment, then said, "Well, it would be too bad to beat a little boy." Then the man turned and went away—and the mob followed!

When John was 17 years old, he accepted the Sabbath truth. When he was 20 years old, he joined Captain Joseph Bates and James White in preaching the Sabbath and the second coming of Christ. He became a mighty preacher. And when John was only 23 years old, by his preaching J. N. Loughborough was converted to the Sabbath truth. John Nevins Andrews was the General Conference president from 1867 to 1869, and in 1874 he became our first missionary to Europe. He was mighty in the knowledge of the Scriptures, and he could repeat the entire New Testament by heart! What a man of God he was! But once he was only a junior who simply loved the Lord with all his heart.

Maybe God has a mighty work for you to do too.

DANIEL 3

*Our God whom we serve is able to deliver us from the burning
fiery furnace, and He will deliver us from your hand, O king.
Daniel 3:17.*

July 23

When it has pleased God to do so, He has made people, houses, villages, churches, books, and even boats fireproof. Here is a story from the Solomon Islands during the terrible days of World War II, about a boat that would not burn. The Australian missionaries in the Solomon Islands had all been ordered home, and the British government had taken over our three mission launches, the *Dadavata*, the *Portal*, and the *G. F. Jones*. The Japanese were coming nearer and nearer, determined to use the islands as a stepping-stone toward their attack on Australia. The British officer in charge had been successful in cutting off the enemy scouting patrols, but he knew the day would come when he would have to retreat before superior gunboats. One day a runner brought the news that a large fleet of enemy boats was coming, and it was time for the officer to go. There was nothing else he could do, so the officer gave the order to start the engines of the three launches and get ready to go. The engines of the *Dadavata* and the *G. F. Jones* started easily enough, but the engine of the *Portal* simply refused to turn over. They tried and tried, but it was no use, and rather than let the launch fall into enemy hands, the officer reluctantly gave the order to burn it. Two five-gallon cans of gasoline were poured over it. The officer himself lit a bundle of waste and threw it into the cabin of the launch. Immediately there was a roar, as a sheet of flame leaped as high as the masthead. Satisfied that the flames would do their work, the officer left with the other two launches. As our Seventh-day Adventist Solomon Islanders saw the flames leaping high, they fell on their knees and prayed, "O God, *Portal*, 'e boat belong God. Don't let 'im burn."

And as if in immediate response to their prayer, the flames died down and went out. Convinced that God was keeping the boat for His work, they swam out and poled and dragged the *Portal* into the mouth of a little creek and hid it among the mangroves. Hardly had they done so when 14 enemy gunboats went by. Our men worked all night and took the engine to pieces. They distributed the parts among the people for safekeeping, and covered the *Portal* with palm trees and branches till no one would know a boat was there.

Perhaps someday God will put out some destructive fire for you.

In order that the living may know that the Most High rules in the kingdom of men [and] gives it to whomever He will. Daniel 4:17.

July 24

God worked miracle after miracle for Nebuchadnezzar, and there was no possible doubt about who was in charge of the affairs of the people.

Even so, in the affairs of nations today God is permitting and directing toward His own plans. In the battle of the Solomon Islands the enemy came and hindered the work of God for a time, but then the tide turned and the enemy was driven out. One day in May 1945 the American forces landed on one of the Solomon Islands and brought with them Pastor Norman Ferris, who had been a missionary to those islands for more than 20 years. When the Solomon Islanders saw him, there was great shouting and jubilation. In just a little while he saw a group run to the beach and launch a big canoe.

"Where are you going?" he asked.

"We go catch 'im *Portal,*" they said.

"But the *Portal* has been burned. The government has informed us," said Pastor Ferris.

"Government, 'e no know. *Portal,* 'e boat belong God. 'Im, 'e no burn. We get," the men said. And in a day or two there was the *Portal,* tied up to the jetty. The rigging and the awnings were burned, but the body of the ship was all right. Pastor Ferris was delighted. He jumped on board and went to the engine room. Then despair! Every removable part of the engine was gone!

"What can we do without an engine?" he asked.

But the men smiled and said, "Engine, 'e all right. We get 'im." And with their drums they sent out word for the people to bring back the parts of the engine. And for the next three weeks the parts came in. Some had buried their pieces for safekeeping. Some had worn them around their necks. But when they knew Pastor Ferris was back, in came all the bits and pieces. Not so much as a half-inch screw was missing! The parts were cleaned and put together. New rigging and awnings were put in place. The *Portal* was painted and refueled, and stores were put aboard. Then the men pulled with all their might on the starting rope. The engine started, and the *Portal* was put to sea! A miracle? Yes, not only on the boat but also upon the hearts and lives of our dear believers there. Who can doubt that the living God directed in the affairs of those men?

Keep close to God. Make Him first in your life.

DANIEL 5

I have heard of you, that the Spirit of God is in you, and that light and understanding and excellent wisdom are found in you.
Daniel 5:14.

July 25

When people talk well about someone, they build up that person's reputation by what they say. What a wonderful reputation Daniel had! Belshazzar heard that Daniel was wise, and that the Spirit of God was with him, to give him understanding of mysterious dreams and writing. Well, today people are talking about Adventists. Do you know what reputation Seventh-day Adventists have? One thing is that they are healthier and live longer than much of the population. Recently research showed that their good health habits, including not eating meat; their keeping the Sabbath, a weekly day of rest; and their strong faith in God are all the reasons. That's a pretty good reputation to have.

A man named Mr. James and his family moved next door to a Mr. Chinnock. A while later a neighbor asked Mr. Chinnock, "Do you know anything about the family who moved next door to you?"

"Why, yes," he said. "I know them well. They go to the same church I do."

"Oh, so he's a Seventh-day Adventist," said the neighbor with a smile. "Well, that's good. Now I won't have to lock my chicken house at night."

Elder Henry Brown told of a bus company in a certain town in Europe that was having trouble with its conductors stealing the passenger fares they collected. One of the directors said, "I'll tell you what you need. If you could get Seventh-day Adventist conductors, you'd have no more trouble with stealing. But you must give them Saturdays off. They'd rather lose their job than work on their Sabbath."

"What church do you belong to?" asked a nurse of a man who had a badly broken leg.

"I'm a Seventh-day Adventist," he said.

"That explains it," said the nurse. "I understand now why you don't curse and swear even though you're in pain."

"You know, I like it here," said a patient in an Adventist hospital. "I like the way they do things. In fact, if it weren't for their religion, I could be an Adventist myself."

"You'll find it's their religion that makes them that way," her friend answered.

What do people say about you? What is your reputation?

My God sent His angel and shut the lions'
mouths, so that they have not hurt me.
Daniel 6:22.

July 26

Many stories are told of how angels have protected those who put their trust in God. Here is one from the African country of Tanzania.

Joy Buckle was a lovely junior Christian girl. Her father was the manager of a large cattle ranch 60 miles from the town of Arusha. Mr. Buckle was a strong, fearless man who often had to take his flashlight and gun to drive lions away from the cattle at night. He often told Joy exciting stories of his experiences with lions, and he always added, "Joy, if you ever meet a dangerous animal in the wild, never show fear. Just remain calm." Now, that sounds easy when you're with someone who has a gun. But—

Well, one day Joy went to Arusha to see some friends, and after a lovely visit they started back to her home in their car. It had been raining heavily, but the road was well paved, and all went well until they came to the four-mile dirt road that ran from the highway to the ranch. They'd gone only a little way when the car got stuck in the mud. "Never mind," said Joy. "I can easily walk from here. You go back home. I'll be all right." With great difficulty the car was turned around, and off it went, leaving Joy alone—but not really alone. Her angel must have been with her. As it was raining, she wrapped her sweater around her head to keep it dry, and began singing to keep herself company. Suddenly, only a few hundred yards down the road, she saw a huge male lion. His tail twitched back and forth like a tomcat getting ready to pounce upon a mouse. "That looks like a very hungry lion," said Joy to herself. Then her father's words came to her mind: *Never show fear. Just be calm.* She wanted to scream, but that would do no good. She wanted to run, but the lion could run much faster. She could only pray and keep on walking. Her prayer brought courage to her heart, and her father's words came again and again to her mind. Straight toward the lion she went. When he saw her coming, he slunk off into the long grass at the roadside. Joy did not look to see where he had gone, but with her heart pounding and her knees trembling, she kept walking. Once home, all she could say was "Mother, kneel down with me and thank Jesus for saving me from the lion." Just a week later a man was taken from his garden nearby and killed by a lion, perhaps the same lion that Joy had met on the road.

Is your angel near you every minute? Better make sure. Satan's "lions" are everywhere, seeking whom they may devour.

DANIEL 7

I watched till thrones were put in place, and the Ancient of Days was seated. . . . The court was seated, and the books were opened. Daniel 7:9, 10.

July 27

If only we could always remember that angels are making a record of all we do and say, and that in the judgment the books will be opened, I think we would always stay close to Jesus and choose what is right.

Jack, a seventh grader, was always in trouble. The teacher tried everything, but nothing made any difference. One day Jack was in the principal's office *again*, and the man just didn't know what to do. At last he gave Jack a sheet of paper and told him to write down all the bad things he'd done that school year. After five minutes the paper was nearly full. "Is that all you can remember?" asked the principal. "There are more!" Taking out his record book, he said, "Look at that, and that, and that. Now copy all you have missed." With a sigh, Jack wrote and wrote, and finally the list was complete. "Now make another copy, and after each bad deed, explain why you did it," the principal said. By the time it was finished, Jack was tired and hungry, and wanted to go home. "Now," the principal said, "make an exact copy to take to your mother."

"Oh, please, don't let my mom know anything about this," Jack said.

"Why not?"

"Because I don't want her to know . . . how I am in school."

The principal thought for a while, then said, "I'll tell you what I will do. Do you think you could be the kind of son your mother thinks you are?"

"I'll try, sir," he said.

"Then I'll put this record in an envelope and put it in my safe. If you are not sent to me any more this year, I will burn it. But if you are, then you will have to copy it, and we'll send it to your mother. Is that fair?"

"Oh, yes, sir. And I will try." And he did try. In fact, he found he had much more fun being good, and he became a loyal friend to his teacher and principal. Thank God that He has given us a way by which the records of our sins can be forgiven. Keep your record clean in heaven. Then when the books are opened, you need not fear.

*While I was speaking in prayer, the man Gabriel . . .
reached me. . . . And he . . . said, "O Daniel, I have
now come forth to give you skill to understand. . . .
For you are greatly beloved."
Daniel 9:21-23.*

July 28

By studying Daniel 8 and 9, the early Adventists were led to believe that Jesus would return to earth on October 22, 1844. They thought the sanctuary that was to be cleansed was this earth, and great was their disappointment when October 22 passed and Jesus had not come. In Port Gibson, New York, a little town on the Erie Canal, there lived an Adventist by the name of Hiram Edson. The little company of Adventists there looked to him as their leader. They were together on the day of disappointment, and there was great weeping when the next day dawned and they were still on earth. "Have the Scriptures failed?" they asked. "Is there no reward for the saints? Is there to be no judgment day?"

"Not so," said Edson. "There is a God in heaven. He has not failed. Some time soon the mystery will be solved, and this dark secret shall be made as plain as day. Let's go out to the barn and pray." So they did, and soon they felt the assurance that God still loved them, that their prayers were heard, and that soon they'd understand. After breakfast Edson said to one of the men, "Let's go and comfort the others with the assurance we have received." So they started off, taking a shortcut across a field where Edson's corn still stood in the shocks. About halfway across the field Hiram Edson was stopped, as if someone had put his hand upon his shoulder. As he turned and looked up at the gray skies there flashed upon his understanding the meaning of the sanctuary in heaven. He realized that Christ, our high priest, represented us in the heavenly sanctuary and that He then would begin His intercession for us in the Most Holy Place. This was the event that was to take place in 1844, and Jesus' coming would be later.

"Brother Edson, what are you stopping for?" called his companion.

"The Lord is answering our morning prayer," said Edson. As they walked and talked it over, it became clearer and clearer. God had given them a new light, and with this new understanding the Adventist believers were lifted out of their disappointment and comforted.

If ever you are heavyhearted and disappointed, lift your heart to God. He will send light somehow and make things plain for you.

DANIEL 12

Your people shall be delivered, every one who is found written in the book. . . . Those who are wise shall shine . . . like the stars forever and ever.
Daniel 12:1-3.

Long, long ago, according to an old parable, there was an ancient king who ruled over an ancient kingdom. One day, wishing to honor the most worthy citizen in his realm, he sent his ministers of state throughout his land to search for the people who had accomplished the most for the kingdom. Then he set a day when each would appear before him, at which time he would choose the one he thought most worthy of them all. At last the day came. The plaza was crowded with important people, and the king sat upon his throne.

The first minister approached the throne and presented a great lawyer, a man by whose skill good laws had been made, and liberty and justice given to all. And the crowd shouted and applauded, for he was a very worthy citizen. The next minister presented a great financier, and told how he had brought security to the trade of the kingdom. Again the crowd applauded their approval. The third minister bowed and presented a great doctor, whose skill had conquered disease and saved the lives of thousands. Again the crowd clapped and shouted. Then the fourth minister approached the throne, a little old woman on his arm. Her hair was white. Her back was bent. Her clothes were old and shabby. The king was shocked and visibly annoyed.

"Who is this woman?" he demanded, "and what right has she to be classed with these illustrious men?"

"O King," said the minister, "when these great men were just little boys this woman was their teacher." Nobody clapped or made a sound. There was a moment of deep silence. Then the king stood up, walked down from his throne, and with tears in his eyes he placed the wreath of honor around the woman's neck. She was indeed the most worthy citizen in his kingdom.

Many of our great leaders and workers in God's cause owe their success to the skill, the patience, and the understanding of the teachers they had when they were children—their schoolteachers and their Sabbath school teachers. Plan to be a teacher someday—in a classroom or in Sabbath school. God is going to honor teachers in a special way, and they "shall shine . . . like the stars forever and ever."

I will heal their backsliding, I will love them freely, for My anger has turned away from him.
Hosea 14:4.

July 30

Hosea lived in the darkest period of the kingdom of Israel. It is probable that the book of Hosea was written just before the nation was taken captive by Assyria. It is full of pleading for Israel to turn from their idols and to repent. It also contains many precious promises and assurances that God would forgive them and receive them. Forgiveness for those who have rebelled and been enemies is one of the most beautiful things in the world.

During the Revolutionary War there lived in Pennsylvania a faithful gospel minister by the name of Peter Miller. There was a man living nearby who was very bitter toward Mr. Miller. He openly abused him and also his followers. As time went on, Miller's enemy got into trouble with the government. He was arrested, found guilty of treason, and sentenced to death. As soon as Miller heard of his sentence, he set out on foot and went to General Washington to beg for the man's life.

"I am sorry," Washington said, "but your prayer for your friend's life cannot be granted."

"My friend?" said Miller. "He is not my friend. I have not a worse enemy living than that man!"

"What?" said Washington. "Do you mean to tell me that you have walked 60 miles to try to save the life of your enemy? That puts the matter in a different light. I will grant the pardon." As soon as the pardon was made out, Peter Miller set off at once for the town, 15 miles away, where the execution was to take place. He got there just as the man was being led to the gallows. When he saw Miller coming, he said, "Here comes Peter Miller! He has come all the way from Ephrata to have his revenge by seeing me hanged today."

But Peter Miller rushed forward and thrust the pardon into the executioner's hand. "Stay! Stay!" he cried. "I have a pardon from General Washington!" The life of his worst enemy was not only spared; it was altogether changed by this manifestation of Christian love.

That's the kind of love God has for every one of us. Whenever you slip and make mistakes, repent and confess quickly. God will forgive your backslidings and always love you, too.

JOEL 2

Blow the trumpet in Zion; sanctify a fast; call a solemn assembly;
gather the people. Sanctify the congregation; assemble the
elders; gather the children, even nursing infants.
Joel 2:15, 16, RSV.

July 31

Joel prophesied of the last days, and in this verse I think he has given us the blueprint for attendance at the 11:00 church service—elders, children, and infants, or, as we would say, families sitting together to worship God in church. We have Sabbath school, where we study the lesson in age groups. We have special children's meetings at camp meeting and at summer camps. But for the regular, every-week worship, I believe that God wants us to worship Him sitting together in families. God said to Abraham, "In you all the families of the earth shall be blessed" (Genesis 12:3). To Jeremiah, God said He would "be the God of all the families of Israel" (Jeremiah 31:1). One of the most beautiful things I have seen is a family sitting together when I get up to preach in a church.

When William Cady was a 10-year-old, he went with his mother and younger brother and sister to spend a summer at his uncle John's farm. He saw many wonderful things, but the most wonderful was a big bottle with a perfect apple inside. The apple was bigger than the neck of the bottle, and yet the apple wasn't bruised. "Aunt Sarah," he said, "how did the apple get into the bottle?"

"That's Uncle John's secret," she said. "Ask him."

He asked Uncle John, but all he would say was "Keep your eyes open, Willie, and see if you can find out." The next summer Willie came back, and still kept looking everywhere to see whether he could find out how Uncle John got the apple into the bottle. Then one day he saw something shining up in an apple tree. He looked closer, and saw a tiny apple on a narrow twig poked inside a bottle. "I know Uncle's secret! I know Uncle's secret!" shouted Willie as he raced back to Uncle John. "You put the apple in the bottle when it was little, and then it just grew inside the bottle."

And his uncle said, "You're right, Willie. That's exactly how it was. The baby apple is already in the bottle—and it keeps on growing there."

I hope you sit with your family during church service, for I've noticed that kids who sit in church with their parents grow up in the church and stay in the church.

215

"Behold, the days are coming," says the Lord God,
"that I will send a famine on the land, not a
famine of bread, nor a thirst for water,
but of hearing the words of the Lord."
Amos 8:11.

August 1

Not one of us can fully realize what a priceless treasure we have in the Bible—the Word of God. David likened it to a lamp and a light (Psalm 119:105) that would show us the way to eternal life. Paul likened it to a sword that would protect us from the temptations of the evil one (Ephesians 6:17), and Moses likened it to bread that would give life to those who read it (Deuteronomy 8:3). What else do we need to take us safely into heaven? This priceless treasure is ours, yet we read it so little!

A story is told about a wealthy woman who lived in New York. Her husband gave her a beautiful brooch set with pearls for which he had paid $30,000! It was her pride and joy, but one day while visiting friends in Detroit she lost it. Frantically she advertised for it, offering a liberal reward for its recovery. She called on the police to help her. They made a check of all the pawnshops where secondhand jewelry is often sold, but all to no avail. The brooch was lost. Now, in Detroit lived a poor woman who earned a living for herself and her daughter by washing clothes. One day as she walked along the street she saw a brooch on the curb. She picked it up, but she had no idea of its value. It was just a pretty pin to her, and she used it to pin her collar together. She didn't read the papers, so knew nothing of the lost brooch or the reward offered for its recovery. Six years went by. This woman still wore the pretty brooch at her collar, though one of the beautiful stones had dropped out and become lost.

It happened that her daughter was graduating from high school. She decided she would get another little stone put in the brooch, then give it to her daughter for a graduation present. She took it to a jeweler and asked how much it would cost. The jeweler looked at the brooch carefully, then said, "Yes, madam, we can match that pearl for $2,000!"

The woman's eyes bugged out as she gasped, "And to think that for six years I've been wearing a fortune on my collar and didn't know it!"

In life's journey you will need a light, a sword, and bread. Before the famine comes, make this priceless treasure yours, now.

OBADIAH

As you have done, it shall be done to you;
your reprisal shall return upon your own head.
Obadiah 15.

August 2

The Edomites, descendants of Esau, were always bitter and cruel toward the descendants of Jacob. They wouldn't let the Israelites pass through their land on their way into Canaan. They joined enemies of the Jews who went to war against them. And they rejoiced when Nebuchadnezzar destroyed Jerusalem. Obadiah prophesied that their cruelty would return upon their own heads. And it did.

Young Davie's back was narrow and hunched. To others, he looked pitiful—his legs were too thin, his arms were too long, and his back was crooked. But there was nothing wrong with his mind, and he was very strong for his size. But the first day he went to school Tom began tormenting him. "Hey, what have we here? Ha, ha, ha! He looks like a spider!" And I'm sorry to say that many of the other boys joined in laughing with Tom.

Poor Davie ran away from his tormentors. He couldn't help the way he looked. After a while the teasing stopped, but Davie was left out of his classmates' games, and he was lonely. The second week in school Tom began bragging about how well he could climb. Bullies always brag. "Come and I'll show you," he shouted as he ran to a big oak tree. And he could climb! Up, up he went. "Tom, you'd better come down," someone called. "You'll fall."

"Oh, no, I won't! Watch me!" he said, slowly edging toward the leafy end of the limb.

"Come down! It'll break," a girl shouted.

"No, it won't," Tom laughed. But suddenly the bough bent, and Tom felt himself slipping. "Help! I'm going to fall," he shouted.

There was a dreadful silence—then Davie rushed forward. "Hold on!" he cried. "I'm coming." Davie pulled his small, crooked body from limb to limb. He could climb too! And how! Reaching the branch where Tom swayed helplessly, he said, "Don't look down!" Then he stretched his arm and caught Tom's collar and pulled and tugged. Inch by inch, with Davie's help, they were soon both on the ground.

"I'm sorry I treated you so shabbily," said Tom, but no one could hear him, for they were cheering wildly for Davie. If you are ever tempted to bully someone or to pick on someone—think first. Remember, as you do, "it shall be done to you."

JONAH 1; 2

"Arise, go to Nineveh." . . . But Jonah arose to flee to Tarshish from the presence of the Lord.
Jonah 1:2, 3.

August 3

Throughout the years people who have chosen not to believe in God or the Bible have delighted to ridicule the story of Jonah and the big fish.

But to the one who believes in God and in His Word there is nothing impossible about His making a "big fish" large enough for the purpose of preserving Jonah inside it until it got back to the seacoast again. Indeed, here is an extraordinary story printed in the April 4, 1896, *Literary Digest* that shows it is possible for a man to be swallowed by an ordinary whale and still live. In February 1891 the whaling ship *Star of the East* launched two small boats with men and harpoons to go after a huge whale not far from the ship. The men successfully harpooned the whale and captured it, but as it struggled, one of the small boats was struck by the whale's powerful tail and was shattered to pieces. The men in the boat were thrown into the ocean.

Eventually all but two were rescued by the men in the other small boat, and later the body of one of the two lost men was found. But the other man, James Bartley, could not be found anywhere. It took a day and a half to get the huge whale onto the deck of the large boat, where they began to cut it up for processing. And when they cut open the huge stomach, they found James Bartley, unconscious but still alive! For several days he was delirious, and it was three weeks before he recovered his reason and could tell about his terrible experience. But he lived for many years afterward. The only noticeable effect on him was that his skin was tanned by the action of the whale's gastric juices.

The book *Jonah and the Whale,* by Charles G. Bellah, tells of other occasions of men, huge fish, and even of a horse being found in a whale's stomach. So even if I didn't believe the Bible—which I do—I'd have no trouble in believing that a huge fish swallowed Jonah. I even believe that Jonah himself wrote the story of his experience, and that he wrote it for you and me, so that we might know it is no use trying to run away from God or from duty.

JONAH 3; 4

"Arise, go to Nineveh." . . . So Jonah arose and
went to Nineveh, according to the word of the Lord.
Jonah 3:2, 3.

August **4**

En-meg-ah-bowh was a young Indian from eastern Canada who went with some early missionaries to open up work among the Chippewa Indians in northern Minnesota. He married a Chippewa maiden, and promised her people that he would remain with them. But the work was very discour-aging, and eventually he grew so disheartened that he decided to go back to his previous work on the Straits of Mackinac. "Will you go with me?" he asked his wife.

"I am ready to go with you and die with you," she said. So they got passage on a sailing ship from Duluth, and the captain promised that if all went well they would arrive in Sault Ste. Marie in three days. But all did not go well. A few hours after leaving they ran into a dead calm, and at 5:00 a terrible storm hit their ship with wind blowing on them from the wrong direction. The captain was worried. "In 20 years," he said, "I have never seen anything like this. I am afraid there is something wrong with us." En-meg-ah-bowh's face went pale. He felt that he knew what was wrong. He knew that he was fleeing to "Tarshish." Nothing could be done, so the captain had to turn around, and with great difficulty the ship got back to Duluth.

"I believe that *we* are the cause of the storm," En-meg-ah-bowh's wife said to him.

"I fully agree," he replied.

"But will you try to go again?"

"Yes," he said.

"Then I shall follow," she said softly.

The next morning at 2:00 the wind was right once more, and the ship set sail, but about the same time and at the same place they ran into another dead calm followed by an even worse storm. The thunder and lightning and waves were terrifying. The captain threw part of the cargo overboard to try to face the storm, but it was no use. He had to turn the ship around.

"Now what will you do?" asked En-meg-ah-bowh's wife.

"I will stay in 'Nineveh' and preach the gospel," he said. And he did. He stayed for 40 years among the Chippewas. It's true. You cannot run away from God and be happy. When God gives you some duty to do, do it.

They shall beat their swords into plowshares, and their spears into pruning hooks; nation shall not lift up sword against nation, neither shall they learn war anymore.
Micah 4:3.

August 5

This prophecy is one of several that reveal God's original plan for Israel—the plan that they would become His agency for the salvation of the world, bringing the light of the gospel, and peace and happiness, to all nations. However, literal Israel failed, so the prophecy can be fulfilled only by spiritual Israel—God's chosen people today—and by the setting up of the kingdom of Christ. Nevertheless, there have been many attempts to bring lasting peace to the nations of the world. The Palace of Peace was erected in The Hague, capital of Holland, in 1899, and many peace conferences have been held there. After World War I the League of Nations was organized (January 10, 1920), with 59 nations joining. After World War II the United Nations was organized, with 46 nations signing the charter in 1945. The headquarters of the United Nations is now in New York City, and by 2008, 192 nations were members.

Remember when the dove brought a twig from an olive tree back to Noah in the ark? Noah regarded that as a sign that the wrath of God had passed and that there was peace between God and the world again. Ever since then the dove with an olive branch in its beak has been a symbol of peace. Perhaps the most famous peace monument is *The Christ of the Andes,* erected high up on the border mountains between Chile and Argentina. In 1900 these two countries were quarreling over a rich strip of land that lay between them. They were on the verge of war when they were persuaded to submit their dispute to the king of England. He called together a group of experts, and they wisely recommended that part of the land belong to Chile and the other part belong to Argentina. Both nations cheerfully accepted the decision, bitterness passed away, and good will took its place. Cannonballs were melted and made into a statue of Christ 26 feet high. This was placed on a cement foundation 22 feet high, on which was placed a huge granite hemisphere to represent the world. There, high up on the border mountains, stands this statue today. In the left hand the figure holds a cross, and the right hand is lifted in blessing. A copy of this statue has been erected in the Palace of Peace in The Hague.

Remember that you belong to God's chosen people of the last days. Make sure you are a messenger of peace in your home, in your school, and in your church.

NAHUM 1

The Lord is slow to anger and great in power. . . .
The Lord has His way in the whirlwind and in the storm.
Nahum 1:3.

August 6

Today is the anniversary of the first use of an atomic bomb in war. August 6, 1945, was a tragic day, for 100,000 people lost their lives and almost all the buildings in Hiroshima, Japan, were destroyed by that one bomb. Before the war we had about 90 members in the Hiroshima Seventh-day Adventist Church. Many of them had scattered into the country during the war, but 42 Seventh-day Adventists were in Hiroshima when the bomb hit. Yet not one whose name was on the church books lost his life! Brother S. Morita, a dentist, was the church elder at the time. The military police and the "thought control" police kept a constant watch over him and his activities, finally arresting him and putting him in prison for 14 months. Then, satisfied that he was not connected with a spy ring, they released him. During his imprisonment he spent much time reading the writings of Ellen White, and when he got back home he felt impressed to move out of the city to a small village eight miles away. And he was there when the bomb fell. After the explosion he went into the city as soon as possible, to see if he could be of any assistance to our church members. The destruction and the suffering he saw were indescribable. The houses around his former city home were all destroyed, and everyone in them had been killed. He came to the home of an elderly sister of the church, and to his surprise, it was still standing. He found her house open, and there she was—giving first aid to more than 30 people who had crowded inside! However, the city was on fire, and since the fire was coming that way, they had to vacate. In time Mr. Morita was able to account for all the church members. Though their homes were lost, their lives had been saved. God is indeed great in power, and He can cover His children when storms rage, when bombs burst, and when fire burns.

Give God first place in your heart. You will need Him in the tempests of the last days.

HABAKKUK 3

His brightness was like the light; He had rays flashing from His hand, and there His power was hidden.
Habakkuk 3:4.

August 7

Habakkuk lived and worked in a time of deep apostasy. He prophesied the coming of the Chaldeans, and in Habakkuk 3:3-16 is a description of the Lord coming in judgment and for the deliverance of His people. At that time the hands that were pierced on Calvary will be honored for what they stand for. Perhaps you have seen a copy of the beautiful painting called *Praying Hands*. This is how it came about. When Albrecht Dürer was just a young man he went to study painting under a great artist. There he met a man somewhat older than himself who was also studying painting, and they decided to room together to save expenses. It was a great struggle, however, to get enough odd jobs to support themselves and still study art, so one day the older suggested that it would be better for him to work full-time and support them both. Albrecht could study full-time, and when he could earn a living with his paintings the older man would give his full time to studying art. Reluctantly Albrecht agreed, for he felt that he should be the first to work.

His friend found work in a restaurant, washing dishes and scrubbing floors. The hours were long and the work was hard, but he was happy to think that someday his chance to study would come. At last Albrecht sold his first wood carving. It brought enough money to last them a while. "Now it is your turn to study," he told his friend, "and I will be the breadwinner." Joyfully his friend took up his brushes and went back to study. But the years of hard work had stiffened the muscles and enlarged the joints of his hands. And though he tried hard and long, he knew that his hands had lost their skill, and that he would never be a great artist.

One day Albrecht saw his friend's work-worn hands folded in prayer, and a great inspiration came to him. "I can never give back to those hands the skill they have lost," he said to himself, "but I can paint them, and show to the world the gratitude and love I have for his noble deed." And he did.

When you see that painting, remember the story behind it. And someday I hope you will see the Savior's hands with beams of glory shining from them. Then you will remember His love for you forever!

ZEPHANIAH 2

Seek the Lord, all you meek of the earth. . . . It may be that you will be hidden in the day of the Lord's anger. Zephaniah 2:3.

August 8

Zephaniah lived in the days of Josiah, king of Judah. He prophesied the coming judgment on Israel and also pleaded with them to seek the Lord, to seek righteousness, to seek meekness, that they might escape punishment.

The story of the Advent message in all the world is full of experiences in which those who have sought God and made Him first in their lives have been "hid" in the day of destruction. Let me tell you the experiences of Brother Morita's son and daughter when the atomic bomb fell on Hiroshima. Two days ago I told you how Mr. Morita moved out of the city into the country and so escaped death among the 100,000 victims in the city. Well, his son went into the city each day to work in a factory, and his daughter, Setsuko, went each day to the girls' high school. On August 6, 1945, Mr. Morita's son was working with a group of men around a heavy, reinforced table. There was a blinding light, then a terrible crash. The factory was demolished. Almost every workman in the factory was killed. Somehow the Morita boy found himself under the table, perfectly protected from crashing walls and beams, without a scratch.

Setsuko was in school when suddenly a huge ball of fire seemed to enter the room. The 80 girls in her room remained in their seats, but Setsuko jumped up and pressed herself against a pillar in the center of the room. In the crash that followed, the whole building collapsed, crushing to death most of the 350 girls attending the school. The pillar to which Setsuko clung remained standing, and although the debris tumbled down all around her, she was unscathed and able to climb out to safety. You can only imagine the parents' joy when the son and daughter both found their way back home that night.

"The tempest is coming, and we must get ready for its fury. . . . Thousands of ships will be hurled into the depths of the sea. . . . Human lives will be sacrificed by millions. . . . Disasters by rail will become more and more frequent; confusion, collision, and death without a moment's warning will occur. . . . The end is near, probation is closing. Oh, let us seek God while He may be found, call upon Him while He is near!" (*Messages to Young People*, pp. 89, 90).

"They shall come to the Desire of All Nations, and I will fill this temple with glory," says the Lord of hosts. Haggai 2:7.

August 9

You will remember that Haggai was one of the prophets who was among the first exiles to return to Jerusalem. He helped Zerubbabel the governor and Joshua the high priest in rebuilding the Temple. Among his inspiring encouragements was the prophecy that the Desire of All Nations—the Messiah—would come and fill the Temple with glory. He did come. And soon "the Desire of All Nations" is coming again, the second time. Everywhere God is using laypersons, missionaries, and evangelists to get people ready for that great day. And in places where we do not have enough missionaries the Spirit of God is using many strange ways to bring the truth to people who desire to know God. Listen:

Away up in northern Uganda in central Africa there lived a man named Eriya Musoke. One day he decided to visit a relative who lived 150 miles away on the other side of Lake Kyoga. When he reached his relative's home he saw a little book on the table written in the Luganda language. The name of it was *Is the End Near?* He picked it up and began to read.

"Where did you get this book?" he asked.

"A colporteur sold it to me," his relative replied.

"Can I have it?"

"No. That is my book."

"But you can't read, and I can."

"Still, you can't have it, but you can read it while you are here," said his relative. So Eriya stayed five days and read it again and again, till he knew it almost by heart. When he got back to his home, he hunted up a Bible, bought it for 20 cents, and began to read it. Soon he came to Matthew 24. He remembered reading about that in the little book. His heart burned within him. "It's true! It's true!" he said. "Jesus is coming again soon!" Before long he was keeping the Sabbath and telling his friends all about it. I will tell you some more about Eriya tomorrow, for it is wonderful what the Spirit of God can do for a man who *desires* to get ready to meet Jesus.

Are you getting ready for the coming of the Desire of All Nations too?

ZECHARIAH 4

So [the angel who talked with me] answered and said to me: . . . " 'Not by might nor by power, but by My Spirit,' says the Lord of hosts."
Zechariah 4:5, 6.

August 10

The Spirit of God is still doing things that seem impossible. Several years ago the president of a mission station in Uganda received a letter addressed to "the missionary who keeps the Bible Sabbath. Mbale." "I have been preaching the Bible Sabbath," it said, "and now two more are keeping that day. Can you come up?" It was signed Eriya Musoke. "How far away is this, Luka?" Pastor Lind asked the man who was helping him translate Sabbath school lessons.

"About 160 miles. It is a good letter. Shall I go up?" said Luka.

"No, not now. We are too busy. We will send him some tracts." Two weeks later came another letter: "Now there are four of us keeping the Sabbath," it said. "Can you now come up?"

Luka asked if he should go, but Pastor Lind said he must stay for some evangelistic meetings. Two weeks later came another letter: "Now 12 of us are keeping the Sabbath."

"I am going, sir," Luka said, and he went.

He stayed about a month, and when he got back Pastor Lind said, "Well, Luka, did you find 12 people keeping the Sabbath?"

"No," said Luka, "there were 18. And when I left, there were 28! And they want you to come up." So Pastor Lind went up.

"Eriya," he said, "how did you find out about the Sabbath?" And Eriya told him about finding the little book in his relative's house.

"And how did you find the Seventh-day mission?"

"Well," said Eriya, "one day I had to go to town five miles away. I was riding the chief's old bicycle, and when I got to the city I found policemen inspecting all bicycles.

" 'Have you brakes?' they asked. I said, 'Yes, but they don't work.'

" 'Have you a bell?' 'No,' I said, so they took me off to jail. There was nothing to do in jail, so I just sat there and talked with the jailer. 'Do you know anyone who keeps the seventh-day Sabbath?' I asked him.

" 'Yes,' he said. 'There is a seventh-day Sabbath missionary near Mbale,' and that is how I got your address." Today Eriya has eight Sabbath schools with more than 500 keeping the Sabbath. But it was not Eriya's might or power that accomplished this. It was the Spirit of God.

"Bring all the tithes into the storehouse, . . . and try Me now in this," says the Lord of hosts, "If I will not open for you the windows of heaven and pour out for you such blessing that there will not be room enough to receive it." Malachi 3:10.

August 11

Malachi probably ministered during the second period when Nehemiah was governor of Jerusalem. The people were lukewarm and indifferent toward God and His worship, and God used Malachi to call them to repentance. We know Malachi best for his appeal to be faithful in returning the tithes and offerings to God, and for reminding us of the guarantee God gives that great blessing will result.

Here is the greatest story of tithe blessing I have ever heard. In 1913 a young man by the name of Clyde Harris and his brother opened a little box factory in Milton, Oregon. The following year Clyde married, and in a remarkable way a few months later he and his wife became Sabbathkeepers, were baptized, and joined the Seventh-day Adventist Church. They were all-the-way people, and had no trouble giving up tobacco, tea, and coffee. What they believed was right, they did, and that's all there was to it. Clyde Harris believed paying tithe was as basic as keeping the Sabbath, and they always gave more than the tenth, to be sure they were doing their part.

God blessed them so much that after running their box factory for three years they added a sawmill to their business. God still blessed, and Mr. Harris added fruit farms to his business. Again and again God rebuked the devourer for their sakes, and they always had good crops. Soon Mr. Harris moved his plant to Pendleton to be near the railway. Then he added a furniture factory and made arrangements for students from nearby Walla Walla College to work there and earn part of their school expenses. God blessed more and more, until in 1951 his factory produced $4 million worth of goods and had 650 employees. In all of their 39 years of operation there was only one depression year, 1932, that they did not show a profit; they were never unable to pay their workers.

As Brother Harris thought of retiring, he wondered what he should do with his $9 million business. One day he called in the conference president and treasurer, and told them he had decided to give the whole business to the church. And he did!

MATTHEW 1

You shall call His name Jesus, for He will
save His people from their sins.
Matthew 1:21.

August **12**

One of the sweetest stories I have ever heard was told about this text. It happened in Poland after World War I. Our little church in one small town had been used as a barracks and had suffered much at the hands of the rough soldiers. Then one of our Seventh-day Adventist soldiers came back to his hometown and found the church's windows broken, doors torn from their hinges, the yard overgrown with weeds, and the congregation scattered to the four winds. It broke his heart that the light of the church had gone out, but he didn't know what to do. He had very little education. But he had a Bible, and he could read, and as he prayed that God would rekindle the light of truth in that little town, God talked to him in a dream and said, "Arise and build!"

"O Lord, I don't know how!" he pleaded.

"My Word builds," came the voice, and when he awoke, he couldn't forget those words. The more he thought of his dream, the more he was impelled to do something. So he repaired the church and pulled up the weeds. Then he took his Bible and decided to go from house to house and read to anyone who would listen. When the woman in the first house invited him in, he read the first chapter of Genesis, had a short prayer, and invited her to the church service the next Sabbath morning. As he went on to the next house he felt that the story of Creation wasn't very inspiring, so he decided to try the New Testament next time. So after being invited in at the second home, he read Matthew 1. In just a minute he realized he had made a terrible mistake, because he was lost in a wilderness of big names. But he kept courageously on, and soon came to the verse that says, "Thou shalt call his name Jesus: for he shall save his people from their sins."

"That's just what I need," said the woman. "I need a Savior." The young man had prayer and invited her to the church service next Sabbath. And so he went from home to home. When Sabbath morning arrived, the people came to the church. He had no hymnal; he couldn't preach; so he simply read from the Bible. But it was just what they wanted, and they came the next Sabbath and the next and the next. After two and a half months the conference president came to that little town, hoping he would find one or two of the church members still faithful. Instead, he found 41 people keeping the Sabbath and waiting for baptism. They needed what the world needs—a Savior. You need a Savior too. Give Jesus first place in your heart, and He will save you from your sins.

227

An angel of the Lord appeared to Joseph in a dream, saying, "Arise, take the young Child and His mother [and] flee to Egypt." Matthew 2:13.

August 13

At the General Conference session in 1962 Pastor Walter Schubert told of a young man who was the only Seventh-day Adventist in his family. He loved to read his Bible, but his mother didn't like this new religion, and she watched angrily while he read his Bible.

One day while he was away from the house she took his Bible and hid it under the mattress in her room. When the young man came home and couldn't find his Bible, he said, "Mother, did you borrow my Bible to read?"

"Me borrow your Bible!" she replied angrily. "As if I would read that!"

That night the young man prayed that God would help him find his Bible, and that night he had a dream. In it he saw an angel, and the angel said, "Your mother has hidden your Bible under the mattress of her bed. You will find it there." The next morning he went to his mother's room and lifted up the mattress.

"What are you doing?" asked his mother.

"I'm getting my Bible," he said.

"How did you know it was there?"

"Last night an angel told me in a dream that you had hidden it there," he replied.

His mother was speechless. "There must be something to this new religion after all," she said to herself. The next Monday night she went to the church with her son, and when Pastor Schubert made a call, she went forward without any hesitation. Later both she and her husband were baptized and became church members.

Keep your heart right with God. Maybe someday He will send an angel to talk to you in a dream.

MATTHEW 3

Bear fruits worthy of repentance.
Matthew 3:8.

August **14**

When we have been disobedient, unkind, dishonest, or discourteous, we must do more than feel sorry. We must bring forth the fruits of repentance. In other words, we must show by our actions that we are sorry and that we are trying to correct our mistakes.

A train was waiting at the station, almost ready to start. Standing near the platform of one of the coaches stood a casually dressed man. He had a disability, and looked as though he had neither wealth nor influence. "All aboard, Limpy!" shouted the conductor.

"Time enough, I reckon," replied the stranger.

"Get on, Limpy!" The man made no reply, but walked in and took a seat. In a few moments along came the conductor. "Your ticket, quick," he said to the stranger.

"I don't pay," quietly replied the man.

"We'll see about that," the conductor said as he moved on down the aisle collecting his tickets. "I'll put you off at the next station."

Just then a passenger stopped the conductor. "Do you know who you were talking to just then?"

"No, sir."

"That is Peter Warburton, the president of this railway company."

"Are you sure?"

"Yes. I know him well." The color rose in the conductor's face. He was in trouble now. When he had finished taking the tickets he came back and stopped beside Mr. Warburton. He placed his books and tickets in his hands and said, "It serves me right, sir. I resign my place."

"Sit down, young man," said Mr. Warburton. "You have indeed been very impudent. Treating passengers that way badly injured the company's reputation. Remember, you cannot judge someone by the clothes they wear, and even the poorest passenger should be treated courteously. Take up your books. If you change your course of action, I shall tell no one about it."

That's it—change your course of action. You may make a mistake, but you should not make the same mistake again and again. Make it right, then change your course of action. Don't make that mistake again.

Man shall not live by bread alone, but by every word that proceeds from the mouth of God. Matthew 4:4.

August 15

The precious Word of God is likened to a light, because it shows the way into the future; to a sword, because it protects us from the temptations of Satan; and to bread, because it supplies us with spiritual life and growth.

Many years ago during my service in Burma a little old grandma came into my clinic. She waited till all the other patients had gone. "Have you got fever?" I asked kindly.

"No, not that," she said. "I'm starving, I tell you!" Then she told how her son had gone to Moulmein to work in a lumber mill. He had promised to send her money every month. "But he hasn't sent me any money at all in his letters," she wept, "and when you go to the city, I want you to—"

"How often does he write you, Grandma?" I interrupted.

"Every two weeks I get a letter," she said.

"And doesn't he send anything in those letters?"

"Only some crazy little bits of paper with English printed and written all over them," she replied almost angrily.

I was immediately interested in those crazy little bits of paper, so I said, "Grandma, go home and get all of his letters and all of those crazy little bits of paper and bring them to me. I want to see them." The next morning she came with them all wrapped carefully in a banana leaf, and I think you have guessed it. Each of those "crazy bits of paper" was a money order for 10 rupees!

"Grandma, Grandma," I said, "all you have to do is to take these to the post office and put your thumbprint on them, and the postmaster will give you 10 rupees for each one of them." I wish you could have seen her face.

"I can? He will?" she gasped. Then, hugging the money orders to her heart, she said, "And there I was starving! With all this fortune in my hands!"

And we might add: Why are so many juniors starving spiritually with the precious bread of heaven in their hands? Are you reading the Bible faithfully? Don't let yourself starve.

MATTHEW 5

Blessed are you when they revile and persecute you. . . . Rejoice and be exceedingly glad, for great is your reward in heaven. Matthew 5:11, 12.

Ever since Satan started the war in heaven, those who have taken his side against God have persecuted those who have chosen to love God and follow Him. Some years ago one of our pastors in central Africa told this story.

During evangelistic meetings in a certain town, among those who joined the Bible study class was a young woman named Nyangwira. At the end of the year she was promoted to the baptismal class. She told her husband about what she had learned and tried to persuade him to come with her, but he became angry. "I don't want this kind of religion in my home," he shouted, "and if you keep on, I'll kill you." Nyangwira, however, kept on. Sweetly, patiently, gently she refused to brew beer, and her husband's anger increased. Another year end came, and she planned to be baptized at the camp meeting. Before going to camp meeting she knelt in front of her husband, as respectful wives did, and told him she was now ready for baptism.

"I have told you not to get baptized," he said. "And you have to obey me." He went to the wall and picked up a large hunting knife. Shaking it in her face, he said, "The day you are baptized I will kill you." Nyangwira was determined to obey God rather than man, whatever the cost, so off she went to camp meeting and was baptized. When she got back, she went to the wall where the hunting knife hung, and, picking it up, she took it to her husband.

"Have you been baptized?" he said angrily.

"Yes," replied Nyangwira. "Here is the knife."

"Are you ready to be killed?"

"Yes, I am." But her courage completely unnerved him, and he put the knife away and said no more. The Spirit of God was with Nyangwlra. She entered the colporteur work shortly after this and brought the light of the gospel to many homes. Not only did God bless her here and now, but there is laid up for her a rich reward in heaven.

Do not fear persecution. Let people call you names if they will. Be sweet, kind, and gentle, and God will bless you here on earth, too.

In this manner, therefore, pray: Our Father in heaven, hallowed be Your name.
Matthew 6:9.

August 17

Do you know why Jesus taught His disciples to say, "Our Father in heaven"? I think it was because He didn't want them to be afraid or nervous when they prayed. If Jesus had taught them to say "King of kings" or "Great Ruler of the universe," they might have been scared. I would be nervous about talking to the president or even a senator of our country. But few are afraid to talk to a father. I am a father. I have two sons and two daughters, and they are not afraid to talk to me.

One day when my eldest son, Lenny, was just a little fellow 4 years old, he awoke at 4:00 a.m., crawled out of his crib, sat on top of me, then started: "Daddy, Daddy, Daddy! Please, Daddy, will you make me a toy car? And paint it green all over and put a toot-toot on it like an engine train, and a seat in it for the pussycat to ride on? Will you, Daddy? Huh?"

I was so sleepy that I said, "I'll do anything if you will only let me sleep."

So later on he ran over to where his little friends Barnabas and Stephen lived. "Daddy's going to make me a toy car. He said he would," he shouted. And all day long, every time I saw him, Lenny said, "You *are* going to make me a toy car, aren't you, Daddy? You said you would!"

At last the day was done, and he lay asleep in his crib.

"Isn't he sweet!" said his mother as we looked fondly at him.

"Yes," I said, "when he's asleep! He has toy-car'd me all day long." But I *was* his father, and I *did* love him, and I *had* promised, so while the little fellow slept I went downstairs and worked till midnight. I made him a toy car with a toot-toot on it like an engine train. I painted it green all over, and made a seat in it for the cat to ride on, and I put it right beside his bed where he could find it in the morning.

God is King of kings, but He also is our heavenly Father! Never be afraid to tell Him everything, or to ask His help for every occasion. He is your Father. He *has* promised to supply all your needs, and He will!

MATTHEW 7

Judge not, that you be not judged. For with what judgment you judge, you will be judged. Matthew 7:1, 2.

It is so easy to criticize or condemn. Like a flash you can decide that someone has done wrong. But you'd better be careful! You'd better look at both sides of the question and find out all the circumstances before you judge; things are not always what they seem to be at first sight.

Not long ago at a church youth meeting I was going to show some color slides on Burma and New Guinea. A friend had taken me to the church quite early, and I had the projector and the tape recorder all set up and checked over before the people began to come in. More and more people arrived. It was just about time for the meeting to begin when in came a tall woman dressed in a fur coat. She brushed heavily along the back of the pew where I was sitting, and bumped my head as she went by. *Dear me*, I said to myself, *what a clumsy person!* I was afraid she would bump into my equipment and knock it over, but fortunately she didn't, and she finally found a seat in front of me.

The meeting began. I gave my talk and entirely forgot about the clumsy woman until my friend said, "I want you to meet our faithful blind sister. She comes to every meeting." And he introduced me to the tall woman in the fur coat. My face went red at the thought of my unspoken judgment. How glad I was that nobody knew what I had thought. My heart nearly stood still.

"I'm sorry you couldn't see the pictures," I finally stammered.

"But I can hear," she said cheerfully, "and what you said and the music in the background made a very enjoyable evening for me." I suppose she has forgotten all about that meeting by this time, but I will never forget how near I came to making a regrettable judgment. I'm going to be doubly careful evermore.

"That which we do to others, whether it be good or evil, will surely react upon ourselves, in blessing or in cursing. . . . Everyone who has been free to condemn or discourage will in his own experience be brought over the ground where he has caused others to pass; he will feel what they have suffered because of his want of sympathy and tenderness" (*Thoughts From the Mount of Blessing*, p. 136). Won't you promise God that you will be careful about what you say and how you judge?

August 19

A certain scribe came and said to Him, "Teacher, I will follow You wherever You go." And Jesus said to him, "Foxes have holes and birds of the air have nests, but the Son of Man has nowhere to lay His head." Matthew 8:19, 20.

A little boy from a Buddhist home in Hawaii was enrolled in the Adventist kindergarten. Day after day he came and enjoyed every activity—the games, the songs, the stories. But the stories about Jesus, he loved the best. "Jesus" was a new name for him and a new kind of teacher—one born as a baby in a stable, because there was no room for Him in the inn. Day by day the story told how Jesus grew up and went around doing good to everybody. Then came the day when the teacher told the story about the scribe, and she solemnly said, "Jesus said: 'Foxes have holes and birds of the air have nests, but the Son of Man has nowhere to lay His head.' Just think! Poor Jesus had no place He could call His own."

The little boy listened carefully and took it all in, and when the story was finished he went up to the teacher, caught hold of her hand, looked earnestly into her face, and said, "Teacher, this Jesus. Didn't He have any home?"

"No, sonny, not here."

"And you say He's coming back here again?"

"Yes, very soon."

The little fellow looked very pleased and said, "Then, Teacher, you tell Jesus when He comes again that we have plenty of room for Him at our house!" Precious little lad! No wonder Jesus said, "Of such is the kingdom of heaven!"

Would you find plenty of room in your house, too, for Jesus when He comes again? But you don't have to wait till He comes. You can make room for Jesus now, in your heart.

Mabel J. Rosemon wrote a beautiful song. The chorus says: "Dear Savior, come to me, I'll ever welcome Thee. Within this heart of mine Thy dwelling place shall be; O Savior, come to me, for there is room for Thee; within my heart there's room for Thee."

MATTHEW 9

Those who are well have no need of a physician, but those who are sick. Matthew 9:12.

August 20

Jesus called Himself a doctor to those who were sick with sin. This helps us to understand how He could hate sin but love sinners. We know that doctors often have to hurt or operate on patients because they care about them and want them to get better. Sometimes God permits us to be hurt, punished for our sins, so we can get rid of sin and be well again.

One day, in Burma, I went to our Awbawa village school to give the half-yearly exams. Afterward the village sick people flocked into the school for treatment. There were some with sore eyes, some with malaria, and some with teeth to be pulled. While I was hard at work a man came groaning up the ladder with a big boil on his wrist. "Quick, Doctor!" he said. "Get your knife, cut it deep, and squeeze all the matter out."

"It will hurt you if I cut it!"

"Never mind if it does hurt," he said.

"Do you like for people to hurt you?" I asked.

"Of course not," he said, "but I can't sleep and I can't work. Come on, get your knife and cut it." Then he added, "If you think I'll wriggle too much, get those six big men to sit on me so I can't move." And so I did. Then I lanced the boil. It *did* hurt, and he groaned with pain.

"Shall I stop now?" I asked.

"No, keep on till it's all finished," he cried.

I squeezed it, and he groaned again. "Shall I stop now?" I asked.

"No! Keep on till it's all finished," he said. So I kept on hurting him until it was all finished. Then I put a nice clean bandage around his wrist. Then the men got off him, and he sat up. For a moment he looked at his sore arm, then he moved over beside me and took my hand in his—the hand that had cut him—and he wept for joy, saying, "Thank you. Thank you so much."

And that's the way it is with God. He hates sin, but He loves *us*. Sometimes He has to let us get hurt in order to take away our sin. Next time you must be punished or corrected, remember this and say, "Thank You, Jesus. Thank You so much. Please help me not to sin again."

Whoever confesses Me before men, him I will also confess before My Father who is in heaven. Matthew 10:32.

August 21

I will always remember the day when Ohn Bwint decided to be baptized. He was my biggest boy in school, and he had been at our mission school for four years. One night he knocked on my office door and said, "Thara, I want to go home."

"But, Ohn Bwint," I replied, "there are only three weeks before school closes."

"Yes, but Thara, I want to be baptized at camp meeting time, and I want to ask my parents' permission to be baptized."

"Oh, that's different," I said. "Of course you can go." And off he went, radiant and happy. But when he came back, the joy had gone out of his face. "I can't do it, Thara," he sobbed. "My father says that if I am baptized he will disown me and tell the devils I am dead."

Each person must make his own decision to follow Christ and be baptized, so I just said, "Keep your heart right, my boy, and the right time will come." School closed. Camp meeting began. On the last Sabbath seven big boys were baptized. We sang, "Happy day . . . when Jesus washed my sins away." And everyone was happy but Ohn Bwint. He sat alone, weeping.

Late that night he knocked on my door. "Thara," he sobbed, "I'm going home again. I'm going to tell my father that even if he disowns me, I must be baptized. As I saw the boys going into the water today, it seemed I could see heaven open, and I could imagine Jesus standing before His Father, saying, 'This one is Mine, Father. Look at My nailprints. I paid the price for him. And this one, too, Father; and this one, too. He's not ashamed to confess Me before men. I'm not ashamed to confess him before You. But not that one under the bush over yonder, Father. He is afraid of being disowned. Not him!'" Ohn Bwint broke down and cried. "I couldn't stand it! To think that Christ was ashamed of me. I must go tell Father that I must be baptized." Ohn Bwint went. He came back and was baptized, and a happier boy you couldn't find anywhere!

Do you want the joy of having Jesus claim you as His own? All you need do is to confess Jesus before your friends here on earth. Confess Him where You are, and He will surely confess you before His Father in heaven.

MATTHEW 11

Come to Me, all you who labor and are heavy laden,
and I will give you rest.
Matthew 11:28.

August **22**

The invitation to come to Jesus is for all. Many have come to Jesus and found freedom from the slavery of sin and rest for their poor tired souls. But there are some who keep struggling along, bound with bad habits, longing to be free, but failing to realize that what they need is Christ.

One time the king of one tribe was taken prisoner by a bitter enemy and carried off to his distant territory. There he was chained to a heavy iron weight but allowed to move about as he wished. Of course, his movements were slow and limited to the distance he could drag or carry the heavy weight. How he longed to be free and to return to his own tribe again.

One day a European traveler passing through the country saw the poor man and pitied him. He dared not try to help him openly, however, because he was closely watched, but he did get permission to give the poor captive a Bible. The captive king wasn't interested in the Bible. He wished the traveler had given him food or clothing or money. He put the Bible to one side and never looked at it. Three years went by, and then one day, bored with nothing to do, he picked up the Bible and looked through it. All of a sudden he felt something hard inside the back cover. He felt it and pulled at it, and what do you think it was? It was a file! Slowly he made his way to the woods, then began to file away on his chain. He worked and worked till at last the chain fell off—and he was free! At once he set out for home, traveling by night to keep out of sight, and before long he was safe at home again. But just think, he could have been free three years before! He had endured three needless years of slavery just because he didn't look inside the Book!

Are you tied up to some bad habit? Are you enduring slavery to sin? Jesus invites you to come to Him. He is the way, the truth, and the life, and He will give you rest. It is not enough just to *have* a Bible. You need to *read* your Bible and *find* Christ in it. Only Christ can make you free.

*But I say to you that for every idle word men may speak,
they will give account of it in the day of judgment.
Matthew 12:36.*

August 23

Sam, Curly, Red, Mike, and Lee were in the same Sabbath school class. They also had a club called Scouts for Jesus. One day a new boy, Eddie Jones, and his mother came to town and moved into a little house nearby. A few days later Sam, president of the club, said, "Has anyone asked the new boy to join our class?"

"No way! It's all off with Eddie Jones," said Curly. "We don't want him in our club, and I'll tell you why. He's a thief!"

"What did he steal?" demanded Mike.

"This morning he stole the bottle of milk right off our front porch!" said Curly. "Believe me, I told him plenty, and he brought it back."

"You mean a big kid like one of us stole a bottle of milk?" Sam asked.

"And that's not all. I watched him out of the corner of the window, and he no sooner got into the street than he went next door and stole Mr. Andrews' milk. He's a thief, all right."

"Wait a minute," said Sam. "Let's not call him names until we figure out why he did it. You guys wait right here. I'll be back soon." Before long, Sam was back, and everyone crowded around to hear his report.

"OK, guys, here's the story. Eddie's mother is sick. They're all out of cash after moving here, but Eddie's mom is a nurse, and she'll soon get work when she gets better. Eddie has been looking everywhere for a job. They are renting their house from Mr. Andrews, and this morning Eddie saw him on his way to the train. He asked Eddie to tell the milkman not to leave any more milk till he got back, and he told Eddie to pick up the bottle of milk on his porch and use it."

"Somebody kick me," moaned Curly. "Mr. Andrews' house and ours are painted the same, and I suppose he just . . ."

"Yes, he just, and Curly, *you* just— Say, what about asking Eddie to join our class and our club?" And everyone shouted, "Yes!"

Is your tongue quick on the trigger? Better tie a knot in it! Or you'll have a hard time in the judgment.

MATTHEW 13

The kingdom of heaven is like treasure hidden in a field.
Matthew 13:44.

In Matthew 13 the kingdom of heaven is likened to several things that show how valuable and precious it is. In verses 3 to 8 it is likened to seed that brings forth an abundant harvest to all who receive it. In verse 46 it is likened to a pearl of great price that was worth all that a man possessed. In verse 44 it is likened to treasure hid in a field, treasure worth more than everything a man had. I wonder if we realize how valuable the kingdom of heaven is, how close it is to us, and how easy it is for us to obtain. According to a story by Russell H. Conwell, there once lived an old Persian sheik named Al Hafed. He owned a large farm not far from the Indus River. He was a wealthy and contented man. But one day a Buddhist priest visited him, and as they talked together the priest told him about diamonds that were more precious than gold.

Once Al Hafed had heard about diamonds, that was all he wanted. "I want a mine of diamonds," he said, and he lay awake at night dreaming about it. Eventually he sold his farm, left his family in the care of a neighbor, and went off in search of a diamond mine. He searched through the Mountains of the Moon in Africa, wandered through Palestine, then on into Europe, but he couldn't find a diamond mine anywhere. At last his money was all spent, and he was in rags. In his wretchedness and despair he threw himself into the bay at Barcelona, Spain, and drowned himself. But that is not the end of the story. One day the same old Buddhist priest came to visit Al Hafed's successor. As he entered the house he saw a flash of light on the mantel. He rushed up to it and shouted, "It's a diamond! Has Al Hafed returned?"

"No! Al Hafed has not returned, and that is not a diamond," said the man. "It is only a pretty stone I found here in the garden."

"But it *is* a diamond," said the priest. And it was indeed. They went into the garden, stirred up the white sands, and found more of the valuable gems. Thus was discovered the famous Golconda diamond mine. Think of it! There were priceless diamonds all around him, hidden in his field, all within reach, but Al Hafed didn't recognize them.

The precious, priceless kingdom of heaven is all around you, within your reach. Have you made it yours?

When he [Peter] saw that the wind was boisterous, he was afraid; and beginning to sink he cried out, saying, "Lord, save me!" And immediately Jesus stretched out His hand and caught him. Matthew 14:30, 31.

August 25

I think it was more than the boisterous waves that made Peter sink. I think there was a little bit of a show-off spirit in Peter, which made him take his eyes off Jesus and turn around to see whether the other disciples were admiring him. That unlovely show-off spirit always causes boys and girls to go down in the estimation of their companions.

Jerry was a strong, smart 10-year-old boy. He could do everything well, but unfortunately, he was always calling for attention and praise by saying, "Watch me hit this ball" or "Watch me ride my bike!" "Watch me" seemed to be a part of him, and nobody liked to hear him brag. Well, one day he and his family were at the seaside. His folks hired a rowboat, and Jerry could handle it quite well. But he spoiled it by saying, "Watch me!" "Watch me!" "Watch me!"

One lovely morning he shouted, "Watch me race the boy in that boat!" He bent his back and pulled hard, but one oar slipped out of the oarlock. Jerry tipped over backward, his feet went up in the air, and the oar fell into the water and went floating away. But Jerry was a bright boy. He picked himself up, looked around, then moved one of the oarlocks to the back of the boat. He put the one oar that was left in it and, moving it from side to side with a twisting motion, began moving forward. "Watch me!" "Watch me!" he called triumphantly. But just then the oar slipped out of the oarlock, and Jerry lost his balance and fell headlong into the sea. Fortunately there were lots of people around. One rescued Jerry, another pulled the boat to the beach, and another saved the two oars. It was a sorry picture, but suddenly someone in the crowd shouted, "Watch me!" And everybody laughed. Jerry went red, then he laughed too.

But Jerry really was a bright boy, and that day he caught on to one of the best ideas he ever had. He stopped saying "Watch me" and never said it again.

Listen in to yourself, and if you find yourself saying "Watch me! Watch me!" then *you* stop it too.

MATTHEW 15

Great is your faith! Let it be to you as you desire.
Matthew 15:28.

Again and again Jesus performed miracles according to the faith of the people who came to Him for help. Jesus was always pleased when He found someone with "great faith."

Here is a story that everyone should know. About 175 years ago there lived a man in England whose name was George Müller. He had unusually great faith in God. In his heart he had a great burden to make Christian homes for the poor orphan children in Bristol. He believed that God wanted him to do this work, and he believed that God would help him do it. And to make sure that it was God doing it, he decided he would never ask anyone for money. He would just pray, and if the money came in, then he would know for sure that God was doing the work. So George Müller prayed—and along came the money. He rented one house and filled it with orphans. Every day he prayed. More money came in. He rented more houses and filled them with orphans. By 1841 he had 96 orphans in his houses. He kept praying, and within 60 years he had built five of the largest orphanages in the world, and had cared for more than 10,000 orphans!

One day George Müller told the Lord he would like to give his 2,000 children a little treat, for it was his birthday. He would like to provide each child with a banana. But 2,000 bananas would cost a lot of money. He looked in the safe to see how much money he had, then went to town to see whether he could buy 2,000 bananas. Imagine his surprise, when he got there, to find that a firm of importers of bananas had already sent a shipment of bananas to the orphanage. When he got back and counted them, there were 4,000 instead of 2,000. So the orphans had two bananas each instead of only one! George Müller is a wonderful example for us all. God honored his life of prayer and faith.

We have a mighty God, with whom all things are possible. But how much faith have you? "Without faith it is impossible to please Him" (Hebrews 11:6). And remember: "Prayer is the key in the hand of faith to unlock heaven's storehouse, where are treasured the boundless resources of Omnipotence" (*Steps to Christ*, pp. 94, 95).

If anyone desires to come after Me, let him deny himself, and take up his cross, and follow Me. Matthew 16:24.

August 27

We often speak of the things we have to give up, and the things we have to suffer to be real Christians, as "the cross" we have to carry. Did you ever think your cross was too big and too heavy? Listen.

There came a day during World War I when Turkey entered the war as an ally of Germany. With the declaration of war came the decision that Turkey would rid its land of the hated Armenian Christians. The poor Christians were driven from their homes and marched off to some unknown destination in the Arabian Desert. Many died on the way. Many became slaves of the Arabs. Some of the Arab masters were kind, but some were very cruel. In the nearby countries of the Western Allies the Americans set up relief camps, and to these camps many refugees found their way. One day among the refugees that came to one of these camps was a young Armenian girl. As she waited in line to see the doctor everyone saw she was in terrible pain.

"Lean on me," said one person next to her, "I am strong."

"I cannot lean," replied the poor girl.

"Have you been hurt?"

"I am bearing the cross," she said. "I know now how Jesus suffered." Just then a nurse came by and, seeing how sick the girl looked, bent over to help her.

"Wait," said the girl. "I must show you first." She then slipped her loose dress from her shoulders and showed them the form of a cross that had been burned across her shoulders with a red-hot iron. It was swollen and terribly inflamed.

"Day by day they added to my cross," she explained. "They would ask me 'Muhammad or Christ?' and when I said 'Christ,' they brought the hot iron and burned the cross bigger and bigger. I thought I would surely die for Christ. Then, miraculously, I escaped and found my way here." Lovingly she was led to the hospital and tenderly cared for. She will bear her cross as long as she lives.

Now, how big is *your* cross? How heavy is *your* cross?

MATTHEW 17

This is My beloved Son. . . . Hear Him!
Matthew 17:5.

To Moses and Elijah was given the greatest honor human beings could know—the privilege of comforting and strengthening Jesus before He was crucified. Both Moses and Elijah had experienced much suffering and disappointment. At the end of his life Moses prayed, "Please, let me go over and see the land of Canaan." But God said no. Once Elijah prayed, "Let me die." But God said no. God had something better for both of them.

While we were on our mission station in Burma, one Christmas I gave my 7-year-old Lenny a little steam engine. It was a real engine. You could put water in it and fire under it, and it turned a wheel and it whistled. Oh, it was marvelous! How excited he was about it. That afternoon, however, a letter came from his three little cousins—Edwin, Wilfred, and Buddy—saying that in February they were coming up to spend three months with us, and they added, "We got a Mechano set for Christmas." As soon as I read that letter, in my imagination I could see Lenny's engine turning a Mechano merry-go-round. But that was two months away, and in two months Lenny's engine might be all broken. So I said, "Son, let's put the engine away till your cousins come with their Mechano set. Then it will still be new, and you'll have more fun." But he couldn't see two months ahead, and he said, "No, no, Daddy, I want to play with it now."

I thought it over carefully. I was sure I was right, so I said, "I know it will be better this way, son." And we put the engine away. Poor Lenny cried. He couldn't understand. But the weeks passed quickly. The cousins came. They unpacked their Mechano set. I brought out Lenny's brand-new engine. In a little while the engine was turning a Mechano merry-go-round, and four little boys were squealing with delight.

"Now aren't you glad that I put the engine away, Lenny?" I asked. And what do you think he did? He jumped onto my knee, threw his arms around my neck, hugged me tight, and said, "How did you know it would be better this way, Daddy?"

Really, parents and teachers and God do know what will be best for you in the future, and if ever they have to say no to some of your plans, take it kindly. Someday you will know it was best.

Where two or three are gathered together in My name, I am there in the midst of them. Matthew 18:20.

August 29

Grandma Batty always went to prayer meeting, and usually she was the only one there besides the minister. Everybody else seemed to be too busy to go. But Grandma Batty said, "Anyway, I'm number two! And that means that the Lord will be there too. So she was always there. But one day Grandma Batty broke her leg and had to stay in bed. Her little grandson found her weeping on the afternoon of prayer meeting day.

"What's the matter, Grandma?" he asked.

"Bobby, I can't go to prayer meeting tonight, and I'm number two. If I don't get there, maybe the Lord won't come either, for the Bible says, 'Where two or three are gathered together in My name, I am in the midst of them.' "

Bobby's eyes opened wide as he took it all in, then he said, "Don't worry, Grandma. I'll go and say my prayers with the minister. I'll be number two tonight. Then God will come, won't He?" And after supper, instead of just playing around, Bobby marched bravely down the street toward the church. On the way he met old Peter Quirls.

"Hi, Bobby. Where are you going?" he asked.

"Granny broke her leg and can't go to prayer meeting, so I'm going to be number two and say my prayers with the minister, so the Lord will come too," said Bobby. And into the church went Bobby.

"Granny can't come tonight," Bobby told the minister. "So I came to be number two, so the Lord won't be disappointed." Tears came to the minister's eyes.

"All right, Bobby," he said. "Let us pray." Bobby said his little prayer, then the minister prayed. He prayed as he had never prayed before, and as he prayed old Peter Quirls came up to the front; then he prayed, too. He had followed Bobby in to see what he would do. What a lovely prayer meeting the four of them had together. The Lord surely was there, and as they rose from their knees Peter said, "Pastor, I'll never be absent from prayer meeting again. I'll be number three." Then Peter told everybody else about little Bobby's prayers, and they all began to come to prayer meeting.

Say, won't you be number two or number three at family worship or prayer meetings?

MATTHEW 19

If you want to enter into life, keep the commandments.
Matthew 19:17.

August **30**

Jesus told the rich young ruler of a simple way to enter into eternal life. The way is simple, to be sure, but it is not easy, and the young ruler soon found that out—and went away sorrowful. Then Jesus said to His disciples, "It is easier for a camel to go through the eye of a needle than for a rich man to enter the kingdom of God" (Matthew 19:24).

In this verse Jesus was using a common Eastern proverb that implied impossibility. But let me tell you something interesting that I know about camels. When I was a junior, we lived for about a year in a town called Broken Hill, on the edge of the great central desert in Australia. My father raised up a church there. I was always fascinated by the camel caravans that took supplies to the mining settlements far across the desert sands. I was always interested to see how the camels were loaded each morning. The men simply spoke a word that the camels understood, and the camels would all get *down on their knees.* Then, while they were on their knees, the boxes, the bundles, the lumber, and the iron sheets were loaded on the saddles and tied securely. When they were all loaded, the camels got up from their knees and started on their journey. During the day if anything went wrong with one of the loads so that it became uncomfortable, that camel would flop down on its knees, and the master would straighten it up again. Then, at the end of the day, when they reached the journey's end, all the camels would get down on their knees and wait patiently till the men took off their burdens. Then, without a care, they would eat and drink and rest for the night.

I think that is the way we can carry our burdens successfully. In the morning we can get down on our knees and ask the Lord to place upon us just the right amount of duty. Then during the day, if ever anything goes wrong, we can fall on our knees and call for help. At night when the day is done we can fall on our knees once more and ask the Lord to take off all our cares and forgive all our mistakes and sins. Then we can lie down to sweet refreshing sleep.

Whether a person is rich or poor, I think that's the only way anyone can keep the commandments and find the way to life eternal.

"Is it not lawful for me to do what I wish with my own things?" . . . So the last will be first, and the first last.
Matthew 20:15, 16.

August 31

In many ways Jesus taught the people what the reward of a meek and unselfish spirit would be. In the parable of the workers in the vineyard, the "last" were not last because they were lazy, but simply because no one had hired them earlier in the day. To me it is quite evident that after they were hired they worked hard. They made no demands, but trusted the master to pay them what was right. And he did.

In a faraway country in which there was suffering and hunger, welfare workers began to distribute bread to the hungry children. Little Sally went to the bread line, but there were people there when she arrived, and when others came they pushed in ahead of her so that she was the last in the line. Of course, the bigger loaves were taken first, and when Sally got to the basket there was only a small loaf left for her. "That will do for Grandma and me," said Sally sweetly to the woman in charge. "We thank you so much." The next day Sally was last again, and got the smallest loaf that was left. The next day it was the same, but Sally always smiled and said thank you. The woman in charge took notice of her kind, unselfish ways. The next day the woman played a lovely little trick. She made a special small loaf and put it right on top of all the loaves in the basket. As usual, the bigger loaves were taken first, and Sally got the small loaf. But when she got home and Grandma cut into it, there was a folded piece of paper money right in the middle of it! The next day Sally took the money back, and when the gate opened she called out, "There must be a mistake. There was some money in the loaf I got yesterday,"

"It was not a mistake," said the woman. "I put it there for you."

"It isn't fair." "Wish I had taken the small loaf now," said a dozen voices.

"You could have taken it if you wanted it," said the woman. "I put it right on top. But Sally is the most unselfish of you all. Now she can buy some warm clothes for winter."

Really, now, how *meek* are you? Do you push and shove to be first, or are you content to be last sometimes? Remember, in God's plan, someday the "last" are going to be "first."

MATTHEW 21

Son, go work today in my vineyard.
Matthew 21:28.

September 1

Today, September 1, is the anniversary of the beginning of World War II in 1939. It is interesting to notice that the parable of the two sons in today's Scripture reading contains the reason for all wars and trouble between people or nations. The second son said, "I will go, sir," but he didn't. He did not keep his word. He did not live up to his promise! He was not trustworthy. His father could not depend on him.

Ken came home angry one day. "I'm not going to belong to their old club any longer!" he said.

"And why?" asked his big brother Dirck.

"They didn't vote for me to be president, that's why. They put Merv Kingston in instead."

"And why?" said Dirck.

"They said that he's responsible," Ken said. "I suppose that means I'm not!"

"Wouldn't they give you some other office?"

"I should say not! If I can't be president I don't want to be in their club at all."

"Maybe they did mean you're not dependable, Ken," said his brother. "Better keep your eyes open and see." Ken went out to water the garden, but the hose was not there. "Who's taken the hose?" he said to himself. Then he remembered. He had left it at Mr. Conley's place when he was washing his car a few days ago. He started off to get it, and met Rip Watkins.

"Any word from your uncle about Milt getting that job?" Rip asked. "Remember, you'd promised to write."

"No. Haven't heard yet, but I'll let you know as soon as I do," stammered Ken. As Rip went off he said to himself, "Why did I forget to write that letter? Never mind. I'll phone Uncle tonight." Then when he got back with the hose he found a card to him from the public library. He'd forgotten to take back a book, and now he owed a fine.

"I guess I don't rate to be club president yet," Ken muttered.

Would you? Are *you* dependable?

Jesus said to him, "You shall love the Lord your God with all your heart, with all your soul, and with all your mind."
Matthew 22:37.

September 2

How good and how just is our heavenly Father! He never requires us to do any-thing impossible. He just expects us to serve Him with all our heart, soul, and mind. The 2-year-old with all her heart; the 10-year-old with all his heart; the 20-year-old with all her heart. I love to serve a God like that, don't you?

One day over in Burma I stepped into the head teacher's house for a few minutes. It was dinnertime, and I found Thara Myat Po with his 3-year-old son, Solomon, sitting at the table. Little Solomon looked up at his father's face and said, "I love you, Daddy."

The father smiled and said, "How much do you love me, Solomon?"

The little fellow stretched his chubby arms as far apart as he could and said, "This big!"

"Then," said the father, "if you love me that big, you jump up and bring me a drink of water." Solomon jumped up and ran over to the waterpot, but the waterpot was too high. For just a moment he looked at it, then looked at the tin cup that hung on a nail near the waterpot, but it was too high too.

Without a moment's hesitation he stood on his tiptoes with his little stomach pressed flat against the post and his little arm reaching toward the cup. He could just touch it. But he did all he could for all he was worth, and while his little finger made the cup go *tinkle, tinkle, tinkle,* he called, "Daddy, Daddy, Daddy!" Joy filled his father's face as he quickly got up from the table and walked over to his little boy. Then he lifted him in his arms until his little hand could reach the cup and dip the water. Then he put him down on the floor again, and the little boy took the cup of water to the table.

I saw the father drink the water and heard him say, "That's the sweetest cup of water I've ever had in all my life." That's the way it is with you and your Savior. He wants you to love Him with all your heart and soul and mind. That is, He wants you to obey Him all you can, for all you are worth.

You pay tithe of mint and anise and cummin, and have neglected . . .
justice and mercy and faith. These you ought to have done,
without leaving the others undone.
Matthew 23:23.

September 3

God Himself established the principle of supporting His work by the tithe of the income of His people. And our text this morning shows that Jesus had no idea of changing that plan. Tithe paying has always had the blessing of God upon it, and it still does.

Once there was a boy named Samuel. When he was 16 years old, he set off to find a job in New York City. On the way he met an old canal-boat captain who was a friend of the family. "Be sure you start right, lad," he said, "and you will get along fine. Let me pray with you, and then I'll give you a little advice." After a fatherly prayer the old man asked Sam what work he would try to get.

"I can make soap and candles," said Samuel. "Father taught me to do that, and I will try to find that kind of work."

"Good," said the old man. "Someday someone will be the leading soapmaker in New York. You can be that man as well as anyone. I hope you are. Be a good boy; give your heart to Christ. Give the Lord all that belongs to Him of every dollar you earn. Make a good soap. Give a full, honest pound, and I'm sure you'll be a rich man someday."

Samuel went to the city. He found work in a small soap factory. He remembered the advice of the old friend. He paid an honest tithe. Soon he was a partner in the business; then the owner. Then he decided to give the Lord two tenths of every dollar. His business kept growing. Soon he was giving three tenths to the Lord—then four, then five! Before he died, he was the leading soapmaker in New York, and his soaps and beauty preparations could be bought all around the world. Maybe you've heard of him—Samuel Colgate!

Why don't you, too, take the advice of the old canal-boat captain? First, give yourself to God. Second, pay a faithful tithe. Third, be thoroughly honest with everyone. Then see what God can make out of you.

Nation will rise against nation, and kingdom against kingdom. And there will be famines, pestilences, and earthquakes in various places. Matthew 24:7.

September 4

How good Jesus is to give us so many signs to tell us that His second coming and the end of the world are near. That day need not come upon us like a thief.

Here is a pathetic description of the distress and famine that followed the war in Algeria some years ago. Ninety percent of the European population and a million Muslims fled to France. The harvest was left to rot, factories were plundered, and 60 percent of the laboring classes were without work, without money, and without food. Our welfare workers from Denmark quickly collected 12 tons of clothing and food, and soon they had set up at three locations in Algeria.

One day a young man came to one of the dispensaries asking for work. His clothes were worn and he looked thin and hungry, but he said he'd rather work than receive charity. So although there really was no work for him, the manager told him to come the next morning at 8:00 and he would give him work. The man came at 6:30 a.m. the next day

"Why did you come so early?" asked the manager.

"I must leave my home before my children are awake. They ask for bread, and I have nothing to give them. It breaks my heart." He was only one father among the thousands of starving Algerian families.

Jesus is indeed coming soon. The desperately poor all around the world are a sign that this is so. Are you ready for Jesus to come?

MATTHEW 25

Then the King will say to those on His right hand, "Come, you blessed of My Father, inherit the kingdom prepared for you from the foundation of the world."
Matthew 25:34.

I have had a preview of the dividing of the "sheep" from the "goats" at the time of Christ's coming. When we were walking over the border mountains between Burma and India during our escape from the war, we camped every evening. And every evening we found that there were two distinct kinds of people in the group. The good people liked to be together, and the bad people liked to be together. On one side of the camp the people were kind and helpful, and every night they sang songs of praise to God. But on the other side of camp they were unkind and selfish. They pushed and shoved, cursed and swore, grumbled and growled, murmured and complained. Nobody told the people what side of the camp to go to. They just went where they wanted to go. But I could see that the good people always stayed together in one part of the camp because they had always been good and they could be happy only among good people. And the bad people gathered together in their part of the camp because they had always been bad and they could be happy only among bad people. They couldn't be happy among good people.

One evening when we had just finished our soup, someone called out, "Mr. Hare, won't you play your trumpet for us?" So I took my trumpet out of my bundle and began to play "Take the Name of Jesus With You." Now, sitting on a rock near me was a man who always stayed on the other side of the camp. When he heard me begin to play, I wish you could have seen him. He listened for just a few seconds to see whether I might play "Roll Out the Barrel" or something like that. When he recognized that I was playing a hymn, he dropped his spoon and his plate, clapped his hands over his ears, and ran off to the other side of the camp, shouting, "I don't belong here! Let me get out of here quick!"

Truly, bad people can't be happy with good people, and bad people could never be happy in heaven. Do you want to be at the right hand of Jesus when He comes, and hear Him say, "Come, you blessed of my Father"? All you need do is to get on the right side with the good people now, and stay there every day. Then when Jesus comes you will be there.

251

What! Could you not watch with Me one hour? Matthew 26:40.

September 6

When Jesus entered Gethsemane with Peter, James, and John, they did not know that Jesus was about to endure the most important hour in His ministry on this earth. If they had only known, they could have been the most privileged of all people on earth—to be able to encourage and comfort the Savior when He struggled in the darkness to make His final decision to die for our sins. If they had known, they would not have failed the Lord Jesus by going to sleep.

John could have spoken words of comfort to the Savior, but he went to sleep, and an angel had to do it. Peter could have lifted the Savior's head and held it lovingly on his chest, but he went to sleep, and an angel had to do it. Jesus longed for human sympathy, but His dearest, closest, most favored friends failed Him. They must have been ashamed about it, for neither John nor Peter ever mentioned it in his writings.

You and I have been chosen to witness faithfully for Jesus in the very last days of the earth's history. Will we measure up to our privilege, or will we fail Him by going to sleep? Perhaps this little story will help you remember to stay awake! Fifteen-year-old Ron was busy putting a model airplane together when he heard a knock at the front door. His mother opened the door, and a boy about Ron's age asked if he could come out for a while. So she went to Ron's door to tell him.

"Who is it?" he asked.

"I don't know his name," Mom replied.

"Oh, well, tell him I'm too busy," Ron said, bending back over the model plane. So Mother went back to the door and said, "Ron says he's too busy."

"When Ron knows it's me, he won't be too busy!" he said, running around to Ron's window. "Hi, Ron!" he called. "It's me! Come on out!"

"Oh, sure!" cried Ron, "if it's *you!*"

That's the way it is with us. We're often too busy to do missionary work for our teachers and leaders, but if we knew it was Jesus calling us to be true and faithful, how easy it would then be to watch with Him for one hour.

MATTHEW 27

What then shall I do with Jesus who is called Christ?
Matthew 27:22.

Try to imagine how the people felt, and what they did, and what they said, as they turned their eyes upon Jesus hanging on the cross at Calvary that day. The centurion was there. He was a hardened man. He had seen many criminals put to death, but as he looked upon Jesus he cried out, "Truly this was the Son of God!" (Matthew 27:54).

Joseph of Arimathea and Nicodemus were there. They secretly believed in Jesus, but were too timid to follow Him openly. But as they looked upon Jesus, suddenly they were ashamed of their timidity. They boldly went to Pilate and begged to get Christ's body for burial. And after that, they gave their wealth to the church, so that the cause of Christ might triumph in the world.

Peter must have been there too. Peter who had gone to sleep and had denied his Lord three times. But as he looked upon the compassionate Savior his heart was broken with repentance. Out into the darkness he went. He ran to the very place Jesus had agonized in the garden, and, kneeling in the same place, poor Peter wished that he could die. But he came out of the garden a new Peter, never again to deny his Lord. He truly followed Jesus even to the cross.

Two thieves were there, and as one looked upon Jesus, he believed. While the multitude mocked, he expressed his faith openly, and said, "Lord, remember me when You come into Your kingdom" (Luke 23:42). I wonder whether Barabbas was there. I wonder what he did and said.

The priests were angry and jealous. The people were astonished and afraid. But there was one happy man on Calvary that day. "Just think, *I* had the privilege of carrying His cross! Me! I came to Jerusalem hoping to see Him and hear Him, and—think of it—they let me carry His cross for Him!" All the way back home he must have told everybody he met. When he got there he must have gathered his children and grandchildren around him and said, "Listen while I tell you about the day I carried the cross for Jesus."

Don't you wish you could have had that honor? Only Simon the Cyrenian carried the Savior's cross of wood, but you can carry His cross of humility and service! Won't you gladly do it?

All authority has been given to Me in heaven and on earth. . . . And lo, I am with you always, even to the end of the age.
Matthew 28:18-20.

September 8

God has given us the "going" and the "teaching" and the "baptizing." He's given us the obeying, the being kind, the overcoming of temptation.

But we must always remember that the power to do these things belongs to Christ. There's no need for us ever to be without that power, however, because Christ has promised to be with us "always, even to the end." We can see electric bulbs and electric wires, but we cannot see electricity. We know the electric power is there, however, because when we flip the switch the light shines. Even so, we can see junior boys and girls, and although we cannot see the power of God, we can know the power is in them—because they shine!

A boy was flying a kite when an old man came along. "What are you doing?" he asked.

"I'm flying a kite, mister," the boy replied.

"Kite?" said the old gentleman. "Where is your kite?"

"Up there beyond the tops of the trees. Can't you see?" asked the boy, pointing.

"No, I can't see anything way up there. Are you sure you have something on the end of that string?"

"Oh, yes, mister. It's there, all right. Look! Can't you see it over there?" The old gentleman looked, then shook his head.

"No, I can't see anything at all. How do you know you've really got something up there on the end of the string?"

"Aw, mister," said the boy, "I can tell by the pull."

That's just the way it is with all of us. If the power of Jesus is in your life, you'll know it by the "pull." Is your life pulling toward obedience, respect, truthfulness, and faithfulness? It should be, and it can be. Just make Christ first in your life, and everyone will know it.

"Every soul is surrounded by an atmosphere of its own—an atmosphere, it may be, charged with the lifegiving power of faith, courage, and hope, and sweet with the fragrance of love. . . . By the atmosphere surrounding us, every person with whom we come in contact is consciously or unconsciously affected" *(Messages to Young People*, p. 417).

MARK 1

Now in the morning, having risen a long while before daylight, He went out and departed to a solitary place; and there He prayed. Mark 1:35.

September 9

Jesus kept the Morning Watch; do you? Jesus got up early and went to a quiet place to pray. You don't have to get up early and go to a special place to keep your Morning Watch. You can do it right in your own bedroom. As soon as you awake, with your very first thoughts, say in your heart, I am not my own; I belong to Jesus. Then take your Bible and read your daily devotional text; then drop to your knees and ask Jesus to be with you all day, to help you to be good. Then get dressed and see how frequently those first thoughts will come to your mind throughout the day.

Carl kept the Morning Watch, and his mother often reminded him, "Someday those texts will shine like jewels in the dark." One evening Carl went to the library to look up some facts for his homework. He found the book he needed and curled up in a comfortable chair in the corner to read. Then he went sound asleep. At 9:00 the bell rang. Everybody left the library. The librarian put the lights out and locked the front door, but Carl slept on with his book on his lap. It was midnight when he woke up, and for a minute he didn't know where he was. Oh, yes! He'd gone to sleep in the library. But smoke hung in the air. His eyes stung! He was choking. There was fire somewhere! For a second or two panic seized him; then his Morning Watch jewels began to shine in the dark. "Whenever I am afraid, I will trust in you" (Psalm 56:3). "Fear not, for I am with you" (Isaiah 41:10). He said aloud, "I will trust." His brain cleared. He was thinking now. *There's a telephone! Of course!* In the darkness he felt his way to the librarian's table. Could he find it in time? The smoke was getting worse! There it was! He called home. "Dad, I'm locked in the library, and there's a fire somewhere!"

Almost by the time he found his way to the front door, he could hear the sirens of the approaching fire brigade. "Good work!" they said, as they came in and soon got things under control. And by the time he could explain, Carl was the hero of the day.

"But, Mom," he confided afterward, "I couldn't have done it without those 'jewels in the dark.'"

Do you read your daily devotional every morning? Are you keeping the Morning Watch?

The Sabbath was made for man, and not man for the Sabbath. Mark 2:27.

September 10

We can never fully tell what a blessing the Sabbath has been to the people of God. But here is one story that tells how one man was blessed.

Down in Brazil there lived a poor man named Rui. He was a humble water carrier, and he was so poor that he even had to borrow the can in which he carried water. Then he heard about the seventh-day Sabbath and decided to keep it. Although he was earning hardly enough money to buy food for his family, Rui decided to pay tithe. His faithfulness to God made him faithful and honest and happy in his work. Soon he had so many customers that he bought his own water can and began to save a little each week in a small bank on his kitchen shelf. Soon it was full, and he bought a little donkey. Soon the bank was full again, and he bought another donkey. He taught his older son to help him in the water business. Soon the bank was full again, and Rui bought a store, and turned the water business over to his son.

After the sun set on every Sabbath evening, he put up a sign that said, "First day of the market." Sunday evening he put up another sign: "Second day of the market." He did that every evening until Friday evening— when the sign read "Sabbath." Then he closed his store, and as the sun set he gathered his family and they all sang as the Sabbath began. Since there are mother and father and 13 children in the family, the whole village knew when Sabbath began.

One time a pastor spent the weekend with Mr. Rui's family, and since they were all ready a little before Friday sundown he suggested they begin to sing. "No, no, Pastor," said Mr. Rui. "If we sing now, it will throw the village folks out of time. We always sing at a certain time, and the village folks set their clocks and their watches by our Sabbath songs."

No wonder God blessed Mr. Rui and his family! No wonder the Lord says, "Blessed is the man who does this . . . who keeps from defiling the Sabbath, and keeps his hand from doing any evil" (Isaiah 56:2).

Are you faithful and regular in welcoming the Sabbath? Try it, and see what blessing God will pour out upon you.

MARK 3

Whoever does the will of God is
My brother and My sister and mother.
Mark 3:35.

September **11**

The late dear old Brother Spicer used to say, "The Advent family is a good family to belong to," and it surely is! There is something about doing the will of God that binds people together even closer than a blood relationship. Once Mrs. Hare and I were traveling by ship to Australia, where I had several Sabbath school institutes to attend. As our boat left Vancouver, British Columbia, a large group of Adventists were at the wharf to see us off. An hour or two later our boat touched in at Victoria, and there we saw another group of Adventists. They were seeing off a couple and their children who were going to New Zealand. We were introduced and, of course, were in each other's company quite frequently after that.

"Are they relatives of yours?" asked Mr. Blakers, a fellow passenger.

"Oh, no!" I said.

"Then they must be old friends."

"Never saw them before."

"Then how come you're so friendly?"

"Why, we belong to the same church!" I explained.

At Honolulu another large group came down to meet us. They welcomed us with song and beautiful leis, as the Hawaiian people do. They took us ashore and later brought us back in style to the boat. "Just who are you, Mr. Hare?" asked friend Blakers. "Are you some prince traveling incognito?"

"Oh, no," I said. "They are just members of our church!"

At Fiji another big delegation was there to meet us. At Auckland, New Zealand, there were some more, and at Sydney there was a big crowd.

"Just what I expected," said friend Blakers. "Everywhere the boat stops there is a big delegation down to meet the Hares! I do declare, before I take my next tour, I'm going to join up with the Adventists! Then I'll have people at every port to welcome me."

Do you belong? Better join up before you take your next-world tour!

*With the same measure you use,
it will be measured to you.
Mark 4:24.*

September 12

Today's text contains a solemn truth. You do reap what you sow.

There was once a farmer who had rented a certain farm for years. He was a good farmer—he kept the soil well fertilized, he struggled to keep down the weeds, he kept the buildings well painted and in good repair, and he had no trouble renewing his lease year after year. However, one day the agent came to see him and said, "The son of the farm's owner is getting married, and he plans to live here on the farm. When your lease expires this year, you must look for another place."

The poor farmer was terribly discouraged. He begged again and again for the owner to change his mind and let him lease the farm again. But it was no good. "All my care and my faithful work for nothing!" he grumbled. The more he thought about it, the worse he felt, until one day, just for spite, he decided to take revenge. He went around gathering up weed seeds from the worst weeds he could find. Then one dark night just before he had to vacate, he walked up and down over the nice clean fields and sowed the weed seed everywhere he went. "There now!" he said to himself. "That will serve him right for taking the farm right from under my nose."

The next morning the agent came while he was still doing his chores. "You'll be glad to know," he said cheerfully, "that the owner's son has changed his plans. He's decided to live in the city, so you can lease the farm again." The poor farmer could hardly believe his ears! He stood there speechless for a moment or two, then realizing what he had done, and the days of toil and trouble it would take to undo what he meant for revenge, he began to tremble. "What a fool I've been," he muttered. "What a fool!"

The dear Book of God says: "Repay no one evil for evil. . . . Do not avenge yourselves, but rather give place to wrath; for it is written, 'Vengeance is Mine, I will repay,' say the Lord" (Romans 12:17-19). And this is God's way.

Life is too short for hatred and cross words. You are sure to get back what you sow anyway, so why not sow kindness, courtesy, and helpfulness? Then the reaping will be so much more pleasant.

MARK 5

*They came to Jesus, and saw the one who
had been demon-possessed . . . sitting
and clothed and in his right mind.
Mark 5:15.*

September **13**

The power of God is just as great today as it was 2,000 years ago. Some years ago the leader of the Haiti Mission wrote a remarkable story. A certain woman was envious of a younger woman, and wanted her job, so she went to a devil priest and paid him to torment her with evil spirits. For a year and a half the poor young woman was thrown about by evil spirits, who made her cry and shout and say all kinds of terrible things, so that she couldn't work. At last this woman's mother took her to another devil priest for help. For eight months he tried all kinds of things to free her from the evil spirits, but she just got worse and worse. Then someone told the mother that Seventh-day Adventists had power over evil spirits, so she sent for the elder of our church in town. He explained that he had no power—the power belonged to Jesus. He told them that if they would turn to Jesus and give their hearts to Jesus, He would cast out the evil spirits.

"We will. We will! Please help us. Tell us what to do," the mother said.

"First you must take off all your devil charms," the elder said. So they did. This made the spirits furious, and they threw the poor girl around till she cried out with pain and fear. Then the elder sang a hymn, read a psalm, and prayed. As he prayed, peace came to the heart of the young woman, and she was calm. She was so happy that she went to prayer meeting that week. But fearing that the evil spirits were not finished with her yet, a group of Adventists went to her house a few days later to pray again. While they were there a strange woman who had traveled many miles by bus arrived. As she came in there was a terrible noise, as when an angry mob is present, and the girl was seized again. Then the spirit spoke: "I am Lucifer. For 18 months I have been after this girl. Today I brought 300 spirits with me, but unfortunately for me, you Adventists got here first, and we found the house surrounded with the angels of Jesus." The Adventists sang, read another psalm, and prayed, then commanded the evil spirit in the name of Jesus to depart. And it did. And the dear woman has been free ever since.

Here in Christian lands we don't speak of people being possessed with devils. But I have seen some juniors throw tantrums and get into fits of temper, and I'm sure it's not the Spirit of Jesus that makes them do that. Do you need some evil spirits cast out of you? Jesus can do it.

MARK 7

For from within, out of the heart of men, proceed evil thoughts. Mark 7:21.

September 14

How many good-looking juniors are spoiled by the meanness and unkindness that comes forth out of their hearts and from their lips? I once read a story about boy named Pat. Not too far away there lived an elderly woman in a little rundown cabin. Pat and his sister Jeanie frequently saw her gathering sticks in her wheelbarrow, and now and then they saw her counting her pennies very carefully when she bought her groceries at the store. They never learned her name, but I'm sorry to say that Pat called her "Old Mrs. Penny Pincher."

"There she goes again," he called one day. "Old Mrs. Penny Pincher picking up sticks."

"You shouldn't talk like that," Jeanie said. "It's real mean of you."

But Pat just laughed. "When it's dark tonight, I'm going over to Old Mrs. Penny Pincher's and scatter her sticks all over the yard," he said.

"That's a mean, shabby trick to play on a poor old woman," said Jeanie. And when the snow began to fall that afternoon, she made up her mind that she was going to run over and help her put her sticks carefully inside where Pat couldn't touch them. It didn't take her long to reach the little cabin, and she was just going to knock when she heard a voice inside. "She must have company," she said to herself. She was so close that she could hear what the woman was saying.

"Dear Father—"

"Why, she's praying," said Jeanie, as she held her breath.

"Please let these sticks of wood keep me warm until my boy comes home in the morning. My Jim will have money, and he won't let me be cold and hungry any longer."

Jeanie couldn't stand to hear another word. She raced home and told Pat what she had heard. Pat looked sick. "Suppose we put our allowance together and buy her a sack of coal," he said at last.

"Let's do," she agreed. Mother filled a basket with food. Then over to the little cabin they went. They put their gifts quietly down, knocked on the door, and hurried softly away.

"I wish I hadn't been so mean," confessed Pat. "I feel so much happier this way."

Are you ever mean and unkind? Give your heart and your lips a good bath, and come clean. It really is more fun.

MARK 6

And He called the twelve to Himself, and began to send them out.
. . . So they went out and preached that people should repent.
Mark 6:7-12.

September 15

In 1858, only 14 years after the early Adventists began to keep the Sabbath, a converted Polish Catholic priest, M. B. Czechowski, attended some tent meetings in Ohio and accepted the Sabbath. Six years later he wanted the church to send him to Italy as a missionary. When he was told there were not sufficient funds, he became impatient and went to the first-day Adventists. They agreed to send him to Europe. But, strange to say, as he traveled around through Italy and into Switzerland, he preached not only Christ's second coming but also the seventh-day Sabbath! A company of Sabbathkeeping Adventists was organized near Basel, Switzerland, and in a few years they sent one of their men to America to become acquainted with the American Sabbathkeepers. A few years later they sent someone else to plead for help, with the result that in 1874 the General Conference selected J. N. Andrews to be their first overseas missionary. He was sent to organize the Adventist work in Europe.

Today, September 15, is the anniversary of the day that Andrews sailed. What a lot has happened since then. And what strange ways God has chosen to open up the way for the message to be preached! One Sabbath morning, soon after Andrews arrived, the little company in Basel was having Sabbath school when they heard a knock on the door. The woman of the house opened the door, and there stood a beggar.

"Come in," she said. He came in and sat down, and listened to the Sabbath school lesson.

"These people are keeping the Sabbath like the Jews," the beggar said to himself in surprise. Then he remembered another group of Sabbathkeepers he had met in Elberfeld, Germany. As they talked together after the Sabbath school lesson he remembered that the leader's name was Pastor Lindermann. J. N. Andrews wrote down the name and the town, and the next year he found the Sabbathkeeping Adventists in Germany. Pastor Lindermann had begun to keep the Sabbath from his own study of the Bible, and did not know of any other Christians keeping the Sabbath till Andrews found them.

What a wonderful God we serve! Study hard, for if time lasts He may need to send you out, too.

261

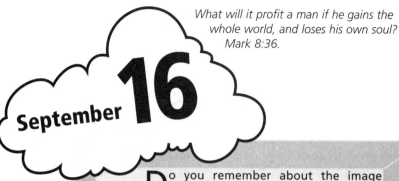

What will it profit a man if he gains the whole world, and loses his own soul? Mark 8:36.

September 16

Do you remember about the image Nebuchadnezzar saw in his dream? Then you will remember that the toes of the image were of part iron and part clay, which showed that the smaller kingdoms into which the Roman Empire broke up would never join together to make another world-wide empire. Someday in a history class you may learn the names of those kingdoms: Ostrogoths, Visigoths, Franks, Vandals, Suevi, Alamanni, Anglo-Saxons, Heruli, Lombards, and Burgundians.

Well, now, listen. In the year A.D. 768 Charlemagne became king of the Franks (later called French), and in his heart he decided to conquer his smaller neighbor nations and rule the whole world. So he conquered the Lombards in Italy, the Saxons in Germany, and after 50 campaigns he was made emperor of Rome in A.D. 800. He then ruled practically all the western part of the Roman Empire. But he died in 814, without his dream of a world empire coming true, and was buried in a large marble tomb.

Nine hundred years went by; then one day his tomb was opened. There was his skeleton, still clothed in kingly robes, sitting on a marble slab. His golden scepter was still in his skeleton hand. On his knee was an open scroll, and a bony finger was pointing to the words "What shall it profit a man, if he shall gain the whole world, and lose his own soul?"

Never be deceived by worldly ambition or wealth. The salvation of your soul is worth more than anything else in all the world. Make your soul's salvation the first and most important aim in your life.

MARK 9

If anyone desires to be first, he shall be last of all and servant of all.
Mark 9:35.

September 17

Truly great people take pleasure in serving others, and the faithful performance of helpful little acts that no one else takes time to do is a sign of true greatness. Ellen White says: "The youngest child that loves and fears God is greater in His sight than the most talented and learned man who neglects the great salvation. . . . Those who feel that they are God's servants will be . . . trusted anywhere. Citizens of heaven will make the best citizens of earth. A correct view of our duty to God leads to clear perceptions of our duty to our fellow men" (*Messages to Young People,* p. 329).

Some years ago a man was walking down a busy street in New York City when he saw a Black man walking along carrying two heavy suitcases. Immediately his heart prompted him to help. He put his hand on the man's shoulder and said kindly, "Pretty heavy, brother, isn't it? Here, let me take one. I'm going your way."

There was no use to protest, and soon they were walking along together. The bighearted man learned that his newfound friend was walking from the railway station to a hotel several blocks away because he couldn't afford a taxi, and that made his helpful deed all the sweeter. He arrived at the hotel before he learned that the man was Booker T. Washington, who later became the famous founder of the Tuskegee Institute.

And who was the bighearted man who carried one of the suitcases? He was Theodore Roosevelt, who later became one of the greatest of American presidents. In the Mount Rushmore National Memorial in South Dakota his head is carved in imperishable granite along with Presidents Washington, Jefferson, and Lincoln.

Always keep your eyes open and faithfully do the helpful little things that you can find to do for others.

September **18**

Jesus answered and said to him, "What do you want Me to do for you?" The blind man said to Him, "Rabboni, that I may receive my sight." Mark 10:51.

My heart goes out to anyone who is blind. Think of poor old Bartimaeus sitting in darkness day after day, year after year, being able only to listen to the happiness of those who could see. How discouraged he must have felt! Then Jesus came and changed his night to day. It is hard even to imagine his great happiness when he looked up and saw the lovely face of Jesus. In our modern times we often hear of people who have been blind for a few years having an operation and being able to see again. But here is a story from our Kwahu Hospital in Ghana, West Africa, that tells of a miracle in answer to prayer that brought sight to a young mother named Theresa.

She came to the hospital to have her baby, and all went well till the evening after the baby was born. Then Theresa became hot with fever, began to go stiff, and had a kind of seizure that doctors everywhere dread. Dr. Hyde was called, and everything possible was done with medicines, treatments, and prayer. After three days the seizure gradually went away and her fever cooled down. But then they noticed unnatural movements with her hands. She had to feel around for her baby's hands and feet. She had to feel around for the food on her tray. They quickly called the doctor, and tests showed that poor Theresa was now completely blind. It was a terrible shock to all the hospital staff. They called in her relatives; then they all knelt in a circle around her bed and prayed. They prayed that God would forgive all their sins and that He would lead Theresa to know more of His will for her, and if it would be to His glory, that He would perform a miracle right there.

When they arose from their knees they didn't need to ask whether she had been healed. There was a light in Theresa's eyes. "I see! I see!" she said, and a wave of joy and happiness swept through the whole hospital.

There is another kind of blindness that many juniors have. "I *don't see* why I can't go," they say. "I *can't see* why this and why that." If you ever get this kind of blindness, pray to God that you can receive your sight too. Then you will be able to understand that your parents and teachers know what is best for you.

MARK 11

Have faith in God. . . . Whatever things you ask when you pray, believe that you receive them, and you will have them. Mark 11:22-24.

September **19**

Paul tells us to come boldly unto the throne of grace, that we can find help in the time of need (Hebrews 4:16). But unless we have faith in God and in His promises, we can never be bold and courageous in prayer. One day some years ago in Burma I was working at my desk when a timid little boy came in and stood beside me. He stood first on one leg then on the other, and opened his mouth to speak, but the words simply wouldn't come.

"Come on, sonny," I said. "Tell me what you want. Don't be scared. I won't eat you."

He opened his mouth with a tremendous effort and said, "Please, Thara . . . I . . . please, Thara . . . I want . . . a new . . . shirt."

"All right," I said. "We have plenty of cloth and plenty of big girls to sew shirts for little boys. That's nothing to be scared about."

"But, Thara, I . . . I haven't any money."

"Oh, oh!" And come to think about it, I too would be scared to go into a shop and ask for a shirt if I didn't have any money, wouldn't you? I soon made arrangements to put his shirt on his account, and away he went as happy as could be. I was still thinking about how scared he was, when another little boy burst into my office, put two pice down on my desk, and blurted out, "Please, Thara, two pice worth of soap."

Now, I was the director of the mission. I didn't sell soap in the store. I had big girls spend regular hours in the store selling soap and pencils. But he was so earnest, so bold, so courageous, and he had his money. I just didn't have the heart to tell him to come back some other time, so I got up and gave him the soap.

"Thank you, Thara," he said pleasantly, and off he went as happy as could be.

When you get on your knees to pray, are you timid about your requests to God, or are you bold? Have *faith* in God and in His promises; then *you* too can ask and receive.

The stone which the builders rejected has become the chief cornerstone.
Mark 12:10.

September 20

During the building of Solomon's Temple great big stones were brought in from the quarry to be built into the foundation. Among these huge stones there was one that didn't seem to fit, so it was rejected and laid to one side. But when they finally came to the last corner of the foundation they found that the rejected stone was an exact fit, and it had already been tested with all kinds of weather, so it became the chief cornerstone.

What a perfect illustration this is of Jesus the Messiah. How many people today reject the only One who can help them build a strong character in this world and give them eternal life in the world to come!

The story is told about one of the soldiers of Alexander the Great who was searching for booty in the ruins of the palace of Darius. He was a simple fellow, and he knew nothing about precious stones. He found a leather bag containing priceless unset jewels, but he did not recognize the great value of the shiny little stones. So he shook them out onto the rubbish heap and eagerly claimed the leather bag. He girded it onto his belt and went around boasting to everybody about the splendid bag he had found in which he could carry his food. Poor, simple man. He threw away a fortune and got only a leather bag.

Be sure you don't make the same mistake. Make Christ the chief cornerstone in the foundation of your life.

MARK 13

Heaven and earth will pass away, but
My words will by no means pass away.
Mark 13:31.

September 21

In 1949, while in London, England, I went to the British and Foreign Bible Society to obtain a new copy of the Bible in the Karen language of Burma. My old copy had been lost during the war, and it seemed impossible to get one from Burma. Four years had passed since the war ended, and as I approached the building I was shocked to see so much destruction still visible in London. I went into the salesroom and made my request. The salesman went to a shelf and came back with a Karen Bible.

"Can you read it?" he asked.

"I surely can," I replied, and opened it and began reading. The salesman was delighted. "Just a moment," he said. He disappeared for a minute or two, then came back with the manager of the Bible Society.

I told them of my 20 years of mission service among the Karens. I told them I had sold hundreds of copies of the precious Karen Bible. Then the manager said, "Mr. Hare, let me show you around." He took me upstairs. He showed me the room where nearly 1,000 different translations of the Bible were on the bookshelves. He showed me the "Mary Jones Bible," one of the first to be published. Then he took me into the huge pressroom and told me to look out of a window on the west side.

"What do you see, Mr. Hare?" he asked.

"Just heaps of broken brick buildings," I replied. We went to a window on the north side and another on the east side. It was just the same—nothing but piles and piles of bricks from the broken-down buildings that had been destroyed by the bombs.

Then the manager, with tears in his eyes, said, "Mr. Hare, all during the war, while the bombs fell all around us and destroyed these buildings, our presses kept running! The windows were smashed and we had to board them up, but we kept on printing the Word of God!" Then we came down to the front lobby of the building, and there in great letters a foot high all around the top of the walls I read the words "Heaven and earth shall pass away: but my words shall not pass away" (KJV). I think I know why those presses kept running, don't you? There is miracle power in the Word of God. Make that power yours.

And immediately, while He was still speaking, Judas, one of the twelve, [came] with a great multitude. . . . Now His betrayer had given them a signal, saying, "Whomever I kiss, He is the One."
Mark 14:43, 44.

September 22

Because of the despicable act of betraying the Lord Jesus, we are apt to conclude that Judas was all bad—a horrible, ugly, selfish, covetous thief.

But wait. Don't be too fast to judge. Judas was a Judean. He believed that Jesus was the Messiah, and he actually volunteered to follow Jesus! Jesus didn't want him to get the idea that this would bring him wealth and honor and fame, so He told him, "Foxes have holes and birds of the air have nests, but the Son of Man has nowhere to lay His head" (Matthew 8:20). Then we read in *The Desire of Ages,* "The disciples were anxious that Judas should become one of their number. He was of commanding appearance, a man of keen discernment and executive ability, and they commended him to Jesus as one who would greatly assist Him in His work" (p. 294). "He had some precious traits of character that might have been made a blessing to the church. If he had been willing to wear the yoke of Christ, he might have been among the chief of the apostles" (p. 295).

He was capable and so clever that the disciples made him their treasurer! How then could this promising man become the betrayer? You can read why in *The Desire of Ages:* "Judas was blinded to his own weakness of character, and Christ placed him where he would have an opportunity to see and correct this. . . . But while listening daily to the lessons of Christ and witnessing His unselfish life, Judas indulged his covetous disposition. . . . Often when he did a little service for Christ, or devoted time to religious purposes, he paid himself out of this meager fund. In his own eyes these pretexts served to excuse his action; but in God's sight he was a thief" (pp. 717, 718). So you see that Judas hardened his heart when he had opportunity to do good. He refused to heed the Savior's counsel, and followed his own selfish practices until his very name became repulsive.

Would you like to know what to do so that you will never be a Judas? When your mistakes are pointed out, confess them, and stop your own selfish ways.

"Selfish interest, if given room to act, dwarfs the mind and hardens the heart; if allowed to control, it destroys moral power" (*Messages to Young People*, p. 150).

He saved others; Himself He cannot save.
Mark 15:31.

September 23

No truer statement was ever made than that Christ could not save Himself. Jesus came to save the world, and the price of our salvation was His precious blood. Christ could have come down from the cross, but He would not. That is why every sinner can find pardon for his or her sins and receive the gift of life—eternal life!

The Ahoada County Hospital in east Nigeria was staffed by Seventh-day Adventist doctors and nurses. At one time I heard Nurse Maria Moletta, who had just returned from a visit there, tell this story about Dr. DeShay, the physician in charge at the time. The doctor had worked a full, heavy day in the 70-bed hospital. He'd had morning worship with the staff, and visits to the hospital patients. Then there were two or three hours in surgery, and the usual host of patients in the afternoon clinic. And by the time the day was done he was looking forward to a good night's rest, when suddenly he heard a group of people hurrying in.

"Master, Master," they called plaintively. "Our friend is dying. Please come and help!" Quickly Dr. DeShay ran outside, and there at the gate, carried in a blanket, was a poor man who was bleeding in spite of the rough bandages they had put on him.

"Yes," said the doctor, "I can help, and I will. But this man needs some blood. Who will volunteer to give this man a pint of blood?" No one answered. They were all afraid. "Will no one give a pint of blood to save this man's life?" he asked again. But still there was no response. "Then," he said, turning to his assistants who had come to help, "take a sample of my blood and see whether it is compatible. Then prepare this man for an immediate operation." The doctor's blood was compatible, so he had his assistants draw one pint of his blood and give a transfusion to the patient. Then the doctor operated, and saved the man's life. After surgery he waited long enough to make sure that all was well, then went out to the group of fearful friends with the glad news, "He lives! He lives!" At that, a clamor of thankful voices arose. Another life had been saved with blood.

Have you taken advantage of the blood of Jesus that was shed for you? "If there had been but one lost soul, Christ would have died for that one" (*Christ's Object Lessons*, p. 187).

269

Go into all the world and preach the gospel to every creature.
Mark 16:15.

September 24

The word *gospel* means "good news," and wherever the gospel is preached, it makes people happy. Not everyone can preach this good news from a pulpit in a church, but everyone can preach it in his or her daily life by speaking words of kindness and good cheer, which will make people happy. Kind words passed along throughout the day make a lot of people happy.

One morning the manager of a big city store said to one of his department heads, "Mr. Parker, you always keep things running smoothly in your section. I like the way you do it."

The kind words didn't cost the manager anything, but they made Mr. Parker very happy, and it wasn't long before he said to one of his clerks, "Miss Belle, you have a very successful way of handling difficult customers. I'm so glad you're in my department."

Miss Belle's eyes sparkled with pleasure, and when she went to lunch she couldn't help saying to the girl who filled her order, "It's great of you to be so prompt. Now I'll have time to do a little errand during this noon hour."

The heart of the little server sang all the rest of the day, and when she got home that evening she said to her young brother, "Jimmy, I'm so proud of you—working on your homework the way you do. It isn't every girl who has a brother she can be proud of."

Jimmy looked up in surprise, and all he could say was "Aw, now." But there was a warm glow in his heart, and the next day, after his teacher had explained a problem to him, he said, "You surely know how to make it clear. I wish I knew as much as you."

The tired look vanished from her face. When the teacher bought her newspaper on her way home, she smiled at the newsboy and said, "Billy, you surely are dependable. You'll make a good businessman someday."

And Billy whistled all the way home. At supper he said, "Mother, you sure are a good cook. A guy can't help working hard—with a supper like this and a mom like you waiting for him at home." And Mom smiled and wasn't quite so tired. And so *many* people were made happy, yet nobody thought they were preaching the good news.

When Jesus said to go and preach the good news, He meant you, too. Are you doing it?

The angel said to him, "Do not be afraid, . . .
for your prayer is heard."
Luke 1:13.

September **25**

An angel came to Zacharius. Maybe Zacharius had been praying for a son, or maybe for the Messiah to come in his lifetime. In either case, the angel came to tell him that his prayer had been heard. John the Baptist was born to make people ready for the ministry of Jesus on this earth. Six months after John's birth, Jesus was born. When the angel appeared to Zacharius, he said, "Do not be afraid." And when the angel appeared to Mary, he again said, "Do not be afraid." You know, when people want to get ready for Jesus to come, Satan tries his hardest to make them afraid. But I am glad to tell you that there is always a power connected with loving Jesus that helps people overcome all fear.

In Ethiopia, three days' journey from our Gimbie Mission station, there lived a witch doctor up on the hillside overlooking a village. He had several children. His third son, Alemu, had the care of the sheep and the goats. "Did you listen to that stranger down by the river?" the witch doctor asked angrily one day as Alemu brought the sheep back from the river.

"No, Father," said Alemu. But he did not tell him he had heard a few words that had made him hungry to hear more, and had caught a glimpse of a picture that was more beautiful than anything he had ever seen. The next day he lingered a little longer, and the next day a little longer. He couldn't sleep at night. *Heaven, Jesus, no more sickness, no more fear*—the words kept ringing in his ears. The next day as he lingered his two big brothers came down the hillside and grabbed him and dragged him back to his father.

The witch doctor shouted, "Didn't I tell you that this Jesus power would spoil my power to bewitch!" Then he cursed Alemu, beat him severely, and shut him up in the hut. But what he had heard was so beautiful. It had to be true. As he thought about Jesus his heart was filled with peace. He was not afraid anymore. He knew what he would do. The mission was only a three-day journey away. He could find his way there. Then he wouldn't be tired or hungry again. One night he slipped away into the darkness and became a pupil at our school.

Has the hope of seeing Jesus taken all fear from your heart?

Why did you seek Me? Did you not know that I must be about My Father's business? Luke 2:49.

September 26

Wonderful Jesus! He was only 12 years old, but He knew already what He was going to be when He grew up; and there He was, doing His Father's business! A few years ago I heard a thrilling story about a 12-year-old boy in Rome who also was determined to be about his Father's business. He had just been baptized and was selling books to earn his way through school. God had blessed him, and he already had 50,000 lira saved up. One day he came to a very big house. For just a second or two he was tempted to go past it. But he remembered that he had promised to go to every house. So he went to the house and rang the bell.

"May I see the lady of the house?" he said politely to the maid who opened the door.

"You mean you want to see the countess?" she asked in surprise. "You cannot see her."

"But I have something so important to show her. I'm sure she would want to see me," he pleaded. And he was such a gentleman that the maid finally took him into the front room. When the countess came, he told her all about his books. The countess was thrilled.

"What are you going to be when you grow up?" she asked.

"I want to be a minister," he said.

"Oh, you mean a priest?"

"No, I mean a minister—a Seventh-day Adventist minister. I am selling books to earn my way through school," he said.

"Now, look here, sonny," said the countess. "If you will agree, I will adopt you as my own son. I will give you a million lira and I will educate you for the priesthood."

The boy looked kindly into the woman's face and said, "Countess, many years ago there was a man named Judas who sold his Lord for 30 pieces of silver. But I would not sell my Lord for 1 million lira." When the countess saw his earnestness, she didn't say any more. She just bought his books. That's all we know for the time being, but of one thing I am very sure. The countess will never forget that junior boy who had made up his mind to be about his Father's business.

What are you going to be when you grow up? Have you made up your mind yet?

LUKE 3

He who has two coats, let him share with him who
has none; and he who has food, let him do likewise.
Luke 3:11, RSV.

When John the Baptist spoke to the people who came to hear him in the wilderness, he summed up a Christian's duty to friends, neighbors, and the world. Whatever we have, God has given it to us to share. And when we share, God always gives back a greater blessing than we had before.

Many years ago a young man by the name of George Boldt was a desk clerk in one of the large Philadelphia hotels. One evening an elderly man came in and asked for a room. "I'm sorry, sir," said George, "but every room is taken for tonight."

The man turned as if to go, but paused to say, "I'm sorry, too, because my wife is ill and I need a room. I have not been able to find one anywhere tonight."

"I am very sorry, sir," said George. "There isn't a room left." The man started to walk away, but George called him back. "Wait a minute, sir," he said. "I did not say you couldn't have a room. I just said there wasn't a room vacant in the hotel. But if your wife is ill, and if you will accept it, you shall have my room. I can sleep on one of these chairs when I go off duty. Please follow me." And George took the couple to his own room and made them comfortable.

Early the next morning the old man called the hotel manager on the telephone and said, "You have a clerk named George who was on duty last night?"

"Yes, we do," said the manager. "George Boldt. May I ask what you want him for?"

"Want him for?" said the old man. "I am John Jacob Astor, and I am going to build the biggest hotel in America. I want that boy for my business manager. For years I've been looking for a man who knows how to be kind to strangers."

The Waldorf-Astoria Hotel became very famous, and equally famous was George Boldt, who managed that hotel for 40 years. George didn't have two rooms. He had only one, but he gladly gave it up for the night and received a 40-year blessing.

Try sharing with those in need and see what God will do for you.

And as His custom was, He went into the synagogue on the Sabbath day, and stood up to read. Luke 4:16.

September 28

Jesus always went to church on Sabbath. No doubt His mother took Him when He was little, and He just kept on going every Sabbath, rain or shine, hot or cold, until it became His habit, or custom. Millions of Seventh-day Adventists have the same habit. They simply couldn't think of staying away from Sabbath school for anything.

Among the many inspiring acquaintances I made during my visit to Brazil in 1956 was that of an influential lawyer named Americo Coelho. Now, *coelho* is the Portuguese word for "rabbit," so as I was introduced to him, I smiled and said, "Our names are almost the same. Mine is Hare!" He was then 73 years old and had been an Adventist for 33 years. For most of that time he had taught a Sabbath school class in the little Victoria church in the state of Espirito Santo (Holy Spirit). He had been so highly respected for his honesty and his integrity that once when there was a vacancy in the position of secretary of state, he was asked to serve in the position until a new secretary could be elected. In addition to this, he also had served eight years as a judge in the court of Victoria. On one occasion the president of Brazil was to visit the city of Victoria, and elaborate plans were made for his reception and entertainment.

"Mr. Coelho," said the chairman of the committee, "as one of our prominent citizens we want you to be one of the honored ones to meet the president at 10:00 on Saturday morning, and you will sit on the platform with him when he addresses us."

"I'm sorry, gentlemen," said Americo Coelho, "but I have another appointment, and I cannot be there."

"But this is the president of our country!" they urged.

"Yes, I know," he replied. "But I am the teacher of a Sabbath school class at that time, and I must be there." And Americo Coelho was there.

I can well imagine the kind of welcome Jesus, the King of kings, will give him when he goes to Sabbath school in the New Jerusalem. Can't you?

Do you have the go-to-church-on-Sabbath habit?

LUKE 5

Those who are well have no need of a physician, but those who are sick. I have not come to call the righteous, but sinners, to repentance.
Luke 5:31, 32.

September **29**

In order that we can readily understand how Jesus can hate sin but at the same time love sinners and have mercy on them, Jesus likened Himself to a physician. In our scripture today we read of the healing of the leper and the man who had palsy. How kind and sympathetic Jesus was to these poor sufferers! Truly He was the loving physician. In the front lobby of the Johns Hopkins Hospital, in Baltimore, there is a beautiful marble statue of Christ called *The Divine Healer*. I have seen it several times. On the base of the statue are carved the words "Come unto Me, all ye that labor and are heavy laden, and I will give you rest." The hands are outstretched in blessing, and the face, filled with tender sympathy, is looking down in love. Many people visit the Johns Hopkins Hospital just to see that statue, and everyone who sees it is impressed with the Savior's mercy revealed there.

A story is told about a certain infidel who heard people talking about the statue, and about the way they felt when they saw it. He heard so much that he determined to go and see it for himself. He went. He looked at the statue, but felt nothing. It was only a piece of cold marble to him. And he was disappointed, for in spite of his unbelief, he had secretly hoped to feel the charm that others talked about so enthusiastically. He looked at it from one side, then the other, and with disappointment showing on his face, he was about to leave the building when a child's hand slipped into his and a sweet voice said, "Don't go away disappointed, mister. You haven't seen Him from the right place yet. Come, I'll show you where to look." And the child led the man to the foot of the statue and said, "There, mister. Now kneel at His feet and look up!"

It does make a difference how you look at the Savior. If you feel tired and weighed down with problems, if you have made mistakes, if you are so discouraged that you don't feel like trying anymore, why don't you kneel at His feet and look up? "The Lord is near to those who have a broken heart, and saves such as have a contrite spirit" (Psalm 34:18).

*Give, and it will be given to you: good measure,
pressed down, shaken together, and running over.
. . . For with the same measure that you use,
it will be measured back to you.*
Luke 6:38.

September 30

It may be only a coincidence, but after giving His disciples the beautiful promise in Luke 6:38, Christ's next words were "Can the blind lead the blind?" This morning we'll meet a blind woman who gave in good measure to thousands of people all over the world, and who received again the same kind of generous abundant blessings by which she blessed others. Fanny Jane Crosby lost her eyesight at 6 weeks of age through a mistake made by a country doctor unqualified to practice. It was a sad day for her family when they learned that their little girl would never see again. But God had bestowed upon her the gift for writing poetry, and she soon found a way to write verses without seeing with her eyes. When she was only 8, she wrote:

O what a happy soul am I!
Although I cannot see,
I am resolved that in this world
Contented I will be.

At age 15 Fanny was finally able to go to a well-known school for the blind in New York City. She was thrilled, and, after graduating, stayed on to teach for 11 years. She married a classmate, a musician, and he wrote music for some of her poems. As a result of her Christian witness in Congress, Fanny became friends with well-known political leaders such as John Quincy Adams, Jefferson Davis, William Cullen Bryant, and the U.S. presidents of her day.

Fanny wrote about 8,000 hymns. Some that we sing over and over are "Tell Me the Story of Jesus," "Jesus Is Tenderly Calling You Home," "Safe in the Arms of Jesus," "'Tis the Blessed Hour of Prayer," "Rescue the Perishing," "Pass Me Not, O Gentle Savior, and "I Am Thine, O Lord." When you sing "When my lifework is ended and I cross the swelling tide" you cannot help feeling the pathos of the closing words—"I shall know Him by the nailprints in His hands." Only a blind person would think of identifying the Savior by feeling the prints of the nails. And you cannot help sharing her great joy expressed in the chorus of the hymn "Saved by Grace," where she says, "And I shall see Him face to face, and tell the story—saved by grace." Fanny Jane Crosby blessed the world by giving of her talent, good measure, pressed down, and running over.

What are you doing to bless the world with *your* talent?

This is he of whom it is written: "Behold, I send My messenger before Your face, who will prepare Your way before You." Luke 7:27.

October **1**

Jesus Himself said that John the Baptist was to prepare the way for Him, and Matthew adds these words to what Luke reports Jesus said about John at that time: "If you are willing to receive it, he is Elijah who is to come" (Matthew 11:14). John was indeed doing the same kind of work that Elijah had done. He was doing it just before the first coming of Christ, and he was partly fulfilling the prophecy of Malachi 4:5. This prophecy indicates that the same kind of work will be done in the spirit and power of Elijah before Christ's second coming. We believe this is being done by those who are preaching the three angels' messages of Revelation 14. Search throughout the world, and the only people you will find preaching the three angels' messages are the Seventh-day Adventists.

Today, October 1, is the anniversary of the day in 1860 when our denominational name, "Seventh-day Adventist," was chosen. As you know, there were many Adventists in the various churches before 1844, people who believed in the second coming of Christ. But in that year one group of Adventists began to keep the seventh-day Sabbath. Little by little, Adventists from the other churches joined with the Sabbathkeeping Adventists, until, after 14 years, there were about 3,000 members among 100 groups. Then at a meeting in Battle Creek, Michigan, church leaders discussed choosing a legal name for the publishing house and the denomination. During the early years many names had been used to refer to the group—"the brethren," "the little flock," "the remnant people," "Sabbathkeepers," and "The church of God," but finally David Hewitt suggested "Seventh-day Adventist," and it was voted and accepted.

Do you remember the name David Hewitt? He was an interesting person. When Joseph Bates first visited Battle Creek, he went to the postmaster and asked who was the most honest man in town. And he was directed to the home of David Hewitt. At that time he was a merchant who sold small household articles from a wagon as he drove around town. He was so honest that the whole town knew him as the most honest man in town. He was the first convert in Battle Creek, and had the honor of suggesting our denominational name.

Are you an honest Seventh-day Adventist?

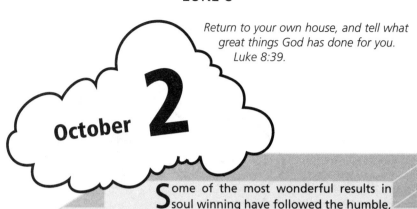

Return to your own house, and tell what great things God has done for you. Luke 8:39.

October 2

Some of the most wonderful results in soul winning have followed the humble, personal testimony given among friends and relatives. Because the two healed demoniacs went around showing what great things God had done for them, about nine months later, when Jesus came to that part of the country again, more than 4,000 people flocked to hear Him and stayed with Him for three days (see Mark 8:1-10).

Pastor Antonio Nogueira, from Brazil, tells this story of the wonderful results of the personal testimony of a young man in that country. In a certain town lived a young man who was full of life and very talented. His mother was a Seventh-day Adventist, but he had no time for God or religion. He gave himself entirely to the world—its pleasures and its evils. Then one terrible day he discovered that he had leprosy! As there was no hospital for the disease in that town, the doctor treating him required that he be confined to his own bedroom. He was terribly lonely. His friends forgot him, and he was tempted to take his life.

Then one day a colporteur came along and sold him a book. He read it, and it changed his life. He became a Seventh-day Adventist, and his heart burned to tell his friends about his newfound faith. But how could he do it? Then a missionary gave him a Picture Roll. He looked at the colorful pictures, prepared a talk on each picture, then hung the Picture Roll out of his window. One day as one of his former friends passed by, he stopped to look at it. What was it? What did it mean? From his window, the young man explained the story behind the picture, and asked him to stop again the next time he went by. That friend told others, and others came. They, in turn, told even more people. The earnestness with which the young man told what God's love had done for him appealed to them, and by the time the man's leprosy was cured, 42 people were ready for baptism. They all worshipped together in the Adventist church in that town. It is true that there is no preaching more powerful than the simple telling of what God has done for you.

Has God given you happiness, faith, satisfaction, and hope? Go tell your friends what great things God has done for you.

LUKE 9

No one, having put his hand to the plow, and looking back, is fit for the kingdom of God. Luke 9:62.

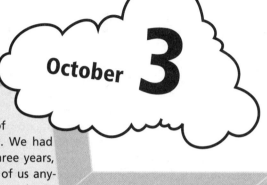

October 3

I can never forget the day that Thara Peter and I opened a school among the Karens at Ohn Daw, on the banks of the beautiful Salween River in Burma. We had been doing medical work there for three years, and the jungle people weren't afraid of us anymore. Many were asking when we were going to open a school, so the mission appointed a fine young Karen man, whose name was Peter, to be the teacher. With great enthusiasm we told everyone, "Next Monday morning we're going to open school. Be sure to come next Monday morning."

"Sure, sure!" they said as they heard the happy news. So next Monday morning we opened school—but nobody came. "Maybe they'll come tomorrow," said Peter. "The jungle people don't know the days of the week very well." So we opened school the next day, but nobody came. The next day we went to a village where we knew we would get two students, and sure enough, they were ready. So we brought them back, and the next morning we really did open school.

While Peter taught the two students I went out to gather in some more, but no more came. The next day Peter taught the two students again while I went out to find some more, but again no one came. And no one came the next day or the next or the next. For three weeks poor Peter taught school with only two students. He became so discouraged that he decided to quit. So early one morning he put his bed bundle and his box on his head and went off to the little river steamer landing one mile away. He had had all he could take. He wasn't going to do this one more day! The steamer came, the gangplank was put down onto the sandy bank, and then this morning's text came to Peter's mind: "No one, having put his hand to the plow, and looking back, is fit for the kingdom of God." For just a second he hesitated. Then he thought of me there all alone, and he said to himself, "I can't turn back. I won't run away." And he came back—and taught school with those two students one more day. Then something happened. The next day two more students came; the next day, one more; then two more; and by the end of the next week we had 10 students! The next year we had 26 students; the next year, 34; the next year, 63; and later there were more than 200 in the school.

Have you put your hand to a plow? Stay by it through thick and thin. A blessing must surely come at last.

*Behold, I give you the authority to trample on serpents
and scorpions, and over all the power of the enemy,
and nothing shall by any means hurt you.*
Luke 10:19.

October 4

Many promises of comfort and encouragement were given to the 70 disciples Christ sent out to preach the gospel and heal the sick. It would be foolish for anyone to be presumptuous and deliberately handle serpents and scorpions, and then expect God to fulfill the promise given in our reading for today. But when you are as careful as can be, and yet accidentally fall into danger, then you can indeed claim this promise. And the experiences of many people have proved that God's promises are fulfilled.

Years ago two colporteurs in Brazil claimed this promise. They were delivering books to the people who lived on the cattle ranches, where they had taken orders some time before. They had heavy packs of books on their backs, and when they came to a big gate that opened into the property of one of these ranches, they opened it and went through. When the gate didn't shut by itself, one of the colporteurs stepped into the tall grass to pull it shut—and was immediately bitten just above his ankle by a bushmaster snake. His friend picked up a stick and killed the snake, but what could he do for his suffering companion? They had no antivenin with them. The only thing he knew to do was to make a fire and cauterize the wound with the red-hot coal at the end of a burning stick. It hurt terribly, and certainly didn't guarantee a cure!

But the man who had been bitten said, "No! I'm going to claim that promise in Luke 10:19. This is either the Lord's work, or it is not. If it is His work, and He wants me to deliver these books, then I'm going on. If He does not wish me to do so, then His will be done." So saying, he picked up his pack and went on his way. The wound did not even swell, and in a few days there was no trace of the bite. The promise had been fulfilled indeed, and the young man went forward with new assurance that God was with them while they were doing His work.

Remember this promise. You may need to claim it someday.

LUKE 11

Ask, and it will be given to you; seek, and you will find; knock, and it will be opened to you. Luke 11:9.

October **5**

Our loving God is an all-powerful God with whom nothing is impossible. He does the giving, the finding, and the opening for us. But we have to do the asking, the seeking, and the knocking. Here is a story from a pastor that illustrates the point very well.

During the pre-Christmas season a certain store advertised that children's toys would be given away by a live Santa Claus at a certain hour, and that the program would be televised. So a fond mother took her 7-year-old Johnny to the store, hoping that he would receive something. The program started. The master of ceremonies took child after child up to Santa and told Santa their names. Then the boy or girl made their request and received their toy. It was very exciting! Soon the master of ceremonies noticed Johnny, so he took him to Santa Claus. "This is Johnny," he said.

"And what do you want, Johnny?" asked Santa. But Johnny was speechless. He was too timid and shy to say a word. "Would you like a bicycle?" Santa asked. Johnny nodded his head, but said nothing. "Or would you rather have a train?" Again Johnny nodded his head, but wouldn't say a word. "Maybe you would prefer a wagon," encouraged Santa. Still Johnny could only nod. The master of ceremonies smiled and said, "Johnny, you have us all confused. We don't know what you really want. Here's a lollipop for you to suck on while you make up your mind." And while Johnny ate his lollipop the program went on, and child after child received a toy. Toward the end of the program Johnny was given another chance, but he still was afraid to ask.

"Oh, well, son," said Santa at last, "you'll never get it if you don't ask for it." And the program went off the air. Johnny could have had a bicycle or a train or a wagon—if he had only asked for it. But because he wouldn't ask, all he got was a lollipop.

What would you like for God to give you? Victory over a bad habit? Strength to say no to temptation? Ability to get good grades at school? Grace to be sweet and patient?

Ask, and you will receive.

Therefore you also be ready, for the Son of Man is coming at an hour you do not expect.
Luke 12:40.

October 6

Many of the sermons that Jesus preached and the parables that He told focus on the importance of our being ready for His coming. In today's scripture He warns us of covetousness, assures us of His loving care for us, then tells us to seek first the kingdom of God. After this follows the parable of the servants waiting for their master's return. Then comes our text: "Therefore you also be ready, for the Son of Man is coming at an hour you do not expect."

A traveler visiting in Switzerland came across a lovely home in the midst of a beautiful garden on the shore of a beautiful lake. It looked so inviting that he thought he would like to visit awhile with the owner. So he knocked at the garden gate. Soon an aged gardener appeared and opened the gate. The gardener seemed glad to have a visitor, and he showed the man all around the wonderful garden. "How long have you worked here?" asked the traveler.

"Twenty-four years," said the old gardener.

"And how often has your master been here during that time?"

"Four times."

"When was he here last?"

"Twelve years ago."

"Then from whom do you receive your wages?"

"From his agent in Mailand."

"Does the agent come here often?"

"He's never been here."

"Then who does come?"

"Except for an occasional visitor like yourself, I am almost always alone."

"Yet you keep the garden in such perfect order, just as if you were expecting your master to come tomorrow."

"Not tomorrow, sir. As if he were coming today."

If every one of us could only get ready to meet the Master, then stay ready, just as did the gardener, wouldn't that be wonderful! I'm going to try. Won't you try too?

LUKE 13

Strive to enter through the narrow gate, for many,
I say to you, will seek to enter and will not be able.
Luke 13:24.

October 7

The Greek word translated "seek" in today's text also means "desire." So a careful study of this verse indicates that many people will desire to enter in at the gate that leads to life, but will not be able to because to "desire" is not enough. A person must strive to enter in. God wants people who serve Him with all their heart and soul and strength, people who not only desire to read their Bible and come to church but who do something about it.

I like this story about a happy old couple in Brazil. The man earned a few cruzeiros by cutting firewood for his neighbors, and the woman, with hands all wrinkled and trembling, washed clothes. They could barely make a living. They could neither read nor write, but one day they heard about Jesus' love and began to attend Sabbath school. This was all so new to them—the singing, the lesson study, and the happy faces of those who raised their hands to show they had studied their lesson seven times. How they wished they were able to put their hands up for studying seven times. But they more than *desired;* they did something about it. And then one Sabbath they were the happiest couple in Sabbath school—for they, too, raised their hands to show they'd studied the lesson seven times. Now they did this every week. The teacher knew they couldn't read, so one Sabbath afternoon she went to visit them to find out how they did it.

"Have you learned to read?" she asked them.

"No," they replied. "We can't read."

"Then," said the teacher, "how can you study your lesson seven times?"

The couple looked at each other with a big smile. "Our neighbor has a nice little boy," the woman said. "He reads very well, so he comes every day and reads the lesson to us."

"What a nice little boy he must be," said the teacher, "but does he come every day? Doesn't he miss sometimes?"

"He comes every day, all right," said the man. "You see, we pay him!"

Well, that's what I call *striving* to enter in. They *desired* to learn about Jesus so much that they were willing to pay a little boy to read their lesson to them. It makes me ashamed to think how little I *strive* to enter in.

Don't you think you ought to strive a little harder too?

Whoever exalts himself will be humbled, and he who humbles himself will be exalted.
Luke 14:11.

October 8

Wonderful are the ways of our loving God. He notices the times that you let others go first, and the times that others received the honor or the credit that should have been yours, but that you so unselfishly let them have. And then, in His own way and in His own time, God lifts you up and gives you more glory than you ever deserved.

During the Civil War there was a fine old soldier whom everyone loved by the name of General O. O. Howard. During General Sherman's last campaign he had been put in command of a special division, taking the place of a general who had retired.

When at last the Civil War was over, a great parade was planned that would go through Washington, D.C. Now, even though he was retired and no longer in the army, the former general of Howard's division insisted that *he* should ride at the head of the division in the parade because he had served longer with that division than had General Howard. It was an awkward situation, and General Sherman did not know what to do.

But he called General Howard in and said, "I know you are in the command of that division, and it is your right to lead it in the parade. But you know, Howard, you are a Christian, and you can stand the disappointment better than the former general can. So would you mind letting him have that honor?"

"Oh, well, General, if you put it that way," said General Howard, "that's all right with me. Let him have the honor. Let him ride at the head of the division."

General Sherman smiled. "I thought you'd do that, Howard," he said. "Now, I want you to report to me at 9:00 in the morning and ride by my side at the head of the whole army!" What an honor! But it could only be given to one who was humble.

What is your humility rating? Are you ready yet to be exalted?

LUKE 15

There is joy in the presence of the angels
of God over one sinner who repents.
Luke 15:10.

If there is one great truth that Jesus tried to impress upon the hearts of His hearers above all others, it is that our heavenly Father is always more than ready to forgive those who come to Him in humble repentance and make confession.

Jim was a good boy when he was small, but as he grew up he got into bad company. He lied, he stole, and he got into all kinds of trouble. Again and again his heartbroken father and mother pleaded with him to make things right and live differently. But the more they pleaded the worse he got, till one day in a fit of anger he shouted, "I've had enough! I'll never darken your door or come into your house again as long as I live."

He packed a few things in a suitcase and left. But life away from home was not as rosy as he thought it would be. It is not easy for a young man who is not honest to keep a job, and it wasn't long before he was jobless and broke. The still small voice that had often tried to make itself heard now spoke louder than ever before: *Go back home! Say you're sorry!*

"I'm too ashamed," he argued with the voice. "Mom and Dad could never forgive me." *Go back! Go back!* said the voice. "But they would never let me back."

But at last he thought of a plan. "Dear Dad and Mom," he wrote, "I've been a terrible disgrace to you. I've lied and stolen and spoken so rudely to you that I'm afraid you can never forgive me. But the first day of next month I'll be on the train that passes our house. If you can forgive me, put a blanket on the clothesline. As the train goes by I'll see it and know I can come back to tell you how sorry I am."

He mailed the letter, and on the first day of the next month he took the train that went past his home. As he neared the familiar scenes—the woods, the factories, the parks—his heart beat faster and faster. "Would they—?" he wondered. "Can they forgive me?" At last the train rounded the last bend. There was his home! And on the clothesline were hanging, not one, but seven blankets.

Our heavenly Father and our earthly parents are just like that. Why be miserable with a heavy sinful heart? Go back and say you're sorry. And you'll find joy on earth while waiting for joy in heaven.

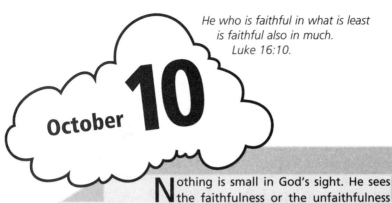

*He who is faithful in what is least
is faithful also in much.
Luke 16:10.*

October 10

Nothing is small in God's sight. He sees the faithfulness or the unfaithfulness with which we do our tasks. Young people who do their work faithfully seldom realize that anyone is taking notice, and maybe they will never know the influence of their faithfulness.

A few years ago, in Paris, some Seventh-day Adventist young people were working for a certain airline. We don't know their names; we don't know what work they were doing; but we do know something about the influence of their faithfulness. Listen to this. The Paris Youth Congress was just over. And as you can imagine, the youth leaders had had a busy time getting so many young people on their way to their home countries again. At last Pastor Watson went to the airport to fly back to London. He went to the desk to check in, pulled out his wallet, took out his reservation slip—but there was no ticket! Where could—? Then he remembered! His ticket was in his other coat pocket, packed in a trunk that had been sent by freight to London.

"I'm sorry," said the agent, "but you must have a ticket." He tried to telephone the office in London where the ticket had been bought, to get confirmation, but the office was closed for a holiday. Then as Pastor Watson searched his pockets again, he pulled out the Seventh-day Adventist youth congress brochure. "I've been attending a youth congress," he explained.

"I've read about that," said the agent. "Are you an Adventist?"

"Yes, sir, I am," replied Pastor Watson.

"Well, that changes things," said the agent. (Now listen!) "I have some Seventh-day Adventist young people working for me. I can trust every one of them, so I know I can trust you, too." He immediately wrote out another ticket and, handing it to Pastor Watson, said, "If you don't send me your ticket after you get home, I'll be out of pocket for its cost, for I'm paying for this ticket myself. But I'm not worried. I know I can trust a Seventh-day Adventist."

Say, how does your faithfulness measure up in regard to things that really count, such as doing your schoolwork, helping around the house, and keeping your clothes hung up and your bedroom neat and tidy? There are no unimportant things with God.

LUKE 17

And one of them . . . returned, and with a loud voice glorified God, . . . giving Him thanks. . . . So Jesus answered and said, "Were there not ten cleansed? But where are the nine?" Luke 17:15-17.

October **11**

It's sad, but far too many people are just about as ungrateful as those men we read about this morning. Only about one person in 10 takes the time and effort to say thank you. We are inclined to take for granted all that God does for us, and what our parents and teachers do for us, and to think that the world owes us a living and we ought to be paid just for being in it. We are quick and eager to grumble and complain, but how many of us stop long enough to say thank you?

A legend tells of two angels who were sent down to earth on a special mission. To one was given a large basket. He was told to gather up all the "thanks" he could find. To the other was given a small basket, and he was told to gather up all the grumbles and complaints. "I don't think I'll have much to do," said the angel with the small basket. "The earth is so beautiful, with an abundance of food, flowers, birds, and sunshine. Surely no one will be grumbling or complaining today! I'll be able to help you gather up the thanks. I'm sure there will be many of them."

But it was not that way at all. As evening came they met, and the angel with the large basket had gathered scarcely enough thanks to cover the bottom, while the other angel had carried back three full loads of grumbles and complaints.

Feel the pleasure and see the brightness in this little thank-you story from Ethiopia.

"What can we do for you?" a doctor in our Addis Ababa hospital asked a patient who was standing in line.

"Oh, nothing, thank you," he said. "I was a patient here a few months ago, and I was cured. So I just came back to kiss the hospital ground and to thank the doctors and the nurses." Do you wonder why the hospital workers went around with a song in their hearts all the rest of the day? There is magic in a sincere little word of thanks. Why don't we use it more? If you want to feel that kind of magic, just think of a half dozen things your father, mother, brothers, and sisters have done for you. Then give each one a nice, sweet thank-you and just see what happens!

Men always ought to pray and not lose heart.
Luke 18:1.

October 12

To teach the disciples to be persistent, Jesus told the parable about the widow who would not give up making her request to the unjust judge. How much we all need to learn the lesson of sticking at something until it is completed. Too often we get tired and quit.

The story of Christopher Columbus gives us a splendid example of persistency, or just plain stick-to-itiveness. Columbus was born in Genoa, Italy, in 1451, and as a boy he loved to watch the sailing ships as they entered and left the port. When he was 19, he went to sea, and after an eventful seven years he settled in Lisbon, Portugal. By this time thinking people believed that the world was round, and little by little Columbus got the idea that he could find his way to India by sailing due west, instead of going all the way around South Africa. He tried to interest the king of Portugal in the undertaking, but he would not think of such a foolish thing. But Columbus would not give up. In 1484 he went to Spain and offered his services to King Ferdinand and Queen Isabella, and little by little he persuaded them to finance the expedition. On August 3, 1492, he set out with three sailing ships and 87 men. In nine days he reached the Canary Islands, and then the excitement began. A week went by. They kept going. Two weeks went by. The men had never been out of sight of land for so long. They were getting homesick.

"The men are discouraged, and they want to go back," said the mate to Columbus. "What shall I tell them?"

"Tell them to sail on!" he replied. And two more weeks went by with the men seeing nothing but the boundless ocean.

"The men are sick and weak. God wouldn't even know where we are if we died. I'm afraid the men will mutiny," said the mate. "What shall I tell them?"

"Tell them to sail on!" said Columbus. "If in three days we do not sight land, then we'll turn back." So they sailed on, and the second night, at 2:00 a.m., the morning of October 12, 1492, they saw the light of a fire. And on that day they landed at San Salvador in the Bahamas. Because of the fearless persistency of Christopher Columbus, a new world was found that day.

Today is the anniversary of that day. It is a good day for you to get out your "persistency" and clean it up, to make sure it is working.

LUKE 19

*"Look, Lord, I give half of my goods to the poor; and if I have
taken anything from anyone by false accusation, I restore fourfold."
And Jesus said to him, "Today salvation has come to this house."
Luke 19:8, 9.*

October 13

The day that Zacchaeus saw Jesus—the day salvation that came to his house—was the greatest day of his life. He would never forget that day. A beautiful legend is told about Zacchaeus in his old age. They say that he continued to live in Jericho and was a very humble and godly man. Every morning at sunrise he would leave his house and go for a walk. When he returned, his face was always radiant and his heart was filled with joy and peace. His wife often wondered where he went and what he did on these morning walks, but he never told her. So one morning out of curiosity she followed him. Down the main road he went till he came to the sycamore tree into which he had climbed that day when he first saw Jesus. He picked up a waterpot that he kept there, went to the nearby spring, filled it with water, then brought it back and watered the tree. He didn't want that tree ever to die. He pulled the weeds from around the foot of the tree, then looked up into the branches where he had sat on that wonderful day. And as he looked he relived that wonderful experience. He remembered the great joy that filled his heart as he saw his blessed Savior and heard those wonderful words, "Today salvation has come to this house." He wanted to remember that happy day always; and he did. And that is why he was so humble and godly.

Can you remember the day you first gave your heart to Jesus? Can you remember the day you were baptized? Can you remember how happy you were? Think of those days often; talk about them often. Never let them die. Your face will be radiant and your heart filled with joy and peace too. In *Steps to Christ* Ellen White says: "Have there not been some bright spots in your experience? Have you not had some precious seasons when your heart throbbed with joy in response to the Spirit of God? . . . Are not God's promises, like the fragrant flowers, growing beside your path on every hand? Will you not let their beauty and sweetness fill your heart with joy?" (p. 117).

Render therefore to Caesar the things that are Caesar's, and to God the things that are God's. Luke 20:25.

October 14

Jesus taught that it is our duty to give our allegiance to the rulers of the country in which we live, and there is nothing I love to see more than a group of juniors, either in school, Pathfinders, or at camp, pledging allegiance to the flag of their country. God has set up governments and rulers, and He desires that we obey them so that we might have liberty. I suppose the most popular statue in America is the Statue of Liberty, "The Lady With a Torch," on Liberty Island in New York Harbor. Have you ever seen it?

The Statue of Liberty was a gift from the French people to commemorate the establishment of American independence, in which France had given help. The statue was dedicated October 28, 1886. The "Lady" is made of copper sheets over an iron framework and weighs 225 tons. From her feet to the top of the uplifted torch measures 152 feet. She stands on a pedestal about 150 feet high, so the torch shines out more than 300 feet above the sea. The figure is only made of metal, but the spirit of The Lady With a Torch has an indescribable effect on almost everyone who sees it. If you ever have a chance, take the ferry that goes by the island where Lady Liberty stands. It's awe-inspiring by day, and even more so at night.

I remember when we came back home as refugees after the war. It was early morning as our ship came into the harbor, and suddenly we heard a great shout. Instinctively everyone knew what it was for, and 1,200 passengers and 300 sailors crowded to the decks to see "Old Liberty." Some were crying, some were praying, and when two women began to sing "Praise God from whom all blessings flow" we all joined in. One sailor waved his hand affectionately and shouted, "Oh, Mother, I'd like to jump right over to you and put my two arms around your neck and give you a big kiss, I would." And everybody cheered, because that's the way everybody felt. I can never forget that day, and every time I see that statue it makes my heart tingle.

Say, juniors, open your eyes wide. Try to realize what liberty and justice for all really means. Then see that you cheerfully render to Caesar the things that are Caesar's.

LUKE 21

He saw also a certain poor widow putting in two mites. So He said,
"Truly I say to you that this poor widow has put in more than all."
Luke 21:2, 3.

God measures our gifts to Him, not by the amount of the gift, but by the relation it has to what we have left. The poor widow had nothing left; that's why her gift was greater than all the others.

I found a touching little story in an Australian missions-appeal magazine not long ago, about a little Solomon Islands boy named Gileni. Gileni's father, Pastor Oti, went as a missionary to the New Guinea islands of Mussau, Emirau, Manus, and Bougainville. Pastor Oti was very successful in opening up new work among primitive peoples, and spent half his lifetime bringing happiness and hope to those who lived without modern conveniences. His children were born on these islands and grew up there, so of course they knew very little about their own relatives.

When Gileni was about 12 years old, Pastor Oti was given furlough back to his home island, and on their way the family arrived in Rabaul, at the union mission headquarters. Sad to say, several members of Pastor Oti's family were desperately ill with dysentery, and although the missionaries did all they possibly could, it was too late to save Gileni's life. He was buried beneath the palms in the nearby village cemetery.

A few days later Pastor Oti brought Gileni's little suitcase to one of the missionaries who lived there. "Please take these things and give them to someone who has need of them," he told her. "Gileni does not need his books or his clothes anymore, and it makes us sad to look at them." In an envelope right on top of his clothes were four 10-shilling notes. Gileni had saved it, and it was all that he had. His father could have used the money, but he said, "Gileni wanted to be a missionary someday, but since he cannot be a missionary now, I'm sure he would want his money to help someone else to be a missionary in his place." So Gileni also gave all that he had. And no doubt, because of his offering some little boy or girl was helped through school, and possibly became a missionary to those who still sit in darkness.

Would you like to know how large your offerings are? Don't measure your giving by what you put into the envelope; look at how much you have left.

Satan has asked for you, that he may sift you as wheat. But I have prayed for you, that your faith should not fail.
Luke 22:31, 32.

October 16

Poor Peter. He surely needed someone to pray for him. He thought he was strong, but he was weak. He said he was willing to go to prison and even die for the Lord Jesus, but he denied Him three times in an hour. Sometimes there is a big difference between what we are, and what we think we are, and what others think we are. I was talking to a 12-year-old girl in one of my baptismal classes one day, and I asked, "Are your parents Christians?"

"I don't think so," she said. "They watch awful stuff on TV, they quarrel and fight, and we never have family worship."

"Oh, but," I said, "haven't I seen them at church?"

"Oh, yes," she said. "They're church members." No doubt that father and mother thought they were Christians, but their daughter thought they were not. It was something like that with Peter. The people in the high priest's courtyard had three counts on him. First of all, Peter had been seen with Jesus. He had helped pick up the leftover fish and bread the time Jesus fed the 5,000. He'd been there when Jesus healed the sick and made the blind see. Even Peter's own mother-in-law had been healed by Jesus. Then there was his accent. When he talked, he sounded like someone from Galilee. And he was just different.

"Weren't you with Jesus?" asked the servant girl.

"I was not!" said Peter. Then along came a relative of the man whose ear Peter had cut off. He had seen Peter keeping company with Christ. This was the second count they had on him.

"You must know Him," the man said. "I saw you in the garden with Him."

"I do not!" said Peter. Then someone else came along with the third count.

"Of course you're one of His followers," they said. "You talk like one." And Peter cursed and said, "I don't know Him." They said Peter was a follower of Christ. Peter said he was not. Who do you think was right? Peter had been following the Lord Jesus for three and a half years, yet he sinned and he needed to repent. Thank God, he did repent, and then he knew and everybody knew he would follow Jesus till the day he died. Say, do you look like a Christian? Do you go to church with Christians? Do you talk like a Christian? Do you think you truly are?

LUKE 23

Then Jesus said, "Father, forgive them,
for they do not know what they do."
Luke 23:34.

How could Jesus plead forgiveness for the people who killed Him? He came to save them, and they mocked Him and spat on Him—and nailed Him to a cross. "Father, forgive them," He prayed. How could He do it? But the wonderful truth is that He did do it, and to those who open their hearts to Him, He offers the same loving forgiveness. If you know God, you can forgive too.

Abelino's heart burned to share Jesus in a town near where he lived, so he got some tracts and started off. But at the very first house the man yelled that he wasn't interested and slammed the door. Abelino went to the second and the third house, and was treated just the same. Then an angry mob pounced on him, threw him to the ground, beat him with clubs, and threw stones at him. When they finally left, poor Abelino limped to a house at the edge of town. Here the people were kind to him and let him stay for the night. In the morning he could hardly walk, but he went right back to the first house again. "Maybe they'll listen this time," he said to himself. But the man was angrier than before, and soon the mob was back. They beat him and left him for dead. But he was not dead, and somehow he managed to get back again to the house where they'd been kind to him. You won't believe it, but the next morning he went back the third time to the same first house.

"You again?" said the astonished man. "I thought we killed you yesterday. How many lives have you got?"

"If you only knew how much Jesus loves you," said our brother. "I want to tell you about it so much that I'm willing to die—if only you will listen." The man had never seen or heard of anything like this before.

"Well, come in," he said,

"Get your friends so that I can tell them, too," said Abelino. So the man gathered 11 of the men who'd beat him, and Abelino told them of the love of Jesus. "We've never heard anything like this before," they said. "Come again!" Abelino went again and again, and he formed a branch Sabbath school. Soon 70 people were there every week. Then they sent for someone to come organize a regular Sabbath school. When he arrived, he found 104 people keeping the Sabbath! There is divine power in a forgiving spirit. Do you have a forgiving heart?

Why do you seek the living among the dead? He is not here, but is risen!
Luke 24:5, 6.

October 18

When Jesus rose from the dead, He rose to a new life. All who are baptized are "buried with Him . . . into death, that just as Christ was raised from the dead . . . , even so we also should walk in newness of life" (Romans 6:4).

I love to tell about people who've found a new joy in life when they live as Jesus lived. I once heard a story that illustrates this perfectly. It told of an elderly woman who was very sick and barely able to walk. Almost every day she had her chauffeur drive her to the cemetery where her son was buried. One day she stopped at the clerk's office and said, "I am Mrs. Adams. You may remember that for the past two years I have sent money every week for flowers to be put on my son's grave."

"Oh, yes, of course," said the clerk.

"Well, I came here today because the doctors say I have only a few more weeks to live, and I wanted to have one last look at my son's grave. Then, too, I wanted to thank you."

The clerk looked at her kindly and said, "You know, ma'am, I'm sorry you kept sending the money for flowers."

Mrs. Adams was shocked. "Sorry!" she gasped. "Why?"

"Because," said he, "no one ever sees them."

"Do you realize what you are saying?" asked Mrs. Adams angrily.

"Oh, indeed I do. I often visit state hospitals and nursing homes. The people there dearly love flowers, and they can see and smell them. Only living people can enjoy flowers, ma'am."

Mrs. Adams was too shocked to reply. She hurried to her car in tears. But some months later the clerk received another visit from Mrs. Adams, but this time *she* was driving the car! And this time she was well and very much able to walk. A wonderful smile brightened her face as she said, "I take the flowers to the living now. You were right. It does make them happy, and it makes me happy, too. The doctors don't know what is making me well—but I do! Now I have something to live for."

It's true! And if you are not getting real satisfaction in living, maybe you need to find a new way of life.

JOHN 1

I saw the Spirit descending from heaven like a dove, and He remained upon Him. . . . He who sent me to baptize with water said to me, "Upon whom you see the Spirit descending, . . . this is He who baptizes with the Holy Spirit."
John 1:32, 33.

October **19**

As the years have gone by since the baptism of Jesus, people have come to regard doves, or pigeons, as symbols of the presence of the Holy Spirit, and in front of many of the big churches in Europe you find flocks of pigeons today. Tourists love to watch them and feed them.

A pastor shared this surprising story several years ago. In a certain town in which there was a big church with a nice flock of pigeons our Seventh-day Adventist believers built a church. It was a simple church building because they could not afford anything grand. So it had no steeple. There was only a sort of attic between the ceiling and the roof, and for ventilation there was a round hole in each end of the attic. The townspeople had never seen such a strange-looking church. Many of them laughed, and many of them shook their heads in scorn.

Well, one day a pigeon from the flock at the big town church discovered the nice little opening into the nice little attic above the nice little Adventist church. It flew in, and it flew out, and went right back and told all the other pigeons about it! And what do you think? One sunny morning the whole flock of pigeons flew away from their home in the big church tower and flew right over to the Seventh-day Adventist church and moved right into the attic! At first the surprised people thought the pigeons were only making a temporary visit to the little church, but the pigeons stayed. Then the townspeople said to one another, "The Holy Spirit has left the old church and has gone over to the Adventists. We must go and see what is going on there too!" And many people from the town came to see and to listen, and many of them stayed and became members of the Adventist church.

Now, of course, no church really needs pigeons, and *you* probably don't need pigeons either. But every church and every Christian most certainly needs the Holy Spirit. Have you opened your heart to let it become the temple of the Holy Spirit?

JOHN 2

Zeal for Your house has eaten Me up.
John 2:17.

October 20

In today's scripture we read about the first miracle Jesus performed (John 2:11) and also about His great enthusiasm, or zeal, as He began His ministry by cleansing the Temple. Today is the anniversary of one of the most enthusiastic events in Adventist history—when our missionary ship, the *Pitcairn*, began taking missionaries to the South Pacific Islands. The *Pitcarin's* story began when a 16-year-old boy, John I. Tay, became interested in the tale of the mutiny that occurred on the ship *Bounty*. It made him curious about Pitcaim Island and its people. In 1874 John became an Adventist, and his heart burned to take the Adventist message to Pitcairn. At last he was able to sign up as a ship's carpenter and go to Pitcairn Island. He stayed there five weeks, and the islanders began keeping the Sabbath and wanted to be baptized. Of course, Tay could not baptize them, but he promised he'd send someone to baptize them as soon as possible.

When John Tay returned to America, his story caused great rejoicing, and the Adventist Church was convinced it was time to send missionaries to the South Pacific. An attempt was made to send Elder A. J. Cudney to Pitcairn to baptize the people there, but the ship he was on was wrecked, and Pastor Cudney was lost at sea. After that tragedy, Adventists began talking about having their own missionary ship, and in 1890 the General Conference authorized the building of a ship and gave the Sabbath schools the privilege of raising the money. Talk about enthusiasm! Fathers and mothers, grandfathers and grandmothers, boys and girls, began saving dimes and nickels and dollars as they'd never saved before. In six months they had $12,000—a *lot* of money back then—and the ship was built! It was named the *Pitcairn,* and on October 20, 1890, it set sail with its first group of missionaries on board. In all, this wonderful ship made six voyages to the South Pacific Islands carrying missionaries. Then, because steamship connections had greatly improved, the brave little ship was sold. But the influence of those 10 enthusiastic years during the life and service of the *Pitcairn* will be felt throughout eternity.

Today there are many more opportunities for youth to be missionaries than has ever been. It's fairly easy to go on a short-term mission trip. As in times past, all it takes is money and a willing heart. You can fund-raise as juniors did long ago. Plan to go on a mission trip as soon as you can.

JOHN 3

*For God so loved the world that He gave His only
begotten Son, that whoever believes in Him should
not perish but have everlasting life.
John 3:16.*

October 21

As we think for just a few moments
on the words of John 3:16—one of
the best-loved verses in all the Bible—we
can only say, "Behold, what manner of love the
Father has bestowed on us" (1 John 3:1). We know
that Jesus would have gone through the agony of
Calvary just to save one sinner. He would have
come to earth and lived and suffered and died just for you—because He loves you.

Rena was in a serious accident and had lost a lot of blood. She was rushed to
the hospital, and a call was made to her family to come and give her some blood.
Everyone's blood was tested, but only 12-year-old Danny's matched. He agreed to
give his blood to his sister, so a needle was inserted in his arm and the blood drawn
out. The transfusion was made. Rena had surgery, and soon she was out of danger. But Danny lay in bed, looking scared to death. "You saved Rena's life. Aren't
you proud of that?" a nurse told him.

"Yes," he said in a squeaky little voice.

A little later the supervisor tried to cheer him up. "You were very brave,
Danny. You've done a beautiful thing for your sister." But Danny didn't say a
word. He was crying.

So the doctor came to see him. "What's the trouble?" he asked, pulling the
covers off Danny's face.

Danny swallowed hard. "Doctor, how soon do I die?" he asked.

"What?" the doctor said. "You're not going to die. You can get up right
now and go home." Danny blinked and looked so relieved that suddenly the
doctor understood. "Didn't anyone in this great big hospital tell you that giving blood wouldn't hurt you?" he asked.

"No, sir," Danny said. "I thought I was giving my life."

Now, just think for a moment. When Rena recovered, do you think
she'd try to think of things she could do to please Danny? If he asked to borrow something from her, was she going to say no? Of course not. She'd do
all she possibly could to show Danny how much she loved him for saving
her life.

And that's what Jesus did for you. But He gave more than His blood.
He gave His life! Will you love Him as much as Rena loved Danny when
she got well again?

297

"Whoever drinks of the water that I shall give him will never thirst." . . . The woman said to Him, "Sir, give me this water, that I may not thirst." John 4:14, 15.

October 22

We know that when Jesus talked with the woman at the well, He was talking about the spiritual water of life—a knowledge of the truth that would result in eternal life. And we know what it means to be hungry and thirsty for righteousness. If ever people searched and studied the Scriptures to find this truth, it was the early Adventists. In fulfillment of the first angel's message of Revelation 14:6, 7, between 1831 and 1844, many messengers arose around the world and began to preach the judgment and the second coming of Christ. Men such as William Miller, Charles Fitch, Joseph Bates, and James White preached it in America. In England it was Edward Irving; in Europe, Joseph Wolff. And in Scandinavia, where adults were not permitted to preach, small children gave the message.

As the Adventists in America eagerly and earnestly studied the prophecies of Daniel 8 and 9 they concluded that the cleansing of the sanctuary meant Christ would come on October 22, 1844. As that day drew nearer and nearer they "drank" more eagerly and earnestly of the "waters of life," and prepared their hearts for Jesus to come and take them to heaven. At last they whispered to one another, "Tomorrow is the last day! We shall never see the sun set again, or hear the unbelievers cursing and scoffing. Tomorrow we will see Jesus!" Then tomorrow came. They dressed in their best clothes and gathered in their homes and meetinghouses.

The unbelievers trembled. "Suppose it *should* be the last day!" they said to themselves; but outwardly they were as mean as could be toward the trusting ones. The day passed slowly, one hour after another. At last the sun set, the day was over, and Jesus had not come.

"Go up! Go up! Why don't you go up?" shouted the unbelievers.

And the children asked, "Why didn't He come, Father? Why didn't He come?" Of course, they soon learned that Jesus had not failed them. They soon learned that cleansing the sanctuary meant the beginning of the judgment connected with the cleansing of the heavenly sanctuary. But today is the anniversary of that sorrowful day, always referred to in the history of our church as the Great Disappointment. It is a good day to remember. But *every* day is a good day in which to make sure that your sins are confessed and that you are *ready* for the judgment.

JOHN 5

You search the Scriptures, for in them you think you have eternal life; and these are they which testify of Me. John 5:39.

October 23

In Wales, more than 200 years ago, lived 10-year-old Mary Jones. In those days Bibles were very scarce and very expensive. The nearest Bible that Mary knew about was at Mrs. Evans' farm two miles away. One day Mary dressed up and walked to the Evanses' farm, and asked Mrs. Evans if she might read the Bible for herself for a little while. "Of course you may, if you're very careful," said Mrs. Evans, and she left Mary alone in the front room with the Word of God. Mary was almost afraid to touch it. Then she carefully opened the Bible, and among the first words she read were "Search the Scriptures . . . these are they which testify of Me."

"Oh, I will! I will," cried Mary. "If only I had a Bible of my own!" And that day she determined that she was going to work and save every penny she possibly could till she could buy a Bible. It took her six years! Then one sunshiny day she set off for the little town of Bala, 25 miles away, where a Dr. Thomas Charles had some Welsh Bibles for sale. She walked barefoot to save her shoes and stockings, but there was a song in her heart because she would soon have a Bible of her own. She stayed that night at a Mr. Edwards' home, and very early the next morning she went across the street to Dr. Charles's house. She put her money in his hands, then tremblingly asked for a Bible. She looked so hopeful that Dr. Charles hardly knew what to say. At last he sadly shook his head and said, "I'm sorry, Mary, my child, but there's not another Bible for sale. I have a few Bibles here, but they have all been paid for. There is not one left." Mary couldn't hide her disappointment. She just broke down and cried. Dear old Dr. Charles couldn't bear to see her crying, and at last he said, "Dry your tears, Mary. I will let you have one of these Bibles. Someone else can wait."

Mary walked the 25 miles home again, rejoicing, but Dr. Charles couldn't forget her tears. He told her story to his friends in London, and they determined that anyone who wanted a Bible should have one. In 1804 they formed the British and Foreign Bible Society, which has printed millions and millions of Bibles since then. When Mary died, they put her Bible in a glass case in the society's building. I was there a few years ago and saw it. And as I looked upon that precious, well-worn book I determined to read the Word of God more and more.

Won't you do that too?

JOHN 6

I am the bread of life. He who comes to Me shall never hunger, and he who believes in Me shall never thirst. John 6:35.

October 24

If you normally eat about four slices of bread a day, then in the past year you have eaten at least 80 loaves of bread. In New Testament times people didn't know the nutrients that bread contained, but they still ate it every day. And so Jesus called Himself the Bread of Life—for there can be no spiritual life without Him. Knowing now what wheat contains—thiamine, niacin, iron, zinc, riboflavin, and several trace minerals—makes Jesus' comparison of Himself to bread even more important.

But Jesus, the Bread of Life, is not in the paper on which the Bible is printed. The life of the Bible is in Jesus, our Savior, of whom it tells. Just as healthy, growing kids get hungry for ordinary bread, spiritually healthy kids get hungry to read about Jesus in the Bible.

Many exciting stories have been told about what people have done to keep their Bibles from being taken away from them during times of persecution. Many years ago there was a family named Schebolt, who lived in the Czech Republic. During this time the rulers and the priests didn't want the common people to read the Bible for themselves. A law had been made prohibiting anyone from owning or reading a Bible, and frequently soldiers were sent to search the homes of those suspected of having one. One day when Mrs. Schebolt was making bread one of the children came running in from outside and said, "The soldiers are coming!" Mrs. Schebolt wasn't about to give up her precious Bible. She thought quickly, and then opened the dough she had just put in her bread pan, shoved the Bible inside, closed the dough over it, and popped it into the oven. The soldiers came. They searched the house. They even looked into the oven. But they didn't find the Bible! When they had gone and the danger was past, Mrs. Schebolt pulled the Bible out of the loaf of bread, none the worse for its baking. The baked Bible was in the possession of the grandchildren who lived near Maumee City, Ohio, for many years.

How much do you love your Bible? How hungry are you for the Bread of Life your Bible tells about?

JOHN 7

If anyone thirsts, let him come to Me and drink.
John 7:37.

October **25**

If you have ever been really thirsty, then you can understand how essential it is for your spiritual thirst to be satisfied too. You and I might live for 30 to 40 days without food, but a person can live only seven to 10 days without water. Our bodies are two-thirds water, and we need about one ton of the precious liquid in food and drink every year. Maybe you've been on a summertime hike when you ran out of water. If so, you know—just a little—what it's like to crave water and not have it. During World War II some desperately thirsty people were sustained by the water of life, which only Jesus can give. It happened like this.

A ship sank near Trinidad. It was not a large ship, so it carried only nine passengers and a crew of 50. But among the passengers were two missionary families coming home on furlough from West Africa, and those two families had four children. Four rafts succeeded in picking up all but 17 of the crew. In the captain's raft, which was just a small one, eight by 10 feet, there were 18 people, and among them were Mrs. Bell and the four missionary children. It's hard to sit still, all cramped up hour after hour, but these children did. It's hard to have only one cracker and a swallow of water for a meal, but there was no grumbling. It was frightening to see the sharks swimming all around them, but 7-year-old Carol said, "It's almost like being Daniel in the lions' den." Some of the seamen didn't know who Daniel was or what happened to him, so Mrs. Bell told the Bible story about him. The men loved it. So Mrs. Bell told Bible stories every day. After a few days the captain died, and finally the drinking water was all gone. What could they do?

The children had the answer. "Why, we'll pray for rain," they said. So Mrs. Bell prayed. And it rained. They all filled their empty water bottles. Mrs. Bell prayed for it to stop raining so that they could get dry again, and it stopped raining. Then an airplane found them and dropped them some food. Days later a convoy picked them up and took them to Barbados. Every man on the raft agreed that it was the faith of those little children that had kept them all alive.

Of course, we seldom suffer with thirst. You and I have plenty of water to drink every day. So why do we sometimes let our spiritual life get all dried up?

You can read about Jesus, think about Jesus, and talk to Jesus every day. Be sure that you do.

I am the light of the world. He who follows Me shall not walk in darkness, but have the light of life. John 8:12.

October 26

"You are the light of the world," Jesus told His followers. Now, we all know that Jesus was talking not about physical light, but about spiritual light; and we all know equally well that nobody can do deeds of love, purity, kindness, and truth unless Jesus lives within them and shines out of their heart. Here is a story I read a long time ago that illustrates this very well. A certain good man brought a Native American, Chief Eagle Eye, from the northland to the United States to be educated and sent back as a teacher to his own people. Chief Eagle Eye had never ridden on a train before. "What make him go?" he asked. "No dogs pull. Nothing pull!"

The man showed the chief the engine and said, "There's a fire inside! Fire makes him go!"

From the station they took a taxi to the hotel. There was no steam engine pulling the taxi, and Chief Eagle Eye was still puzzled. "What make him go?" he asked again, and the man replied, "There's a fire inside."

Arriving at the hotel, they stepped into a box that whisked them up to their room. At this, an elevator, Chief Eagle Eye was afraid. "What make him go?" he asked. "Fire inside?"

"Yes," replied his friend. "Fire inside."

Then the man switched on a light. "U'mm," said Chief Eagle Eye, "where light come from? You no strike match." The man switched off the light. "Ugh, where light go?" So the man took out the bulb, flipped the switch, and told him to place his finger there. Chief Eagle Eye then nearly jumped out of his skin. "Ugh! Fire inside!" he cried. Then one day a man called the chief on the phone. By now he knew the answer. "Box, he talks," he said wisely. "Fire inside."

Then one day came a violent thunder and lightning storm, and all the city fuses were blown. The room was in darkness and everything stopped. Eagle Eye thought for a moment, then said, "Light, he gone. Up-and-down basket, he dead. Little box, he no talk. What matter? No fire inside?" Chief Eagle Eye had discovered the reason, all right. And if ever you see a young person whose light has gone out, someone who is unkind, impure, or dishonest—it is simply because there is no "fire" inside anymore.

JOHN 9

One thing I know: that though I was blind, now I see.
John 9:25.

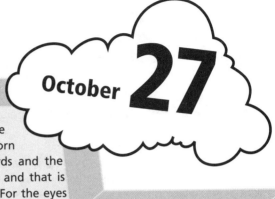

October **27**

The haughty Pharisees refused to believe that Christ had opened the eyes of the man who had been born blind. To refuse to believe the words and the work of Christ is spiritual blindness, and that is even worse than physical blindness. For the eyes of the physically blind who believe will see throughout eternity, but the eyes of those who refuse to believe will not see beyond this short life on earth. The man who was born blind rejoiced. He'd always been blind, but now, through the power of Christ, he could see.

Do you know that this same power is being manifested today? Listen! Over in Angola, in a little village not far from our Bongo Mission Hospital, lived a man by the name of Manjata. According to the story told by Dr. Roy Parsons, Manjata had worked hard, and he owned a farm, two bullocks, and a plow. His only son, Dolino, had grown to manhood, and Manjata should have been the happiest man in the village. However, he had become blind and was unable to work in his fields. For three years Manjata's wife did the plowing, planting, and harvesting, but by then his house needed repair and he couldn't do it, so he and his wife had to live with his son. But Dolino was terrible to his old blind father. He secretly sold his father's farm, his plow, his bullocks, and even the corn that had just been harvested. Then one night while his father and mother were asleep Dolino sneaked away with his family to a faraway village, leaving poor old Manjata and his wife to get along as best they could.

Two more years went slowly by, and old Manjata wished he could die. Then an Adventist man, Samuel Borigue, bought a garden near Manjata's house. Now, Samuel had worked in the clinic years before, and when he saw Manjata's eyes, he said, "Why, Manjata, you have cataracts! The doctor at our Bongo hospital can operate and make you see again!" Manjata believed him, and Samuel brought him to the hospital, where Dr. Roy Parsons operated on his eyes. In 10 days off came the bandages, and he could see! Manjata stayed at the hospital for nearly one month, rejoicing every day. By that time his spiritual eyes were open too, and Manjata went back to his village a new and happy man.

Don't be satisfied because the eyes in your head can see. Pray that your spiritual eyes will be able to see too. That is what counts most.

The sheep hear his voice. . . . And when he brings out his own sheep, he goes before them; and the sheep follow him, for they know his voice.
John 10:3, 4.

October 28

The voice of God sounded like thunder at Mount Sinai, and also when He glorified Christ on the last day of His public ministry (John 12:28, 29). But when God spoke to Elijah, He used the still small voice of the Holy Spirit. It is the still small voice with which we are most familiar. "Another way in which God's voice is heard is through the appeals of His Holy Spirit, making impressions upon the heart" (*Messages to Young People*, p. 156). Many people have had such clear, distinct impressions that it almost seems they heard an audible voice. Sometimes the still, small voice gives reproof, sometimes instruction, and sometimes encouragement.

I will always remember the time I heard the "voice of God." It was in the early days of my ministry in Burma. I had learned the language. That was easy. I was having success in my little clinic. That was easy. But I couldn't get the jungle people interested in the gospel. They wouldn't come to Sabbath school. I took my trumpet and a bag of medicines and a Picture Roll to a village, and sheer curiosity made them listen to the first meeting. But when I came the next week, as I had announced, the village was empty except for three old grandmas who wouldn't even listen to me when I began to tell about Jesus with the Picture Roll. I was so discouraged. I sent Mrs. Hare and our clinic helper back home by canoe, but I walked home through the jungle. I wanted to be alone. I had tried everything I could to get them interested in the gospel, but nothing seemed to do any good, and in the agony of my heart I cried, "Lord! I can't do it!"

Then I heard it, just as clear as a voice. It was the voice of God—I know it was—and it said, "I know you can't do it. I've been waiting for you to realize that you don't have the power to change hearts. That's My work. I alone have that power. Just be faithful sowing the seed. I will give the increase. My word shall not return unto Me void."

Oh, what wonderful words! My discouragement vanished. "Yes, Lord," I said, "I can keep sowing the seed, and I will." And I did. And as the voice had promised, before long the change came. When *you* talk to God, take time to wait and listen to see what the voice of God will say to you.

JOHN 11

Jesus wept. Then the Jews said, "See how He loved him!"
John 11:35, 36.

October **29**

Verse 5 of today's Scripture reading tells us that Jesus "loved Martha and her sister and Lazarus." And when the messengers went to call on Jesus they said, "He whom You love is sick" (verse 3). The love of Jesus is the most wonderful love in all the world. It is so wonderful that sometimes it is hard to understand. Jesus could have gone to Lazarus as soon as He was called, and He would have performed a miracle and healed his sickness, and everybody would have been happy. But in His great love Jesus waited until Lazarus was dead. Then He went. And then He performed a much greater miracle. He raised Lazarus from the dead! This in turn produced much greater happiness. That's the way Jesus loves everybody.

Jesus' love is like a father's love, a mother's love, a friend's love. Writers have used many words to describe it. They have called it great, wonderful, and everlasting, but Paul sums them all up when he says, "The love of Christ which passes knowledge" (Ephesians 3:19). Poets and musicians have written countless songs about the love of Jesus, but I think the most loved and most widely known is "Jesus loves me, this I know, for the Bible tells me so." Those precious words were written by Anna Warner, a Sunday school teacher at West Point, New York, in the 1850s. She wrote the poem little dreaming that the whole world would fall in love with it. Soon after it was published it was set to music, and spread round the world. You will remember that we date the beginning of our Sabbath schools from the 1850s. So that lovely little song is as old as our Sabbath schools, and it is interesting to know that wherever our missionaries go, as soon as the name of Jesus is known, and a Sabbath school is formed, that beautiful song is translated into the language of the people first of all. Then fathers and mothers, grandfathers and grandmothers, little and big children, all join in singing, "Yes, Jesus loves me, yes, Jesus loves me . . . the Bible tells me so." Always remember that Jesus loves everybody—the people who are kind and who love Him and those who are mean and do not love Him.

Yes, He loves you, too, when you're good or when you're bad. He dislikes the bad things you do, but He always loves you. And that's that!

305

And I, if I am lifted up from the earth, will draw all peoples to Myself. John 12:32.

October 30

Because Jesus died on the cross, multitudes of every nation, language, and people have been drawn to Him. And if Christians lift up Christ in their own lives—if they are kind like Jesus, patient like Jesus, and thoughtful like Jesus—then all people will be drawn to Him.

Some years ago I found a story about a Christian nurse called Annabelle who did this very thing in one of our sanitariums, and found that it was true. A fretful woman was brought to a room on Annabelle's floor. She was sick, irritable, and restless, and Annabelle did all she could to make her as comfortable as possible. When she came in to say good night, she patted the woman's hand sympathetically and asked, "Would you like me to pray for you before I go?"

"No," the woman said sharply.

"Well, then, have a restful sleep and pleasant dreams," said Annabelle with a smile as she went out.

"She's so cross and unappreciative," she confided to her roommate that night. "No wonder she's sick."

"Forget it," said Grace. "Tomorrow will be a new day, and maybe she'll be different." Tomorrow came, but the woman didn't sweeten up one bit. And she was just the same the next day and the next and the next. Annabelle continued to care for her, but sometimes found it all she could do to remain gentle and kind. She often asked God to help her and, of course, He did. When finally the woman got better and went home, Annabelle was almost glad to see her go.

A year went by. Then one day Annabelle received an urgent invitation to come to this woman's home for a visit. Why? she wondered. What could she want? She almost dreaded it, but what a surprise awaited her! A gracious, charming woman welcomed her. "You were so kind to come," she said. "Do you remember the night you asked me if I would like to have you offer a prayer and I said no? I have never forgotten your kindness and cheerfulness in spite of my peevish impatience. You are a Seventh-day Adventist. Please tell me what Adventists believe. I want to be the kind of Christian you are."

Would anyone want to be the kind of Christian *you* are? They will if you lift Jesus up in your life.

JOHN 13

What I am doing you do not understand now, but you will know after this.
John 13:7.

October 31

Jesus said and did many things that the disciples could not understand at the time, but even as Jesus promised, in the words of our Bible text for today, the time surely did come when they understood not only what He said and did but also why. I think many of the answers to our prayers are hard to understand now, but I am sure that in the "hereafter" we shall know and understand.

Moses prayed, "O Lord God," "let me cross over and see the good land beyond the Jordan" (Deuteronomy 3:24, 25).

But the Lord said, "No, you cannot cross over there." But some time *after,* Michael the archangel came and resurrected Moses and took him to heaven! Then Moses understood why God had said No. It was because He had a better answer for him.

Elder Steen Rasmussen used to tell a story about six Seventh-day Adventist miners in Yugoslavia. One day as they were being paid their wages the manager said, "Men, I have to lay off 20 employees. So do not come back to work till we call you again."

"But, sir, we have wives and families. Why don't you lay off only the single workers?" they pleaded. But it was no use. The manager wouldn't listen, and the men went home discouraged. They prayed about it at home and pleaded with God to help them get their work back again. The next day they went back to the manager of the mine and begged to be reemployed, but without success. They must have felt that the Lord had forgotten them or had turned a deaf ear to their prayers.

But a few days *after* their dismissal, a terrible explosion occurred in the mine where they had been working, killing scores of the workers, including the men who were working where they had been. Then, of course, they understood why God had permitted them to be laid off, and they praised His name for saving their lives.

When you have committed your way to the Lord, trust Him to give you the right answer even though you may not understand it now. You will surely know "hereafter."

*Let not your heart be troubled; you believe in God,
believe also in Me. In my Father's house are many
mansions; if it were not so, I would have told you.
I go to prepare a place for you. And if I go and
prepare a place for you, I will come again
and receive you to Myself; that where
I am, there you may be also.
John 14:1-3.*

November 1

The promises recorded in John 14 sustain and support us when our hearts are troubled. They fill our hearts with hope, because the day will come when there will be no more sorrow, no more tears, and no more death.

As an example of the sustaining hope the words "I will come again" can give, let me tell you about General Douglas MacArthur. After a colorful and successful military career he was appointed military adviser to the newly created Philippine Commonwealth. Then on December 7, 1941, Japan made a surprise attack on Pearl Harbor, forcing the United States into World War II.

In the face of superior forces, the U. S. division in the Philippines suffered a terrible defeat, and in March 1942 General MacArthur was ordered to Australia to become commander of all the South Pacific troops. His job: to make preparation to liberate the islands from the hand of the enemy. As he left Corregidor by night in a Navy torpedo boat, he said to the Filipinos, "I shall return!" What wonderful words! They were whispered from trench to trench, from village to village, from prison camp to prison camp, and from hospital to hospital. "He will come again. He said he would."

The people knew MacArthur. They believed he would come, and in a little more than two years, on October 20, 1944, he *did* come back. His return struck terror to the hearts of the enemy but brought great rejoicing to the suffering people. Step by step his troops marched forward; island after island was liberated; and in six months the Philippines was free! Only those who were there can picture the rejoicing. Prisoners were released; families were reunited. People wept for joy and danced in the streets.

Perhaps you have waited for someone to return. How excited you are as the days get closer and closer, and what joy and fun it is when they finally arrive. It will be even better than that when Jesus comes again. He said He would come, and He will. Believe it. He is *coming* someday, and it must be soon. What a day of rejoicing that will be!

JOHN 15

I am the vine, you are the branches. He who abides in Me, and I in him, bears much fruit; for without Me you can do nothing. John 15:5.

November 2

The longer you live, the more you will realize that you need power and life from the Lord Jesus in order to make a real success of anything. Truly, without Him you can do nothing.

A little girl and her mother were staying at a hotel in Switzerland. The mother insisted that her daughter keep up her piano practice while they were on vacation, so every day right after lunch the little girl would go to the piano in the lounge and do her five-finger exercises and play her one-finger tunes. Again and again for a whole half hour she would do them, till the guests couldn't stand it, and one by one they would get up and leave the room.

As the days went by, the guests became very weary of the performance, but they were too polite to complain. Then one day one of the guests came and stood beside the little girl for a moment, then said, "Move up a little and make room for me." She scooted up on the piano bench, and the guest sat down beside her. "Now play those exercises again, and I'll play with you," he said. And while she strummed away on her same five-finger exercises, the guest put his arm around the little one and with his two skillful hands improvised a most beautiful melody. The guests heard the difference at once! Who could it be? When they'd left the room the girl was still sitting at the piano, but she couldn't be responsible for this beautiful harmony. Hurrying back to the lounge, they saw a man sitting beside the girl, his large hands creating a melody that somehow made her little tune beautiful. "Who is that?" they asked the hotel manager.

"The great pianist Josef Hofmann," he whispered. "He is spending his vacation here under another name just to have a little rest." The little girl alone nearly drove them crazy. But together she and the great pianist produced pleasing, delightful music.

That is the way it is with us. Alone we often play the wrong notes and do not get the timing right. At best our efforts are not at all melodious or satisfactory, but if we will "move up a little" and make room for the Master in our life, then His life and ours together will produce sweet harmonies.

I will see you again and your heart will rejoice, and your joy no one will take from you.
John 16:22.

November 3

There is such a difference between the clean, satisfying joy of a Christian and the fleeting pleasure that the world offers and that so often is mixed with regrets. Jesus said, "Your joy no one will take from you." In contrast, in Job 20:5 we read, "The triumphing of the wicked is short, and the joy of the hypocrite is but for a moment."

A number of years ago while we were living on our Karen mission station in Burma, our three little nephews—Edwin, Wilfred, and Buddy—and their mother came to visit us. One day 7-year-old Wilfred was blowing soap bubbles in a room next to my office. He was having tremendous success and wanted me to share in his pleasure. "Oh, Uncle, come and see," he called with great enthusiasm. "What a beauty! Oh, Uncle!" But I was very busy and made no response. "Oh, Uncle, there's another! What a beauty! Oh, Uncle, there's another! What a beauty! Oh, come quickly!" His enthusiasm was so contagious that at last I stood up. "Come on, Uncle! There's another. Oh, what a beauty." I went to the door, and, encouraged by my movement, Wilfred shouted still louder. "There's another, oh, Uncle!" I opened the door, but as I did I heard him say, "Aw, Uncle, it's busted!"

That reminded me of that verse in Job that says the joy of the hypocrite is but for a moment. Probe into the reasons for the great army of alcoholics and drug addicts that are found in the world, or look into the background of the thousands of suicides we have every year, and you will find that the pleasures of life proved disappointing for these sad people. You'll see that their laughter and excitement could not heal their pain, and so they found a terrible way of escape. They reached for the beautiful bubble, but it "busted" before they even touched it!

Don't you be disappointed. Make God first and last and best in your life, and no one can take your joy from you. David says, "In Your presence is fullness of joy; at Your right hand are pleasures forevermore" (Psalm 16:11). And Seventh-day Adventist young people the world around bear witness to the fact that those who find their recreation where Jesus can be present do indeed have fullness of joy in physical and mental activities, unmarred with the sorrows of regret and remorse.

JOHN 17

*The world has hated them because they are not of
the world, just as I am not of the world. I do not
pray that You should take them out of the world,
but that You should keep them from the evil one.
John 17:14, 15.*

November 4

What a beautiful thought—that Jesus prayed for His children. And this prayer—that His children who are in the world should not be of the world in thought or word or action—has been granted again and again down through the centuries.

Oakwood College is built on an old plantation near Huntsville, Alabama. When it was purchased for a school, the soil was depleted out and the buildings were run-down. But worse than that, the neighbors were very hostile toward having a school near them that was sponsored by Northerners. However, the principal and his students worked hard, and they soon had the buildings in shape for use and the farm doing as well as possible. Then a terrible misfortune misfell one of the neighbors who was most bitter in his tirades. His barn burned down, killing his work animals and destroying the farm machinery. The next morning Principal Jacobs called the boys together for worship, and after prayer they briefly discussed the neighbor's plight. "Do any of you want to give him a helping hand?" he asked. Of course they all did. So they promptly hitched the horses to the cultivators and drove over to the neighbor's place.

"What do you want?" the farmer asked.

"Why, we've come to plant your corn," said Mr. Jacobs. It took a few seconds for the angry man to get the idea.

"Is that the kind of people you are?" he demanded in surprise.

"Yes, that's the kind of people we are," they answered.

"Well, just a moment before you get started," said the man. "I've said some mighty hard things against you people for starting that school. Now I ask you to forgive me."

"We have forgiven you long ago. That's why we're here," said Mr. Jacobs. And they all went to work. They plowed the field and planted the corn, and stopped at noon to eat their lunch.

"Oh, no, you don't," the farmer called. "Dinner's ready! We'll all eat together today." As you can imagine, the grateful farmer told the story all around, and that was the end of the hostility and the bitter words—from anyone. That's the spirit this bitter old world needs.

If my kingdom were of this world, My servants would fight, so that I should not be delivered to the Jews; but now My kingdom is not from here.
John 18:36.

November 5

Most Seventh-day Adventists are loyal citizens in whatever country they live—and they should be! They are honest. They pay their taxes, salute the flag, sing the national anthem, and repeat the Pledge of Allegiance. They believe that the principles of government were established by God, and in harmony with the teaching of Christ they are proud and happy to "render to Caesar the things that are Caesar's." However, they also believe that there are certain things that are God's, and they are equally as loyal in rendering to God the things that are His.

In 1863, in the middle of the U.S. Civil War, the Seventh-day Adventist General Conference organization was made a legal body. As soon as possible, church leaders composed a statement giving the reasons Seventh-day Adventists were noncombatants—did not carry guns. The next year, 1864, J. N. Andrews was sent to Washington, D.C., to present our position to the provost marshal general. He was kindly received by Brigadier General James B. Fry, and we were finally classed with the Quakers and granted exemption from bearing arms.

Our men who were called up by the draft were assigned to hospital and other noncombatant duties. During World War I, however, our position was not well enough known to benefit all of our men who were drafted, and a number of them suffered court-martial and imprisonment for keeping the Sabbath and/or refusing to bear arms. After the war E. N. Dick, who'd been a marine during the war, felt the church ought to do something to prepare our young people for hospital work in the event of a future war. And so the Medical Cadet Corps was founded. Those who organized the Corps chose for their motto "To serve, To serve, and To serve." The Medical Cadet Corps gave intensive basic and medical training to thousands of our young men and women, with the result that all who took the training were readily classed IAO and were given noncombatant duties. However, after the United States stopped the draft, this training was no longer taught at our schools.

Nonetheless, it's important to remember the value that Jesus puts on the life of even one person. And to think very carefully before agreeing to put yourself in a place where you might have to kill a fellow human being.

JOHN 19

So when Jesus had received the sour wine, He said, "It is finished!" And bowing His head, He gave up His spirit. John 19:30.

November 6

From the foundation of the world, from the time Adam and Eve sinned, Christ had been coming nearer and nearer to the time He would pay the price for our salvation. For 4,000 years all heaven had looked on at the great controversy between Satan and his forces and Christ and His forces. What sadness there had been when Cain killed Abel, and when the world mocked at Noah, and when again and again Israel returned to worshipping idols. But what great rejoicing there had been when Enoch walked with God, when Noah and his family entered the ark, when faithful Abraham followed God's leading, and when Moses chose to suffer affliction with the people of God rather than to enjoy the pleasures of and power of Egypt. Then Jesus came to earth. Mary, Martha, Lazarus, Peter, James, John, and a few more than a hundred others believed on Him. But His own nation received Him not. They mocked Him. They spit on Him. They crucified Him. But there on the cross the price of redemption was paid, so that whoever believed on Him could have eternal life.

There's a lovely story told about a little boy who made a boat. With his father's help it was shaped and painted. He put a mast in it and put some sails on it, then proudly took it to the park to sail it in the lake. He had a long string tied to it, and joyfully he watched his little boat sail farther and farther out on the water. Suddenly the string slipped out of his hand, and he could not bring his boat back. He called for help, but there was none, so he ran home to get his father. But by the time they got back to the lake the little boat was gone. Someone had found it and taken it. The little boy was heartbroken.

One day while downtown he saw *his* boat in a toy shop window. Of course it was his boat. He could tell by the size, the paint, the mast, and the sails. But rather than start an argument with the shop owner, he went in and bought it. He paid the price for it. Then he went home, hugging his little boat to his heart while he said, "Dear little boat, how I love you! You are mine, twice mine, for I made you, and now I have bought you."

That's what Jesus says about you and me. "Oh how I love you. You are Mine, twice Mine, for I made you, and I have bought you!"

Won't you believe Him and accept Him—today, and always?

Jesus said to him, "Thomas, because you have seen Me, you have believed. Blessed are those who have not seen and yet have believed."
John 20:29.

November 7

The name of Thomas has come down through the years as one who would not believe unless he saw with his own eyes and felt with his own hands. Remember, Jesus blessed those who believed on Him without seeing!

Once upon a time, the story goes, a young man who didn't believe in God was traveling on a boat. Traveling on the same boat was a godly old minister. One day as they talked the young man ridiculed the idea of believing something they hadn't seen. "But you believe many things *you* haven't seen," said the minister.

"No I don't," said the young man.

"You believe there's a country called England, don't you?"

"Of course!"

"But you have never seen it."

"No, but others have."

"Oh, I see," said the minister. "Then it's only the things you or someone else has seen that you believe."

"That's it!" the young man said confidently.

"Have you ever seen your brain?" the minister asked with a little smile.

"Well—er—"

"Has anyone else ever seen your brain?"

"No, but—" The young man went away feeling very uncomfortable.

I like the answer a good old fisherman gave to a man who asked him how he knew there was a risen Savior. He said, "I go fishing on the lake very early in the morning. By and by I see the glory and brightness of the sunrise reflected in the windows of the homes on the lakeshore. I don't have to turn around and see whether the sun has risen. I know it has risen because I can see its reflection. So when I see love, kindness, and thoughtfulness for others shining in the faces of men and women, and being given out in their words and actions, I can tell by the reflection that there is a risen Savior."

Do you believe in a risen Savior? Can others see His reflection in Your life?

JOHN 21

*"Cast the net on the right side of the boat, and you will
find some." So they cast, and now they were not able
to draw it in because of the multitude of fish.
John 21:6.*

November 8

Near the beginning of His ministry
Jesus performed a miracle, and
Peter, James, and John caught a "multitude of fish" in their net. Now, near the end of
His ministry and just before He ascended to
heaven, Jesus performed another miracle for His
discouraged friends, and they caught 153 fish!
Notice that on each occasion there was absolute obedience to His command. Jesus
is always the same—yesterday, today, and forever—and where He finds absolute
obedience He can still work miracles.

When I was in Brazil years ago, Pastor Rasi pointed out a village in which a
faithful family of fishermen had experienced a miracle. There the fish are caught
in a big bamboo trap that is made in such a way that when the tidewaters rise,
the fish easily swim in, but they can't get out. There were 14 traps in all, belong-
ing to 14 different families. Soon after our Adventist fishermen were baptized
they had a severe trial. No more fish came into their trap. A whole week went
by; still no fish. Then a month with no fish! Soon they owed the equivalent of
$350 at the grocery store.

"It's because you're keeping the Sabbath," taunted their friends. "Come
on, give up your Sabbath, and you'll catch more fish."

But our good believers said, "We won't deny our Savior. We'll die first."
They knelt down and told the Lord they were determined to be true, and they
asked for His help. Then one Thursday night a huge fish weighing 200 pounds
got into their trap! They knelt down right there on the shore and thanked
God. Friday morning there were three fish that size in their trap, and by sunset Friday there were six more huge fish in their trap. But our men wouldn't
touch them.

"No," they said, "not till after the Sabbath." Their friends called them fools.

"They'll break your trap if you don't take them out," they said. But our
people kept the Sabbath, and Saturday night they found in their trap 22 large
fish and 400 pounds of smaller fish—5,000 pounds in all! They worked all night
getting the fish ready for market. They paid off all their debt, put money in
the bank, and supplied half the cost of a new chapel in their village!

Don't be surprised if God tests your obedience sometime. Be sure you
keep true, and He could perform a miracle for you, too.

ACTS 1

You shall be witnesses to Me in Jerusalem, and in all Judea and Samaria, and to the end of the earth. Acts 1:8.

A witness for Christ is someone who says or does something that brings honor to the Savior's name. Mary, the sister of Martha and Lazarus, did something for Jesus that has been told wherever the gospel has been preached.

Now let me tell you about another young woman who lives away over in New Guinea, whose kind deed for Jesus has been told all around the world. She was one of the daughters of Faole, whom you read about on June 17 to 19. She had gone to school at one of our missions and had been trained to do clinic work there. Later on she married and, with her husband, moved to one of the outstations far up in the Owen Stanley Mountains.

One day during World War II an American pilot crashed into the jungle not far from Faole's home village. Faole's first-aiders found the pilot unconscious, with both legs broken. Tenderly they carried him into the village. They had no clinic, but Faole's married daughter took over. She gently straightened the pilot's legs and put them in bamboo splints as well as she could. She sewed up his wounds with a needle and thread, and tenderly nursed him back to health and strength again. Frequently they had to move because of the nearness of the enemy, but they took the pilot with them. Then after 70 days they were able to carry him through the jungle to his base hospital.

"Officer," said the pilot to the doctor in charge, "I want you to give this good woman anything she may desire. Never mind the cost. Put it to my account. I am alive and back here with my friends because of her excellent service." They asked Faole's daughter what she would like to receive as a gift for caring for the pilot. What do you think she said?

"Sir, if I can have anything I want, please give me a medical kit with everything in it so that I can help someone else who may get injured."

The physicians couldn't believe their ears. They had never heard of such devoted witnessing. She got the medical kit, and most likely she has forgotten all about her kind deed by this time. But the pilot hasn't forgotten, and the medical officers at the base hospital haven't forgotten—and they have told her story all around the world.

ACTS 2

*I will pour out of My Spirit on all flesh; your sons and
your daughters shall prophesy, your young men shall
see visions, your old men shall dream dreams.
Acts 2:17.*

November 10

What a wonderful experience the early Christians enjoyed when the Holy Spirit was poured out on them on the day of Pentecost. Peter said it fulfilled Joel's prophecy (Joel 2:28). We believe that again, in these last days, there'll be a mighty outpouring of the Holy Spirit, and I believe that the wonderful things we are seeing around the world are because of it.

Several years ago the Holy Spirit used an 8-year-old girl in the city of Tunis to do a great work for Him. Nancy was the daughter of our church pastor there. When her family moved there, she became friends with the little girls who lived on her street. Now, the chief of police lived close by, and he had a little girl the same age. Nancy and Linda soon became good friends, and played together every day until Saturday. On Sabbath Nancy went to Sabbath school. Then that afternoon, still in her Sabbath clothes, she went to visit her little friend.

"Why didn't you come play with us today?" Linda asked.

"I went to Sabbath school," Nancy said. "You see, today is the true Sabbath, so that's why I was in church." Then she told Linda and the other little girls about Creation and how God made Sabbath on the seventh day. That evening Linda told her father and mother, and they were very interested. The next day Linda brought home the news that Nancy's family didn't eat pork. The chief of police was so interested that he told the other police officers when he went to work.

"Why do they believe Jesus is coming soon?" he asked his little girl one evening.

"I don't know. I'll ask my friend tomorrow," she said. And so Nancy asked her pastor father, and he wrote down a few texts on a slip of paper. Then the pastor's little girl told the policeman's little girl all about it and gave her the piece of paper. Then the police chief read the texts and told his fellow officers the next day. And that's the way it went, step by step, day by day, till at last the chief of police asked for Bible studies, and today five police officers and their families are members of our church.

It's time for the Holy Spirit to be poured out everywhere. Are you ready for the latter rain to be poured out upon you?

Silver and gold I do not have, but what I do have I give you: In the name of Jesus Christ of Nazareth, rise up and walk.
Acts 3:6.

November 11

What a wonderful gift the poor lame man received the day that Peter told him to walk. The ability to walk was much more precious to him than silver or gold. No wonder the happy man leaped up and down as he praised God!

Today is the anniversary of another day when something more precious than silver or gold was given to the people of this world. For four long years 16 nations with 65 million soldiers had been fighting in World War I. More than 8.5 million had been killed or had died of wounds. Another 21 million were wounded. But at last the peace treaty was signed at the eleventh hour of the eleventh day of the eleventh month.

For two minutes, around the world, all traffic stopped, and everybody remained silent in gratitude for the peace that had been restored. Then, after taps sounded out over the radios, people went wild with joy. Whistles blew, bells rang, car horns honked, and millions of people leaped up and down with joy. They called it Armistice Day, and during the next few years monuments were built in the great cities of the world, and the bodies of unknown soldiers were buried in many special places so the people could remember the millions of soldiers who died to bring back peace again. France's unknown soldier was buried under the Arc de Triomphe, and above the grave a flame representing sacrifice is kept burning day and night. England's unknown soldier was buried in Westminster Abbey in London. The United States unknown soldier was buried in Arlington National Cemetery, with the inscription: "Here rests in honored glory an American soldier known but to God." Sentries, who are changed every hour during the day and every two hours during the night, keep guard over the tomb.

Sadly, World War I was followed by World War II, and since then many more wars have been fought and millions more have died as a result. Perhaps even a family member or friend has been wounded or killed fighting for freedom.

Only Christ's coming will bring lasting peace. Make up your mind to have a place in His eternal kingdom, where there always will be peace.

ACTS 4

*By the name of Jesus Christ . . . this man stands here
before you whole. . . . Nor is there salvation in any other,
for there is no other name under heaven given among
men by which we must be saved."
Acts 4:10-12*

November 12

It matters not one bit whether a person is a Pharisee or a scribe, a publican or a sinner, a body builder or a weakling, a Jew or a Gentile. There is only one way to be saved, and that is to believe on the name of the Lord Jesus Christ. I am reminded of a story William Stidger told about a friend of his who fell down into a well. Fortunately, the well was dry, with only a little soft mud in the bottom. But it was 30 feet deep and quite a distance from the man's house. He yelled and shouted for an hour, hoping to attract someone's attention. But it was no use. Nobody heard, and nobody came to help him. At last the seriousness of his position came to him, and as he began to get chilly and numb, he was terrified. He tried to think, but he couldn't. Then he tried to pray, and as he looked up, there above him at the top of the well he saw a circle of light with a star clearly visible in the sky. The sight of that star brought hope to his fearful heart, and he said to himself, "The only way out of this dark, miserable well is up, up toward that star."

He took out his pocketknife and dug two toeholds in the clay walls of the well about a foot up from the bottom. Then he cut two more a foot or so above them, then two more and two more. Then step by step, with his toes in the toeholds, he kept on climbing up. It took him five hours to climb up and out, but there was no other way, no shortcut. The only way was "up," and he kept going up until he made it.

And so it is with us—the only way out of this world of sin, sorrow, and temptation is to believe on the precious name of Jesus. It's easy to get discouraged. Whether your problem is a history class you can't seem to master, parents who don't get along, a friend who's betrayed you, or anything else, the only way out is to look to Jesus. Ask Him for guidance. Ask Him where you should go for help.

Whether you are weak or strong, baptized or not, whoever believes in Him should not perish but have everlasting life. Have you made Jesus your Savior?

November **13**

They brought the sick out into the streets and laid them on beds and couches, that at least the shadow of Peter passing by might fall on some of them. Acts 5:15.

What kind of "shadow" do we cast on friends and strangers? We certainly want to be ready to meet Jesus, and our shadow, or influence, has a great deal to do with our hearts and minds. Peter was so humble, so good, so cheerful—so Christlike—that wherever he went the sick were healed and people were happier and felt better. Maybe you don't yet realize that you too have an influence, that makes people feel glad to see you—or not.

I well remember the first time I realized that I had a shadow. I was 19, and a college junior, spending a weekend with friends in Mount Gambier. I had lived there when I was 11, and now Pastor Brown asked me to preach on Sabbath and take the young people's meeting. I was thrilled. I stayed in the Browns' home, and that evening I sat around the fire with Pastor and Mrs. Brown, 10-year-old Lionel, and his two sisters. As we talked, I felt young Lionel's eyes on me the whole time, and when it was time for the little folks to go to bed he said, "Oh, Dad, can't Eric sleep with me in my bed tonight?" And when I nodded yes, he bounded happily away. But he was sound asleep when I finally crawled in beside him, and didn't know anything about it till he woke up and found me in bed with him in the morning. "Eric," he sputtered in surprise, "did you sleep with me?"

"Sure," I said.

"All night?"

"That's right," I said. Then we talked till it was time to get up. I got up first, poured some water from a big pitcher into a porcelain basin, and washed my face. Then I opened the window so that I could throw my dirty water out—for that's what we did long ago. But Lionel sprang out of bed, grabbed the basin, and said, "Aw, Eric, can't I wash my face in your water?" My heart nearly stood still. I didn't know what to do. But I couldn't disappoint him, so I let him use my water. It was then that I realized that this boy wanted to be like me, and I lifted my heart to God. "Dear Lord," I prayed, "help me to live so that it will always be safe for boys and girls to wash their faces in my water."

Your shadow will fall on someone today. Make sure your influence will help them to be ready when Jesus comes.

ACTS 6

And Stephen, full of faith and power,
did great wonders and signs among the people.
Acts 6:8.

November 14

Stephen was a wonderful man of faith and courage, and his good works were amazing to all. But the secret was very simple. He was full of the Holy Spirit (Acts 6:5).

Many, many Stephens have worked for God all around the world. Let me tell you about one way over in Burma. Ohn Bwint, one of the first students in our mission school, came from a village 38 miles away. After four years he was baptized, and when he had finished the sixth grade, Hte Po, the headman of La Po Ta village, 18 miles away, pleaded so hard for a teacher that we let Ohn Bwint go there. Now, Ohn Bwint was full of faith and the Holy Spirit, and at the end of his first year he came to camp meeting with five bullock wagons filled with people, and with Hte Po, the headman, ready for baptism. Ohn Bwint went back to La Po Ta for a second year.

Now on the first Sunday of each new quarter all the workers from our outstations came to the mission for a meeting. They brought in their school reports, medical reports, and Sabbath school reports. They got their wages and supplies, then returned, refreshed and encouraged, to their outstations. The end of the third quarter of Ohn Bwint's second year found the country flooded. The great Salween River had overflowed its banks and covered the whole country with water and mud right back to the foothills. Our other outstations were on the riverbank, and we were able to bring the men in by launch and canoe, but La Po Ta was 18 miles inland. It was impossible to think of his coming in till after the flood had gone down. Nevertheless, on the first Sunday of the fourth quarter, in came Ohn Bwint!

"However did you make it?" we asked. "Wasn't the whole country under water?"

"Oh, yes," he replied cheerfully, "but it wasn't so bad in the hills. I had to swim across 20 rivers in the little valleys between the hills, then when I came to the plains I had to walk through mud and water, often up to my neck, for six miles. But I brought in my report on time!" You won't be surprised to know that in time Ohn Bwint was ordained to the ministry and was used by God to raise up several churches. What inspired him to be so faithful? The same Spirit of God that inspired Paul to say, "None of these things move me; nor do I count my life dear to myself, so that I may finish my race with joy" (Acts 20:24). Won't you pray that God will fill you with His Holy Spirit and make you a faithful Stephen too?

S-11

And they stoned Stephen as he was calling on God. . . . Then he knelt down and cried out with a loud voice, "Lord, do not charge them with this sin." Acts 7:59, 60.

November 15

When Jesus was being crucified, He prayed, "Father, forgive them, for they do not know what they do" (Luke 23:34). Nothing could be more Christlike than to pray this for people who are determined to destroy you. Many years ago, during the fearful Mau Mau rebellion in Kenya many of our African Seventh-day Adventists were persecuted and tortured because they had adopted a White religion. The Mau Mau leaders tried to force all Africans to take an oath that included obscene acts and a promise to worship the Mau Mau leader. Gakui, a teenage girl who had been at our mission school only one year, determined she would not take the oath. Her parents coaxed her to do it for their sake, and the Mau Mau threatened her with death. For a while she hid in the bush when the Mau Mau came to her village. Then a neighbor woman betrayed her, and she was seized and taken to the ceremonial hut some distance away.

"Will you take the oath?" they demanded.

"I cannot," she replied. "I am a Christian."

They slapped her face in fury. "Do you want to die?" they shouted.

"I don't want to die," she replied, "and I know Jesus will save me." The men beat her with clubs till she was unconscious, then dragged her body to the wall of the hut. When she regained consciousness she watched in horror as other young people performed filthy acts and swore the terrible oath. "O God," she prayed, "save me. Save me!" And as she prayed she felt strong hands grip her feet, and she was pulled slowly but steadily through a hole in the wall. Once outside, she rose carefully to her feet, and quietly slipped away to the home of an Adventist family who hid her until the trouble was over. When the government officials asked Gakui to identify her tormenters and lay charges against them, she quietly said, "No, I don't want to do that. They did not realize what they were doing. I have hope that they will be Christians someday." What a lovely spirit! The officers examined the walls of the ceremonial hut, but there were no signs of the hole through which she had been pulled. God does not let anything hinder Him when He performs His miracles. He needs only to find a Christlike spirit in the life. Then He can do anything. Have you that Christlike spirit?

ACTS 8

And the multitudes with one accord heeded the things spoken
by Philip, hearing and seeing the miracles which he did. . . .
And there was great joy in that city.
Acts 8:6-8.

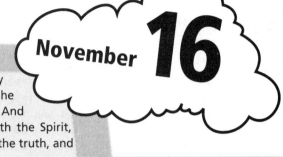

November 16

Philip had power to bring great joy to the city of Samaria because he was filled with the Holy Spirit. And wherever we find people filled with the Spirit, we find miracles, people accepting the truth, and great joy.

In a certain town there lived a very poor shoemaker. He was a good man, and wanted to do what was right. One day he listened to the Voice of Prophecy radio program and was convinced that it was God's truth. He listened every week and was thrilled with what he learned about the Bible. So when a colporteur came by, selling books published by the church that broadcast the Voice of Prophecy, he was glad to buy one and asked the colporteur to come explain it to him.

"I surely will," he said, and he visited the shoemaker nearly every evening. The shoemaker rejoiced over one truth after another, but when it came to the Sabbath he said, "Oh, no. I couldn't keep Sabbath. That is my biggest day for business." The colporteur urged him to step out in faith and see what God would do for him, but he was sure he would starve if he closed the shop on Saturday. On the first Sabbath, though his heart said it was God's rest day, he went to work. He opened his shop and got out his leather—but his hammer was gone! He looked everywhere, but it was nowhere to be seen. At last he said, "It seems I'll have to keep this Sabbath anyway." So he went home.

When he went to work the next day, there was his hammer, as plain as could be, right on his workbench. "Well, now! Where was that hammer yesterday?" he wondered out loud. The next Sabbath he made a decision to go to work again. This time he'd locked his hammer in the drawer, and it was there, all right. "Now I shall work, and no one will stop me," he muttered, but with the very first blow the hammerhead broke in two! There was nothing to do but go home. "It must be a sign from the Lord that the Sabbath is true and that He wants me to keep it," he told the colporteur.

A few months later this good man and his wife were baptized. After the baptism the pastor presented him with a brand-new hammer that had never worked on Sabbath. "I am sure you and your hammer will both enjoy keeping the Sabbath after this," he said. And they did.

Are you filled with the Spirit? Do you bring great joy to your community, wherever it is?

ACTS 9

At Joppa there was a certain disciple named . . . Dorcas. This woman was full of good works and charitable deeds.
Acts 9:36.

November 17

To be full of good works and charitable deeds is almost the same as being full of the Holy Spirit, for it is the Spirit who makes us kind and thoughtful toward the needy. What a blessing Dorcas was to the church in Joppa and to the needy ones there. Now centuries later her spirit of helpfulness lives on in the lives of other women and men in the Community Service workers of the Christian church. Let me tell you of a present-day Dorcas.

Several years ago the church at Worcester, Massachusetts, decided to open a welfare center. "Anything can happen," said their pastor, "and we should be ready." Myrtle Meyer was made leader, and for years the Dorcas women gathered clothing, bedding, and supplies of all kinds. They had more than enough for the needy in their community. But "anything can happen," said Myrtle, so they kept putting things away and kept getting ready for a catastrophe.

One June Tuesday was an ordinary day at the center. Nineteen families had been cared for. The place was cleaned, and the women went home. But then a terrible thunderstorm broke. The wind roared, and lightning lit the sky. Then the rain stopped, and an ominous quiet filled the air. Then, in the distance, came an awful roar. "It's a tornado!" Myrtle's husband shouted. And it was. Hundreds of people were killed or wounded, and thousands were left homeless. And Myrtle Meyer was ready! This was the hour they had prepared for. She hustled off to the community center. When morning came, the hospitals were full; thousands were homeless; children were crying. All was confusion and chaos except in one building. There Mrs. Meyer and her Dorcas women were all in uniform and ready. A big sign in front of the church said "Relief Center," and breakfast was cooking in the kitchen. Then the people began to come. They needed clothes, and they were given clothes. Newborn babies were given layettes. Whatever they needed was there and ready to go. And when the center ran out of sheets and blankets, people in the homes that had not been destroyed took them from their own beds. The "green-clad angels" worked all day and all night for the first few days, feeding 500 to 700 people a day. Bakeries gave them bread; a dairy donated milk. Stores gave slippers and baby carriages, cribs, and high chairs to the Dorcas women to give out because they were ready.

Are you full of good works? Is your heart ready to respond in time of need?

ACTS 10

So Cornelius said, "Four days ago . . . I prayed in my house, and behold, a man stood before me in bright clothing, and said, 'Cornelius, your prayer has been heard. . . . Send therefore to Joppa and call Simon here, whose surname is Peter.'"
Acts 10:30-32.

How many times we read or hear of the Holy Spirit leading, guiding, and bringing people together by dreams and visions to hear the gospel story! Here is one sent in by Pastor J. M. Miranda, telling about one of his experiences as a missionary in Angola.

Pastor Miranda, with his wife and a group of helpers, was conducting evangelistic meetings in a district about 78 miles from Nova Lisboa, their headquarters mission station. They went to the town where the meetings would be held, and divided the villages among them so that every house would receive a personal invitation to the evening meetings.

The home of the king of the tribe was in Pastor Miranda's territory, and the king and his three wives listened with great interest as Pastor Miranda spoke about salvation through Jesus Christ. They closed their visit with prayer. Then just before leaving, Pastor Miranda asked the king whether he had anything to say. "Yes," the king replied. "A few days ago I had a dream. I saw a great multitude dressed in white, singing hymns as they were marching toward the great city of heaven. I wanted to go with them, but one of the glorious multitude told me I would have to have a passport to go with them. But he said there are people on a mission station that has four buildings, in Nova Lisboa, who can give you a passport, and soon a White man and a teacher from the Quioco tribe will come to your village. They will tell you what to do and how to get the passport to go to heaven."

The king paused, and Pastor Miranda said, "Today your dream is fulfilled. I am here, right in your village. Our mission in Nova Lisboa has just four buildings, and my assistant pastor is of the Quioco tribe!" Needless to say, the king attended the meetings and joined the baptismal class, where he was getting ready to bury his past in the waters of baptism.

Stay close to God. In the last days the Holy Spirit is to be poured out on all people—even young people. Who can tell? Maybe God will direct you to go to the help of someone, someday, by a dream.

ACTS 11

And they sent out Barnabas. . . . For he was a good man, full of the Holy Spirit and of faith. And a great many people were added to the Lord. Acts 11:22-24.

Did you ever wonder why they called Barnabas a good man? He was a rich man, but he wasn't good because he was rich. He was a successful evangelist, but he wasn't good because he baptized many people. He was of the tribe of Levi, but his goodness didn't come from social standing. If you read carefully about him you will find one outstanding fact about Barnabas—he was kind and thoughtful of others. That's why they called him a good man. Barnabas sold his property and donated the proceeds for the support of the needy in the Jerusalem church. Barnabas befriended Paul, the converted persecutor, and helped him to get started in the ministry. Barnabas stood by his young cousin, John Mark, who had failed during his first missionary trip, and gave him another chance to make good. Good old Barnabas! No wonder everybody said he was a good man.

Once upon a time there were two brothers called Ahmed and Omar. They were both rich; they were both well educated; and they both wanted to do something that would cause people to remember them forever. So Omar erected a great stone obelisk in the desert near a road that passed from one country to another. Upon it he carved his name in big, deep letters among many beautiful designs. The hot winds blew and the desert sands gathered around it, and after a year or two no one ever stopped to admire the great stone pillar or to read the name. But Ahmed found a place in the desert where he could dig a well, a well that would cheer the thirsty travelers. Around it he planted date palms to make cool shade for weary pilgrims and to provide sweet fruit for the hungry. He carved no name, but as the years went by, almost everyone who passed by stopped at the well and rested in the shade of the trees. And everyone remembered the name of Ahmed, for he was a good man, one who had made kindness to others first in his life. Did you know that "goodness" is one of the fruits of the Spirit (Galatians 5:22)? And it is the "goodness of God" that leads to repentance (Romans 2:4).

Are you a good junior? I don't mean rich. I don't mean clever. I mean good—to others.

ACTS 12

*And when Peter had come to himself, he said, "Now
I know for certain that the Lord has sent His angel,
and has delivered me from the hand of Herod."
Acts 12:11.*

November **20**

One Friday evening 21 armed bandits surrounded our Karen boarding school and kidnapped 10 of our young people. They were taken across the Salween River and forced to carry stolen food and clothing to the bandits' camp about 15 miles away. The next day one young man was sent back with a note demanding 25,000 rupees. If the money wasn't brought, the nine remaining prisoners would be shot. It was raining, the mosquitoes were bad, and they were given no shelter. A bowl of rice twice a day was their only food. No wonder some of them began to cry. But Mo Chit Aye, a young woman teacher, took control and said, "Now listen. It won't do us any good to cry. We are Seventh-day Adventists, and we don't cry. We sing! Come on, let's sing." One by one the others joined in, and as they sang the bandits listened and listened.

"What kind of people are you?" asked the chief. "Everyone else that we capture curses and swears, but you sing."

"We are Seventh-day Adventists," said the teacher, "and after we sing we will pray. And we will pray for you, for Jesus told us to pray for our enemies."

"You needn't think your God can deliver you out of my hands," scoffed the chief. "Nothing can deliver you but money!" But day after day our young people kept on singing and praying. About a week later one of the girls was released to take back the final word that if the money was not produced in three days, the eight remaining prisoners would be shot. Our poor people could find no more money. All they could do was to pray, and they prayed that the great God of heaven would preserve the lives of our students. Back in the bandits' camp the prisoners sang and sang, preached and preached, and prayed and prayed—and those wicked men listened and listened and listened. Every day the captives thought this would be their last. But after three weeks a messenger from the district bandit chief brought a message to the bandit camp: "Release immediately the eight young people you are holding as prisoners."

"All right! All right!" shouted the chief angrily. Calling our students, he said, "Follow me." He led them to eight newly dug graves. "I was going to shoot each of you into a grave," he said. "But your God has delivered you." Then he led them to the trail and let them go back to school!

The God who can deliver is your God. Always stay close to Him.

It was necessary that the word of God should be spoken to you first; but since you reject it, and judge yourselves unworthy of everlasting life, behold, we turn to the Gentiles.
Acts 13:46.

November 21

Acts 13:46 is one of the saddest verses in the Bible. God chose the children of Israel to be His own people. He planned to make them the most enlightened people on the earth, physically and mentally. They were to be the head and not the tail—light bearers to the whole world. But again and again they turned from God. They rebelled against the leadership of God and demanded a king so they would be like the other nations. When the world's Savior was born among them, they crucified Him; and when Christ's messengers preached the last message to them, and gave the last invitation, they contradicted and blasphemed. If they had only known that this was the last message to be given them as a nation, that this was their last chance to excel as a nation, and that after this the invitation would be given to all nations, how different their history could have been. This danger of putting off until it's too late comes to us all.

A Persian prince divided his adult life into four periods—10 years for travel, 10 years for government work, 10 years for pleasure, and 10 years for God. He thought his plan a good one, but the trouble was that he died during the first 10 years! If he'd only known, how much more wisely he could have planned.

A man from outside North America came to Chicago and rented a room in a hotel. Soon after getting settled he took a walk around the shopping section and got lost. He wandered around trying to find his way back, but in his excitement he had forgotten the name of the street and the name of the hotel. He was too embarrassed to ask for help, and at last he had to rent another room. He tried for five days to find the first hotel, where his luggage was, but nothing looked familiar. Finally he was compelled to ask the police for help. They telephoned around to some of the hotels and soon found his name in the register of the hotel *next door* to where he had been staying! He was so near, but he was lost!

God wants you to be one of His special children. He wants to bless you physically and mentally and spiritually above all others, so you can be a light bearer to the world. Make sure you have accepted Him now. Don't put it off until it is too late. It is too sad to think of being almost saved, but lost.

ACTS 14

In Lystra [was] a certain man . . . who had never walked.
This man heard Paul speaking. . . . "Stand up straight
on your feet!" And he leaped and walked.
Acts 14:8-10.

November **22**

I love to think of the joy and happiness that must have come to the man Paul healed. He had never walked before. Try to imagine him sitting there day after day, year after year, watching the happiness of others who could run and walk and play, but not having any of the happiness for himself. No wonder he leaped with joy when he was healed.

I know juniors who have never walked to visit the lonely, or walked to collect money for missions. They don't realize how much happiness they're missing.

Once there was a timid girl who had never wanted to go Ingathering. But one year she decided she must get over her timidity, so she took a bundle of magazines and some Ingathering leaflets and started off. "If I'm too scared to ask for money," she said to herself, "I'll give them a paper anyway."

She went down the street and selected the poorest looking house of all for her first call. She knocked on the door, and when a woman with a baby in her arms opened it, she was so scared she couldn't do anything but say, "Please take these papers." And she put the whole bundle of them in the woman's hands and fled in embarrassment. The woman didn't want the papers, but she took them, and put them up on top of a kitchen cabinet. Weeks went by, and one cold winter day she sat shivering with her baby in her arms.

"If only I had some paper I could paste it over those cracks in the wall," she said. Then she remembered that bundle. "Just the very thing," she said, and soon the cracks in the wall were covered with those pages. How much more comfortable her room was now! Another day as she sat rocking her baby her eye caught the title of an article on a page of a paper on the wall. "That looks interesting," she said, and read it to the end of the page. Then she looked all over the wall till she found the rest of the article. Day after day, week after week, she read the articles pasted on the wall, and as she read she accepted salvation and, in time, found her way into the church. The day she was baptized, the minister asked to see the hands of those whose first contact had been through literature, and this woman told her story.

A vision appeared to Paul in the night. A man of Macedonia stood and pleaded with him, saying, "Come over to Macedonia and help us."
Acts 16:9.

November 23

In response to the call for help that came to Paul, he and Silas took the gospel to a new continent. In the same way, thousands of youth have gone to un-reached peoples around the world. I answered the call, too, and with my good wife joyfully went to Burma to minister to the Karens. However, I was greatly disappointed. My spirit worshippers didn't want the gospel. They were quite satisfied with ignorance and superstition. They called me a dawtaka—an evil spirit that eats babies. With my trumpet, a Picture Roll, and a bag of medicines I could get them to listen to me—once! But the next time, I would find the village empty. I invited them to Sabbath school, but nobody came. At last I decided to have Sabbath school in a nearby village. I visited every house, treated every sick person, and told them to come when they heard the trumpet. And they came—200 of them. They clapped their hands and said, "Fine, fine. Now sing for us." So we sang. I was starting to tell them about Jesus when they clapped and said, "Fine, fine! Now tell your wife to dance for us."

I was so discouraged. I turned to Acts and studied Paul's experience again. I was surprised to find that his Macedonia trip took a year, and he preached in only three cities. In Philippi he was put in jail; in Thessalonica he escaped from the city by night after a riot; and in Berea, after another riot, his friends sent him out of the country into Greece! But Paul was not discouraged. He sang in prison at midnight, and made a second and even a third trip into this difficult field.

I fell on my knees and asked God to show me what made the difference. Why was I discouraged and Paul was not? And God showed me. The man of Macedonia was a *symbol*. Paul understood that he meant that the Lord had called them to preach the gospel there (Acts 16:10). What a difference it made to Paul. He was helping the Lord Jesus save souls! The dear Lord Jesus, whom the people crucified! Of course, Paul could do anything and suffer anything for Him. And when I understood that God had called me to Burma to help *Him* preach the gospel, it made a world of difference. Little by little the people opened up. Many gave their hearts to God, and my 20 years there were the happiest of my life.

When you are called to witness for Jesus, don't expect everyone to meet you with open arms. But go forth anyway! You'll see what a difference it makes to you.

ACTS 17

The brethren immediately sent away Paul and Silas by night unto Berea. . . . These were more noble . . . in that they received the word with all readiness of mind, and searched the scriptures daily. Acts 17:10, 11, KJV.

November **24**

How thankful we are for the noble Bereans, who studied their Bibles every day. What a wonderful example they are to all Christians. Throughout the years many Bible reading or study groups have taken the name Berean. But remember, the Bereans did more than just read their Bibles—they searched them. They studied the Word of God.

Long ago I heard of an experience in South Africa that illustrates perfectly the difference between only reading the Bible and studying the Bible. Thirteen-year-old John lived in the part of Africa in which there are diamond fields. Because his mother was a widow it was necessary for him to get work when he finished grade school and save money so that he could go to high school. So with a partner he chose a piece of unclaimed ground and began digging for diamonds. Each week they found enough diamonds to pay expenses and live well, but the fortune they dreamed of never turned up. Now, diamonds are generally found in a layer of gravel near the surface. So young John and his partner worked the gravel thoroughly right down to the basic dirt. They noticed that their neighbors were digging deeper, but thought only that the surface gravel over there was deeper than their own. They did not think of digging a hole to see whether there was more gravel under what appeared to be the basic dirt, and when they had thoroughly worked the surface gravel, they moved on.

Later on, someone else came along and dug a hole on their old plot. They found more gravel deeper down, and in that gravel was a fortune. Many thousands of dollars' worth of diamonds were dug from that plot of ground. If John and his partner had only dug a little deeper they could have found that fortune! But they had been satisfied to skim over the surface, so they missed it.

There is a "fortune" in the Word of God, but you have to search for it. You have to dig for it. Skimming over the surface and getting the story will give you some blessing, but the richest blessing comes when you study, when you think, when you compare one text with another, and when you compare your life with the ideas found in the Word of God.

When Paul had laid hands on them, the Holy Spirit came upon them, and they . . . prophesied. . . . So the word of the Lord grew mightily and prevailed. Acts 19:6-20.

November 25

I think that among the many, many things we have to be thankful for, the Spirit of Prophecy in our church is one of the best. All through the years God has spoken to His people and led them by His servants the prophets. When this Advent movement began in 1844, God needed a prophet He could use as a mouthpiece to lead and encourage His people. Among the early Adventist preachers was a young man, Hazen Foss. He was an eloquent speaker and well liked. One night God gave him a vision in which he saw the Advent believers traveling on a straight, narrow path high above the world, leading to the heavenly city. A light shone from the beginning of the path all along the way, so that the travelers would not stumble. Jesus was leading the company, and as long as the people kept their eyes on Jesus they were safe. But some lost sight of Jesus. Then their light went out, and they were left in darkness.

Foss watched and watched till he saw the righteous dead rise from their graves and caught up to enter the City of God. Then God said to Hazen Foss, "Make known to others what I have revealed to you." But Hazen Foss was afraid that people wouldn't believe him, and that it would hurt his influence, so he wouldn't do it. God sent him the vision a second time, and again he was told to make it known to others. Still he would not.

Then God chose a sickly 17-year-old girl. Her name was Ellen Gould Harmon. She was given the same vision, and she heard the same voice commanding her to tell it to others. She was timid and weak, and her voice was not strong, yet in a meeting of believers she courageously began to tell what she had seen. And as she talked her voice grew strong. Outside the meeting room, listening to her message, was Hazen Foss. "That's it. That's it," he said to the man standing beside him. "That's the vision God gave me. I was told to tell it to others, but I refused."

The next morning he met Ellen and said to her, "I heard you talk last night. I believe the visions are taken from me and given to you. . . . Be faithful in doing your work."

Aren't you thankful that Ellen Harmon accepted the responsibility and became God's mouthpiece for this Advent movement? What a blessing she has been and still is to each one of us! Are you careful to follow the instruction God has given through her?

ACTS 18

Do not be afraid, but speak, and do not keep silent;
for I am with you, and no one will attack you to hurt you;
for I have many people in this city.
Acts 18:9, 10.

November **26**

Again and again when Paul was preaching, mobs of angry people, shouting and blaspheming, rushed upon him. But again and again God delivered him, and this time God came to Paul in a vision and gave him the beautiful promise found in today's devotional text. This same promise has been fulfilled again and again for God's faithful Adventist preachers. I remember a time, on a small island called Alor, between Java and New Guinea, where God delivered the pastor in a mighty way. Pastor J. A. Raranta was holding a series of meetings there, and the other Protestants were angry about it.

One night the city's headman got together a mob of strong men. He armed them with sharp knives, clubs, and axes and sent them to break up the meeting and to kill Pastor Raranta. The pastor saw them coming—yelling and shouting, sharpening their knives and swinging them over their heads. But he kept on preaching, trusting in the Lord for help. He was halfway through the meeting when the mob entered the building. Then something wonderful happened. They took one look, then turned around and ran back to the leader. "That place is filled with people bigger and stronger than we are," they said. "We've never seen anything like it before."

"You cowards!" snarled the headman. He decided that on the day of the baptism he would lead the mob himself. Then they would kill the pastor for sure. The day came. Seven were to be baptized, and a large group of interested believers gathered by a quiet river. In the midst of the service the mob rushed down to the riverbank. The pastor quietly invited them to watch the service first, before making any trouble. They quieted down and watched, and as they watched, the Holy Spirit came upon them and made them so weak that they couldn't even stand up. After the baptism Pastor Raranta invited them to give their hearts to Jesus and obey His Word. For a while they couldn't even talk. Then the headman said, "The Adventists are being led by God. I can't do anything against them. In the future I will leave them alone." Then one by one the mob picked up their knives and axes and went quietly away.

What a wonderful God we have! What a wonderful promise He has given us! Keep close to Him. You may need this promise to be fulfilled for you someday.

But none of these things move me; nor do I count my life dear to myself, so that I may may finish my race with joy.
Acts 20:24.

November 27

Good old Paul! What a man he was! Chains and hurts awaited him, but nothing could intimidate him. Nothing could make him turn back.

He was determined to finish his life race with joy, and he has inspired millions to do the same. It reminds me of Elder and Mrs. Orley Ford, who gave 45 years of service to the Indians in Peru and Inter-America. It was my privilege to meet them at the General Conference session in San Francisco. I was there when Inter-America gave its report, and I heard Elder Ford say, "Were we to begin life anew, we would choose to follow the same course. The Lord has been so precious to us in giving us good health and in saving our lives in times of extreme peril. I have been shot at many times, handcuffed and chained to a soldier guard, and thrown into dirty dungeons. On one occasion I was stoned, beaten to unconsciousness, and left for dead. But here we are, as good as new. Once, while I was away from home, Mrs. Ford's life was miraculously spared when 20,000 Indians on the warpath began looting and burning.

"We leave three little mounds, monuments to our little ones, laid away out there in lonely graves waiting to see us again. It is our desire to continue until the work is finished. Although officially retired, as all old Fords finally must be, I find in the used-car lot that the older the car the greater its sales value. So, as the oldest Ford on the road, I take courage and feel that I don't need to be retired but just need a retread. We have greatly enjoyed our work out there where darkness and poverty cause the light to shine with greater brilliance. We have lived with these people, treated their sick, conducted their marriages and their funerals, and we love them and desire to go home together with them. After hearing the wonderful reports here of what others are doing and have gone through, we feel that our lot has been too easy and our efforts insufficient. So we hope that these Fords will still run a little longer."

Aren't you proud of wonderful missionaries who want to finish their race with joy like that? Now, how are you going to finish your race someday? I can tell you the answer—it will be exactly the same way you finish your chores, your homework, and your schoolwork now.

Are you satisfied with that kind of finish?

*What do you mean by weeping and breaking my heart?
For I am ready not only to be bound, but also to die at
Jerusalem for the name of the Lord Jesus.
Acts 21:13.*

November 28

What a noble spirit of devotion is often expressed in the words of Paul! Just think of it. Paul—who imprisoned, persecuted, and even killed the followers of the Lord Jesus—is now ready himself to be imprisoned and to die for the Lord. The words of our text have inspired youth all around the world with the same spirit of devotion to the cause of our Savior. I doubt you've ever heard of Felipe Corcoro. Born in the Philippines, Felipe traveled to California with other young men whose one object was to get rich. There he found the truths of the gospel, a gospel more precious to him than silver or gold. With the truth came an intense longing to take the message to his own people. So a few years later he set sail for the Philippines again. His father's entire family accepted the third angel's message, and a new church was built in their village. Felipe then became a colporteur, and with his heart burning with love and enthusiasm, he decided to go to the darkest part of the island—to the Bontok tribe in the mountains.

"We would advise you not to pass along that road alone," said the gatekeeper at the beginning of the mountain road. "It is dangerous to go alone. The Bontoks are bloodthirsty headhunters, you know." Of course, Felipe knew. The day before, he had mailed a letter to the church office, enclosing two pesos for his Sabbath school offering. In his letter he said, "This is all I have left. I could use it to buy a seat on the bus, but I will walk. I want Jesus to have that money. You may not see my face again, for somehow I feel that I may never return. But for Jesus' sake I am determined to go. Farewell."

Poor Felipe did not return. While on that mountain road he was attacked by four young Bontok men and killed. His lower jaw was severed from his head as a trophy, and his body thrown into the river below. Two weeks later the sad news was brought to our Philippine college. What do you think our young people did when they heard of Felipe's noble devotion? Five young men stood up and said, "We will go in his place."

How great is the spirit of devotion to the work of God in *your* heart? God may not ask you to go to prison or to die for Him, but it would please Him to see you serving Him where you are.

The God of our fathers has chosen you that you should know His will, and see that Just One, and hear the voice of His mouth. For you will be His witness to all men of what you have seen and heard. Acts 22:14, 15.

November 29

In today's Scripture reading Paul tells the story of his dramatic conversion. The process of conversion differs with different people. With some it is quick and sudden, like that of Paul. He could always point to the time and the place of his conversion. With others it is so gradual that they cannot remember any particular time or place when they were converted—as in the lives of Samuel and of Timothy. In *Steps to Christ* we read, "A person may not be able to tell the exact time or place, or trace all the chain of circumstances in the process of conversion; but this does not prove him to be unconverted" (p. 57). I was so happy when I first read that paragraph, because like Samuel, I was born into a family that loved and obeyed God; and like Timothy, I had known the Scriptures since I was a child. I couldn't remember a special day when I was converted, as some of my schoolmates could. Those words make it very clear. The passage goes on to say: "Who has the heart? With whom are our thoughts? . . . If we are Christ's, our thoughts are with Him, and our sweetest thoughts are of Him" (*ibid.*, p. 58).

Billy Sunday, a well-known evangelist, had the simplest rule whereby we can tell positively whether we have been converted. He said, "If a sheep falls into a mudhole, it tries to get out as quickly as possible, but if a pig falls into a mudhole, it is in its glory, and stays there as long as it can." So when a Christian makes a mistake, if they feel miserable and try at once to make it right, they have a changed heart. They've been converted. Only a converted heart hates sin. But if someone does something wrong and is not found out, and they say, "Great! Nobody knows what I did; I guess I'll do that again sometime," what would you say about that person's heart?

Think about your own life. Do you truly hate sin? When you've done wrong, do you hate yourself till you've made things right? Have you been converted? You may be able to remember the time and the place you withdrew your affections from the world and fastened them upon Christ, or you may not. That is not the proof of conversion. But if you hate sin and love Christ, *then* you have been converted.

ACTS 23

Men and brethren, I have lived in all good
conscience before God until this day.
Acts 23:1.

A conscience is a strange thing. You can't see it, smell it, or taste it, but you can hear it, and everybody has one. Isaiah called it "a word behind you, saying, 'This is the way'" (Isaiah 30:21). Elijah called it "a still small voice" (I Kings 19:12), and a creative Christian called it a "three-cornered thing" that pricked him whenever he did wrong. Let's thank God this morning for the voice of conscience, and pray that it will never, never stop speaking to us.

Years ago a boy took a bus ride without paying his fare. The little voice kept telling him that to do this wasn't right, but the voice was so small that he closed his ears to it. Forty-five years went by, and the "little voice" spoke time and again. At last he sent the company four times his stolen fare—and then he had peace. Once upon a time a woman took two towels from a hotel room in which she was staying. For 20 years the little voice told her to make it right. At last she sent money to pay for them to the hotel. Then she could sleep peacefully again.

Once upon a time a girl cheated in an algebra examination. She passed the test, but she was unhappy. "Make it right. Go and confess," said the little voice, but she was too ashamed. She grew up and became an overseas missionary, but she couldn't get away from that voice. One day she couldn't stand it any longer, so she wrote a letter to her teacher: "Twenty-five years ago I cheated in an algebra exam. It has troubled me ever since. I have decided that my peace of mind is worth more than my pride, and so I am confessing my wrong. Please forgive me."

Then there was the schoolboy in Indiana who stole a watermelon. When he grew up, he was converted, and the voice of conscience got after him. The man from whom he stole the melon was dead, so he sent a letter to his daughter: "I am on my way to heaven, and have run up against that melon. It has grown so large that I cannot get over it. Please forgive and forget."

There is something very interesting, but also very sad, about this voice of conscience. The more we listen to it and obey it, the nearer it draws us to God, for it is the voice of God's Spirit. But if we refuse to obey it, its voice will become weaker and weaker till we can hear it no more, for God has said, "My Spirit shall not strive with [people] forever" (Genesis 6:3). And since there is no other voice to call us to repentance, how can we repent?

How is your conscience? Do you keep it in good working order?

337

As he reasoned about righteousness, self-control, and the judgment to come, Felix was afraid. Acts 24:25.

December 1

Paul was only a minister of the small early Christian church, which was hated and despised by the world, but when he stood before the greatest rulers in the land and explained his faith in Christ, they trembled (KJV) with fear. In *Education* we read that many a youth, "growing up as did Daniel in his Judean home, studying God's Word and His works, and learning the lessons of faithful service, will yet stand in . . . halls of justice . . . as a witness for the King of kings" (p. 262). This has been fulfilled many times as in times of war our young people have witnessed before high military officers, and God has given them words to speak and courage to speak them, and honor has come to God's name. In England three of our men were brought before their commander because of difficulty in getting their Sabbaths off. "I too am a Christian," he said. "In civilian life I am strict about Sunday observance. But in the army I forget my Sunday."

The eldest of the three soldiers replied, "Sir, the Sabbath is not our day. It is God's. We cannot change His law."

"You're a bunch of cowardly hypocrites," the officer shouted. "You are not fit to live. I'll turn the machine guns on you. Christians! Bah! You'd sit on your bed and read your Bible all day Saturday, and if the hospital should catch on fire, you'd just fold your hands and pray."

"No, sir," our young man replied. "In such an emergency we would work all day if necessary. Punish us if you must, sir. We are not afraid to suffer in prison. We do not drink or smoke. We do not go to shows, play cards, or gamble. If you want, you could put us in the guardhouse every Saturday, and we would be ready for business as soon as the sun sets."

The captain was astonished. "Is this man telling the truth?" he asked their officer. The man said yes, he was. "Well, then, call in all the noncommissioned officers at once," he ordered. When they came in, he said, "Do you see these three men? From now on, a half hour before sunset on Friday, no matter where they are or what they are doing, send them back to the barracks." And for all the rest of the time they were in the army they had no trouble.

Make sure you put God first in *your* life. He will give you words to speak and courage to speak them someday if you are called to stand before rulers.

ACTS 25

Now when they bring you to . . . magistrates . . . , do not worry
about how or what you should answer. . . . For the Holy Spirit
will teach you in that very hour what you ought to say.
Luke 12:11, 12.

December 2

After being kept in prison for two years, Paul was brought before Festus, the governor of Judea. Again the Holy Spirit gave him just the right words to say. And again and again the Holy Ghost has given our youth the right words to speak as they've stood before military officers appealing for permission to keep God's Sabbath. I think of the young man who was secretary to the president of the Latin Union Conference just before World War I. He was called into the French Army, and went to his captain to ask for Sabbath privileges. The captain flew into a rage. "Are you a fool?" he bellowed. "Do you think you are going to run the French Army?"

"No, sir," said the young man respectfully. "I do not wish to dictate to the army, and I do not think I am a fool. I only believe my first duty is to God."

"In the army you have to forget all other authority!" replied the captain.

"I can't do that in disobedience to God, sir."

"Then I'll send you to the worst place I can—the worst climate and the worst criminals."

"I can go there, sir, but I cannot disobey God."

At that, the captain marched him to the colonel. The colonel questioned him; then the colonel and the captain talked together for a while. Then the colonel dismissed them, and they went back to the captain's office. "How do you feel now?" the captain asked the soldier.

"I feel the same, sir."

"Can't work on Saturday, eh?"

"No, sir."

"You say you were a secretary?"

"Yes, sir."

"How would you like to be my secretary?"

"Why, Captain, I would like it fine," our soldier replied. "Only no work on the Sabbath."

"Very well," said the captain, "that's understood. You can begin right away." And he did!

Are you willing to go to prison rather than disobey God? God's Holy Spirit does wonders for those who obey at all cost.

339

December **3**

Agrippa's words to Paul are some of the saddest words found in the Bible. Agrippa was the king of the territory northeast of Judea. He was paying a courtesy visit to Festus in Caesarea. Out of curiosity he wanted to hear Paul speak. Paul told him the simple story of his conversion, and the Holy Spirit gave power to his words. Agrippa was convinced of the truth, and almost accepted it. He almost gave his heart to Christ, but he didn't. I wonder why he didn't.

Sad to say, there are some young people who do the same. They go to youth camp or on a mission trip or attend a Week of Prayer, and *almost* make their decision to accept Christ—but they don't. I wonder why. Megan was like that. She believed in Christ, but she wasn't quite ready to take up her cross. She wanted to have a good time in the world first. One day her mother got sick and was put in the hospital. Megan got some pretty flowers and went to see her. The nurse was a lovely Christian woman who understood the struggle Megan was having to give herself to Christ. She saw an opportunity to give Megan a good object lesson, so she said, "Oh, those flowers are so beautiful, but I think we'll keep them here for a few days till they get a little older before taking them to your mother."

"No way!" Megan said indignantly. "Mom will like them so much more while they're bright and fresh."

"You're right, of course," the nurse said. "I think your mom should have those flowers right now. And I wonder if Jesus wouldn't rather have your life right now, too, while you are young and your life is at its best?"

Megan saw the point, and that very day she gave her heart to Jesus. I hope you have already given your heart to Jesus. But if you happen to be a young person who has only *almost* done it, won't you do it today?

I read recently of a man who drowned only 20 feet from the shore of an East Coast beach. He seemed to be a good swimmer, but suddenly he called out, "Which way to shore? Which way to shore?" No one took any notice, for he was so close to safety. But he drowned. Later his two weeping sisters explained that John was blind. Poor John. He was *almost* safe, but he drowned. His words "Which way to shore?" still haunt me.

If *you* are almost persuaded to give your heart to Christ, do it *now*. The Holy Spirit is saying, "This is the way."

ACTS 27

Paul said to the centurion and the soldiers, "Unless these men stay in the ship, you cannot be saved."
Acts 27:31.

December 4

Paul, a prisoner, was on his way to Rome. The ship he was on ran into a terrible winter storm, and all hope of saving it from destruction was lost. Then an angel appeared to Paul and said, "Do not be afraid, Paul; you must be brought before Caesar; and indeed God has granted you all those who sail with you" (Acts 27:24). What a precious promise that was. But there was a condition given for their salvation—they must stay with the ship. There are few things more terrifying than a shipwreck, and no joy like being saved from certain death.

Some years ago a ship wrecked off the coast of the Pacific Northwest. A crowd of people from a nearby village stood on shore and watched in horror as the ship was pounded to pieces on the rocks. A lifeboat was sent to the rescue, and after a terrific struggle it came back with all the sailors but one. "There was no room in the lifeboat," they said, "so we told him to stay by the ship and someone would come back for him."

"Who will come with me?" shouted a young man as he sprang into the lifeboat, and immediately others joined him. Just then a woman cried out, "Don't go, Jim. Don't go! You're all I have left. Please don't go!" It was true. Her husband had drowned in the sea, and her other son, William, had sailed away, never to return." Jim listened to his mother's cry, then kindly said, "But I must go, Mother. It is my duty."

On shore everyone watched as the lifeboat fought its way toward the wreck. Anxiously Jim's mother wept and prayed. They saw the boat start back, a frail little shell tossed about by the angry waves. At last it came close enough to hear, and they shouted, "Did you get him?"

And Jim shouted back, "Yes! And tell Mother it's William!"

Oh, what a joy there can be when we do our duty and work together and stay together. Just try to imagine the double joy of that mother when she got back not only her brave son Jim but also her long-lost son.

One evening, when I lived in California, I picked up the paper, and there in great headlines read: "Wrecked, Just Outside the Golden Gate." A ship had gotten lost in the fog and broke into pieces on the large rocks near the shore. God forbid that any youth should be wrecked just outside the heavenly golden gate!

These signs will follow those who believe: In My name they will cast out demons; . . . they will take up serpents; and if they drink anything deadly, it will . . . [not] hurt them.
Mark 16:17, 18.

December 5

The promise made by Jesus to the believers was meant not only for His disciples but also for all Christians who would follow them in preaching the gospel in all the world. It included Paul, whose experience we have read about today. And here is another miraculous experience in the life of Captain O. F. Jones, the beloved trailblazer of the South Pacific.

In May 1908 Jones landed on the west coast of the island of Sumatra and hired a horse to make a journey into the interior. Most of the journey was through dense jungle inhabited by elephants, tigers, and large howling monkeys. The people were Muslims, and when they found that Captain Jones did not eat pork and did not smoke tobacco or drink alcohol, they called him a "learned man of God" and accepted him kindly. Then one day while he was resting at noon, a large poisonous snake attacked the grazing horse and bit it on the mouth. The horse's owner, who was in the group of people accompanying Captain Jones, was terrified. He was sure that the horse would soon die, and began to weep and wail at losing his means of earning a living. The people looked upon the snakebite as a sign of God's anger, and the poor man began to blame himself for having anything to do with Captain Jones, who was not a Muslim.

"God is punishing me," he wailed. The feelings of Captain Jones's companions changed. Suddenly they became hostile, as the horse showed symptoms of suffering from the snake's venom. For a moment Jones wondered what to do. Then he knelt in view of them all and prayed. He told the Lord how necessary it was, for his sake and for the people's sake, that the horse should not die. Then he claimed the promise in today's reading. When he got up from his knees, he said to the people, "My God will not let the horse die. He has heard my prayers." Then he mounted the trembling horse and rode on. The people followed, and were astonished to find the horse quite well at the end of the day. And you can imagine how much more they respected the captain for the rest of the journey.

What God did for Captain Jones, He can do for you. Remember this precious promise, and have faith in God.

ROMANS 12

I beseech you therefore, brethren, by the mercies of God,
that you present your bodies a living sacrifice, holy,
acceptable to God, which is your reasonable service.
Romans 12:1.

If every morning as we wake up we would say, "Dear Lord, today my life belongs to You; may my eyes, my ears, my hands, and my feet do only those things that please You," and if we would remember all day, every day, that we are not our own—that would be giving our bodies as a living sacrifice to God.

I once met a true "living sacrifice." A young couple, Louis and Zoila Gomez, with their four small children, were sent to open a new mission among the Sipibo Indians 1,000 miles upstream from Iquitos. Their only connection with the outside world was a little river steamer that came from Iquitos and passed their place once every two months. God blessed their work, and soon they started a school for the children and were holding night classes for the adults. This made a certain rich landowner angry. "If those Indians learn to read, I won't be able to work them like slaves anymore," he said to himself. So he hired men to poison Louis' food while he was with some Indians in their harvest field one day. Poor Louis was carried home. He had time only to tell Zoila and the children to be faithful; then he died. Zoila wrote their supervisor, Elder Hayden, and begged him to come visit them. He did come. He saw the school, baptized 30 new believers, then said, "Zoila, we can't understand why God has permitted Louis to die like this. The work is just nicely started, but you can't stay here alone. You must pack up your things and take the steamer and go home."

"No, no," said Zoila. "I can't leave these dear Sipibo Indians without a teacher. They have begged me to stay, and I've promised them I would."

"But Zoila, how can I go away and leave you alone?"

"Please say no more," pleaded Zoila. "See those tall men over there? They traveled four days to come here to beg for a teacher. I cannot go. I must stay."

And Zoila stayed. She stayed *alone* on that isolated mission station for eight years! Then a new missionary couple came to take her place, and Zoila took her little family to our college near Lima, Peru. I had the pleasure of meeting her there. I shook the hand of that noble woman, and thanked her for her faithfulness and her courage. That's what I call a living sacrifice.

Now take a look at the little things you might be asked to give up for Christ. Could you call any one of them a sacrifice?

And now abide faith, hope, love, these three;
but the greatest of these is love.
1 Corinthians 13:13.

December 7

Paul reminds us that true love is indeed the greatest power in the world. Without love there could be no obedience and no salvation. Without love there could be no homes and no heaven. Here is one of the most outstanding illustrations of the power of love that I have ever heard about. It occurred in connection with the death of Kathryn Lawes in October 1937.

Kathryn was the wife of Lewis E. Lawes, the famous warden of Sing Sing Prison. For 17 years she had walked in and out of this prison, befriending the unfortunate men who were shut off from society. She listened to the cries of worried fathers. She wrote letters for hopeless young criminals. She visited the families of the prisoners, taking food, clothes, and even money to the wives and children of the imprisoned men. And when men were newly released after years of isolation, it was often Kathryn who helped them adjust once more to freedom.

When news of her tragic death, resulting from an accident, was whispered from man to man and from cell to cell, it brought a gloom and sadness felt over the entire prison. As the day of her funeral approached, a representative of the prisoners went to Warden Lawes and begged in behalf of hundreds of devoted men the privilege of paying their last respects to one they so deeply loved. Warden Lawes listened sympathetically, then nodded his consent. The night before the funeral the south gate of Sing Sing Prison swung slowly open, and a long, silent procession of thieves, swindlers, murderers, and criminals of every kind walked to the warden's house a quarter of a mile away. There were no guards. There were no guns. But not a man broke ranks. After reaching the house, they filed past the coffin. Each paused a few seconds in front of the casket, then heartbroken and weeping, he moved on. Re-forming the lines, they slowly walked back to their lonely prison cells.

No wonder Paul says that love is the *greatest* power on earth. Ellen White says love is a *precious gift* from God, and Henry Ward Beecher says love is the *river of life* in this world.

If the Christian love of that good woman had power to do this miracle, then why can't God do something like that with *your* love?

2 CORINTHIANS 9

He who sows sparingly will also reap sparingly, and
he who sows bountifully will also reap bountifully.
2 Corinthians 9:6.

December 8

A young man, Will Sullivan, and his wife, Mary, built a little cabin in a spot where the prairie met the vast forest. One day down the trail to the cabin came a tall Indian warrior. But he looked weary, and as he came closer the young wife peering through the window saw by his face that he was sick and thirsty. "Can I get a drink of water?" the Indian asked Will.

But Will replied roughly, "Go away! I give nothing to Indians."

The rude answer hurt, but he tried again. "Please, I can go no farther. Just one drink?"

"Get out of here!" Will hissed, and slowly, with anger burning in his heart, the Indian turned to go. Will's wife had heard the man's request and was troubled by her husband's rough answer. She watched the Indian slowly walk away, but he had not gone far before he staggered and fell. At once the kind woman took bread, parched corn, water, and a jug of milk, and, slipping out, ran to help him. He had fainted with exhaustion, but with cool water and kind words she revived him.

"Please forgive my husband's unkind words," she said, "and take this food to strengthen you." The man ate and revived and was able to go on. But before leaving he handed Mary a long white heron feather. "Take this, little dove," he said. "When your mate is hunting in the red man's hunting grounds, tell him to wear this." Some months passed, and Will, with other settlers, set out to hunt. Despite his protests, he wore the feather Mary insisted on sewing into his cap. The hunters were successful, getting meat they'd have for winter's use, but somehow Will got separated from his friends. He wandered exhausted, unable to find neither them nor his way home. He grew frightened as night drew near, imagining he was watched by both wild animals and Indians. Then he heard a snort and breaking branches as a buffalo rushed toward him. A shot split the air, and the beast fell dead. A moment later a tall form knelt beside him, giving him food and saying, "If the weary hunter will rest till morning, the eagle will show him the way to his nest." At daybreak the Indian led him through the forest and to his home. Only then did he speak, saying, "Many moons ago you called me 'Indian dog' and drove me from your door. But the white dove fed me, and for her sake I spared her mate."

Do you want to reap kindness? There is only one way to get it—sow kindness yourself.

Do not be deceived, God is not mocked; for whatever a man sows, that he will also reap. Galatians 6:7.

December 9

Paul had a real burden to teach the members of the early Christian church that they could not sow "works of the flesh" and reap "fruit of the Spirit." To reap "fruit of the Spirit," they had to sow love, peace, goodness, and the like.

Pedro was only a boy when his father accepted the Advent message in Argentina. When he was 17, Pedro became a colporteur, and later he entered our new school in Entre Rios. After only three months of study, however, he was drafted into the Argentine army. The army officers had never heard of a Seventh-day Adventist and had never seen a conscientious objector, so when he asked for Sabbath privileges, he was told he must obey orders—or else. But those officers were soon to discover what a Seventh-day Adventist is! The first Sabbath when Pedro refused to work, they didn't know what to do, but the second Sabbath they made him stand stiffly at attention till his feet were so swollen he could hardly walk. The next Sabbath he was told to go to the river and wash clothes. When he wouldn't do it, they brought a tub, put water, soap, and his clothes in it, and told him to wash. When he refused, one soldier took one hand and another took the other hand, and they moved his hands up and down, up and down, till they were tired. But when they stopped, he stopped. Then they whipped him till the whip broke. They begged and they threatened, but Pedro would not work on Sabbath.

At last he was sent to work in a stone quarry with common criminals. The Catholic chaplain intervened and secured liberty for him on Sabbaths. Soon one of his fellow prisoners was converted. After four months of this he was transferred to a special disciplinary department of the army. Pedro thought the ordeal would begin all over again, but the commandant, listening carefully to Pedro's explanation, was convinced that his imprisonment was unjust. He freed him from Sabbath service and put him in charge of his garden. Later this officer brought Pedro's case to the attention of the minister of war, with the result that all Seventh-day Adventist youth thereafter drafted into the Argentine army were to have complete Sabbath liberty! Pedro later became one of the great missionaries in South America. What a man! What a wonderful result of sowing faithful obedience to God's commandments.

What are you sowing now? You will surely reap it, for good or for ill, someday.

EPHESIANS 6

Take the helmet of salvation, and the sword
of the Spirit, which is the word of God.
Ephesians 6:17.

December **10**

In a thousand ways the dear Word of God has protected those who love and obey it.

Paul sold Bibles and portions of Scripture, and one week he was working in a little town some distance from his home. After a hard week, on the last day he became nervous as he realized that he was being watched by a tall stranger. At last it was time to take a bus to the station, where he'd catch a train for home. The bus came. Paul got on. But the stranger got on too! Paul felt relieved when he got off at the train station. The train pulled in, and he quickly got on board and found a small compartment. He was about to lie down when the compartment door opened, and in came that same stranger. "Do you carry much money with you?" he asked.

Paul said that he didn't. "Have you got 500 lira?" the man asked. Again Paul told him no, and asked him who he was. Instead of answering, the man asked Paul, "Are you armed?"

Paul hesitated, then said, "Yes. Are you?"

"Yes," the man said, pulling out a large pistol. "Now show me yours."

Paul took out his Bible. "Here's mine," he said.

"You're crazy," said the stranger. "That's not a gun. That's a book."

"It shoots better than yours," said Paul. "Your gun can shoot only the person it is pointing at, but this Book is certain death to every wicked person who will listen to its words. I've shot at least six wicked men with this Book."

"How do you shoot with a book?" the stranger asked, puzzled.

"Put your gun away, and I will show you." Then Paul opened his Bible and read verse after verse, telling the terrible story of how sin entered the world and the wonderful story of Jesus, the Son of God, who died to save sinners and is now preparing a place in heaven for all who believe.

"Tell me more. Tell me quickly. My station is the next stop," said the man. And Paul told of the new earth, where there will be no more sin or sorrow or death. The stranger grasped Paul warmly by the hand, and as the train stopped and he stood up to leave, he said, "No one will know what your gun saved me from!"

The Word of God is indeed the sword of the Spirit. Be sure you are always armed with it.

PHILIPPIANS 4

My God shall supply all your need according to His riches in glory by Christ Jesus.
Philippians 4:19.

December 11

There were so many good texts in today's Scripture reading that it was hard to decide which one to talk about. At last I chose the promise of Philippians 4:19, because someday you may need to remember it and claim it. There is a difference between "needs" and "wants." There is a difference between "necessities" and "luxuries." Notice that God has promised to supply your needs—your necessities—and He does!

Mr. and Mrs. Peter Jensen could tell you that He does. Mr. Jensen was a painter by trade and faithful in paying his tithe and supporting the work of God. But painting jobs aren't too numerous during the cold winter months, and one winter he found himself out of work. The Jensens prayed earnestly, but no work opened up. Then one day their oil-burning heater ran out of oil and went out. The weather was bitterly cold, and heat was definitely a "need," so they claimed the promise in this morning's text. They scraped around and found enough money to buy two gallons of fuel oil—just enough for one more day. But the next day they were able to find enough money to buy two more gallons, so they had heat for one more day. Then Mr. Jensen disconnected the two oil drums at the side of the house, and by tipping them up he managed to get two and a half more gallons of oil. This he put into the container connected with the stove, and prayed to God for help. It would burn for one more day anyway. But it burned for two days, three—four—five—*six* days! Then Mr. Jensen happened to look through his wallet and found a $7 check that he hadn't cashed. With this he bought some fuel oil and enough gas for his car so they could go to church on Sabbath. When they came home from church, the flame finally sputtered and went out. But on Monday Mr. Jensen found work, and the crisis was over.

God often permits us to be tested and tried so that we can be certain that it is *He*, and not we, who is able to supply our needs.

What a wonderful God we serve! What wonderful promises He has made for us! Have you gone into partnership with Him?

COLOSSIANS 4

Praise the Lord! . . . Let everything that has breath praise the Lord.
Psalm 150:1-6.

It was on our second visit among the Karen hill folk that the idea was born. The boys questioned whether it was worth holding a meeting in such a small village, but we put up the sheet on which we projected the pictures, then I and the two other men who were with us got out our cornets and began to play. It worked like magic. Soon everyone in the village was there. And when the students saw that, they said, "Wouldn't it be lovely if we all had cornets!"

And then came the big idea. "Boys," I said, "when I go home to Australia next year, I'll see if I can't bring back a half dozen cornets."

So throughout our furlough I told the story of the boys' desire for cornets. And the people were so warmhearted and generous that when I returned to Burma I brought 23 instruments with me. Oh, the boys were excited. But wait a minute. I'll tell you a secret. You must have something more than brass instruments for a brass band. If you don't believe me, I wish you'd have been there when we opened the boxes. "Here you are," I said, giving out instruments right and left. They were so excited. I showed one boy how to play a big bass and he went into a corner to practice, and you should have heard the awful sound! I gave a cornet to another, and the sound he made was horrible! Multiply that by 20, and you'll know why Mrs. Hare fled to the jungle—and why I took to bed with a fever. It was terrible. I soon wished I'd never been to Australia and had never promised the boys that we'd have a band. I had a tremendous problem on my hands.

The third day we tried to tune up, but no one could blow the same note twice. They practiced, oh, they did. They blew their instruments until they were soaked with sweat, but it was no use. But do you know why they wanted to "blow the band"? It was so they could better preach the gospel, and so they pleaded, "O Lord, help us to blow the band. Help us." And He did. It sounds more like fiction than fact, but after 30 days we lined up in a beautiful shining ring and held our first open-air meeting in a nearby village. We played only five exercises and "Abide With Me," but it was a start. It revolutionized our jungle preaching. After that when we came to a village and began to play, everyone came to hear! Then one of our students would preach.

I know that when rewards are given out in heaven, there will be many bright stars in the crowns of the boys that "blow the band."

December 13

The Lord Himself will descend from heaven with a shout. . . . And the dead in Christ will rise first. Then we who are alive and remain shall be caught up together with them in the clouds to meet the Lord in the air. And thus we shall always be with the Lord. 1 Thessalonians 4:16, 17.

What a privilege it is to be "children of light," and to have the hope of Christ's soon return. Napthali was a Fijian missionary on the island of Mussau, but the people there would have nothing to do with him. They wouldn't listen to him preach or even look at his pictures of Bible scenes. Nobody, it seemed, took any notice of the gospel. Then both Napthali and his wife got very sick. Tina, their 12-year-old daughter, and Joe, their 8-year-old son, were the only ones there to look after them. Then one day a man came from a village 10 miles away. "Teacher," he said, "a man in our village has died, and with his last breath he said he wanted to be buried like a Christian. Can you come?"

"I'm sorry," said Napthali, "but I'm too sick. I can't get out of bed."

"Then we'll have to bury him like a heathen," said the man.

But Tina came to the rescue. "Let me go, Father," she said. "I know the verses to read. And Joe can go with me."

Napthali was worried, but still he let them go. When they got to the village, 200 heathen people gathered around to see what they would do. Tina showed them how to wrap the dead man in a mat and told them to dig a grave. Then that brave girl read our text for today. After that she and Joe sang "When He cometh . . . to make up His jewels," and Tina prayed that angels would mark the grave because she was sure the man had loved Jesus as he understood, and that he wanted to go to heaven when Jesus came. After the funeral Tina and Joe walked the 10 miles home again, alone. In a few days another messenger came from another village to request another Christian funeral. And a few days later came still another request. Three times Tina and Joe conducted Christian funerals and comforted heathen hearts while Napthali was too sick to go. When at last he was better he found that something wonderful had happened. In every village everybody wanted to listen now. That was the turning point, and today everybody on that island comes to Sabbath school.

Tina, of course, is grown up, and while visiting our Fiji Sabbath schools not long ago I met a fine-looking woman. As we shook hands she said, "I'm Tina! My father was Napthali." I was so happy to meet her. I thanked God again for "children of light." Are you one of the "children of light" too?

2 THESSALONIANS 2

Let no one deceive you by any means.
2 Thessalonians 2:3.

December **14**

In today's scripture Paul is warning us against "the working of Satan, with all power, signs, and lying wonders" (2 Thessalonians 2:9). Isn't it strange, but just about the time the three angels' messages of Revelation 14 went to call out a people who would keep the commandments of God and the faith of Jesus, Satan began his movement of modern spiritualism, which—by signs and lying wonders—he tries to deceive even those who trust God the most. Here is how it began.

In 1848 Mr. and Mrs. John Fox and their two youngest children, Margaret, age 15, and Kate, age 12, lived near Rochester, New York. Soon after moving into this house they were disturbed by strange knocking sounds. At first they thought it was mice or rats, or maybe the windows rattling in the wind. But on the night of March 31, after making sure the windows were tight, Kate thought that "something" imitated the knocks she made, or even replied to them. So she snapped her fingers and said aloud, "Here, old Splitfoot, do as I do." ("Splitfoot" was their name for Satan, based on drawings of Satan as a creature with split hooves and a tail.)

Immediately they heard the same number of sharp distinct taps. This scared the girls nearly out of their wits, and they didn't want to continue any more conversation with "old Splitfoot." But their mother was interested. She worked out a code of knocks and was soon getting intelligent messages. One of the first things the coded knocks told her was that years before, a man had been murdered in this house, and that his body was buried in the cellar. They dug through the dirt floor of the cellar, and sure enough, they found a skeleton.

Margaret soon became a spirit medium, and from that day to this, people are fascinated by the belief that they can communicate with the dead. You can hardly turn on the TV without finding a program based on the idea that the dead are not dead at all, but exist in some other place. And *that* was the first lie Satan told to Eve: "You will not surely die" (Genesis 3:4). That lie opens the door to terrible evil, but you and I need never be deceived. We know that Satan and his fallen angels tremble because time is short, and they want to take as many people as possible with them to their death. Keep your eyes on Jesus. Never give Satan anything with which he can pry open a door into your heart.

351

Godliness with contentment is great gain. For we brought nothing into this world, and it is certain we can carry nothing out. And having food and clothing, with these we shall be content.
1 Timothy 6:6-8.

December 15

At some time or other we all will be tempted to give up a little godliness for a little more money. Satan knows just how to tempt us to be discontent with our wages, and to make us think we could earn so much more if we were not particular about the Sabbath and the work of God.

Some time ago a Seventh-day Adventist missionary hired a man to cook for his family. The cook in turn hired a little boy to bring the water, peel the potatoes, and light the charcoal fires. He was called the cook's assistant, and he was so faithful and polite that the missionary took quite a fancy to him and sent him to the mission school. As the years went by he became a Christian and was baptized. Then one summer he decided to sell books to earn a scholarship. God blessed him with success, and one hot day he called at the home of a missionary of another denomination and showed his books. This man was impressed with his courteous, efficient manner, and invited him in. After talking awhile and finding out who he was, the missionary said, "Look here, young man, I need somone like you to look after one of my village schools and churches. My assistant has just passed away." He then offered him a very good wage and said, "You can preach anything you like except the Sabbath and the second coming of Christ." When the young man hesitated, the man saw it and quickly said, "Don't give me your answer now. Stay with me tonight and think it over. Give me your answer in the morning." The young man stayed. He had a good dinner and spent a very pleasant evening, and early the next morning he knocked on the missionary's door.

"Goodbye, sir," he said.

"You mean you are not going to take the job?" asked the man in surprise.

"No, sir. I'm sure you wouldn't want me. You see, it is the second coming of Christ and the Sabbath that have made me what I am. If I couldn't preach the Sabbath and the Second Coming, all you would have would be a cook's assistant boy." After thanking his host for his kindness, he went on his way rejoicing. That's the spirit we all need. Pray God to make you content, and strong to resist the temptation to give up some godliness for worldly gain.

2 TIMOTHY 4

I have fought the good fight, I have finished the race, I have kept the faith. Finally, there is laid up for me the crown of righteousness, which the Lord . . . will give to me on that Day.
2 Timothy 4:7, 8.

December **16**

Paul was himself a good Christian soldier; no wonder he exhorted Timothy to "endure hardness, as a good soldier of Jesus Christ" (2 Timothy 2:3).

Down through the years young people have caught the inspiration and the challenge of these words, and have gone forth everywhere doing great things for God. In the year 1864, there was in Yorkshire, England, a minister by the name of Sabine Baring-Gould. One day his Sunday school was to join another Sunday school in a nearby village for a rally, and he wanted his children to sing as they marched into the village. He looked through all the songbooks he had for a suitable marching song, but couldn't find one, so decided to write one himself. He sat up late into the night, and gave, not only to his children but to all the children in the world, the greatly loved song "Onward, Christian Soldiers!"

Onward, Christian soldiers! Marching as to war,
With the cross of Jesus going on before.

His children loved it, and they sang it so enthusiastically that it became popular immediately, and soon found its place into several hymnbooks. The tune to which the hymn is sung today is not the original tune. This tune was written sometime later by Sir Arthur Seymour Sullivan. This wonderful hymn, with its popular words and tune, is known all around the world, in every nation, and brings inspiration and challenge to all. Whether it is played by brass bands or cathedral pipe organs, whether it is sung by church choirs or mission school students, its spirit is irresistible.

Can you sing this great hymn? Do you get goose pimples when you hear a great choir sing it? Goose pimples are not enough. Determine that you yourself will also be a worthy soldier of the Lord Jesus Christ.

TITUS 2

Teaching us that . . . we should live soberly, righteously, and godly . . . , looking for the blessed hope and glorious appearing of our great God and Savior Jesus Christ. Titus 2:12, 13.

December 17

What could we do without Jesus? And what could we do without the "blessed hope" of His soon coming? Do you really long for Jesus to come? Listen!

Many years ago Dr. C. F. Schilling spent his three-week vacation in my jungle clinic in Burma. It was a wonderful time for us, and we kept the doctor busy day and night looking after the surgical cases that were beyond our skill and ability. The news of the doctor's visit spread far and wide, and five days after he had gone back to his hospital in India two men came to ask him to come examine a poor woman who had a huge watery cyst in her abdomen. I explained that the doctor had gone away again.

"Then can't you do something?" they begged.

"I can do only a little," I said, and I went with them.

With my instruments I drained off five gallons and three quarts of fluid. The poor woman was so happy. She thought that I was the doctor, and that the operation was all over. I said to the husband, "Tell her that you missed the doctor, and that all the water will come back again."

"No, no! I can't tell her," he said. "You tell her."

So I had to tell her. I told her that I was only a nurse, that I couldn't operate, and that in a few weeks the water would come back again. I told her that I would try to get the doctor to come back again next year, but that this time they were five days too late. Then I saw one of the saddest things I've ever seen in all my life. I saw the smile crushed from her happy face. For the longest minute I've ever lived she looked off into space, and then she said, "All right, then. All right. You write and tell the doctor that I'll be lying here on my back, counting the moons away, till he comes again. You say he might come again in a year? I've been lying on my back for seven years, and one more year won't seem so long. I'll be waiting here."

I'm glad to tell you that I was able to arrange with a surgeon in Moulmein to remove the cyst (it weighed 49 pounds) and that she had a wonderful recovery. But I cannot forget her pathetic words, "I'll be lying here counting the moons away till the doctor comes."

Do you long that much for Jesus to come?

PHILEMON

I appeal to you for my son Onesimus, . . . who once was unprofitable to you, but now is profitable to you and to me.
Philemon 10, 11.

December 18

Onesimus was a slave to Philemon, a Christian gentleman in Colossae. For some reason or other he ran away. In those days if a slave ran away and was found again, according to the law of the land he could be put to death at the will of his master. But Onesimus had been converted and had repented of his mistake, and in this letter to Philemon, Paul begged him to give his slave another chance to make good. This lesson is good for us all to learn. One mistake or one failure need not spoil a whole life. We can make things right, we can try again, and we can make good. Here is a story told in a mission paper that is typical of the success that can come to those who may fail once.

Tadayga, a young man attending one of our mission schools in Ethiopia, was studying to become a teacher. But unfortunately, he failed in math. In fact, he failed it twice. Without passing his math classes, he could not even hope to get a teacher's certificate. And now that he had tried and failed twice, he would not even be permitted to stay on in school. What could he do?

About then a call came to the mission for a teacher to come to the village of Abonsa and start a school for first graders. The mission at which Tadayga had been studying had no teachers to spare, so they asked Tadayga if he would like to go and try. Tadayga went. He received no pay—only his food and a place to sleep—and the school was only a shed with one small blackboard. But the first week 50 children came to Tadayga's first-grade classes. The next week there were 62; the next, 85; and the next, 90! Tadayga could not take any more. Even now he had to have a morning session and an afternoon session, for the schoolhouse would hold only 45 children. He taught them numbers and reading and writing. They learned to read the Bible, and the children read the Bible to their parents, and more than 100 people came to his Sabbath school. And what do you think Tadayga did in the evenings? He studied math, and at the end of the year he passed his examination!

If at first you don't succeed, try, try, try again. It works!

Faith is the substance of things hoped for,
the evidence of things not seen. . . . Without
faith it is impossible to please Him.
Hebrews 11:1-6.

December 19

Hebrews 11 is known as the faith chapter of the Bible. Our hearts thrill as we read the list of Bible heroes mentioned there, and recall what their faith accomplished. But the list of heroes given is not complete by any means, for many followers of the Lord Jesus in every land have been giants in faith.

Let us take Dr. Ida Scudder for an example. She was born in India, where her parents were medical missionaries. As a young woman she saw that India had need of women doctors, so after studying medicine in the United States she went back to India, determined to establish a medical school. She began in a little room eight by 10 feet, with one bed in it for an inpatient, and a window through which she could talk with outpatients and dispense medicines. Some people laughed at the idea of her starting a medical school, but two years later a friend gave her money to build a 40-bed hospital. By 1909 she had started a nurses' training school, and in 1918 she opened a medical college with 34 women students! In 1965 (just after this book was first printed) the *761-bed* Vellore Christian Medical College had 159 full-time doctors and 224 graduate nurses on the staff. Look up this incredible school on Google, and you will see thousands of entries. The hospital and school have more than 100 different units and departments and see 5,000 patients a day.

I remember a story told by the doctor who was then head of Vellore Christian Medical College. One day he was sitting by a railway bridge that crossed a deep ravine and saw a man and little girl come walking along the railway track. "The little girl will be too frightened to cross the bridge," he said to himself. But when they got to the ravine, where they had to walk on the railway ties to get across, the girl took her father's hand, looked at the ties, then looked up into her father's face, and talked pleasantly all the way. In a few seconds they were safely across. The ravine was there, but the little girl barely saw it.

That's the way you can exercise faith too. When you meet with difficulties, simply take your heavenly Father's hand. Then look up into His face and talk pleasantly all the way.

JAMES 3

See how great a forest a little fire kindles! And the tongue is a fire. . . . it . . . sets on fire the course of nature.
James 3:5, 6.

December **20**

On the evening of October 8, 1871, a Mrs. O'Leary, who lived on the west side of the hustling frontier city of Chicago, lit her little kerosene lantern and went out to her barn to milk her cow. She fastened the cow's head in the stall, put her lantern on the floor, then sat down on her little stool and began to milk. For some reason or other the cow was in a contrary mood that night, and without warning, it let fly a vicious kick. It knocked over the kerosene lantern, and caused Mrs. O'Leary to lose her balance. Before she could pick herself up, the straw on the barn floor was on fire. In spite of all she could do, in no time, the flimsy barn was in flames. There had been no rain for several weeks; the grass around the barn was dry, and a high wind carried the blaze to the nearby houses. In those days most of the houses in Chicago were built of wood, and soon the fire was beyond all possible control. The fire quickly spread up to the Chicago River, leaped over it, and spread desolation far and wide, to the south first and then to the north side. An area of about 3.5 square miles was destroyed, including 17,500 buildings and property valued at $196 million. About 300 people were burned to death, and many thousands were made homeless. And it all started from a little kerosene lantern that was meant to be a blessing.

The apostle James tells the truth when he says, "The tongue is a fire." God meant for our tongues to be a blessing—to speak kind, helpful, cheerful words. But if we let them gossip and criticize and tell falsehoods, good names may be ruined, friendships broken, and fond hopes turned to ashes.

The Bible talks about the "gift of tongues." I can remember one of our pioneer preachers saying, "The gift most of us need is the gift to *hold* our tongues." And I think he was telling the truth. Don't you?

Never let your tongue say anything about anyone until you ask yourself whether it's true, whether it's kind, and whether it will do any good to tell it.

Be sober, be vigilant; because your adversary the devil walks about like a roaring lion, seeking whom he may devour.
1 Peter 5:8.

December 21

I don't know anything about roaring lions, but for 20 years I lived in a land that had roaring tigers, and I know how roaring tigers seek whom they may devour. One day my Burma brass band was on its way to hold an evening meeting in Lapota village. In the cool of the evening, as we were approaching the village, suddenly on the hills to the right we heard an animal call "Squ-e-e-eak!" It was a high reedy note, and I said, "Boys, listen! There's a deer over there somewhere." For there were lots of deer in our jungle that called just like that.

The students listened. The sound came again—"Squ-e-e-eak"—but they shook their heads and said, "That's not a deer, Thara. That's a tiger."

I said, "But tigers don't go squ-e-e-eak. Tigers go roar-r-r-r."

"No," they said. "Not always. It all depends on what animal the tiger is hunting. He makes a sound like the sound of the animal he is trying to catch."

Just then we heard another "squ-e-e-eak" on the hills to the left. And I said, "Listen! There's another tiger."

The students listened, then whispered, "No, no. That's not another tiger. That's a deer."

"Well, I can't tell the difference," I said.

"We can," they said. "We live in this jungle country, and our fathers have taught us the difference. The tiger's call is a little more throaty. Listen!" So for the next half hour we listened to one of the tragedies of jungle life. "Squ-e-e-eak," called the crafty, deceitful tiger. "Squ-e-eeak," answered the unsuspecting deer, who thought its mate was calling and ran a little closer. "Squ-e-e-eak, squ-e-e-eak." "Squ-e-eeak, squ-e-e-eak." Closer and closer they came together, till the tiger was close enough to spring. Then it opened its mouth and roar-r-r-r-r-red. The poor little deer was paralyzed with fear, and the tiger sprang upon it and killed it! Believe me, the devil does not do his hunting wearing a pointed goatee and narrowed, evil eyes. He's handsome and smart, and loves to have a good time. He gets into your computer games and iPods, magazines, and DVDs. He tries to make you think he's your best friend. He tries to lure you closer and closer to him, then when it's too late he laughs at your terror and mocks your regrets. Ask God to help you recognize the crafty old devil, then keep as far away from him as you can.

2 PETER 3

*The Lord is not slack concerning His promise . . . , but is
longsuffering toward us, not willing that any should perish
but that all should come to repentance.*
2 Peter 3:9.

December 22

It doesn't matter what God does—whether He creates, forgives sin, performs a miracle, or makes a promise—you can expect someone to come along and try to make fun of it and say it isn't so. And this is just what Peter said would happen. He said that in the last days scoffers would come and ask, "Where is the promise of His coming?" (2 Peter 3:4). But quite often God has given His children words to speak that have shut the mouths of these scoffers and put them to shame.

I remember a story told by the greatly loved evangelist Phillip Knox. A notorious drunkard was converted, and sometime later one of his old drinking buddies thought he would hold him up to ridicule, so he said, "I hear you've been converted."

"Yes, thank God," replied the new Christian.

"And I suppose you believe the Bible now."

"Yes, indeed I do."

"And I suppose you believe the miracle of Jesus turning water into wine."

"I surely do," the new Christian replied. "And if you will come to my house I'll show you a bigger miracle than that. I'll show you where Jesus has changed beer and whiskey into carpets, chairs, a piano, and new dresses for my wife and children!"

The scoffer's mouth was stopped, and he never tried to ridicule that man's religion again.

There's another story I like about a pious old Christian who spent much time in prayer and fasting. One day a wild young fellow came to poke fun at him. "Father," he said, "if there is not another world after this one, what a miserable time you have had."

"True, my son," said the old man, "but if there is another world after this one, what a miserable time you *will* have!"

Don't be surprised if someone comes along to mock and scoff at you and your religion. You are safe if you stay on God's side and hold fast to His promise.

Do not love the world or the things in the world. . . .
The world is passing away, and the lust of it; but
he who does the will of God abides forever.
1 John 2:15-17.

December 23

While Ingathering in Burma, I met the chief engineer of a large rice mill and shared some of our dramatic experiences. I told him about the girl with the "burned" finger, and how we amputated her arm below the elbow and saved her life, and the man who had been "stung" by an elephant, and how we washed his bowels and put them back and sewed him up.

"Remarkable!" Mr. Sinclair said. "But how can you two men be happy way up there in the never-nevers—with no whiskey and sodas?"

I said, "We get more pleasure out of seeing happy mothers with healthy babies and hearing them each say, 'My baby was nearly dead, but you cared enough to help, and now look! If it hadn't been for you, my baby would have died.'"

"Yes, yes!" said Mr. Sinclair. "But you have no jazz orchestras and no dances!"

"But I have a brass band of 25 instruments and a choir of 83 voices that can sing anthems in six parts. That gives me more pleasure than any orchestra could ever give."

"You're right," he said thoughtfully. "But you have no movies!"

"Ah, but we have real life," I said. And I told him of the woman with a terribly scarred face and only one arm who fell at my feet and sobbed out her thanks: "Oh, if you hadn't come the night the marijuana fiend attacked me I surely would have died. But you weren't afraid of the night. You weren't afraid of the tigers. You came, and now I am alive." And I said, "Mr. Sinclair, no movie could ever give me joy like that."

"Yes, I suppose," he said. "But it's just you two White men among all the jungle people."

I said, "Mr. Sinclair, nothing satisfies like seeing men and women who have found Christ because of what you've done. The last night of school one of my big boys stepped into my office and said, 'I wanted to come and say thank you. When I came to school, I had no hope of heaven, but it's different now, because you and MaMa have been so kind and patient with me.'"

For a moment Mr. Sinclair struggled with his emotions, then said, "Mr. Hare, I'd give the world to experience a joy like that."

"That's exactly what I gave," I said. "I gave the world for that joy."

That's what it will cost you, too—the world. But no happiness, no satisfaction, can compare with the joy of serving Jesus.

REVELATION 1

Behold, He is coming with clouds, and every eye will see Him.
Revelation 1:7.

December **24**

One of the most exciting days of my life was when I was only 7, and played third cornet in our publishing company's brass band. The Prince of Wales was coming to town. In 1901 George, the Duke of York (who later became King George V), was made Prince of Wales. That same year he visited Australia. The procession was to pass along a street in our town at 10:00 a.m., and we were told to be sure to be there early. My father played one of the bass horns, and my brother Reuben played the baritone, so we got up very early. I wasn't hungry, but Mother said, "You'd better eat a good breakfast, and you'd better take some lunch. You can never tell what might happen to a procession like this." But I was too excited to eat, and I didn't want to carry anything but my horn.

"He's coming at 10:00, Mother, and we'll be home for dinner," I argued. And Mother said, "All right! But you know—"

All our band members were there at 9:00, their horns shining and bright. We stood in formation and played our piece, just for practice. Then we waited. Crowds came and lined the streets on both sides. That was one of the longest hours I have ever lived, but at last 10:00 came, and we all snapped to attention. But the prince didn't. Nobody came. Eleven o'clock came, but the prince didn't come. We were getting tired. We weren't standing at attention anymore. The crowd was getting restless; some were grumbling and complaining, and many just left! Noon came, but still no prince! We were hungry. If only I had brought the lunch Mother tried to send. Father went to a bakery and brought back a roll. One o'clock. Two o'clock! Three o'clock! No prince! We were so tired.

"Maybe he'll never come. Let's go home," said some.

Four o'clock! Suddenly we heard cheering way up at the other end of the street. We looked. Two couriers with trumpets came riding along. Everybody stood up and cheered. A mounted guard followed the couriers—and then came the Prince of Wales in the royal carriage. The bandmaster gave the signal, and we began to play. You should have heard us! The prince looked right at us. He took off his hat and smiled. And we weren't tired anymore. We weren't hungry anymore. We had seen the prince!

Jesus is coming soon. Make sure you are ready. Make sure you don't get tired and give up watching and waiting.

REVELATION 2

To him who overcomes I will give some of the hidden manna to eat. And I will give him a white stone, and on the stone a new name written which no one knows except him who receives it. Revelation 2:17.

December 25

Today is Christmas. No doubt you will receive many gifts and surprises, but none can ever equal the gift spoken of in this text.

A story is told about the Persian king Shah Abbis, who reigned long ago. It says he disguised himself and visited with his subjects to find out whether they were happy. He ate in their eating houses, and worked beside them in their fields.

One evening he stopped to talk with a workman who was tending a furnace. The man was cheerful and talked about his work, his wife, and his children, thinking that his visitor was only a poor man who wanted to rest where it was warm. The next night the king came again, and the next and the next. The workman was so friendly and kind that he even shared his lunch with his visitor. They became such good friends that at last the king confessed that he was not a poor man who needed a warm place to rest, but the king in disguise.

The workman was too amazed for words. Then the king added, "Now that you know who I am, I suppose you have some request to make of my generosity."

"No, no, my king," the man said. "I have nothing more to ask. To think that my king has visited me and shared my humble food—this is the greatest gift you could have given me. The memory of your friendship will stay with me forever."

So it is with Christmas. A lot of myth and legend is connected with it, but Jesus, our king, *did* live on earth as a man, walking the city streets, eating in the homes of friends, teaching and healing, and making children glad. And it is because Christ's name is connected with Christmas that the weary old world pauses and forgets things that are mean and selfish, and tries its best to make others happy.

Be sure that you keep Christ in this Christmas. Make this the happiest one of your life by following the example of Christ by forgetting yourself and doing everything you can to make others happy.

REVELATION 3

Behold, I stand at the door and knock. If anyone hears
My voice and opens the door, I will come in to him and
dine with him, and he with Me.
Revelation 3:20.

December 26

If all of us only knew that Jesus longs to come into our heart, and if we only knew what Jesus could do for us, and how much we need Him, none of us could ever refuse to let Him in, or ever send Him away. See if you can find the lesson in this story about Barry, the Saint Bernard dog.

Up in the Alps, on one of the mountain passes between Switzerland and Italy, is a rest house where 12 monks live. They keep a number of Saint Bernard dogs there that have been trained to lead travelers across the pass and to find travelers who are lost. One bitter cold winter day as two travelers struggled up the trail toward the rest house, a blinding snowstorm overtook them. They soon became tired, and one man decided to drink some brandy to stimulate him and help his circulation.

"Don't do it," begged his friend. "The effect will soon wear off, and then you'll feel worse than ever."

But the man would not listen. He drank heavily, forged ahead a short distance, then sank down in the snow, utterly exhausted. The other man struggled on and finally found the rest house. He told the monks about his fellow traveler, and they immediately sent the dog, Barry, to find him and lead him to safety. Barry sped off and quickly found the man asleep in the snow. He did everything he could to waken him. He barked, he nudged him, and little by little the man came to. But he wasn't coherent, and somehow he thought he was being attacked by a wild animal. Taking his knife, he stabbed Barry in the neck. Suddenly he realized his terrible mistake, so with all the strength he had he struggled to his feet, and half leaning on the big dog, he managed to reach the rest house. Barry's blood had stained every step of the way back, and the noble dog fell exhausted on the doorstep and died.

In a cemetery in Paris a monument was erected to the memory of this faithful animal. On it is written "Barry: He saved the lives of 40 persons and was killed by the forty-first."

Be sure you do not resist the Savior. When He knocks at your heart, recognize Him and let Him in.

I looked, and behold, a great multitude which no one could number, of all nations, tribes, peoples, and tongues, standing before the throne and before the Lamb, clothed with white robes. Revelation 7:9.

December 27

I am definitely planning on being among the redeemed who will stand before God's throne clothed in white robes. Aren't you? But there is a kind of white robe we must get here on earth before we ever get to heaven. If you don't first get this robe, you'd feel terribly embarrassed among the people who have white robes there.

One evening, after the day's work was finished at my mission station in Burma, I was sitting on my front veranda in fresh clean clothes, waiting for supper. A cool breeze was blowing from the river, and it was very pleasant. Just then one of the students came upstairs and said, "Thara, Mg Tin is downstairs and wants to see you." Mg Tin was our leaf-thatch contractor. He came every year, and we estimated the number of leaf-thatch strips we needed to get the houses ready for the rainy season. So I said, "Good! Tell him to come right up."

The boy was back in a minute, and said, "Mg Tin is afraid to come up. He wants you to come down."

"Fiddlesticks," I said. And going to the back veranda, I called, "Come on up, Mg Tin. It's nice and cool up here. I have a chair all ready for you."

You should have seen the poor man. He was so miserable and uncomfortable. He looked here and there, then went over to a bush and spat out his mouthful of betel nut. "Oh," I said to myself, "his mouth was dirty!"

Then he washed his face and hands and feet at the big waterpot. "Oh," I said. "His face and hands and feet were dirty."

At last he brushed the dust from his travel-stained garments, and, smiling and confident, he came upstairs into my nice clean house and sat with me on my front veranda. Soon Mg Tin went away with a good order for thatch and a pocketful of money, but I will never forget how embarrassed he was before he got cleaned up.

Young people, the white robe we must get here before we go to heaven is the robe of Christ's righteousness. To get it, we confess our sins and obtain Christ's forgiveness. Then every day we ask forgiveness for our mistakes and shortcomings. That isn't hard, but it is very important.

REVELATION 14; 15:1-4

Here is the patience of the saints; here are those who keep the commandments of God and the faith of Jesus. Revelation 14:12.

December **28**

We are not born with fully developed patience. Indeed, no! We have to be taught to be patient, and one of the teachers is Miss Fiery Trial. That's why Peter says, "Do not think it strange concerning the fiery trial which is to try you . . . ; but rejoice to the extent that you partake of Christ's sufferings" (1 Peter 4:12, 13). When you recognize that teacher, and know what it is trying to teach you, then little by little you will become long-suffering and patient. In some cases these teachers are small and quite gentle. But in other cases they are big and very severe.

In a certain town in Bolivia lived a good Seventh-day Adventist man. He was so nice that the villagers felt condemned by his life, and they hated him. After a while the father of this good man came to live with him, but before too long he took sick and died.

Then the villagers said, "Here's our chance. We'll say that this Adventist killed his father, and then he'll be put in jail." So they accused him before the town judge, and although he was perfectly innocent, he was put in jail. It was hard for him to understand why God would permit this trial to come to him. But he was patient, and while in jail he was a true and faithful Christian. After a few months one of his accusers had a dream in which he saw a heavenly being who said to him, "Something terrible will happen to you for condemning that innocent man." He was very much afraid, and when he woke up he went to one of his companions and told him about the dream.

"I had the same dream exactly," said his companion. So they asked each of the accusers, and were amazed to find that several others had also had the same dream. They were so terrified that they went to the judge and confessed their sin, and the Adventist brother was set free. "Now," said the freed man's lawyer, "this is your chance to get even with those evil men."

"No, no! I'm a Seventh-day Adventist Christian. I don't want to do them any harm," he said. And soon most of the people in that village were Seventh-day Adventists too.

How good it was that our believer recognized the "teacher" God permitted to come to him. Are you planning to be among the patient ones that are found keeping the commandments of God when Jesus comes? Then don't be afraid of Miss Fiery Trial. She can be a great teacher.

REVELATION 20

And books were opened. And another book was opened, which is the Book of Life. And the dead were judged according to their works, by the things which were written in the books. Revelation 20:12.

December 29

First there is the book of remembrance, in which are recorded the good deeds of those that fear God (Malachi 3:16). Second is the record of evil deeds (*The Great Controversy*, pp. 481, 483). And third is the book of life, which contains the names of all who accept Christ (*Patriarchs and Prophets*, p. 326).

Not long ago Miriam Bruce was teaching a junior Sabbath school class about the books in heaven, and she asked, "What do you think the book of death looks like?"

"It's full of sins," said one. "It's all red like scarlet," said another.

But Carlos had another idea. "I think it is full of erasures," he said. "Erasures?" the class laughed. But as they thought about it, they decided Carlos was right.

Then Miss Bruce asked, "Have all *your* sins in the book of death been erased?" And everybody felt very serious for a while.

One day a junior youth went into a drugstore and slipped into a telephone booth. Because he didn't close the door the clerk nearby overheard this one-sided conversation: "Hello. Is this Main Street Grocery? Is this Mr. Jones? . . . Mr. Jones, do you need a good lively errand boy? . . . Oh . . . Well, are you going to keep him? . . . Is he OK? . . . Well, all right, thank you. Goodbye."

"Never mind," said the clerk as the boy went out, "you're a smart-looking guy. I'm sure you'll find a job somewhere."

"Me find a job?" the boy said with a grin. "I have one! I'm Mr. Jones's errand boy. I was just checking up on myself." I like that idea of checking up on oneself. Why don't you do it? When you pray, ask God whether all your sins have been erased. Ask Him whether your name is still shining brightly in the book of life. And the still small voice will let you know right away. It is better to make sure now than to wait till the day of judgment and find unforgiven sins against your name. "Oh, that we might control our words and actions!" Ellen White wrote. "How strong we would become if our words were of such an order that we would not be ashamed to meet the record of them in the day of judgment" (*Messages to Young People*, p. 328).

REVELATION 21

And God will wipe away every tear from their eyes;
there shall be no more death, nor sorrow, nor crying.
. . . For the former things have passed away.
Revelation 21:4.

December **30**

We are on our way to the kingdom of God. What a wonderful place that will be, with all the joys we have ever known, and more—but no death or sorrow or crying or pain! The danger in our life on this earth is that, like Lot's wife, we might let our hearts become so enamored with the things of this world that we are not willing to give them up.

One day during the battle of Rangoon, in World War II, I was packing some of our most valuable possessions in our mission headquarters building when a well-to-do woman came in and asked for the superintendent. I pointed to Mr. Meleen's door and told her he was in. She knocked on the door, and when Mr. Meleen opened it, I heard her say, "Oh, Mr. Meleen, I have to go, and I can't take anything with me except one little suitcase and a rug for the journey. I live in that big house a few blocks away where the big mango trees are. I hate to think of thieves breaking in to steal and loot and destroy. Won't you mission people go over and take all of my lovely things—my beds and tables, my chairs and beautiful rugs? I will feel so much happier if I know you mission people have them."

And I heard Mr. Meleen say, "I'm sorry, but it's too late now! We are all packed up, and we expect to have to leave any day now. Three months ago we could have used every bed, every chair, and every rug. We were trying to set up our city clinic then. But our doctors and nurses have all gone now; so it's too late, too late!"

I saw the tears come to her eyes. "Too late?" she cried, then covering her face with the shawl she had on her shoulders, she went sadly away, bitterly crying, "Too late! Oh, how I wish—" Then emotion choked her voice, and she left us to fill in the wish. But I knew what she wished. Do you?

We really are on our way to the heavenly kingdom, and we can't take any of our worldly belongings with us. Our homes, our cars, our computers, our iPods—everything we have—will all be burned up someday. God will give us so much more, of course.

Pray that God will make you content with only what is necessary, so that you will have no heartache when you leave it all behind.

The Spirit and the bride say, "Come!" And let him who hears say, "Come!" And let him who thirsts come. Whoever desires, let him take the water of life freely. Revelation 22:17.

December 31

Whoever desires." That is your part of your salvation. Jesus has paid the price. But you must want to be saved. You yourself must will to do.

Many years ago an old man came to my clinic and asked for medicine for his broken thumb. I was shocked to see that the thumb was dead, black, and rotting. In alarm I said, "Uncle, you must sit right down and let me cut off your thumb. It is dead, and no medicine will ever make it better."

"No, no, no, Thara," he pleaded. "Put some medicine on it. You put some medicine on Saw Wa's broken arm and you tied it up with a stick and some rag, and it got better."

"But Uncle," I said, "it's too late now. If you had come 10 days ago, then maybe I could have put a splint on it. But now I must cut it off, or you will die." I showed him a finger I had amputated preserved in alcohol. "Look! Here's a finger I cut off. It didn't hurt a bit. I have medicine that—" But he refused.

"My dear man," I said earnestly, "we have no time to lose. Come, let me do it now."

"No, not now. There's a medicine man in a village across the valley. He's got strong medicine. I'll try his medicine for 10 days. Then if it's not better, I'll let you cut it off."

"But you can't live 10 days with that dead thumb," I pleaded. "Come on, I have the medicine. I have the time. I'll do it right now." But in spite of all I could do or say, he left, saying he'd come back in 10 days. Every day I asked patients who came from his direction about Uncle Soo Sar. Nine days later a patient came in who said, "Oh, yes, I know Uncle Soo Sar."

"Is he better?"

"We burned him five days ago" was the sad reply. (The Karens cremate their dead.)

But now you tell me, why did Uncle Soo Sar die? Was it because he broke his thumb? Was it because there was no balm in Gilead and no physician there? No, no. It was because he was not willing.

God will *never* shut you out of the kingdom because you have sinned. We all have sinned! But Christ is the physician, and Christ has the remedy. He has the time to cleanse you and heal you from sin. But you—*you*—must be willing.